FROM THE KITCHEN OF

THE

COUNTRY COOKING

of

ITALY

THE
COUNTRY COOKING
of ITALY

by **COLMAN ANDREWS**
foreword by **MARIO BATALI**

photographs by

HIRSHEIMER AND HAMILTON

CHRONICLE BOOKS

SAN FRANCISCO

Library of Congress Cataloging-in-Publication Data available.
ISBN 978-0-8118-6671-2

Manufactured in China
Designed by Brooke Johnson
Prop and food styling by Melissa Hamilton
Typesetting by Janis Reed

Photo on page 18: Courtesy of Mary Melfi (www.italyrevisited.org); Photo on page
43: Courtesy of Fosco Maraini/Gabinetto Vieusseux Property/ c.Fratelli Alinari/
Mary Evans; Photos on pages 77 and 350: Courtesy of Getty Images; Photos on pages
142 and 167: Courtesy of Library of Congress; Bottom photo on page 149: Courtesy
of Mary Evans/Alinari Archives; Photo on page 230: Courtesy of Dag Sundberg/
StockphotoPro; Print on page 262: Courtesy of Mary Evans Picture Library; Bottom
photo on page 323: Courtesy of Popperphoto/Getty Images.

10 9 8 7 6 5 4 3 2 1

Chronicle Books
680 Second Street
San Francisco, California 94107
www.chroniclebooks.com

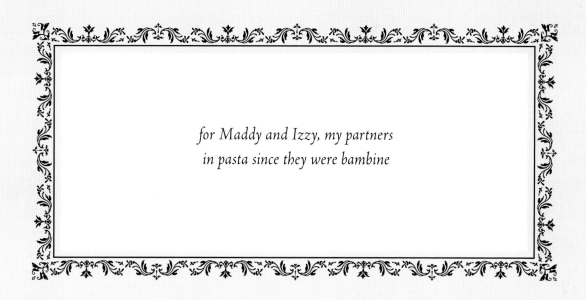

*for Maddy and Izzy, my partners
in pasta since they were bambine*

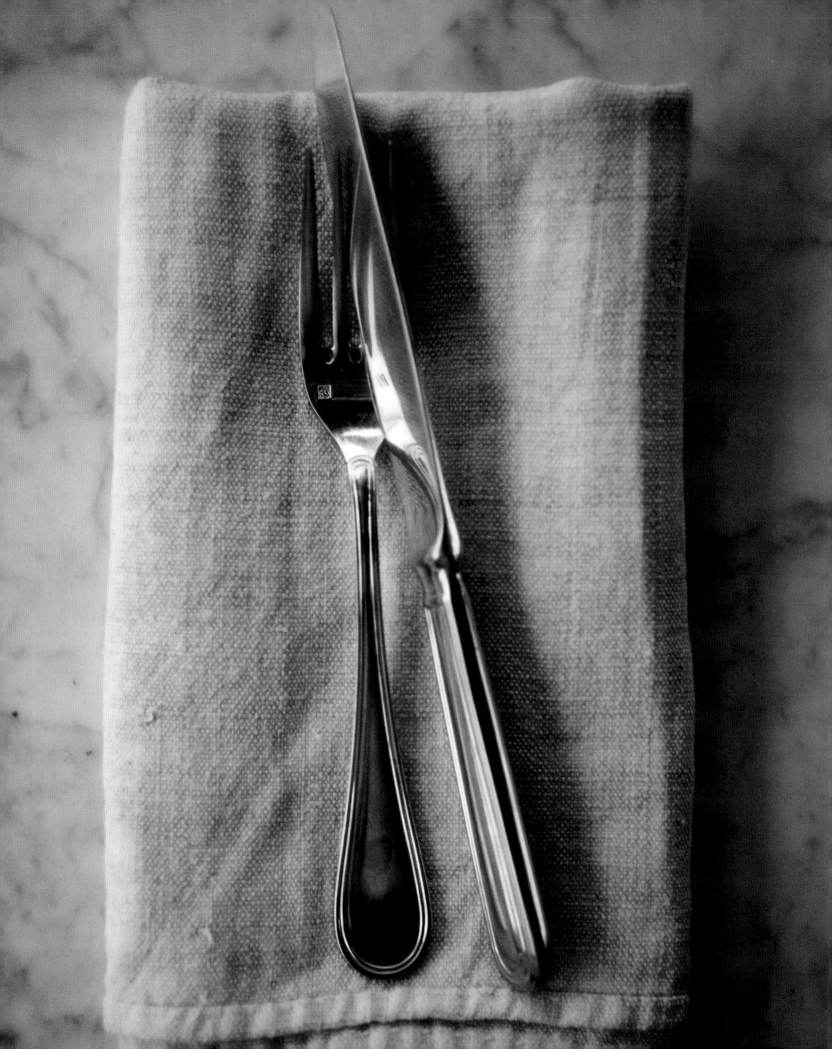

TABLE OF CONTENTS

ACKNOWLEDGMENTS

I must begin by thanking some old friends, both American and Italian, who helped introduce me to real Italian cooking many years ago: Karen (Kelly) Miller, Gianfranco Perrotti, Piero Selvaggio, the late Mauro Vincenti, and Steven Wagner. More recently, the ever erudite and entertaining Darrell Corti (they don't call him Il Professore for nothing) and the similarly gifted Charles Perry answered numerous questions about language, food, and culture. Jonathan Waxman, with whom I've shared scores of meals in Italy (among many other places), was a font of practical culinary information. Although I never spoke to them specifically about this book, Marcella and Victor Hazan have been a frequent source of information and inspiration for more than a decade.

Grazie mille to Michele Russo and Riccardo Russo in Basilicata and Natale Rusconi, Bepi D'Este, and Luca da Vita in the Veneto—and to Domenico Laera in Alberobello, Maurizio Barone at Il Tastevin in Vigevano, and the proprietors of Ristorantino di Columba in Ferrara and of Ristorante Cocchi in Parma, who were generous with their recipes.

I've drawn on my experiences in the early 1990s in Liguria for portions of this book, and so—though I haven't seen them for years—I must also acknowledge the help, way back then, of Giorgio Bergami, Maria Deidda, Diego Moreno, Renato and Gianni Belforte, Franco and Melly Solari, Sandro and Erica Oddo, and Mara Allavena.

Julia Lee and Elizabeth Pearson, a couple of the more illustrious alumnae of the *Saveur* test kitchen, worked with many of the recipes that follow and made them better. Thanks, too, to Rick Mindermann, Anahid Nazarian, and Carlo Petrini for counsel of various kinds—and to my wife, Erin Walker, for her continuing understanding and (in several senses of the word) support.

This book wouldn't exist without the efforts of my agent, Michael Psaltis, who both made the deal and helped me, in many ways, fulfill my end of it successfully. It is always a pleasure to work with my editor at Chronicle Books, Bill LeBlond, and with Chronicle's crack design and production team, who are as good as it gets. Sharon Silva, copy editor *straordinario*, brought logic and consistency to both my prose and my recipes, and saved me from making some silly mistakes.

Finally, but also first and foremost, I owe a whole feast full of gratitude to Christopher Hirsheimer and her colleague Melissa Hamilton. Christopher's delicious and evocative photographs don't just illustrate this volume but bring it to life, and she and Melissa made sense out of some of the most challenging recipes herein and elegantly refined some of the simplest, dispensing plenty of culinary wisdom along the way. This would be half a book, if even that, without them.

PHOTOGRAPHERS' ACKNOWLEDGMENTS

We work on many book projects, but when we work together with the great Colman Andrews it is always such a gratifying collaboration. He shares his breadth of knowledge and authority in such a rich, accessible voice. It was a great honor to photograph this wonderful book and, we thank him for asking us to do it.

Lori De Mori and Jason Lowe gave us their beautiful Italian farmhouse, an agrarian paradise, nestled in the folds of vine planted hills. Thank you for allowing us to pretend-live your dreamy Italian lifestyle.

We would still be lost on the back roads of Italy had it not been for our lovely guide, Katharine Johnson, who led us to secret gardens and hidden hamlets, introducing us to real Italians all along the way.

Thank you Peggy Markel for sharing your jewel of an apartment with us and for showing us the sights and sounds of Italian city life.

We're always grateful to Joan Evans for her generosity in allowing us to benefit from her refined eye and sensibility.

We would like to thank Elizabeth May for sharing her wonderful ways with all things sweet.

Our greatest appreciation goes to Julie Sproesser, our studio colleague, who holds down the fort while we roam the globe.

To the lovely people at Chronicle Books for being so sensitive to the photographers' vision: Bill LeBlond who publishes beautiful book after beautiful book and the extraordinarily talented designer, Brooke Johnson.

FOREWORD

Colman Andrews's long history as a food writer, editor-in-chief, bon vivant, and inside player in the behind-the-scenes worlds of both food producers and chefs is evidenced by his many magnificent tomes and about a million stories published in glossy monthly foodzines. His legendary and definitive books, *Catalan Cuisine* and *Flavors of the Riviera*, on Catalan and Ligurian cooking, respectively, are cornerstones of my 10,000-volume cookbook collection, and *Ferran*, his sashay into biography, has shaped what the world knows and thinks of the enigmatic and influential chef Ferran Adrià.

But why *The Country Cooking of Italy*—and what the hell does that title mean anyway? With this volume, Andrews has thrown himself into a market crowded with books by various divas, alleged *nonne*, TV stars from the Food Network and PBS, and chefs from *trattorie* and *ristoranti* across the land—many of whom may actually have visited Italy at least a couple of times. In their works, distinct food opinion is often blurred by the prism of commercial marketability, and any real voice or presence is lost.

Not so here. *The Country Cooking of Italy* is not the usual jumble of recipes for "unique" versions of spaghetti alla carbonara, lasagna variations from points outside Bologna, and treatments of saltimbocca ad nauseum. Andrews is keenly aware of the pitfalls of books that offer recipes like these, and he is tired of the dishes that well-intentioned restaurateurs serve their foreign guests throughout the Boot.

It certainly isn't tourist fare—or even the fancy dishes from the tables of Firenze and Roma and Venezia—that make me hungry to cook. I am intrigued and delighted by the inclusion in this book of many recipes, such as Ripiddu Nivicatu, a kind of cuttlefish and ricotta risotto from Catania, that are entirely new to me. Or the odd, simple, and truly delicious Calabrian marinated lettuce dish called Mappina ("dishrag" in the local dialect). It is exactly these kinds of dishes that tempt me into my local grocer and into my kitchen to cook.

Andrews reminds us that genuine cooking from the Italian countryside is not based on exotic proteins or super-rare produce available only on Tuesdays at the market in Lerici, but on daily shopping for seasonal vegetables and on a well-stocked pantry. *These* are the keys to creating food authentic to Lombardy, Sicily, and all the regions in between. Understanding that grain of truth will help you create delicious dishes in your own kitchen in Peoria, Hollywood, or SoHo, whether you cook on an outdated electric stove top or a six-burner modern marvel.

The Country Cooking of Italy succeeds in bringing a fresh cart down a well-traveled path, not only with its selection of unusual, simple, and delicious recipes, but also with the conceit that any American—gastronaut or not—can actually find the required ingredients nearby and cook authentic-tasting Italian dishes at home. Welcome to the real Italy, where great recipes can be found in every corner and good food belongs to everyone.

MARIO BATALI
chef-entrepreneur

ABOUT THE RECIPES

When I signed a contract to write two books in the Country Cooking series, the first on Ireland and then this one on Italy, each with about 250 recipes, more than one person asked me these two questions: How are you going to find that many recipes in Ireland? How are you going to limit yourself to that few in Italy? I have to say that the former was a good deal easier than the latter.

Deciding what was and wasn't "country cooking" was the first challenge. In Italy, at least in principle, the farm is never far away from the table. The best Italian dishes, even the sophisticated kind, tend to derive from simpler fare; and while there are plenty of world-class chefs in Italy today, the most influential and respected cook is always Mamma. Even many distinctly urban specialties have rural roots. One of the most famous of Roman pastas, spaghetti alla carbonara, is said to have been brought into the city by charcoal vendors from the forests of Abruzzo; another, spaghetti all'amatriciana, comes from the agricultural capital of Amatrice in northern Lazio. (I have included the latter in these pages, but not the former, which seems too citified to me, whatever its provenance.) On the other hand, risotto alla milanese is clearly a dish of the Lombardian capital (legend has it that it was originally colored not with saffron but with gold leaf supplied by artisans working on mosaics for the Duomo); pizza Margherita was invented in downtown Naples, and nowhere else; risi e bisi (a kind of risotto made with the first spring peas) is as definitive of Venice as the Piazza San Marco. Dishes like these, then, don't appear here. Neither do contemporary variations on traditional cooking, even those with rustic inspiration.

Although I have avoided the specialties of Milan, Naples, Venice, and other large cities, I have included plenty of good things from the countryside that surrounds them—and from provincial capitals and smaller towns and villages in every corner of the country. I have also tried to strike a balance between familiar dishes (done right) and more obscure ones. Many recipes in the pages that follow will seem almost ingenuous in their simplicity; only a handful require any measure of culinary dexterity or will take much time. I don't think you will find anything too daunting here, in any case. There are recipes for offal, to be sure, as no book on Italian country cooking could exist without them, but nothing too intimidating: no fried blood, no spleen or lungs or spinal marrow. You won't find recipes here for horsemeat or donkey flesh, either, though I do mention them and have enjoyed eating both meats in Italy. As much as possible, I have avoided dishes based on ingredients that aren't readily available in the United States. A few exceptions appear, and in those cases I've suggested substitutes and/or offered mail-order sources.

Where do these recipes come from? Unlike my Irish cookbook, for which I did most of my research in a period of a little under two years—just before writing the manuscript—this one draws on my more than forty years of traveling and eating in its subject country, and nearly as many years of cooking Italian food myself back home. I don't remember where some of these recipes come from, or even where I first tasted the dishes some of them represent. They have been a part of my cooking, and my life, for a long time. Where a recipe in the pages that follow has been given to me by a restaurant or a friend, or has been adapted from a cookbook, I have credited the source. In the other cases, I just have to say that they came, well, from Italy.

In naming dishes, I have used descriptive English titles in most cases, employing Italian terms only when they are either well-known (as with the names of shapes of pasta), awkward to translate (panzanella, caponata), or when the Italian—or, more often, dialect—forms seem particularly attractive or evocative to me (malloreddus, peposo, presnitz).

Two final notes: I have never measured olive oil by the tablespoon (or cup or milliliter) in my life, and I doubt that any Italian country cook ever has, either. Unless I'm baking, I don't believe much in exact measurements. A dish will not be ruined if you add an extra tablespoon or so of grated pecorino, or leave one out. Recipes in Italian cookbooks often include the notation "q.b.," for *quanto basta*—as in "flour q.b."—meaning "when there's enough." That's not very helpful for the inexperienced cook, but the more confident you are in the kitchen, the more useful a notion it is. In testing the recipes, I have used conventional measurements, but in most cases I would advise that you take them as guidelines, not gospel.

If the amount of olive oil I have called for in a frying pan, for instance, looks like too much or too little, or the quantity of flour I have specified leaves the dough too dry or too damp, adjust at will.

Also, I have tried to offer the most "authentic" recipes throughout, but in almost every case many versions with equal claims to legitimacy exist. I have chosen those that best reflect my experiences of the dishes in question. I'm sure that some of my knowledgeable friends—not to mention some knowledgeable strangers—will find things to quibble about. All I can answer is that the recipe I offer might not be yours, but it is somebody's.

A NOTE ON INGREDIENTS
AND TERMINOLOGY

INGREDIENTS

Butter means unsalted butter. I'm particularly fond of Kerrygold from Ireland, now widely available in supermarkets, which is very rich, with an attractively elastic texture.

Country-style bread means good-quality Italian or French bread sliced from round loaves (not baguettes). The best bread of this kind has a firm but not tough interior and a crust that will crack and flake a bit when cut.

Eggplant/aubergine means the medium-size globe variety (in fact, more ovoid than spherical), not the thinner, elongated Asian types. The latter may be used in recipes where shape is not important, however, as long as the quantity is adjusted to match the weight of the globes. I don't find it necessary to salt and drain eggplant before using it, though some cooks disagree.

Eggs are large (about 2 ounces/60 grams each) and should be as fresh as possible. Use organic eggs, if available.

Extra-virgin olive oil is specified throughout, even (in most cases) for deep-frying. You can use a lower grade of olive oil if you like, or even oil of other kinds, but the results won't be as good. I hasten to add that I'm not talking about frying dried fava/broad beans in Tuscan olio d'oliva that costs a small fortune a liter. There is plenty of good extra-virgin oil around today for a quarter or a third of the cost, both from Italy (if not necessarily Tuscany) and from Spain, Greece, Tunisia, California, and elsewhere.

Flour means all-purpose/plain white flour unless otherwise specified. Fresh pasta made with water only (not eggs) came out best in my tests when I mixed semolina pasta flour with all-purpose flour, though this type of pasta, almost always dried before using, is typically made with only semolina flour in Italy. (I also use semolina pasta flour for making scacciata, a kind of Sicilian stuffed bread.) What about oo flour? This is a designation, widely used in Italy and on at least one American brand, indicating that the flour is very finely milled, like talc in consistency. It usually also means that the flour has a high protein content (typically 10 to 12½ percent)—though American oo flour is lower in protein, closer to 8 or 9 percent. (Protein affects the texture of the finished product, whether pasta or baked goods.) There are also slightly different oo flours sold in Italy for pasta on one hand and pizza on the other. Italian oo flour is sold in the United States and the United Kingdom, but it's more expensive than domestically milled flour, and I don't think there are noticeable differences in the results it gives.

Fruits and vegetables are medium or standard size and are always washed, trimmed, and peeled, as necessary, before using, unless otherwise specified.

Herbs are always fresh, unless otherwise specified. Whole dried bay leaves are the exception.

Parmigiano-reggiano cheese should be just that, or else good-quality grana padano (a parmigiano relative)—not an American, Australian, or Argentinean imitation. It really does make a difference in flavor and texture. Although not specified in the recipes, the cheese should be freshly grated if possible.

Peperoncini are dried chile flakes, reasonably spicy. I find the ones packaged by the big spice companies, the kind you find in supermarket spice racks, generally don't have the requisite kick for southern Italian dishes. Buy Italian flakes if you can find them. Otherwise, use the Mexican variety.

Pasta should be Italian made (unless you're making your own). How much pasta constitutes one serving? That depends on the richness of the sauce, the size of the meal (will the pasta be preceded by antipasto and followed by a main dish?), and, of course, the appetites of the diners. Nonetheless, recipes that call for 1 pound/500 grams of dried pasta to serve ten or twelve people are ridiculous. Pasta is a course, not a garnish. You will need that much to feed four to six hungry eaters.

Pepper should be good-quality coarse-ground black pepper, either packaged or freshly ground, unless otherwise specified.

Salt should be fine-ground sea salt or kosher salt, unless otherwise specified.

Poultry should always be rinsed inside and out and patted dry with paper towels before preparing.

Where the word *prawn* appears in recipes, it is as the British synonym for *shrimp*, and doesn't refer to Dublin Bay prawns—*scampi* in Italian.

Wine should be Italian, if possible. In recipes calling for white wine, don't use overly fragrant varieties (Gewürztraminer, Muscat, or the like) or overly oaked wines. Most Chardonnays are not good for cooking. "Bottle" means a standard 750-milliliter bottle.

Unless otherwise specified, all ingredients should be at room temperature before using.

TERMINOLOGY

The recipes that follow call for various ingredients to be minced, finely chopped, diced, chopped, or coarsely chopped. *Minced* means very finely chopped, into pieces too small to measure. *Finely chopped* means cut into slightly larger irregular pieces ¼ to ⅓ inch/6 to 8 millimeters square. *Diced* means about the same size or slightly larger, but cut into cubes as uniform as possible. *Chopped* means cut into irregular pieces 1 to 1½ inches/2.5 to 3.75 centimeters square. *Coarsely chopped* means cut into larger irregular pieces, their size not critical.

The cooking vessels most commonly called for are a frying pan, a saucepan, a pot, a Dutch oven, and a baking dish. A frying pan is a large, comparatively shallow pan; I prefer cast iron. My own cast-iron pans are old and seasoned enough that they don't react with tomatoes, lemon juice, and other acidic foods; if you are worried about such reactions, which may lend a faint bitterness to food from leached iron, use enameled cast-iron or nonstick pans instead. A saucepan is a small pot of moderate depth, always with a handle and sometimes with a lid. A pot is a deep vessel with a relatively heavy bottom and a lid. (I don't use a pasta pot, which is a pot with a colander set into it, but these are fine for cooking pasta.) A Dutch oven is a heavy, ovenproof pot with a lid. A baking dish is a glass or earthenware cooking vessel, round, square, or rectangular, with or without a lid, ovenproof, and usually but not always usable on the top of the stove (a Spanish *cazuela* or a *tiella*, its southern Italian equivalent, is a good example).

METRIC CONVERSIONS

For the convenience of readers who use metric measurements, quantity, temperature, and length or dimension equivalents have been given in the recipes that follow. Please note that the conversions are approximate, and have been rounded off for reasons of practicality. For instance, 1 pound has been equated to 500 grams, not 454 grams, which would be more accurate; an oven temperature of 400°F becomes 200°C, not the more precise 204°C. Diameter and volume measurements for pots and baking dishes correspond to sizes that are actually available. For example, a 2-quart vessel becomes a 2-liter one, or a 9-inch round baking dish is a 23-centimeter baking dish, rather than a 22.9-centimeter one.

INTRODUCTION

Italian cookery is the cookery of a poor nation, of people who have scant means wherewith to purchase the very inferior materials they must needs work with; and that they produce palatable food at all is, I maintain, a proof that they bring high intelligence to the task.

—The Marchesa di Sant'Andrea in *The Cook's Decameron: A Study in Taste Containing Over Two Hundred Recipes for Italian Dishes* by Mrs. W. G. Waters (1901)

As they ate, they spoke of eating, as always happens in Italy.

—Andrea Camilleri, *The Shape of Water*

Many years ago, when my age and my body mass index were both in the low twenties, I went to Europe for the first time, with my slightly older and considerably more worldly English girlfriend. Our plan had been to spend most of the summer on the Dalmatian coast, but as an aspiring filmmaker—I never got any further than the aspiration—I had also been invited to attend a film festival in Trieste, and my Uncle Paul, who worked on travel accounts for an advertising agency, asked me if I'd like to spend the week before that at a hotel on the Venice Lido, for free, while I was at it. I said yes to both, of course.

A week apiece on the Lido and in Trieste is hardly a conventional introduction to Italy. It was in these places, though, that I began to discover both the country and its food. Meals were included in the Lido deal, so we mostly ate at our hotel, rather than in Venice itself. In retrospect, I realize that the food was probably pretty mediocre, but I marveled at the simplicity and purity of what we were offered: slices of bright orange melon with curls of butter-soft prosciutto, pasta tossed with just a few shreds of tomato and some garlic, thin veal steaks or plump fish fillets grilled on a wood fire and then seasoned with nothing more than olive oil and salt. Moving on to Trieste, where we were given meal tickets for the

Birreria Forst (a basic trattoria run by a large Italian brewery), I expanded my horizons with unsummery soups full of beans and sauerkraut and intense pasta sauces made with chicken livers or crumbled sausage. I had gone to Italian restaurants all my life, back home in Southern California, but I had never before had food like what I ate in these two weeks.

My experience of Italian food began to grow (as did my waistline, unfortunately) a few years later, when I started spending my vacations with an American friend who had moved to Rome. Sometimes we would go to the market and then she would cook huge meals at home. Mostly, though, we went to restaurants and trattorias around the city, or drove out to the hills of the Castelli Romani or up the coast to Civitavecchia or Ansedonia for lunch. Almost every time I sat down at a table, I was amazed. I loved all the typical Roman specialties—bruschetta, artichokes Roman or Jewish style, spaghetti all'amatriciana or carbonara or cacio e pepe, saltimbocca, stewed oxtail, roast baby lamb—but I also liked it when we went to places serving food from other regions, among them Tuscany, Sardinia, Campania, and Abruzzo. It was in Rome, then, that I also first started to realize that there wasn't one Italian cuisine, but many.

To understand the impact this kind of eating had on me, you have to remember—or imagine—what things were like in America back then: Italian food typically meant antipasto out of a jar or Caesar salad (invented in the little Italian hill town of Tijuana), spaghetti with meatballs or linguine with clams, "shrimp scampi" or breaded veal smothered in tomato sauce and melted cheese, and maybe spumoni or (in the fancier places) zabaglione for dessert. Unless you came from an Italian family that had maintained strong culinary ties with the old country, or had traveled pretty widely in Italy yourself with an open mind and an unprejudiced palate, you simply would never have heard of—much less tasted—sun-dried tomatoes, balsamic vinegar, or porcini mushrooms. Radicchio, which now gets tossed into salads at McDonald's, was an obscure and pricey import. My old friend Piero Selvaggio of Valentino restaurant in Santa Monica remembers buying radicchio from Italy for $75 a crate, including airfreight, and having to throw half of it away when it arrived because it had spoiled en route. When he would put the good leaves into salads and charge a bit more than usual for them, his customers would ask, "What's so special about red cabbage?"

When I first started traveling in France, I realized that real French food was more refined and complex than what I had come to know in the United States; it had been "dumbed down" for American consumption. But Italian food, in a sense, was the other way around: for the most part, Italian cooking in its homeland, I began to figure out on my trips there, was far simpler than the gussied-up Italian American interpretations of it I was used to. It was chicken roasted with garlic and rosemary, not chicken in a wine sauce with sausage, artichoke hearts, onions, and mushrooms. It was fettuccine Alfredo made with just rich butter and parmigiano, not loaded down with cream and ham and peas. American chefs—and for that matter, Italian chefs who come here and quickly learn the American way—don't seem to be able to leave well enough alone. American diners (or so the

perception goes) won't pay good money for simple grilled bread with olive oil and garlic, so "bruschetta" comes topped with heirloom beans, artisanal salami, and white truffle oil. You can't charge a premium price for a plate of pasta with plain tomato sauce, so better throw in the peekytoe crab and balsamic-glazed fennel. Half a dozen grilled fresh prawns look naked on a plate, so let's dress them up with some herb risotto and green beans with prosciutto. The same chefs who fell in love with Italian cooking in Italy for its simplicity and purity, it appears, no longer trust the virtues that attracted them when they look back from the New World. They don't cook Italian food anymore; they cook a version of Italian, inspired by the original but (they believe) improved. Somewhere along the way, of course, the inspiration fades away and the remains of an ancient cuisine, vivid and vital, get tossed into the melting pot. Back in the 1970s, my friend Bill Stern—who had lived in Rome and had much the same reaction to the food there as I did—wrote a magazine article called "There Are No Italian Restaurants in America." This was perhaps hyperbole, but I knew what he meant.

The next stage in what I hope is not too corny to call my love affair with Italian food developed slowly in the 1980s and 1990s, as I broke free of Rome's seductive magnetism and began traveling and eating in other parts of the country. I spent long spells in Tuscany, Umbria, Emilia-Romagna, the Catalan end of Sardinia, the wine country of Friuli and the Alto Adige, and the wine and truffle country of Piedmont. I practically lived in Liguria for a year and a half, researching a book (published as *Flavors of the Riviera: Discovering Real Mediterranean Cooking*). Later, I went south, into Molise, Puglia, Basilicata, and Sicily, and eventually managed to visit every one of the country's twenty regions, however briefly in some cases. As my Italian improved (from nonexistent to pretty shaky, where it remains today), I went beyond restaurants and began to meet and talk—and above all, eat and drink—with farmers and winemakers and shopkeepers and just plain food-loving citizens. And I learned that what I thought I knew about Italian food from my restaurant experiences in Venice, Trieste, and Rome was only part of the story.

I learned that many of the most famous "real Italian" dishes I had encountered, even in Italy, were twentieth-century creations—and that even so definitive a food as pasta was not a daily part of the Italian diet until about a hundred years ago. People ate polenta or bread, and invented scores of ways to use the latter when it became too hard to eat alone. A few basic vegetables—onions, garlic, carrots, celery, fava/broad beans, and later tomatoes, shell beans, and potatoes—were the staples. Protein came from anchovies and sardines, sometimes dried or salted cod, occasionally bits of ham or sausage. The preferred cooking fat in some areas was neither butter nor olive oil but lard. Butter and oil were too expensive, and even those who grew olives and made their own oil often sold it for a profit instead of using it themselves. Until the last few generations, fresh fish was all but unknown unless you lived on the coast, fresh meat was a rarity, and chicken was for a holiday feast for most Italians. When I was researching my book in Liguria, I talked to old-timers in the *entroterra* (backcountry) who as children had lived on little more than dried cod, chestnuts, and wild greens. The romanticized "Mediterranean diet" touted in the latter part of the twentieth century was, I realized—as I wrote in *Flavors of the Riviera*—"more the way people eat at Chez Panisse than the way they eat, and have traditionally eaten, around the Mediterranean."

None of these realizations made me love Italian food any less. In fact, they made me look at it with greater admiration, and, I think, to understand its underpinnings better. Italian food—a lot of it, anyway—grew out of poverty, but it also grew out of fundamental respect for the land and what it yielded. At its best, like all cuisines with modest beginnings, it respects the seasons, wastes nothing, values consistency and simplicity; and it belongs to a place. Over the years, I have been particularly impressed, as I've made Italian friends from one end of the peninsula to the other, at the intensity of local and regional pride that so many Italians, even the young upwardly mobile ones with their iPhones and VWs, maintain in the food products and dishes they grew up with. They love eating—is it an accident that in the language of their predecessors, the Romans, the words for "eat" (*edo*) and "be" (*sum*) share an infinitive form, *esse*? (Edo ergo sum?)—and they love talking about eating. They love telling you about the cheese made just outside town, the salami that their uncle cures each year, the olive oil from down the road so good that Tuscans come and buy it to resell as their own. They love talking about the "unique" pasta shapes found only in their town (which are probably found in lots of other towns, too, if sometimes under different names, but never mind). And they love talking about everybody's favorite cook, Mamma, and what she puts on the table, or used to before she passed on to her much-deserved reward—the food against which all other must be judged.

In introducing my last cookbook, *The Country Cooking of Ireland*, I proposed that, in a sense, all Irish cooking was country cooking. I cannot make the same case for Italy. Too many culinary innovations over the centuries can be traced to the legendary gourmands of ancient Rome, to Renaissance noblemen and prelates or their chefs, to wealthy urban merchants. But I do think that all Italian cooking is in some sense *from* the country, from the region, from the land. This is the key to its identity. This is what makes it great.

Olive harvest on the Melfi family farm, Casacalenda, Campobasso (Molise), 1932

ANTIPASTO

AWAKENING THE PALATE

In [a] sense the antipasto . . . is shop-bought food, and it was used by the
cleverest hosts to fill out the duller phases of the meal.
—*Alberto Capatti and Massimo Montanari,* Italian Cuisine: A Cultural History

Among Italian *antipasti* (hors d'oeuvre) are to be found some of the most
successful achievements in European cooking.
—*Elizabeth David,* Italian Food

Years ago, on the popular TV quiz show *Jeopardy!*, the following clue was given: "It means appetizer, but only when served after pasta." According to the show, the correct answer (phrased as a question, in *Jeopardy!* style) was, "What is antipasto?" Wrong. As I pointed out in a letter to the show's producers (this predated e-mail), the words *pasta* and *pasto* are etymologically unrelated. The former means "paste," that is, "dough," and comes from a Greek word, also *pasta*, meaning a kind of salted porridge, related to the verb *passein*, "to sprinkle" (*pastry* and *paste* derive ultimately from the same root). The latter is Italian for "meal" or "dinner," related to the Latin *repastus*, which has its origin in *pascere*, "to graze" or "to feed," as in *pasture*. Antipasto is thus something served before the meal, not necessarily before the pasta. I got back a rather snippy form response, informing me that the show stood by its extensive and painstaking research. I never watched *Jeopardy!* again.

In any case, antipasto first became part of the Italian eating experience in the sixteenth century—long before the daily consumption of pasta did. The idea was to stimulate the appetite through vivid, salty, simple flavors, which usually meant pickled vegetables, cured meats, and brined or oil-packed seafood (that's why antipasto was frequently "shop bought"). The great cured meat products of Italy—the hams, salamis, and so on—were particularly useful in this context.

At the Italian restaurants I knew growing up in Southern California, antipasto was usually a small plateful of pickled vegetables, often fished out of an immense glass urn, possibly garnished with some cubes of salami and maybe some strips of provolone. I remember how amazed and delighted I was, then, when I first walked into Casale, an ancient country inn on the Via Appia, on the edge of Rome. Just inside the door, I came upon a breathtaking example of what antipasto could be: a long, two-tiered self-service table was crowded with platters and bowls and well-used baking dishes full of the most wonderful-looking foods—marinated cipolline onions, three kinds of meat-and-rice-stuffed vegetables (onions, tomatoes, and bell peppers/capsicums), lentil salad, butter beans in olive oil, borlotti (cranberry) beans in olive oil, fresh ricotta and mozzarella (both glistening with olive oil and sprinkled with peperoncini), marinated anchovies, tuna in olive oil, seafood salad, grilled squid, grilled zucchini/courgettes, grilled radicchio, marinated beets/beetroot, frittatas flecked with spinach and chard, thin slices of hard sausage in several varieties, three or four kinds of olives, and on and on. There must have been forty things to choose from; I think I chose them all.

Of course, most antipasto selections in Italy today aren't this elaborate. In the mid-twentieth century, the array of cold antipasti began to go out of style in many places. Gourmets criticized it for dulling the palate, rather than stimulating it; one Milanese writer called the practice of eating antipasto "absolutely barbaric." Today, many places offer just a few kinds of stuffed or marinated vegetables, maybe some prosciutto, maybe some local salami or the equivalent. Or, there might be something hot—croquettes, fried squash blossoms, some form of melted cheese. That's fine. A huge choice is not essential. The point of antipasto is just to start the culinary conversation.

DEEP-FRIED OLIVES

SERVES 6 TO 8

Deep-fried olives, often stuffed with ground meat, are served in the bars of Venice and the surrounding region as cichetti, *the little snacks often called Venetian tapas. But I've also had them in rural Tuscany and in Puglia, and those of Ascoli Piceno in the Marche are particularly famous. This is a simple version, without filling.*

¾ CUP/45 GRAMS TOASTED BREAD CRUMBS, HOMEMADE (PAGE 378) OR COMMERCIAL

SALT AND PEPPER

¼ TEASPOON PAPRIKA

¼ TEASPOON DRIED OREGANO OR MARJORAM

2 EGG WHITES

50 MEDIUM-SIZE PITTED GREEN ITALIAN OR SPANISH OLIVES

4 CUPS/I LITER OLIVE OIL

Put the bread crumbs into a wide, shallow bowl. Season them generously with salt and pepper, and add the paprika and oregano. Mix together well with a fork. Lightly beat the egg whites in a small bowl.

Select a baking sheet/tray large enough to hold the olives in a single layer without touching, and line it with waxed/grease-proof paper or parchment/baking paper. One at a time, dip the olives into the egg whites, roll them in the seasoned bread crumbs, and place them on the lined baking sheet. Refrigerate for 30 minutes.

Heat the oil in a deep fryer or a deep saucepan fitted with a frying basket to 375°F/190°C. Working in batches, add the olives and fry until golden brown, about 3 minutes. As they are done, drain them on paper towels. Serve warm.

FRIED SQUASH BLOSSOMS

SERVES 6

Fried squash blossoms, either plain or stuffed with mozzarella and sometimes anchovies, are eaten anywhere in Italy that zucchini/courgettes or other summer squash will grow—which is almost everywhere. I got this recipe many years ago from a friend in Liguria.

1½ CUPS/185 GRAMS FLOUR

SALT

I TABLESPOON EXTRA-VIRGIN OLIVE OIL

I EGG, LIGHTLY BEATEN

2 TO 3 CUPS/480 TO 720 MILLILITERS CANOLA OIL

I GARLIC CLOVE, MINCED

2 TABLESPOONS MINCED ITALIAN PARSLEY

36 SMALL- TO MEDIUM-SIZE SQUASH BLOSSOMS, STEMS AND STAMENS REMOVED, THEN RINSED AND DRIED INSIDE AND OUT

Sift together the flour and 1 teaspoon salt into a medium bowl. Whisk in 2 cups/480 milliliters warm water, the olive oil, and the egg. Set the batter aside.

Pour the canola oil into a large frying pan to a depth of about 1 inch/2.5 centimeters and heat over high heat to 375°F/190°C. Stir the garlic and parsley into the batter. Working in batches, dip the blossoms into the batter, allowing the excess batter to drip back into bowl, and add to the hot oil. Fry the blossoms, turning once if necessary to cook evenly, until golden brown, 2 to 3 minutes. As they are done, drain them on paper towels.

Sprinkle the fried blossoms with salt while they are still slightly moist, then serve hot or at room temperature.

FRIED FAVA BEANS

SERVES 4 TO 6

Deep-fried dried fava beans are eaten in many countries, from Portugal to China. I first encountered them in Italy, though, at Il Frantoio, an agriturismo (see page 228) in Fasano, in a portion of Puglia famous for its olives and olive oil. (A frantoio is an olive mill.)

4 CUPS/1 LITER OLIVE OIL

1 CUP/250 GRAMS DRIED FAVA/BROAD BEANS

SALT

Heat the oil in a deep fryer or a deep saucepan fitted with a frying basket to 375°F/190°C. Working in batches, add the beans and fry until dark brown, about 3 minutes. As they are done, drain them on paper towels.

Salt the beans generously while they are still moist, then let cool to room temperature before serving.

FAVAS WITH PECORINO

SERVES 4

A sunny, breezy afternoon in May in the hill town of Ariccia, in the Castelli Romani outside Rome; an impromptu picnic on a low stone wall in the Parco Chigi, its gardens designed by Bernini, its pathways trod by Stendhal and D'Annunzio. Wandering through the town, we've collected miscellaneous foodstuffs, and now we're eating slices of flat-sided, coarse-textured spinata romana salami unwrapped from its butcher paper, juicy local cherries leaking through their paper bag, fava beans that we found sitting in brine in a barrel at the cheese shop, and shards of ivory-hued pecorino romano. It is a perfect meal. Favas and pecorino go particularly well together, and fresh ones are even better than the big, yellow brined ones we found that day. (Use young pecorino if possible, not the hard, pungent pecorino romano found in supermarkets; young pecorino sardo might be easier to find than its Roman counterpart.) Pop a couple of favas into your mouth, then a bit of pecorino: for me, those flavors will always be springtime in Lazio.

2 CUPS/300 GRAMS SHELLED FRESH FAVA/BROAD BEANS (ABOUT 2 POUNDS/1 KILOGRAM IN THE POD)

SALT

6 OUNCES/175 GRAMS YOUNG PECORINO SARDO OR PECORINO ROMANO, BROKEN INTO SMALL, IRREGULAR PIECES

1 TO 2 TEASPOONS EXTRA-VIRGIN OLIVE OIL

Bring a medium pot of unsalted water to a boil over high heat, add the shelled beans, and blanch for about 30 seconds. Drain and rinse under cold running water, then peel them by squeezing gently from one end so they slip out of their skins.

Meanwhile, refill the pot with fresh salted water and bring to a boil over high heat. Add the beans and cook just until they begin to soften, 1 to 2 minutes (depending on size). Drain them and rinse under cold running water, then pat them dry with paper towels.

Scatter the pecorino pieces on a serving plate, then scatter the beans over them. Drizzle with a little oil and season lightly with salt before serving.

CALABRIAN GREEN OLIVE PASTE

MAKES ABOUT 3 CUPS/720 MILLILITERS

This Calabrian "tapenade" is typically eaten spread on country-style bread or slightly more refined crostini. I find that it also makes a good if unusual condiment for simply grilled or roasted chicken.

½ CUP/120 MILLILITERS EXTRA-VIRGIN OLIVE OIL

2½ CUPS/375 GRAMS PITTED GREEN ITALIAN OR SPANISH OLIVES

3 GARLIC CLOVES, COARSELY CHOPPED

½ FRESH SERRANO OR CAYENNE CHILE

2 TABLESPOONS CAPERS

SALT

Combine the oil, olives, garlic, chile, and capers in a food processor and process until a paste forms that is almost but not quite smooth. Season lightly with salt if necessary. This paste will keep, tightly covered, in the refrigerator for at least 1 week.

CAPONATA

SERVES 6 TO 8

"He who has not eaten a caponatina of eggplant has never reached the antechamber of the terrestrial paradise . . . ," Sicilian writer Gaetano Falzone once proposed. This famous sweet-and-sour eggplant specialty is a typical summertime dish in southern Italy, particularly favored in Sicily and Campania. Some scholars think that it is Catalan in origin; others maintain that it was devised by Sicilian sailors, as the vinegar would have acted as a preservative on long sea journeys. Several theories offer explanations as to how it got its name. Some link it to caupona, *a Latin word for "landlady" or "innkeeper," and by extension tavern or inn; others suggest a relation to* chapon, *a French term for oil-soaked bread used in some Mediterranean salads. There is also a very different, almost architecturally arranged vegetable dish from Genoa called* cappon magro, *meaning fast-day capon (that is, a centerpiece for a meal on days when the consumption of meat was forbidden to Catholics), so perhaps a connection exists there.*

I CUP/240 MILLILITERS EXTRA-VIRGIN OLIVE OIL

2 EGGPLANTS/AUBERGINES, ABOUT 2 POUNDS/
I KILOGRAM TOTAL, CUT INTO SMALL CUBES

I ONION, CHOPPED

3 STALKS CELERY, CHOPPED

I CUP/150 GRAMS PITTED GREEN ITALIAN OR
SPANISH OLIVES

½ CUP/90 GRAMS CAPERS

2 SMALL, RIPE TOMATOES, SEEDED AND GRATED
(SEE RAW TOMATO COULIS, PAGE 371)

½ CUP/120 MILLILITERS WHITE WINE VINEGAR

2 TABLESPOONS SUGAR

SALT AND PEPPER

2 TABLESPOONS PINE NUTS

6 TO 8 SPRIGS ITALIAN PARSLEY, MINCED

Heat the oil in a large frying pan over medium-high heat. Add the eggplant cubes and sauté, stirring frequently, until golden brown, about 5 minutes. Using a slotted spoon, transfer the cubes to paper towels to drain.

Add the onion, celery, olives, capers, tomatoes, vinegar, and sugar to the oil remaining in the pan and season with salt and pepper. Reduce the heat to low and simmer the vegetables, stirring occasionally, until they soften, about 10 minutes. Return the eggplant to the pan, add the pine nuts, and cook for about 5 minutes more to blend the flavors.

Adjust the seasoning, stir in the parsley, and transfer the mixture to a bowl. Cover and refrigerate it for at least 24 hours. Bring to room temperature before serving.

PICKLED EGGPLANT PRESERVED IN OLIVE OIL

SERVES 4 TO 6

I had this unusual preparation of eggplant at La Locandiera, a trattoria specializing in local cooking in Bernalda, in Basilicata. Home cook Maria Salfi Russo, mother of my friends from Bernalda, Riccardo and Michele Russo, was kind enough to give me her recipe.

I¼ CUPS/300 MILLILITERS WHITE WINE VINEGAR

SALT

2 EGGPLANTS/AUBERGINES, ABOUT
2 POUNDS/I KILOGRAM TOTAL

24 MINT LEAVES

3 GARLIC CLOVES, MINCED

2 FRESH CAYENNE OR OTHER SMALL RED CHILES,
MINCED

I TO 2 CUPS/240 TO 480 MILLILITERS EXTRA-VIRGIN
OLIVE OIL

Combine 1 cup/240 milliliters of the vinegar, 4 cups/1 liter water, and 2 tablespoons salt in a large, nonreactive bowl and stir to dissolve the salt.

Peel 1 eggplant, then slice it crosswise into rounds between ⅓ and ½ inch/about 1 centimeter thick. As each slice is cut, put it into the acidulated water to avoid discoloration. Repeat with the remaining eggplant. Let the slices soak for about 30 minutes, weighing them down with a heavy bowl if they float to the surface.

Select a clean, dry 1-quart/1-liter Mason or other hermetic jar with a mouth big enough to fit the bottom of a wine bottle (3 to 3½ inches/about 8 centimeters in diameter). Sprinkle a few drops of the remaining vinegar in the bottom of the jar, and add 2 mint leaves and a few bits of garlic and chile.

Drain the eggplant slices, then press them against the bottom of the bowl with your hand to remove as much moisture as possible. Working as fast as possible, put three eggplant slices into the jar and press down on them with the bottom of a clean, flat-bottomed wine bottle. Holding the bottle in place, upend the jar over the sink to drain out any water. Sprinkle a little more vinegar over the top of the eggplant slices, top with 2 or 3 mint leaves, and scatter with a few bits of garlic and chile. Put three more eggplant slices into the jar, and again press down on them with the bottom of the wine bottle and upend the jar to drain out the liquid. Repeat the process until you have used up all the eggplant, vinegar, mint leaves, garlic, and chile, pressing down with the wine bottle and draining off the water after each addition.

When the jar is full, stand the wine bottle (if the bottle is empty, fill it with water) in the jar, cover the bottle with plastic wrap/cling film, extending it down over the top of the jar, and refrigerate the setup overnight. In the morning, remove the wine bottle and drain out any accumulated water.

Pour the oil into the jar to cover the eggplant by about ½ inch/1.25 centimeters. Cover the jar with a tight-fitting lid and refrigerate for at least 3 days before serving. The eggplant will keep for up to 2 weeks.

PICKLED SQUID, ANACAPRI STYLE

※

SERVES 4 TO 8

I'd never had this dish, named for a commune on the island of Capri, but I found the recipe in Elizabeth David's Italian Food *and tried it—and liked it a lot. It's an easy and unusual addition to a cold antipasto selection.*

3 CUPS/720 MILLILITERS WHITE WINE VINEGAR

4 LARGE SQUID, ABOUT 6 INCHES/15 CENTIMETERS LONG AND 3 INCHES/7.5 CENTIMETERS WIDE, OR 8 TO 12 SMALLER ONES, CLEANED AND CUT INTO RINGS

1 TABLESPOON OREGANO OR THYME LEAVES

SALT

4 CUPS/1 LITER EXTRA-VIRGIN OLIVE OIL

Bring the vinegar to a boil in a medium saucepan, add the squid, and cook for 3 minutes. Drain the squid, place in a medium bowl, and set aside to cool to room temperature.

Mix the oregano into the squid, then season with salt.

Divide the squid evenly between two sterilized 1-pint/500-milliliter Mason or other hermetic jars (or put them into one sterilized 1-quart/1-liter jar), then add oil to cover the squid completely (you may need a little less or a little more than what is called for). Cover the jars with sterilized tight-fitting lids and refrigerate for at least 6 weeks before serving. The squid will keep, tightly covered, in the refrigerator for up to 3 months.

STUFFED TOMATOES

SERVES 4 TO 8

The most famous stuffed vegetables in Italy are those of Liguria, but tomatoes, onions, zucchini, eggplants, and the like are filled with rice, bread crumbs, meat, even sometimes seafood in many parts of the country, and rice-stuffed tomatoes are a staple on anti-pasto tables almost everywhere. This recipe comes from Il Casale on the Via Flaminia, a short distance outside Rome—a restaurant famous for its antipasto array.

8 RIPE BUT FIRM TOMATOES

½ CUP/120 MILLILITERS EXTRA-VIRGIN OLIVE OIL, PLUS MORE FOR GREASING

⅓ CUP/65 GRAMS VIALONE NANO OR ARBORIO RICE

2 TABLESPOONS FINELY CHOPPED ITALIAN PARSLEY

2 TABLESPOONS FINELY CHOPPED BASIL

2 GARLIC CLOVES, MINCED

SALT AND PEPPER

Preheat the oven to 400°F/200°C/gas 6.

Cut a slice about ½ inch/1.25 centimeters thick off the bottom (blossom end) of each tomato, and a slice about ¾ inch/2 centimeters thick off the top (stem end), discarding the bottoms but reserving the tops. Working over a medium bowl, use a grapefruit spoon or other small spoon to scoop the flesh out of the tomatoes, being careful not to puncture the walls and reserving the flesh.

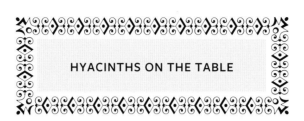

HYACINTHS ON THE TABLE

One of the harbingers of springtime in Connecticut, where I've lived for the past seventeen years, are grape hyacinths, little plants with lavender-blue flowers that spring up in the lawns. When I first read references to the "little onions" known as *lampascioni* that are eaten in Basilicata and Puglia, I had no idea these were the bulbs of those same pretty flowers. Lampascioni (*Muscari comosum*)—also called *lampasciun* and *lamponi* and about twenty other things in various parts of the region—are tiny and do indeed look like onions. I first encountered them at a splendid trattoria called La Locandiera in the town of Bernalda, in Basilicata, where they were served both pickled and fried—scored at the top so that they blossomed, in the latter case suggesting tiny analogues to the "Bloomin'

Onion" at the Outback steakhouses. I had them again at a restaurant called L'Aratro in Alberobello, in Puglia, where they were cooked with lamb and potatoes. They have a faintly fruity or musky flavor, and a distinctive bitterness—not something I would trek across the desert for, but unusual and not unpleasant.

Lampascioni are harvested—they are a wild food, dug from fields and hillsides—mostly in the fall, but they will keep for months in a dark place, alongside the onions and potatoes. Somewhere, years ago, I ran across a fragment of Persian poetry—Persian poetry in the Edward FitzGerald mode—that I always liked: "If you have two loaves of bread, sell one/and with the dole, buy hyacinths to feed the soul." Little did I suspect that hyacinths could feed the body, too.

Lightly oil a baking dish just large enough to hold the tomatoes in a single layer, and stand the tomatoes in the dish. Set the dish aside.

Pass the tomato flesh through a food mill or pulse it in a food processor or blender to form a coarse puree. Return the puree to the bowl and mix in the rice, parsley, basil, garlic, and oil. Season generously with salt and pepper.

Spoon the rice mixture into the tomatoes, then replace the tops. Bake until the rice is cooked and the tomatoes are soft and beginning to char, 45 to 55 minutes. Serve at room temperature.

TUNA PÂTÉ

SERVES 6 TO 8

This unusual purée, which I encountered at Osteria del Portico in Castelvittorio, in the backcountry of western Liguria, might be considered a variation on brandade. Serve it with grilled or toasted country-style bread.

SALT

2 RUSSET OR OTHER FLOURY POTATOES

ONE 6-OUNCE/175-GRAM CAN OR JAR TOP-QUALITY OLIVE OIL–PACKED ITALIAN OR SPANISH TUNA

1 PINCH CAYENNE PEPPER

BLACK PEPPER

2 CUPS/480 MILLILITERS MAYONNAISE

20 TO 24 BLACK ITALIAN OLIVES

Bring a medium pot of salted water to a boil over high heat, add the potatoes, and cook until tender when pierced with a fork, 20 to 35 minutes (depending on size). Drain the potatoes and set them aside to cool. When they are cool enough to handle, peel them and put them into a large bowl. Mash them with a potato masher.

Add the tuna and its oil to the potatoes, breaking it up with a fork and mixing it in well. Add the cayenne pepper, season with salt and black pepper, and then work in the mayonnaise. For a smoother pâté, pass the mixture through a food mill.

Put the pâté into a serving bowl or mound it on a plate, and scatter the olives across the top.

LIPTAUER
(SPICED CHEESE SPREAD)

SERVES 4

My introduction to the spiced cheese spread called liptauer came in London in the mid-1960s, at a then-popular Labor Party politicians' hangout and very good Hungarian restaurant called The Gay Hussar. The spread is apparently Slovakian in origin (it is named for the Liptov region of Slovakia), and is eaten in one form or another all over Central Europe. Since I first encountered it at a Hungarian place, though, and because its most prominent flavoring is paprika, I have always associated it primarily with Hungary—where, incidentally, it is called körözött. I was somewhat taken aback, then, when I was brought a little crock of what was clearly the same thing, a few years later, at a trattoria just outside Trieste. I shouldn't have been, I later realized, since Trieste was the seaport of the Austro-Hungarian Empire, and Mitteleuropean influences are strong there. In any case, when I asked the waiter what it was, he replied, "una spuma di formaggio all'ungherese" (Hungarian-style cheese mousse). Then he added, "But you can call it liptauer." This is a Triestino recipe for same.

5 TABLESPOONS/75 GRAMS BUTTER, SOFTENED

1 CUP/250 GRAMS FRESH RICOTTA

1 TEASPOON PAPRIKA

1 TEASPOON MUSTARD SEEDS

1 TEASPOON GROUND CUMIN

2 ANCHOVY FILLETS, MINCED

2 GREEN/SPRING ONIONS, WHITE PART ONLY, MINCED

6 TO 8 CHIVES, MINCED

SALT AND PEPPER

TOASTED SQUARES OF COUNTY-STYLE BREAD OR CRACKERS FOR SERVING

Put the butter in a medium bowl, and whisk vigorously with a whisk or beat with a handheld electric mixer until smooth. Then whisk in the ricotta, a little at a time. With a wooden spoon, stir in the paprika, mustard seeds, cumin, anchovies, green onions, and chives. Season with salt and pepper, mixing together thoroughly.

Scoop into a serving bowl and accompany with toasts.

FRICO

(FRIULANO CHEESE CRISPS)

MAKES ABOUT 20 FRITTERS; SERVES 6 TO 8

These easy-to-make cheese crisps or fritters are a specialty of Friuli, and are best made with montasio, a firm cow's milk cheese from that corner of Italy. There is also a cheese from the Valcellina in Friuli's Pordenone Province, rarely seen today, called frico Balacia, specifically meant to be fried. Some purists insist that the cheese must be fried in lard. See page 382 for a source for montasio.

1 POUND/500 GRAMS MONTASIO OR ASIAGO, GRATED

2 TABLESPOONS FLOUR

1 TABLESPOON BUTTER

2 TO 3 TABLESPOONS EXTRA-VIRGIN OLIVE OIL

Combine the cheese and flour in a large bowl, and mix together well but gently with your hands.

Melt the butter in a large frying pan over medium-low heat, and add 2 tablespoons of the oil. When the oil-butter mixture is hot, working in batches, use a spoon to form fritters 2 to 3 inches/ 5 to 7.5 centimeters in diameter, using about 2 tablespoons of the cheese mixture for each fritter and gently tamping down each fritter with a spatula. Make sure the edges of the fritters don't touch. Cook the fritters, without moving them, until their edges turn golden brown, about 3 minutes. Then, using the spatula, carefully turn them and cook until golden, about 2 minutes longer. As the fritters are ready, drain them on paper towels.

Serve the fritters at room temperature.

GRILLED SCAMORZA

SERVES 4

The first time I ever tasted grilled cheese—as opposed to grilled cheese sandwiches, which were a staple of my youth—wasn't exactly in the country, but it felt like the country: One of the restaurants my friends and I frequented in Rome in the early 1970s was the rustic Er Cucurucù (Roman dialect for "The Dove"), a now-vanished place perched on a quiet, tree-shaded hillside above the Tiber. There was a huge wood-fired grill/barbecue on one end of the terrace where we always sat, and a white-garbed cook would stand there, cooking quail, little lamb chops, immense porcini mushroom caps, thick slices of bread for bruschetta—and slabs of mozzarella-like scamorza, which would come to the table slightly charred and oozing flavor. Years later, I had grilled scamorza with grilled porcini at an unexpectedly elegant rural hotel-restaurant called Degli Angeli, near Magliano Sabina in the Sabine Hills of Lazio. The combination was almost too much fun. Usually made from cow's milk, scamorza came originally from southern Italy, possibly Puglia, but today is made in many regions, including Molise and Abruzzo and, industrially, in Lombardy and the Veneto. Available in both regular and smoked versions, it closely resembles provolone, which makes an acceptable substitute.

OLIVE OIL FOR GREASING

1 POUND/500 GRAMS UNSMOKED SCAMORZA OR PROVOLONE, CUT INTO SLABS ABOUT 1 INCH/2.5 CENTIMETERS THICK

GRILLED COUNTRY-STYLE BREAD FOR SERVING (OPTIONAL)

Lightly oil a grill/barbecue, then light it and let the coals or wood burn down to medium-hot (if using a gas grill, preheat to about 500°F/260°C).

Place the cheese directly on the grill rack and cook until the cheese begins to melt and grill marks appear on the underside, 2 to 3 minutes. Turn and cook for 2 to 3 minutes on the other side.

Serve with grilled bread, if you like.

FONDUTA

SERVES 4

It is tempting to call fonduta, a specialty of Piedmont, the Italian fondue, but there are important differences: Unlike its Swiss and French counterparts, it contains no alcohol; it does, on the other hand, usually contain egg yolks, which the fondues of France and Switzerland do not. It is served in a shallow bowl or even on a flat plate, not kept warm over a burner, and while it is often served with bread, it is usually eaten with a spoon. For those who can afford it, it is wonderful garnished with white truffles during their short season every fall and early winter. In addition, while the Swiss and French admit various kinds of alpine cheeses to the fondue pot, true fonduta is made with only one variety: fontina from the Valle d'Aosta (non-Italian fontina won't yield good results). Although it can be eaten as an antipasto before a simple meal, and is thus included in this chapter, fonduta is usually served in place of a pasta or risotto course.

6 OUNCES/175 GRAMS FONTINA, TRIMMED OF RIND AND CUT INTO ¾-INCH/2-CENTIMETER CUBES

1½ TEASPOONS FLOUR

1 CUP/240 MILLILITERS WHOLE MILK

2 EGG YOLKS, LIGHTLY BEATEN

1 TABLESPOON BUTTER, SOFTENED

1 SMALL FRESH WHITE TRUFFLE, GENTLY BRUSHED CLEAN (OPTIONAL)

COUNTRY-STYLE BREAD OR TOAST FOR SERVING (OPTIONAL)

Toss together the fontina and flour in a heatproof bowl, then stir in the milk. Cover and refrigerate overnight.

Let the bowl come to room temperature, then stir the egg yolks and butter into the milk-cheese mixture. Bring a medium pot of water to a simmer over medium heat. Reduce the heat to low and rest the bowl over, not touching, the water in the pot. Cook, stirring constantly, until the cheese has completely melted and the mixture is smooth, 15 to 20 minutes.

Divide the mixture between 4 warmed shallow bowls or deep plates. Shave an equal amount of the white truffle over each serving, if using. Serve with crusty country bread, if you like.

MOZZARELLA IN CARROZZA

SERVES 6

After pizza, this is Campania's best use of mozzarella. A carrozza is a "coach" or "carriage," a reference to the way the cheese is enclosed in the bread and egg.

12 THIN SLICES COUNTRY-STYLE BREAD, CRUSTS TRIMMED

½ CUP/120 MILLILITERS WHOLE MILK

ONE 1-POUND/500-GRAM BALL FRESH MOZZARELLA, CUT INTO 6 SLICES OF EQUAL THICKNESS

2 EGGS

½ CUP/65 GRAMS FLOUR

1 CUP/60 GRAMS TOASTED BREAD CRUMBS, HOMEMADE (PAGE 378) OR COMMERCIAL

½ CUP/120 MILLILITERS EXTRA-VIRGIN OLIVE OIL

SALT

Brush one side of each bread slice lightly with the milk. Make 6 sandwiches, with the milk side facing in, positioning the mozzarella slices in the center of the bread and pressing down lightly on the top slice of each sandwich. Refrigerate the sandwiches for 1 hour.

Lightly beat the eggs in a shallow bowl. Put flour and bread crumbs into two separate shallow bowls. Dredge a sandwich in the flour, then dip it into the eggs, then dredge it in the bread crumbs. Press the edges together carefully but firmly to seal in the cheese. Repeat with the remaining 5 sandwiches.

Pour the oil into a medium frying pan and heat over medium-high heat to 375°F/190°C. Working in batches, fry the sandwiches, turning once, until golden brown on both sides, about 1 minute per side. As they are ready, transfer them to paper towels to drain.

Season the sandwiches with salt, then halve each sandwich lengthwise or on the diagonal. Serve warm or at room temperature.

BUFFALO CHEESE

It used to drive the late Roman-born restaurateur Mauro Vincenti crazy when he heard his American customers talking about "buffalo mozzarella." "Colman," he would say, "it's *bufala*. In Italy, it is not possible to get milk from an animal with an *o* at the end of its name." True enough, but the beasts in question—the ones whose milk produces the finest of mozzarella, most notably in the region of Campania, around Naples (but also in other corners of central and southern Italy)—are indeed buffalo, at least to us Yankees; water buffalo, to be precise. What are these Asian bovines doing in Italy? That's a good question. Over the years, credit has been given to everyone from the Goths to the Moors to the Normans (who supposedly brought them up from Sicily). Or, maybe Crusaders brought them back from the Middle East. Il Consorzio per la Tutela del Formaggio Mozzarella di Bufala Campana—"The Association for the Protection of the Bufala Mozzarella of Campana"—has even suggested that the animals might have originated in Italy and gone the other way, to Asia.

However they might have arrived, the animals are undeniably a fact of life in the Campanian countryside today, and it is not uncommon to come upon fields in which they browse by the hundreds. They are big, lumbering, and blackish brown, with serious-looking horns and scraggly moustaches. The first man—or, more likely, woman—to have milked one must have had extraordinary courage. Nowadays, of course, commercial producers of the cheese milk them by machine, twice a day. Mozzarella—first mentioned by that name in 1570 (the word derives from *mozzare*, Neapolitan dialect for "to cut")—is best when eaten as soon after it is made as possible, preferably the same day, which is why some of the best producers refuse to export their wares.

The vast majority of mozzarella made in Italy, in Campania and elsewhere, it should be noted, is based not on the milk of water buffalo, but of cows. In Campania, this cheese is called *fior di latte*, "flower of the milk." A Neapolitan aristocrat once told Elizabeth David scornfully that it was "eaten only by servants"—but good-quality fior di latte is excellent cheese, and preferred today by some connoisseurs for any preparation that calls for mozzarella to be melted.

BRUSCHETTA

※

SERVES 4

All over America today, restaurants—Italian and otherwise—serve something called "brooshedda," which involves various combinations of vegetables and sometimes other substances spooned over bread or limp toast of some kind. If you want to make your own at home, supermarkets now sell little plastic containers labeled "bruschetta," which typically hold mixtures of chopped tomatoes, garlic, and basil, among other ingredients, with nary a morsel of bread in sight. Meanwhile, in Italy, and especially in Rome and the Lazio countryside, people go on happily eating what they *think is bruschetta—that's "bruh-skate-a"—which is nothing more than good country bread, grilled or toasted (the word comes from the Roman dialect verb* bruscare, *meaning "to cook on coals"), rubbed with raw garlic, anointed with olive oil, and seasoned with salt. Some places might strew chopped tomatoes across the top and serve it with a knife and fork, but it is generally meant to be eaten on its own—call it the original "garlic bread"—or as an accompaniment to prosciutto or various salumi. In Tuscany, incidentally, the same thing is called* fett'unta, *dialect for "oiled slice"—a reminder that you should use the best possible olive oil.*

8 LARGE SLICES COUNTRY-STYLE BREAD,
½ INCH/1.25 CENTIMETERS THICK

2 GARLIC CLOVES, PEELED

2 TO 3 TABLESPOONS EXTRA-VIRGIN OLIVE OIL

SALT

Lightly grease a grill/barbecue with oil, then light it and let the coals or wood burn down to medium-hot (if using a gas grill, preheat to about 500°F/260°C).

Grill the bread slices, turning once, until black grill marks begin to appear on both sides. Do not allow it to burn. Alternatively, toast the slices medium-light.

Rub the flat side of a garlic clove gently but firmly over one side of each slice of grilled or toasted bread, using 1 clove for 4 slices. Drizzle the slices with the olive oil, then season with salt before serving.

CHICKEN LIVER CROSTINI

※

SERVES 6 TO 8

Crostini, literally "little crusts," are a favorite antipasto in Tuscany. Pureed chicken livers are one of the most popular toppings, but other purees—white beans, black kale, wild mushrooms—are also used.

4 TABLESPOONS/60 GRAMS BUTTER

1 TABLESPOON EXTRA-VIRGIN OLIVE OIL

1 POUND/500 GRAMS CHICKEN LIVERS, TRIMMED

½ ONION, MINCED

SALT AND PEPPER

1 TEASPOON ANCHOVY PASTE

¼ CUP/60 MILLILITERS CHICKEN BROTH,
HOMEMADE (PAGE 372) OR COMMERCIAL

40 THIN SLICES COUNTRY-STYLE BREAD,
3 INCHES/7.5 CENTIMETERS SQUARE, LIGHTLY
TOASTED ON BOTH SIDES

Melt the butter with the oil in a medium frying pan over medium heat. Add the chicken livers and onion and cook, stirring frequently, until the chicken livers are cooked very thoroughly, 12 to 15 minutes. Season with salt and pepper and remove from the heat.

Puree the chicken liver mixture in a food processor until smooth. Add the anchovy paste and broth and process again until fully incorporated.

Transfer the puree to a shallow bowl and cover it with plastic wrap/cling film, pressing it down lightly onto the surface of the puree to prevent a skin from forming. Refrigerate for about 2 hours. Bring to room temperature, then spread on the toasts to serve.

SARDINIAN CROSTINI

✺

SERVES 4

When I first had these little snacks—not really "crostini," of course—years ago in a caffè off the Viale Trieste in Cagliari, on Sardinia's southern coast, I thought of them as Sardinian nachos. They consist of nothing but three definitive foodstuffs of the island: the crackly flatbread called pane carasau *(also called* carta di musica *or "music-paper" bread for its parchmentlike texture), tangy sheep's milk caciocavallo cheese, and honey made from the corbezzolo (arbutus or madrone) tree. I wouldn't bother trying to make it if you have to make substitutions. See page 382 for sources for the ingredients.*

4 SHEETS PANE CARASAU

¼ POUND/125 GRAMS YOUNG CACIOCAVALLO, VERY THINLY SLICED

¼ CUP/90 GRAMS CORBEZZOLO (ARBUTUS) HONEY

Preheat the oven to 400°F/200°C/gas 6.

Break each sheet of *pane carasau* into four or six large, irregular pieces. Put them on a baking sheet/tray in a single layer, then lay the caciocavallo slices on top. Bake until the cheese melts but does not brown, 4 to 6 minutes.

Drizzle a little honey over each piece and serve.

ARTICHOKE FRITTATA

✺

SERVES 6

I've never much liked eggs, and can't bring myself to eat a fluffy, eggy French omelet. One day in the rural Veneto many years ago, however, I got talked into sampling an artichoke frittata, and found that I like this kind of omelet, in which the egg is merely a binder and the filling itself is the thing, very much.

JUICE OF 2 LEMONS

6 ARTICHOKES

3 TABLESPOONS EXTRA-VIRGIN OLIVE OIL

1 SMALL ONION, MINCED

SALT AND PEPPER

6 LARGE EGGS, VERY LIGHTLY BEATEN

1 CUP/100 GRAMS GRATED ASIAGO

½ CUP/50 GRAMS GRATED PARMIGIANO-REGGIANO

Preheat the oven to 325°F/160°C/gas 3.

Mix the lemon juice with 2 to 3 cups/480 to 720 milliliters water in a medium bowl.

Cut the stems off the artichokes. Follow this whole process with one artichoke at a time: Pull off the tough outer leaves by hand, then trim off more layers of leaves with a sharp knife until only the tenderest leaves, or heart, remain. Scoop out and discard the choke and slice the heart into four or six lengthwise wedges (depending on its size). Immediately put the wedges in the acidulated water to stop them from turning black.

Heat the oil in a large ovenproof frying pan over medium heat. Add the onion and cook, stirring often, until beginning to soften, 4 to 6 minutes. Drain the artichokes and pat them dry. Add them to the frying pan, stirring them well to coat them with the oil, and cook, stirring occasionally, until just cooked through, 6 to 8 minutes. Season generously with salt and pepper, then pour in the eggs and mix well. Stir in the asiago, then raise the heat to medium-high and cook, shaking the pan several times so the frittata doesn't stick, until the eggs are just set, about 5 minutes.

Sprinkle the parmigiano evenly over the top of the frittata and bake until the eggs are firm and top is golden brown, 10 to 12 minutes. Serve at room temperature.

THE ORIGINAL GLUTTON

Apicius was the most famous gourmand in ancient Rome, and is remembered as the author of *De re coquinaria* (which might be translated loosely as *On Culinary Matters*), which some consider to have been the first cookbook ever written. (Others give that honor to Archestratus, a Sicilian-born Greek whose lengthy poem *Hedypatheia*, or *Life of Luxury*, was in fact more of a diner's guide than a culinary manual.) Unfortunately, Rome knew not one prominent Apicius but three, and it is quite likely that not one of them had anything to do with *De re coquinaria*. In his proto-encyclopedia *Dictionnaire historique et critique* (*Historical and Critical Dictionary*), published in 1695, French philosopher Pierre Bayle explained that "there have been three Apicii in Rome famous for their gluttony. The first lived before the change of the republic; the second under Augustus and Tiberius, and the last under Trajan." The original one, Bayle reports, was said to have "outdone all men in gluttony." The second "laid out prodigious sums on his belly, and . . . there were several sorts of cakes which bore his name." This Apicius, according to Bayle, "kept as it were, a school of gluttony in Rome" and poisoned himself when he learned that his remaining fortune was not enough to allow him to continue eating the kinds of lavish meals to which he had become accustomed. The third Apicius was notable primarily for having had "an admirable secret for preserving oysters."

The name Apicius became a synonym for gourmet, and for that reason was attached to a collection of Roman recipes that was probably compiled around AD 400, roughly three hundred years after the time of the third actual Apicius. The collection, consisting of ten books covering a range of subjects—wine and the preservation of food, vegetables, legumes, fowl, seafood, sauces for seafood, and so on—was lost for hundreds of years and rediscovered, according to most sources, by the grammarian Enoch of Ascoli in the fifteenth century. Whatever its origins, it remains our most extensive record of the way aristocrats ate in ancient Rome. That way was, in a word, extravagantly. Among the recipes in *De re coquinaria*—some of which call for more than forty ingredients—is one for double-stuffed suckling pig, with a filling of almonds, lovage, oregano, garum (fermented fish sauce), eggs, (pig's?) brains, the root of silphium (a now-extinct plant sometimes referred to as giant fennel), little birds of unspecified variety, spelt, and pine nuts. Another involved rose petals crushed with garum, brains, and pepper and mixed with eggs, wine, raisin wine, and oil. A note appended to yet another recipe brags, "At table no one will recognize what he is eating."

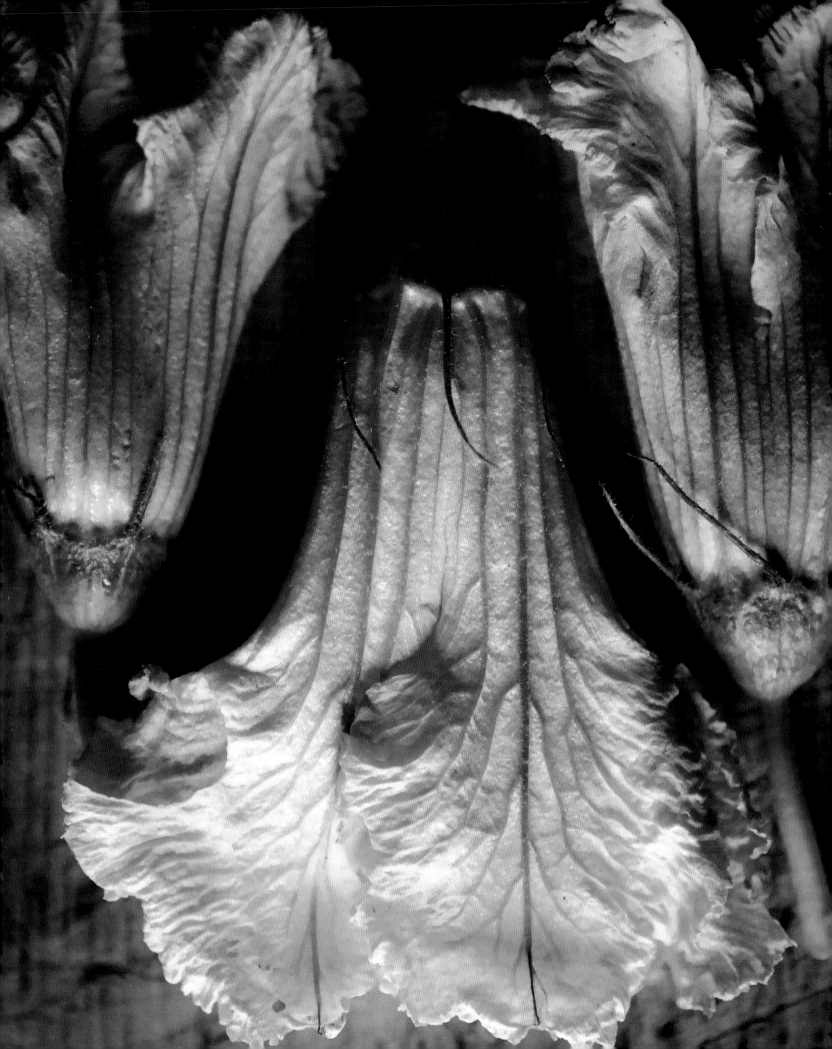

SQUASH BLOSSOM FRITTATA

SERVES 6

Next to deep-frying them (see page 23)—and using them in a couple of Mexican recipes, which needn't concern us here—this is my favorite way to prepare squash blossoms.

3 TABLESPOONS EXTRA-VIRGIN OLIVE OIL

1 SMALL ONION, MINCED

30 TO 36 SMALL- TO MEDIUM-SIZE SQUASH BLOSSOMS, STEMS AND STAMENS REMOVED, THEN RINSED AND DRIED INSIDE AND OUT

SALT AND PEPPER

6 EGGS, VERY LIGHTLY BEATEN

1½ CUPS/150 GRAMS GRATED PARMIGIANO-REGGIANO

Preheat the oven to 325°F/160°C/gas 3.

Heat the oil in a large ovenproof frying pan over medium heat. Add the onion and cook, stirring often, until beginning to soften, 4 to 6 minutes. Add the squash blossoms and cook, turning once, until just softened, about 20 seconds per side. Remove the pan from the heat and season the blossoms generously with salt and pepper.

Pour in the eggs and mix well, then stir in 1 cup/100 grams of the cheese. Return the pan to medium-high heat and cook, shaking the pan several times so the frittata doesn't stick, until the eggs are just set, about 5 minutes.

Sprinkle the remaining parmigiano evenly over the top of the frittata and bake until the eggs are firm and the top is golden brown, 10 to 12 minutes. Serve at room temperature.

MEATLESS "MEATBALLS"

SERVES 4

On my most recent trip to Italy, I had polpette twice in one day. The term usually means "meatballs," but neither of these contained any meat. They were concocted instead from bread, cheese, and eggs. The first ones, at lunch in Basilicata, were big, roughly billiard-ball size, and were draped in tomato sauce as if they were a main dish. The second ones, part of an antipasto selection, were small, like croquettes. These latter were served at L'Aratro, Domenico Laera's restaurant in Alberbobello, in Puglia, and he kindly shared his recipe. "We don't know how old this recipe is," he told me, "but the technique for making these polpette is traditionally passed on from father to son."

8 TO 10 SLICES COUNTRY-STYLE BREAD (ABOUT ½ POUND/250 GRAMS TOTAL), CRUSTS TRIMMED AND SLICES DRIED ON A BAKING SHEET/TRAY FOR 4 DAYS

4 EGGS

¾ CUP/75 GRAMS GRATED CACIOTTA OR PARMIGIANO-REGGIANO

1 GARLIC CLOVE, MINCED

4 SPRIGS ITALIAN PARSLEY, MINCED

SALT

FLOUR FOR DUSTING

3 TO 4 CUPS/720 MILLILITERS TO 1 LITER EXTRA-VIRGIN OLIVE OIL

Put the bread into a medium bowl with water to cover and soak for 30 minutes.

Squeeze as much moisture as possible from the bread, and put the bread into a large bowl. Using a fork, stir in the eggs, one at a time, then work in the cheese, garlic, parsley, and a good sprinkle of salt.

Lightly flour a board or platter. Using 2 teaspoons for each, form the dough into ovals, setting each one aside on the floured surface as it is formed.

Pour the oil to a depth of about 2 inches/5 centimeters into a large, deep frying pan and heat over high heat to 375°F/190°C. Working in batches, add the ovals and fry until golden brown, 3 to 4 minutes. As they are done, drain them on paper towels. Serve hot.

GREEK ITALY

My friend Michele Russo from Bernalda, in Basilicata, was talking about foraging for lampascioni, the edible hyacinth bulbs that are much enjoyed in the region (see page 30). "Sometimes when you dig for them," he said, "you'll find a Greek tomb." He may have been exaggerating slightly, but he made a good point: the Greeks were once all over this part of Italy. The heel of the Italian boot, around the Pugliese town of Tricase, isn't much more than sixty miles/one hundred kilometers from the coast of Greece, and in the eighth and seventh centuries BC, Greek colonists began settling in southern Italy, especially in what are now the regions of Calabria, Puglia, and Basilicata and on the island of Sicily. They brought with them religious beliefs, language, and culinary ideas that were to influence the area and even Rome itself. They even brought the Western Greek, or Cumae, alphabet, which evolved into Old Italic and then into the Latin alphabet used all over the world today. The Romans dubbed the Hellenized area Magna Graecia (Greater Greece).

Two more waves of Greek immigration followed these early settlers, first a flood of Byzantine Christian Greeks in the fourth and fifth centuries AD, and then refugees from the Ottoman invasion of the Peloponnese in the 1500s. Over the centuries, the Greeks in Italy became absorbed into the local population for the most part, though there are still people in Puglia and Calabria who speak a form of ancient Greek called Griko, which, interestingly enough, the Greeks themselves call Katoitaliotika, or Southern Italian. The unique conical houses, or *trulli*, found in central Puglia, incidentally, may or may not be of Greek origin, but their name seems to derive from the old Greek word *tholos*, meaning a cone-roofed building.

One of the most famous early citizens of Magna Graecia was the great philosopher and mathematician Pythagoras of Samos (570 to circa 495 BC). Though born on the Greek island whose name he bears, he moved at the age of forty or so to Crotone, in Calabria, and is said to have died in Metapontum, near what is now Bernalda. Pythagoras had a problem with a staple of the Italian diet: beans, meaning fava/broad beans and other European varieties. He not only forbade his followers to eat them but also to walk through bean fields. Because they were extremely popular in both Greece and Italy, no one is quite sure what he had against them. It may have been simply that he did not like their intestinal aftereffects, or perhaps, as Pliny the Elder proposed some centuries after his death, he may have objected to them because they were so irresistible that they inevitably inspired gluttony. It has also been suggested that Pythagoras might have been afflicted with an extremely unpleasant heredity condition called favism, common in the southern Mediterranean and whose effects are stimulated by the consumption of fava/broad beans. The Canadian classicist R. Drew Griffith, on the other hand, in an essay published in the book *Mystic Cults in Magna Graecia*, thinks that the Pythagorean aversion might have been strictly symbolic. "Beans are seeds . . . ," he writes. "Seeds are obvious symbols of rebirth. . . . Rabbi Meïr explained resurrection to Ptolemy V's wife, Cleopatra, as a kind of sowing wherein the seed, buried in the earth, comes to life again in a new and different form. . . . That is why . . . it can be dangerous to eat even a single seed, if one hopes ever to get free of the underworld."

POTATO AND PINE NUT CROQUETTES

SERVES 4

These small croquettes, or crochette, are a popular bar snack on the coast of Lazio, and a great way to use up leftover mashed potatoes.

SALT

I POUND/500 GRAMS RUSSET OR OTHER FLOURY POTATOES, PEELED AND QUARTERED

I TABLESPOON PLUS 4 CUPS/I LITER EXTRA-VIRGIN OLIVE OIL

½ SMALL ONION, MINCED

I CLOVE GARLIC, MINCED

3 TABLESPOONS BUTTER, SOFTENED

I EGG YOLK, PLUS I WHOLE EGG

2 TABLESPOONS PINE NUTS, LIGHTLY TOASTED IN A SMALL, DRY FRYING PAN

PEPPER

I CUP/60 GRAMS TOASTED BREAD CRUMBS, HOMEMADE (PAGE 378) OR COMMERCIAL

2 SPRIGS ITALIAN PARSLEY, MINCED

Bring a medium pot of salted water to a boil over high heat, add the potatoes, and reduce the heat to medium-high. Cook until tender when pierced with a fork, about 20 minutes.

While the potatoes are cooking, heat the 1 tablespoon oil in a small frying pan over medium heat. Add the onion and garlic and cook, stirring occasionally, until they begin to soften, 3 to 4 minutes. Remove from the heat and set aside.

When the potatoes are ready, drain them, reserving a few table-spoons of the cooking water. Put the potatoes in a large bowl and mash them well, adding a little of the cooking water as needed to obtain a smooth and moist but sticky puree. Add the butter and egg yolk and mix them in well. Stir in the onion and garlic and their cooking oil, then stir in the pine nuts. Season the mixture generously with salt and pepper, then cover the bowl and refrigerate for about 30 minutes.

Form the mixture into 12 or more round croquettes about 1½ inches/3.75 centimeters in diameter.

Heat the 4 cups/1 liter oil in a deep fryer or a deep saucepan fitted with a frying basket to 375°F/190°C. Lightly beat the whole egg in a small bowl. Put the bread crumbs into a wide, shallow bowl.

One at a time, dip the croquettes in the egg, then roll them in the bread crumbs. Working in batches, add the croquettes to the oil and fry until golden brown, 2 to 3 minutes. As they are done, drain them on paper towels.

Serve warm, sprinkled with the parsley.

RISOTTO CROQUETTES

SERVES 4 TO 6

Nothing goes to waste in an Italian country kitchen, including leftover risotto—though these mozzarella-filled croquettes, called arancine or arancini (meaning "little oranges," for their shape and color), have become so popular all over Italy that many cooks prepare risotto specifically to make them. Curiously, since risotto is a dish of northern Italy and, above all, the regions around the rice-cultivated Po Valley, arancine were apparently invented in Sicily.

FLOUR FOR DUSTING

I½ CUPS/225 GRAMS COOKED RISOTTO (LEMON RISOTTO, PAGE I4I, MADE WITHOUT THE LEMON ZEST), AT ROOM TEMPERATURE

¼ POUND/I25 GRAMS FRESH MOZZARELLA, CUT INTO I2 CUBES OF EQUAL SIZE

2 EGGS

2 CUPS/I20 GRAMS TOASTED BREAD CRUMBS, HOMEMADE (PAGE 378) OR COMMERCIAL

3 TO 4 CUPS/720 MILLILITERS TO I LITER EXTRA-VIRGIN OLIVE OIL OR CANOLA OIL

Flour your hands, then divide the risotto into 12 equal portions on a lightly floured work surface. Form each portion into a ball, then flatten it slightly with your palm. Put 1 cube of mozzarella in the center of each portion and form the risotto around it, shaping it back into a ball and concealing the cheese in the center.

Lightly beat the eggs in a small bowl. Put the bread crumbs into a wide, shallow bowl. Dip each risotto ball into the beaten eggs, then roll them in the bread crumbs to coat evenly. As they are ready, set them aside on a baking sheet/tray. Refrigerate the risotto balls on the baking sheet for 30 minutes.

Pour the oil to a depth of about 2 inches/5 centimeters into a large, deep frying pan and heat over high heat to 375°F/190°C. Working in batches, add the risotto balls and fry until golden brown, 3 to 4 minutes. As they are done, drain on paper towels. Serve hot.

FRIED FROGS' LEGS

SERVES 6

I had always thought of frogs' legs as being French (there is even a pejorative for Frenchmen based on their supposed predilection for this delight), so was surprised to find them on the menu one day in a little roadside trattoria outside Pavia, south of Milan. I later learned that frogs are—or were—abundant in the rice marshes of Lombardy, and that they used to be much appreciated in the local cuisine. Fresh, small frogs' legs aren't easy to find anywhere today (I've had the most success in the American South), and the frozen ones, typically imported from Thailand or Japan, can be rubbery. This dish probably isn't worth making unless you have access to the good ones.

2 POUNDS/1 KILOGRAM SMALL FRESH FROGS' LEGS, RINSED AND PATTED DRY

1 TO 1½ BOTTLES DRY WHITE WINE

½ CUP/65 GRAMS FLOUR

2 TO 3 CUPS/480 TO 720 MILLILITERS CANOLA OIL

1 LEMON, QUARTERED

SALT

Put the frogs' legs into a medium bowl and pour in the white wine to cover. Cover the bowl and refrigerate for 3 hours.

Put the flour into a medium bowl, then drizzle in 1 cup/ 240 milliliters of the wine, whisking together to form a medium-thick batter. Add a little more flour or wine to get the consistency right.

Remove the frogs' legs from the wine, and discard the wine. Pat the legs thoroughly dry with paper towels.

Pour the oil to a depth of about 1 inch/2.5 centimeters into a large frying pan and heat over high heat to 375°F/190°C. Working in batches, dip the frogs' legs into the batter, allowing the excess batter to drip back into the bowl, and add to the hot oil. Fry them, turning once if necessary to cook evenly, until golden brown and cooked through, 3 to 4 minutes. As they are done, drain on paper towels.

Arrange the frogs' legs on a platter, squeeze the lemon quarters over them, and salt them generously.

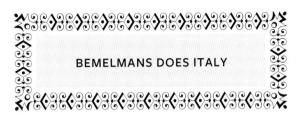

BEMELMANS DOES ITALY

Ludwig Bemelmans (1898–1962), the celebrated writer, illustrator, and gastronome best known today for his Madeline children's books, was born in Italy—sort of. He first made his appearance in the Austrian town of Meran, in the South Tyrol. In the redrawing of national borders after World War II, however, Meran became Merano, part of the "new" Italian region of Alto Adige. His collection of pieces about Italy for Holiday magazine, published in 1961 in book form as Bemelmans' Italian Holiday, unfortunately includes not a word about Merano—but Bemelmans leaves readers no doubt about his preoccupations in other parts of the peninsula, as this passage suggests. I have not tampered with his spelling (fettuccine needs two c's and ends with an e, and is "Verdiso" perhaps "Verdicchio"?), punctuation (surely he meant to install a comma between "agnolotti" and "dishes" in the first sentence), or misapprehensions (goat cheese in pesto?).

We have eaten our way down the length of Italy from Piedmont and its *agnolotti* dishes of mixed boiled meats and its sauces called *fondua* and *bagna calda*. We have had *ossobuco*, a cut of the veal bone with saffron-colored rice which is the specialty of Milano. We've eaten the fish dishes and fish soups of Venice; the *pesto* sauce made of basil, olive oil and goat cheese. We've tasted the *tagliatelle* and *tortellini* and the great sausages of Bologna, *mortadella*, *cotechino* and salami, and its hams. We've stuffed ourselves on Tuscany's roast suckling pigs and the products of the Roman kitchen, the fried meats, the *fettucini*, the *bacalao* and deviled meats. In Naples we've had *pasta asciutta* and *pizza*, with the sauces which increase in fragrance and potency the farther south you go. We also have paid attention to the wines—the Chianti, Lacrima Christi, Barbaresco, Barbera, Soave, Orvieto, Verdiso—after all these pleasures of the stomach it is time to see a doctor who will direct us to a pleasant retreat where the air, water and management combine to restore the victims of good food and to send them back with fresh appetites.

FOOD FOR THOUGHT

The Italians like talking about food almost as much as they like eating it,
and, like many peoples elsewhere, they often express folk wisdom in culinary
terms. Here are a few of my favorite Italian food-based proverbs:

A tavola non si invecchia.
At the table you don't get old.

Ne ammazza più la gola che la spada.
The gullet kills more than the sword.

Troppi cuochi guastano la cucina.
Too many cooks spoil the cooking.

*Quando la fame entra dalla porta, l'amore esce
dalla finestra.*
When hunger comes in through the door,
love goes out the window.

L'avaro è come il porco, è buono dopo morto.
The miser is like the pig, he's good when
he's dead.

Gallina vecchia fa buon brodo.
An old hen makes good broth.

Chi mangia solo crepa solo.
Who eats alone dies alone.

Il diavolo fa le pentole ma non i coperchi.
The devil makes the pots but not the lids.

O mangiar questa minestra o saltar questa finestra.
Either eat this soup or jump out this window.
[That is, take it or leave it.]

A pocu carni, pigghiati l'ossu. [Sicilian dialect]
When there is little meat, take the bone.

SOUP

THE ESSENCE OF LAND AND SEA

Vo' campari quantu voi? Mancia suppa avanti e poi.
[Do you want to live as long as you wish? Eat soup before and after.]
—*Sicilian proverb*

Viëlle marmitta, bouna seupa. [Old pot, good soup.]
—*Valdostani proverb*

Soup—in Italy as elsewhere—is the ultimate "poor" food. Its main ingredient is water, either plain or flavored with otherwise inedible bones and scraps. It can be single-minded, with only one or two main constituents, or it can be a miscellany, accommodating the most ordinary of foodstuffs—beans and other pulses, bits of broken pasta, onions, garlic, herbs, celery, tomatoes, and, if you're lucky, a bit of meat (often pancetta or some other kind of cured pork) or some minor fish too small or too bony to be served alone. Modest though its ingredients may be, soup is famously nourishing. The Calabrese have a saying (and they are surely not alone in believing this) that soup does seven things: It satisfies the appetite, slakes thirst, fills the belly, cleans the teeth, makes you sleep, helps you digest, and colors your cheeks.

Italian has a number of names for soup. *Brodo* is "broth," almost always served with small pasta forms, either plain or filled with cheese or forcemeat, cooked—and floating—in it. (Brodo can also be the basis for other soups and stews; traditional Italian cooking doesn't use stocks in the French sense.) *Minestra* takes its name from the Latin verb *ministrare*, "to minister," and usually implies a thick, hearty soup. But the term is tricky because it can also be used as an umbrella term for soups and pastas. A *minestrina*, or "small soup," is somewhere between *brodo* and *minestra*. *Minestrone*, of course, is "big" soup, in the sense of importance as well as richness (the Genoese sometimes call it *Scignore Menestron*— "Mr. Minestrone"—as a term of respect). *Potaggio* or *pottaggio*, a term rarely seen today (it comes from the Latin *potare*, "to drink," as does the French term *potage*), refers specifically to soup made from pulses. The word *crema* means "cream soup," but neither word nor soup is common in Italy, outside of certain international-style restaurants. *Zuppa* usually describes soups that are served over dried or toasted bread. The Latin word *suppa*, in fact, means bread soaked in broth—not the broth itself (the word *sop* is related).

You'll note that a good many of the soups—and stews (which I think of as just soups with more stuff in them)—in these pages are indeed served over bread. A minestra can also involve bread, as may be seen from this report published in a study of Italian eating habits conducted between 1928 and 1937 by the Istituto Nazionale di Economia Agraria (quoted in Carol Helstosky's book *Garlic and Oil*): "Every evening the housewife makes two or three panfuls of *minestra* with dried beans and black cabbage: she cuts the bread into thin, thin slices, fitting them into a pan and then, a half-hour before serving dinner, she skims the broth from the pot in which the cabbage and beans have been boiling, and then pours the boiling liquid over the bread. When the bread is soaked through, she calls the family to the table."

ACQUASALE
(WATER AND VEGETABLE SOUP)

SERVES 4

This utterly simple soup, whose name means "water-salt," is a piatto povero—"poor peoples' food"—in Puglia and Basilicata. As such, it changes from season to season and household to household according to what's available. Some versions omit the tomato; some add a bit of hot chile. It is often served hot, in which case it might have an egg or two broken into it, or cheese, typically ricotta salata, grated over it. I had a room-temperature version similar to this one at Masseria Barbera, an agriturismo (see page 228) in Minervino Murge, near Canosa in Puglia, and it was one of the highlights of an excellent lunch. A variation on the theme is cialledda (mixture), found in Puglia and Basilicata, a dish of tomatoes, onions, celery, and scrambled eggs served over grilled bread that has absorbed most of the water and oil so that the results aren't quite soupy anymore.

16 RIPE CHERRY TOMATOES, HALVED

I RED ONION, VERY THINLY SLICED, WITH SLICES TRISECTED

½ SMALL CUCUMBER, HALVED LENGTHWISE, SEEDED, AND SLICED CROSSWISE

I TEASPOON DRIED OREGANO

SALT

16 SLICES COUNTRY-STYLE BREAD, 2 INCHES/ 5 CENTIMETERS SQUARE, GRILLED OR TOASTED ON BOTH SIDES

½ CUP/120 MILLILITERS EXTRA-VIRGIN OLIVE OIL

Divide the tomato halves and the onion and cucumber pieces equally between 4 bowls. Sprinkle the oregano over each serving, dividing it equally, and salt the ingredients generously. Add 1 cup/240 milliliters room-temperature water to each bowl.

Brush the bread squares lightly with some of the oil, then drizzle the remaining oil into the bowls, dividing it evenly. Serve the bread alongside the soup.

SALAMURECI
(SICILIAN COLD TOMATO SOUP)

SERVES 4

This is a Sicilian version of acquasale, from Trapani, on the island's western end. The local name for it is 'nsalata r'acqua, or "salad with water"—which, come to think of it, accurately describes it.

3 OR 4 SLICES COUNTRY-STYLE BREAD, I INCH/ 2.5 CENTIMETERS THICK, CUT INTO I-INCH/ 2.5-CENTIMETER CUBES

2 GARLIC CLOVES, PEELED

1½ POUNDS/750 GRAMS VERY RIPE RED TOMATOES, PEELED, SEEDED, CHOPPED, AND DRAINED FOR IO TO 15 MINUTES IN A COLANDER

IO TO 15 LARGE BASIL LEAVES, JULIENNED

SALT

ICE WATER

EXTRA-VIRGIN OLIVE OIL FOR DRIZZLING

About 24 hours before making the soup, spread the bread cubes in a single layer on a large plate or baking sheet/tray and set them aside, uncovered, to dry.

Rub 4 nonreactive soup or salad bowls (preferably wooden) with the garlic cloves. Discard the garlic.

Mix together the tomatoes and basil in a medium bowl, and season generously with salt. Divide the tomato mixture and bread cubes equally between the soup bowls. Pour ice water into each bowl just to cover the tomatoes and bread, then drizzle a little oil on top before serving.

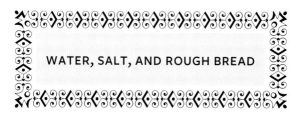

WATER, SALT, AND ROUGH BREAD

*In 1875, the Neapolitan historian and politician Pasquale Villari published
a series of newspaper reports on life in southern Italy and what he called "the social
question" in Italy. At one point he reports:*

A young and esteemed economist from Puglia, when I questioned him about conditions for workers on the country estates, wrote to me: "The farmers in charge of cultivating the more distant properties live there almost the whole year, returning home to their wives and children every two or three weeks. At the estates, they live in tunnels dug into the earth, sleeping in niches carved into the walls. They have sacks of straw, on which they sleep fully dressed; indeed, they never undress. Their boss is a *massaro* [farm manager], who gives each of them a flat, dark loaf of bread weighing about a kilo [two pounds] every morning; it is called a *panrozzo* [rough bread], and is supplied by the landlord. The farmers work from dawn to dusk, taking a half hour break at ten to rest and eat some of their bread. In the evening, when their work is done, the massaro lights a fire in the hall and brings a pot of water with just a touch of salt to a boil. As he does, the farmers line up, slicing their bread and putting it in their wooden bowls. The massaro pours a ladle of water over the bread, and sprinkles it with a few drops of oil. This is what they eat year-round, calling it *acquasale* [water-salt]. They never receive anything else, except during the threshing season, when they're given one to two liters of weak wine, which inspires them to work even harder. These farmers set aside some of their panrozzo each day to sell or to take home to their family; their wages consist of nothing but this bread, about 132 lire a year, and a half a tomolo [a old unit of weight] each of fava [broad] beans and wheat, according to the harvest.

MONTAIGNE'S ACORNS

In his accounts of his travels through Italy in 1580 and 1581, celebrated French essayist Michel de Montaigne at one point notes, "At Viterbo I ate some sort of acorn called *gensole*. These are found in many places in Italy. They are very tasty." What was he talking about? The word was not in any of my Italian dictionaries or books on Italian food, but I eventually found a reference to it on the Internet as a synonym for giuggiole, and that I was able to track down. What Montaigne had sampled was the jujube or Chinese date (*Ziziphus ziziphys*). It has nothing to do with the little gummy candies called Jujubes that were a staple snack at the Saturday matinee when I was in grammar school, but are sweet little fruits with a large stone, with a flavor somewhere between those of an apple and a date.

Jujubes are widely eaten all over Asia and in the Middle East, and may have reached Italy from Syria, perhaps as early as the fourteenth or fifteenth century. In folk medicine, the jujube was prescribed to treat respiratory problems and colds, along with dates, figs, and raisins. It was also used to make preserves, and was candied. There is an annual Festa delle Giuggiole in Arquà Petrarca, in the Veneto, for which the fruit is used to make ice cream, baked goods, and liqueurs, among other things. Brodo di giuggiole, or "jujube broth," is a Renaissance-era recipe from Lombardy—it's a sweetened infusion of the fruit, not a soup—and the jujube figures in an expression heard to this day: Siamo in brodo di giuggiole (literally, "We're in jujube broth"), which is a way of saying, "We're in fat city."

RIBOLLITA
(TWICE-COOKED TUSCAN VEGETABLE SOUP)

❄

SERVES 10 TO 12

This is the definitive soup of Tuscany, enjoyed all over the region. Just as the Marseillaises insist that bouillabaisse cannot be made without rascasse (scorpionfish), Tuscans will tell you that, other than the beans and the stale bread on which it is based, this soup absolutely demands cavolo nero, or "black kale" (also sold as lacinato or Tuscan kale). This may sometimes be found at farmers' markets or in specialty stores; in its absence, red Russian kale, increasingly common in American markets, makes a good substitute. One other essential: this soup must be made the day before it is served, and then reheated—otherwise it is not ribollita *(reboiled).*

2 CUPS/500 GRAMS DRIED CANNELLINI BEANS, COOKED, WITH THEIR COOKING LIQUID RESERVED (SEE PAGE 308)

½ CUP/120 MILLILITERS EXTRA-VIRGIN OLIVE OIL, PLUS MORE FOR SERVING

2 ONIONS, CHOPPED

2 STALKS CELERY, CHOPPED

I BUNCH BLACK KALE OR RUSSIAN KALE, COARSELY CHOPPED

I BUNCH SWISS CHARD, COARSELY CHOPPED

I SMALL HEAD SAVOY CABBAGE, ABOUT I POUND/500 GRAMS, COARSELY CHOPPED

2 RIPE TOMATOES, SEEDED AND GRATED (SEE RAW TOMATO COULIS, PAGE 371)

4 THICK SLICES DRY COUNTRY-STYLE BREAD, TORN INTO PIECES

SALT AND PEPPER

Measure 1 cup/100 grams of the beans and 2 cups/480 milliliters of the bean cooking liquid and set aside. Process the remaining beans and their liquid in a food processor or blender until smooth, and set aside.

Heat about half the oil in a large flameproof earthenware or metal pot over medium-low heat. Add the onions and cook, stirring occasionally, until they soften, 10 to 12 minutes. Add the celery, kale, chard, cabbage, and tomatoes, cover the pot, and cook, stirring occasionally, for about 20 minutes.

Add the pureed beans and the reserved cooking liquid, re-cover, reduce the heat to low, and cook for about 1 hour to thicken and blend the flavors. Add the bread, re-cover, and cook for about 10 minutes more. Season with salt and pepper, then stir in the reserved beans.

Remove from the heat, let cool to room temperature, cover, and refrigerate for at least 12 hours or up to 2 days.

To serve, reheat the soup over low heat, stirring frequently. Drizzle in the remaining oil before serving, and serve with additional olive oil to be added to taste.

ZUPPA ALLA PAVESE
(POACHED EGG SOUP)

❄

SERVES 4

This soup, associated with the ancient Lombardian agricultural and university town of Pavia (Albert Einstein once lived there), is utterly simple. I had a particularly good version one day at Il Tastevin, a restaurant in Vigevano, about twenty-five kilometers northwest of Pavia, and the proprietor, Maurizio Barone, was kind enough to share his recipe with me. "It is a very 'poor' plate," he wrote when he sent it to me, "and easy to make, but diners like it very much." He adds that he sometimes uses broth made from frogs' legs—something of a specialty of the area—in place of veal broth.

5 CUPS/1.25 LITERS VEAL BROTH (PAGE 373) OR COMMERCIAL BEEF BROTH

6 TABLESPOONS/90 GRAMS BUTTER

4 OR 8 THICK SLICES COUNTRY-STYLE BREAD, DEPENDING ON SIZE (1 OR 2 SLICES TO COVER THE BOTTOM OF EACH SOUP PLATE)

4 EGGS

SALT AND WHITE PEPPER

¼ CUP/25 GRAMS GRATED PARMIGIANO-REGGIANO, PLUS MORE FOR SERVING

Bring the broth to a boil over high heat.

Meanwhile, melt the butter in a medium frying pan over medium-high heat. Working in batches, add the bread and fry quickly, turning once, until golden brown on both sides, 30 to 40 seconds per side. Put 1 or 2 slices in each of 4 warmed soup plates just large enough to hold them.

Carefully break 1 egg on top of the toast in each soup plate. Salt and pepper the eggs generously, then sprinkle each with 1 tablespoon of the parmigiano. Keeping the broth boiling as you work, pour about 1 cup/240 milliliters of the broth into each bowl, pouring around the bread, not over the egg and cheese. (The broth will cook the eggs.) Serve with additional parmigiano on the side.

SOUP STORY

Isn't it interesting that so many traditional dishes seem to have been invented—at least according to their creation legends—by or for a monarch or other personage, instead of just having been put together out of necessity or accident by some farm wife or thrifty peasant? In the case of the famous if gloriously uncomplicated soup known as *zuppa alla pavese*, the monarch involved is Francis I, king of France, a contemporary of Henry VIII and Süleyman the Magnificent. In late February 1525, the French army met the combined forces of Spain and the Holy Roman Empire in what became known as the Battle of Pavia, on the plains outside that city, just south of Milan in Lombardy. According to the story, zuppa alla pavese was improvised to feed Francis either during a respite in the battle or just after he had been captured by the enemy. The Irish writer Sean O'Faolain, in one of his two books about his sojourns in Italy, was skeptical, invoking heraldic imagery to describe the dish: "[The soup's] very name is, I suggest, a joke," he wrote, "for *pavese* means shield (I do not think it has anything to do with Pavia), and the specialty of this excellent soup is the fried egg *gules* on the slice of fried bread *sable* floating in it." In fact, the word *pavese*, in addition to meaning "of Pavia," means "bunting" or "flags"—which doesn't necessarily contradict his speculation.

SEUPETTA CONGEINTZE

SERVES 4 TO 6

I first had this soup, a specialty of the mountain town of Cogne, south of Aosta in the Valle d'Aosta, at Lou Ressignon, a superlative restaurant in that town. More solid material than liquid, this is, as Waverley Root once described it, a "dish which smells of the mountains, simply rice in beef consommé, poured over slices of black or white bread spread with melted fontina cheese." That's pretty much the recipe, but here it is in more conventional form.

6 TABLESPOONS/90 GRAMS BUTTER, OR AS NEEDED

2½ CUPS/500 GRAMS CARNAROLI OR OTHER RISOTTO RICE

8 CUPS/2 LITERS VEAL BROTH (PAGE 373) OR COMMERCIAL BEEF BROTH, HEATED TO A SIMMER

SALT

8 SLICES COUNTRY-STYLE BREAD

I POUND/500 GRAMS YOUNG FONTINA, THINLY SLICED

I PINCH FRESHLY GRATED NUTMEG

Melt 3 tablespoons of the butter in a large pot over medium heat. Add the rice and stir to coat well with the butter. Cook the rice, stirring occasionally, until it begins to color faintly, 3 to 4 minutes. Add three-fourths of the broth, reserving the remaining broth for using later, and season with salt. Reduce the heat to low and cook uncovered, stirring frequently, until the rice is tender, 15 to 20 minutes. Some broth should be left unabsorbed.

Meanwhile, preheat the broiler/grill.

Melt the remaining 3 tablespoons butter in a large frying pan over medium-high heat. Working in batches, add the bread and fry quickly, turning once, until golden brown on both sides, 30 to 40 seconds per side. Add a little more butter if necessary. Arrange the toasted slices on a baking sheet/tray and top with the cheese, distributing it equally. Broil/grill until the cheese is melted but not browned, 3 to 4 minutes. Remove the cheese toast from the oven and turn the oven temperature to 350°F/175°C/gas 5.

Put two slices of the cheese toast on the bottom of a Dutch oven or other heavy ovenproof pot or a deep baking dish. With a slotted spoon, spoon about one-third of the cooked rice over the bread. Top with two more cheese toasts, and spoon half of the remaining rice over them. Repeat the process again, using up the remaining rice, then finish with a layer of two cheese toasts. Stir the nutmeg into the broth remaining in the rice pot, then pour the broth remaining in the rice pot down the sides of the Dutch oven. If the broth does not just cover the top layer of bread, add enough of the reserved broth just to cover.

Put the soup in the oven and bake, uncovered, for 5 minutes to heat through. Ladle into warmed soup plates and serve.

MINESTRONE ALLA GENOVESE

SERVES 4

The Genoese were great seafarers, and in earlier times when ships would return to Genoa harbor after long voyages, they would be met by small boats ferrying big pots of minestrone out to feed the vegetable-starved sailors. Genoa's version of the soup is probably the closest regional variation to the minestrone we know in America. It includes one unique feature: this being Genoa, the soup is always finished with a dollop of pesto, the city's heraldic condiment.

I OUNCE/30 GRAMS DRIED PORCINI MUSHROOMS

SALT

2 POTATOES, PEELED AND DICED

I EGGPLANT/AUBERGINE, PEELED AND DICED

I SMALL CARROT, DICED

I SMALL ZUCCHINI/COURGETTE, DICED

¼ POUND/125 GRAMS SPINACH, COARSELY CHOPPED

¼ POUND/125 GRAMS SWISS CHARD, COARSELY CHOPPED

2 TABLESPOONS EXTRA-VIRGIN OLIVE OIL

½ POUND/250 GRAMS TUBETTI OR OTHER SMALL PASTA

2 CUPS/200 GRAMS DRAINED COOKED CANNELLINI BEANS (SEE PAGE 308)

3 TABLESPOONS PESTO GENOVESE (PAGE 374), MADE WITHOUT CHEESE

GRATED PARMIGIANO-REGGIANO FOR SERVING

Soak the mushrooms in 2 cups/480 milliliters warm water in a medium bowl for 30 minutes. Remove the mushrooms from the soaking water, squeezing out the excess liquid over the bowl. Chop the mushrooms finely. Strain the soaking water through a fine-mesh sieve lined with cheesecloth/muslin or a coffee filter and set aside.

Combine the mushroom water and 6 cup/1.5 liters water in a large pot. Salt it generously, then cover the pot and bring to a boil. Uncover, add the potatoes, eggplant, carrot, zucchini, spinach, chard, chopped mushrooms, and oil, reduce the heat to low, and simmer, uncovered, for about 1 hour. The vegetables should be tender and the flavors blended.

Add the pasta and cook until soft but not mushy, about 15 minutes. Add the beans and cook until heated through, about 5 minutes longer. Stir in the pesto, then adjust the seasoning.

Serve hot or at room temperature, with the parmigiano on the side.

MINESTRONE FRIULANO

SERVES 4

Cooks in many parts of Italy make a soup they call minestrone. One broad distinction between varieties is in the kind of starch added: In Milan, it is usually rice, and around Genoa, small forms of dried pasta are preferred. In Friuli, where barley is an important crop, that's what goes into the pot.

I CUP/250 GRAMS PEARL BARLEY

I CUP/250 GRAMS DRIED BORLOTTI (CRANBERRY) BEANS

SALT

2 POTATOES, PEELED AND DICED

I SMALL CARROT, DICED

I SMALL ZUCCHINI/COURGETTE, DICED

I STALK CELERY, DICED

3 TABLESPOONS EXTRA-VIRGIN OLIVE OIL

2 OUNCES/60 GRAMS PANCETTA, DICED

I GARLIC CLOVE, MINCED

6 TO 8 SAGE LEAVES, MINCED

6 TO 8 SPRIGS ITALIAN PARSLEY, MINCED

SALT

GRATED PARMIGIANO-REGGIANO FOR SERVING

Put the barley and beans into separate bowls, and fill the bowls with water to cover each ingredient by about 2 inches/ 5 centimeters. Cover each bowl with a clean kitchen towel and let stand for 10 to 12 hours. Drain the barley and beans and keep separate.

Put the beans and 8 cups/2 liters salted water into a large pot, cover, and bring to a boil over high heat. Add the barley, reduce the heat to low, and cook, uncovered, for 2½ hours. Both the beans and barley should be tender.

SOFFRITTO AND BATTUTO

I remember Marcella Hazan once saying that if you asked most non-Italian "Italian" chefs how they made their soffritto, they would have no idea what you were talking about. I'm sure she was right—and yet the soffritto, or its close cousin the battuto, is the basis of most traditional Italian sauces and stews. As Patience Gray explains it in her classic *Honey from a Weed*, "The Italian *soffritto* or *battuto*, for which there is no Anglo-Saxon equivalent, consists in the fine chopping of aromatic herbs and vegetables which, underfried [that is, slow fried] in olive oil, are the point of departure for imparting flavour to whatever is being cooked."

The soffritto—which, as Gray suggests, literally means "underfried"—has counterparts in Spanish and Catalan cooking, where it is called the *sofrito* and the *sofregit*, respectively, and is closely related to the mirepoix of classical French cuisine. Its basic ingredients are onion, carrot, celery, and parsley, with garlic sometimes included, all very finely chopped with a knife or, more traditionally, a mezzaluna (the crescent-shaped chopping blade, with a handle on each end, that is a basic tool in many Italian kitchens). The mixture is fried over very low heat until it softens. Some cooks keep cooking until the vegetables caramelize and brown, while others maintain that they should not take on much color. Although not everybody uses the terms the same way, a soffritto is usually meatless (some people call it a *trito*, from the word "to chop"), and a battuto combines the vegetables with lardo (cured pork fat) or pancetta that has been crushed or beaten to a paste or minced with a knife. You will find some variation on both in many of the recipes in this book.

About 20 minutes before the beans and barley are ready, add the potatoes, carrot, zucchini, and celery to the pot and stir well. Heat the oil in a small frying pan over medium heat. Add the pancetta, garlic, sage, and parsley, reduce the heat to low, and cook, stirring frequently, until lightly browned, about 10 minutes.

Add the contents of the frying pan to the beans and barley and stir well. Season with salt and continue to cook over low heat for about 30 minutes longer to blend the flavors.

Serve hot or at room temperature, with the parmigiano on the side.

TUSCAN FARRO SOUP

SERVES 4

*A surprising number of references to the grain known in Italian as farro, in publications both popular and serious, identify it as spelt. It isn't. It is emmer (*Triticum dicoccum*), an ancient relative of durum wheat, believed to have been one of the first cultivated cereals in history. (Spelt is another early relative of wheat.) Farro is grown in many parts of Italy, including Abruzzo, Sicily, and Sardinia, but the most famous farro is probably that cultivated in Garfagnana, a mountainous corner of the province of Lucca in Tuscany. Tuscan recipes for farro soup include little more than the grain and onions, but I find this version, with pureed lentils added, more interesting. Pearled (dehulled and polished) farro, which does not require overnight soaking, is widely available at Italian markets and other specialty stores.*

1½ CUPS/300 GRAMS LENTILS, PREFERABLY ITALIAN, SOAKED IN WATER TO COVER OVERNIGHT

3 TABLESPOONS EXTRA-VIRGIN OLIVE OIL, PLUS MORE FOR DRIZZLING

I ONION, FINELY CHOPPED

1½ CUPS/300 GRAMS PEARLED FARRO

⅔ CUP/160 MILLILITERS VEAL BROTH (PAGE 373) OR COMMERCIAL BEEF BROTH

½ CUP/120 MILLILITERS TOMATO SAUCE, HOMEMADE (PAGE 371) OR COMMERCIAL

SALT AND PEPPER

Drain the lentils, put them in a large pot, and add water to cover. Bring to a boil over high heat, then reduce heat to low, cover, and simmer until the lentils are very soft, about 1 hour.

Remove from the heat. With a slotted spoon, transfer the lentils to a food processor or blender, add about ½ cup/120 milliliters of the cooking water, and puree until smooth.

Heat the oil in a Dutch oven or other heavy pot over medium heat. Add the onion and cook, stirring frequently, until it begins to soften, 6 to 8 minutes. Stir in the pureed lentils, farro, broth, and tomato sauce. Reduce the heat to low and cook uncovered, stirring occasionally, until the farro is tender and soup is very thick, about 45 minutes.

Season with salt and pepper, then drizzle in a little oil. Serve in warmed soup plates.

PASTA E FAGIOLI

SERVES 4 TO 6

Pasta e fagioli—literally "pasta and beans"—is another dish found in regional variations all over Italy. Italian Americans like to call it "pasta fazool," an approximation of the Neapolitan dialect term for it. A version made with broad noodles in Ferrara, in Emilia-Romagna, bears the delightful name sguazabarbuz *(page 66). It may be argued whether pasta e fagioli is a soup or a pasta dish. I would be on the side of the former, at least in the present case, because it is liquid enough to be eaten with a spoon. This is a standard recipe for the dish.*

1¾ CUPS/375 GRAMS DRIED BORLOTTI (CRANBERRY) BEANS, SOAKED OVERNIGHT IN WATER TO COVER

2 OUNCES/60 GRAMS PANCETTA, MINCED

I ONION, MINCED

I SMALL STALK CELERY, MINCED

3 SPRIGS ITALIAN PARSLEY, MINCED

2 TABLESPOONS TOMATO PASTE, HOMEMADE (PAGE 371) OR COMMERCIAL

3 GARLIC CLOVES, I MINCED, 2 CRUSHED

I SPRIG ROSEMARY

1½ CUPS/360 MILLILITERS EXTRA-VIRGIN OLIVE OIL, PLUS MORE FOR DRIZZLING (OPTIONAL)

3 SAGE LEAVES

SALT AND PEPPER

½ POUND/250 GRAMS FRESH FETTUCCINE, CUT INTO ½-INCH/1.25-CENTIMETER PIECES

Drain the beans and put them into a large pot. Add the pancetta, onion, celery, parsley, tomato paste, minced garlic, rosemary, 1 cup/240 milliliters of the oil, and 6 cups/1.5 liters water. Bring to a boil over high heat, reduce the heat to low, and simmer uncovered, stirring occasionally, until the beans are very soft, about 2½ hours.

Meanwhile, heat the remaining ½ cup/120 milliliters oil in a medium frying pan over medium heat. Add the crushed garlic and the sage and cook, stirring frequently, until softened, about 5 minutes. Remove and discard the garlic and sage, and set the oil aside.

Remove and discard the rosemary sprig, then transfer half of the soup to a food processor or blender and puree until smooth. Return the puree to the pot and stir well. Stir in the reserved flavored oil and season with salt and pepper.

Bring the soup to a slow boil over medium-high heat. Stir in the pasta, reduce the heat to medium-low, and cook uncovered, stirring frequently, until the pasta is cooked, about 15 minutes longer.

Drizzle more oil over the top of the soup, if you like, then serve in warmed soup plates.

SGUAZABARBUZ
(FERRARESE BEAN AND PASTA SOUP)

SERVES 4 TO 6

I saw this dish on the menu, as a primo piatto, at the Ristorantino di Colomba in Ferrara, in Emilia-Romagna, and ordered it just because I loved the name. It turned out to be a delicious local variation on pasta e fagioli (pasta and beans) whose moniker means "beard- [or chin-]splasher" in Ferrarese dialect. This is my version of the restaurant's recipe. Maltagliati—literally "badly cut"—is irregularly shaped pasta, originally the leavings at the bottom of a dried pasta bin or the scraps left over from homemade pasta, but today manufactured specifically in this form (see page 382 for a source).

2 CUPS/500 GRAMS DRIED BORLOTTI (CRANBERRY) BEANS, SOAKED OVERNIGHT IN WATER TO COVER

¼ CUP/60 MILLILITERS EXTRA-VIRGIN OLIVE OIL

2 ONIONS, FINELY CHOPPED

I STALK CELERY, FINELY CHOPPED

I CARROT, FINELY CHOPPED

¼ POUND/125 GRAMS PANCETTA, DICED

4 SPRIGS ITALIAN PARSLEY, MINCED

2 SPRIGS ROSEMARY

6 SAGE LEAVES

SALT AND PEPPER

½ POUND/250 GRAMS DRIED MALTAGLIATI

GRATED PARMIGIANO-REGGIANO FOR SERVING

Drain the beans and put them into a large pot with water to cover. Cover the pot and bring the water to a boil over high heat. Reduce the heat to low and cook, tightly covered, until the beans are tender but just before the skins begin to split, 45 minutes to 1½ hours, depending on the age of the beans.

When the beans are almost ready, heat the oil in a large frying pan over medium heat. Add the onions, celery, carrot, pancetta, parsley, rosemary, and sage and season with salt and pepper. Cook, stirring frequently, until the vegetables have softened, 8 to 10 minutes.

Remove and discard the rosemary sprigs and sage leaves. With a slotted spoon, transfer about half of the beans to the frying pan. Mash them into the other vegetables with a potato masher or fork, then reduce the heat to low and cook, stirring occasionally, for about 20 minutes to blend the flavors.

Meanwhile, bring a large pot of salted water to a boil over high heat. Add the pasta and cook until al dente, 8 to 10 minutes. If you have turned off the heat under the pot of beans, reheat the beans to a steady simmer. When the pasta is ready, drain it and add it to the pot with the unmashed beans. Stir the mashed bean mixture into the pot, and adjust the seasoning if necessary.

Serve in warmed soup plates, with the parmigiano on the side.

PIACENZA-STYLE BEAN AND GNOCCHETTI SOUP

SERVES 8

This dish, called pisarei e fasò *in the local dialect, is a classic example of the "poor" cuisine of Emilia-Romagna, based on ingredients (dried beans, flour, dry bread, pancetta, wine, oil) that every farmhouse kitchen would have had. The word* fasò, *sometimes written* fasö *or* fasoi, *means "beans" in Piacentino dialect;* pisarei, *the name for the tiny homemade flour–bread crumb gnocchetti that are paired with the beans, means "little penises," a reference to their shape. Such earthy names for pasta varieties and other foods are not uncommon in Italy. Some years ago in Rome, I would sometimes encounter* cazzetti d'angeli, *"little angel penises," similar in appearance to* pisarei, *and within the immense repertoire of Sicilian convent pastries are* fedde del cancelliere, *"chancellor's buttocks," and* minni di virgini, *"virgin's breasts."*

2 CUPS/500 GRAMS DRIED BORLOTTI (CRANBERRY) BEANS, SOAKED OVERNIGHT IN WATER TO COVER

2 CUPS/250 GRAMS FLOUR, PLUS MORE FOR DUSTING

1½ CUPS/90 GRAMS TOASTED BREAD CRUMBS, HOMEMADE (PAGE 378) OR COMMERCIAL

SALT

½ CUP/120 MILLILITERS BOILING WATER, OR AS NEEDED

3 TABLESPOONS EXTRA-VIRGIN OLIVE OIL

3 TABLESPOONS BUTTER

¼ POUND/125 GRAMS PANCETTA, DICED

1 ONION, DICED

2 CARROTS, DICED

2 STALKS CELERY, DICED

2 GARLIC CLOVES, MINCED

1 TEASPOON ROSEMARY LEAVES

4 CUPS/1 LITER CHICKEN BROTH, HOMEMADE (PAGE 372) OR COMMERCIAL

1 CUP/240 MILLILITERS DRY RED WINE

2 RIPE TOMATOES, SEEDED AND GRATED (SEE PAGE 371)

PEPPER

GRATED PARMIGIANO-REGGIANO FOR SERVING

Drain the beans and put them into a large pot with water to cover. Cover the pot and bring the water to a boil over high heat. Remove from the heat, drain the beans, return them to the pot, and add water to cover again. Bring to a boil again over high heat, reduce the heat to low, cover tightly, and cook until the beans are tender but just before the skins begin to split, 45 minutes to 1½ hours, depending on the age of the beans.

Meanwhile, mix together the flour and bread crumbs in a large bowl, then mix in 1 teaspoon salt. Make a well in the center and pour the boiling water and 1 tablespoon of the oil into the well. Stir the water into the flour mixture until a fairly stiff dough forms, adding a little more water if necessary.

Turn the dough out onto a floured work surface and knead it briefly. It should be smooth. Divide the dough into four equal portions. Using your palms, roll each portion into a long strand about ½ inch/1.25 centimeters in diameter. With your thumb, press down at ¾-inch/2-centimeter intervals to cut the dough into short lengths. Set the gnocchetti aside.

Combine the remaining 2 tablespoons oil and the butter in a pot over low heat. Add the pancetta, onion, carrots, celery, and garlic, cover, and cook, stirring occasionally, for about 30 minutes. Stir in the rosemary, then add the broth, wine, and tomatoes. Season generously with salt and pepper, cover, and continue cooking for about 30 minutes. Drain the beans and add them to the pot. Cook for 10 minutes more.

Transfer about one-third of the soup to a food processor or blender and puree until smooth. Return the puree to the soup, stir well, re-cover, continue to cook over low heat for about 15 minutes more.

Meanwhile, bring a large pot of salted water to a boil, add the gnocchetti, and cook for about 1 minute. Quickly lift them out of the water and add them to the soup. Cook for about 5 minutes more.

Serve in warmed soup plates, with the parmigiano on the side.

JOTA
(ISTRIAN BEAN AND SAUERKRAUT SOUP)

✳

SERVES 6

A close cousin of the Austrian staple called Suppen, *this substantial soup of beans and sauerkraut—almost a stew—is eaten around Trieste and down into the (formerly Italian) Istrian Peninsula that is now mostly part of Croatia. This is an adaptation of a recipe from Istrian-born chef-restaurateur Lidia Bastianich.*

1 CUP/250 GRAMS DRIED BORLOTTI (CRANBERRY) BEANS, SOAKED OVERNIGHT IN WATER TO COVER

2 SMOKED HAM HOCKS

1 POUND/500 GRAMS MEATY PORK RIBS

2 BAY LEAVES

¼ POUND/125 GRAMS PANCETTA, MINCED

4 GARLIC CLOVES, MINCED

2 POUNDS/1 KILOGRAM SAUERKRAUT, THOROUGHLY RINSED AND DRAINED

3 RUSSET OR OTHER FLOURY POTATOES, PEELED AND QUARTERED

SALT AND PEPPER

Drain the beans, put them into a large pot, and add the ham hocks, pork ribs, bay leaves, and 3 quarts/3 liters water. Bring to a boil over high heat, skimming off any foam that rises to the surface.

Reduce the heat to medium. Mash the pancetta and garlic in a mortar with a pestle until they form a paste, then stir the paste into the beans. Cover partially and cook until the beans are tender but just before the skins begin to split, 45 minutes to 1½ hours, depending on the age of the beans.

Add the sauerkraut and potatoes to the pot and continue to cook until the potatoes are soft, about 30 minutes more.

With a slotted spoon, remove the ham hocks and pork ribs from the soup and set them aside to cool to room temperature. Remove the potatoes from the pot with the same spoon, put them into a large bowl, and mash them coarsely. Return them to the pot and season the soup generously with salt and pepper. Continue cooking the soup for about 30 minutes longer.

Meanwhile, pick the meat off the bones of the ham hocks and pork ribs and cut into bite-size pieces. When the soup is ready, stir the meat back into the soup and simmer until the meats are hot, then serve in warmed soup plates.

CANEDERLI TIROLESI
(TYROLEAN HAM-DUMPLING SOUP)

✳

SERVES 4 TO 6

Trentino–Alto Adige has two official languages, German and Italian, and the dishes that make up the local cuisine often bear German names. In this case, the name is Italian, but Italian imitating German: canederli *equals* Knödel, *or "dumpling." Eaten all over the region, this dumpling soup calls for speck, a unique juniper-flavored cold-smoked ham made in the Tyrolean Alps, on both sides of the Italian-Austrian border (see page 382 for a source).*

4 TO 6 LARGE SLICES COUNTRY-STYLE BREAD (ABOUT ½ POUND/250 GRAMS TOTAL), ABOUT 1 INCH/2.5 CENTIMETERS THICK, CRUSTS TRIMMED AND CUT INTO 1-INCH/2.5-CENTIMETERS CUBES

¼ POUND/125 GRAMS SPECK OR PROSCIUTTO (NOT SLICED), FINELY CHOPPED

6 TO 8 CHIVES, MINCED

3 TO 4 SPRIGS ITALIAN PARSLEY, MINCED

1 PINCH FRESHLY GRATED NUTMEG

SALT AND PEPPER

2 EGGS, LIGHTLY BEATEN

1 CUP/240 MILLILITERS WHOLE MILK

4 TO 6 TABLESPOONS/35 TO 55 GRAMS FLOUR, PLUS MORE FOR DUSTING

6 CUPS/1.5 LITERS VEAL BROTH (PAGE 373) OR COMMERCIAL BEEF BROTH

In a large bowl, combine the bread cubes, speck, chives, parsley, nutmeg, a big pinch of salt, and a few grinds of pepper. Stir in the eggs and then the milk, and set aside for 20 minutes.

Dust a work surface with flour, turn out the dough onto it, and dust the dough lightly with flour. Using your hands, work the mixture into a damp dough. Sprinkle in enough flour to absorb most of the moisture, then form the dough into dumplings about the size of walnuts, shaping them between two spoons. As they are shaped, set them aside on the floured surface.

Pour the broth into a pot, season to taste with salt, and bring it to a boil over high heat. Reduce the heat to medium, then carefully add the dumplings and cook until they are done, about 15 minutes. The dumplings will float when they are cooking through.

Divide the dumplings evenly between 4 warmed soup plates, then ladle in the broth, dividing it evenly.

BRANCH RESTAURANTS

The traveler in the Friulian countryside, especially around Gorizia, abutting the Slovenian border on the region's eastern side, might occasionally pass a rural trattoria or farmhouse with a leaf-laden branch hung on a wall or gatepost outside. The branch is called a *frasca*, which simply means "bough," but it has symbolic meaning: it is a sign that the establishment it marks serves simple meals made in whole or in part from products grown or produced on the property, wine often included. Frasche are like small agriturismi (see page 228), never fancy, always tied closely to the land. According to a tourist-brochure tale, a nobleman passing through the Carnian Alps sent scouts ahead to seek out inns that served good wine, asking them to mark the places with branches. Wherever the tradition may have come from, in the years when Friuli–Venezia Giulia was part of the Austro-Hungarian Empire, branches outside farmhouses indicated that farm products were for sale within.

By the latter half of the twentieth century, the custom had evolved to identify casual farm-based eating places, and today some frasche are quite large and may offer guest rooms as well as meals. They are also wonderful places to sample the traditional cooking of the region. The fare at frasche is likely to include homemade salumi, rustic soups and pastas (Jota, page 68, is a staple), hearty meat dishes like sausage with polenta or stewed tripe or goulash, and marmalade-filled crepes or apple pastries for dessert. In previous decades, the wines were fairly rough-and-ready, but now they can be among Friuli's best, which is very good indeed.

PASTA SECCA

THE HEART OF A CUISINE

No man is lonely eating spaghetti; it requires too much attention.
—*Christopher Morley, The Arrow*

It will be *maccheroni*, I swear to you, that will unify Italy.
—*Giuseppe Garibaldi (attributed, circa 1860)*

Everybody knows by now, I hope, that Marco Polo didn't bring pasta home to Italy from China. This historically insupportable claim was apparently first made by one L. B. Maxwell in a trade publication called *The New Macaroni Journal*, out of Minneapolis, in either 1929 or 1938 (sources differ, and I have been unable to find the original). Wheat as we know it, along with several cousins like emmer and spelt (see page 103), was domesticated in the eastern Mediterranean as long as ten thousand years ago, and somebody probably figured out how to turn it into flour and to mix that flour with water and make unleavened (or naturally leavened) bread of some description around the same time. It is not unreasonable to assume that in the millennia that followed, somebody also worked out other ways to make flour-and-water dough edible— for instance, by boiling it in water, which would have become possible with the development of watertight cooking vessels around 9000 BC. In any case, references to various kinds of dough cooked in liquid appeared at least two thousand years ago in Greece, Rome, and Palestine, and a document from AD 1154, about a century before Marco Polo was born, mentions the manufacture and widespread exportation of noodles called *itriyya* from Norman-ruled Sicily.

The word *pasta*—which derives ultimately, as noted earlier, from the Greek *passein*, "to sprinkle"—was first used to describe noodles or something similar in the eighth century. (It entered the English language with that meaning as early as 1673, but wasn't in common use until the mid-nineteenth century.) The fifteenth-century chef known as Maestro Martino of Como gives recipes for pasta in his *Libro de arte coquinaria*, but advises that it should be boiled for two hours. The first people to consume large amounts of pasta regularly were the Neapolitans, but this wasn't until the seventeenth century, when the local citizenry, who had jocularly been called *mangiabroccoli*, "broccoli eaters," became known instead as *mangiamaccheroni* (translation presumably not necessary). The pasta-eating habit did not extend to most of the rest of Italy until the eighteenth century, and even then, pasta was not prepared as we know it today: it was seasoned with salt and maybe pepper, possibly with a dusting of dry cheese, but nothing more; old etchings and woodcuts show people eating it with their hands. The widespread popularity of tomato sauce, and then variations on the theme, in the late eighteenth and early nineteenth century changed all that. The serving of pasta with sauce, in fact, is said to have greatly increased the popularity in Italy of what had been a marginal eating instrument: the fork.

Pasta types can be characterized several ways, but one of the most basic is the distinction between *pasta all'uovo* ("pasta with eggs," typically made from soft summer wheat) and *pasta di semola di grano duro* (pasta made from the bran of durum wheat). Another is that between *pasta secca*—also called *pasta asciutta* (*secca* means "dry," *asciutta* "dried"), which is not the same as *pastasciutta* (see page 76)—and *pasta fresca*, or "freshly made pasta," which may be made with either eggs or water, and occasionally both. For present purposes, this is the best distinction. The recipes in this chapter all use store-bought (dried) pasta. Some of those in the following chapter may be made with either store-bought or homemade pasta, while some require domestic manufacture.

Dried pasta was a godsend to the Italians. Like the considerably less-attractive gallette, or sailor's biscuits (hardtack), taken on shipboard in place of ordinary bread, dried pasta lasted for a year or more, and unlike its fresh counterpart (and unlike raw flour), it wasn't subject to mold or infestation by parasites. That doesn't mean that it was always a sterile product. In *The Food of Italy*, published in 1971, Waverley Root writes of his initial distaste for pasta in 1929, the first time he saw it drying over clotheslines in the "insalubrious courtyards" of Naples: "Dirt swirled though the air, flies settled to rest on the exposed pasta, pigeons bombed it from overhead, children invented games to play with it, and the large dog population, finding itself short of lampposts, put up with what it could find. . . ."

But, he continued, "have no fear today: macaroni and spaghetti are now made indoors in spick-and-span automated factories."

Many of the best pasta brands available internationally today, mostly made with eggs, come from Emilia-Romagna, including Barilla, Fini, and Dallari. Other capitals of commercial pasta production, with eggs and otherwise, include Fara San Martino in Abruzzo, home of the ubiquitous De Cecco as well as Delverde and Cocco; Pianella, also in Abruzzo, where Rustichella d'Abruzzo is based; Campofilone in the Marche, home of Spinosi, La Campofilone, and Antica Pasta, among others; and Imperia, in Liguria, headquarters of Agnesi.

PASTASCIUTTA AND PASTA ASCIUTTA

In organizing the recipes in this book, I wanted to group the pasta dishes into two categories: those that use store-bought dry pasta, which is almost always made only from durum-wheat flour and water, and those that require homemade fresh pasta, mostly made from just flour and eggs, or its store-bought equivalent. I had no problem labeling the latter *pasta fresca*; even if you didn't make it yourself, chances are good that it would be soft in texture and quite possibly stored in the grocery-store cooler. The dry stuff was more difficult. *Asciugare* and *seccare* both mean "to dry," and thus both *pasta asciutta* and *pasta secca* mean dried pasta. I was originally going to use the former term as a chapter heading, but it is too close to the term *pastasciutta*, which does not mean quite the same thing. At least I didn't think so. I'd heard *pastasciutta* used in Italy to describe pasta with or suitable for a sauce, as opposed to pasta in soup, but it was not applied to all pasta of that sort. What, I wondered, was the story?

My old friend Darrell Corti, who is of Genoese extraction and who runs an extraordinary grocery store called Corti Bros. in Sacramento, California, knows a great deal about both Italian food and the Italian language, so I asked him if he could conclusively define *pastasciutta* for me and establish once and for all the difference between *pastasciutta* and *pasta asciutta*. This was his response: "You have entered the black hole of italianità [Italianness] with your question. *Tagliatelle alla bolognese* is a pasta with a sauce, but would never be called *pastasciutta*. Spaghetti al pomodoro, yes, but not tagliatelle alla bolognese. Even though the tagliatelle might be dried, it is relatively inconceivable to call it *pastasciutta*. Some shorter shapes, like penne, can be called *pastasciutta*, but really it means long, thin shapes like spaghetti and the like. *Pasta fresca* can be a confusing term, too. Some restaurants may make pasta daily with an extruder in the kitchen, but even though it might still be damp when it's cooked, it's not pasta fresca. In Puglia, orecchiette are nearly always made fresh, and are prized for their 'freshness,' for having just been made. They are called *orecchiette fresche*—but nobody would call them *pasta fresca*. It probably makes most sense to divide the chapters between egg pasta, which you can call *pasta fresca*, and non-egg pasta, which could be termed *pasta asciutta*—two words—or *pasta secca*." Once I unscrambled my brain, that's exactly what I did.

COOKING PASTA

Here are some things I've learned over the years about cooking pasta:

1. You don't need to use a huge pot of water, just enough to give the pasta enough room to cook. About 3 quarts/3 liters of water for 1 pound/500 grams of pasta should be plenty.

2. Salt the water generously before you bring it to a boil.

3. Don't put oil in the water "to keep the pasta from sticking together." It doesn't work. Just stir the pasta as soon as you immerse it, and a few more times while it cooks.

4. Don't overcook pasta. I happen to like pasta secca not just al dente—literally "to the tooth," meaning that you will get a little resistance when you bite into it—but what my Roman friends call *filo di ferro*, "iron string," meaning that a very thin core of barely cooked dough runs down the middle of each noodle. You may not agree, in which case al dente is fine. If you cook pasta too long, though, it gets unpleasantly gummy.

5. Unless you have a consistent supply of pasta or a very good eye, the only way to tell whether store-bought pasta is done is to taste a bit of it. Dried pasta can be three months old or three years old, and the latter will take longer to soften than the former. Homemade pasta, if it is used fresh, should never take more than three to five minutes to cook properly.

6. Drain the pasta but for heaven's sake don't rinse it. It's the starch that remains on it that helps the sauce to cling.

7. In general, cooks in northern Italy transfer the cooked pasta to a big bowl (preferably warmed in advance), then add the sauce and toss it. (I sometimes use the pot in which the pasta was cooked as a stand-in for the bowl.) Their counterparts in the south often dump the pasta into the pan where the sauce is cooking and mix the two together there. This is a matter of personal preference and convenience (your frying pan may not be large enough to accommodate the latter technique, for example), though in general I toss fresh pasta in a bowl and dried pasta in the pan.

8. Most pasta sauces—there are certainly exceptions—can be made in the time it takes the pasta itself to cook.

9. Don't overdo the sauce. It should be a condiment for the pasta, not an end in itself.

10. Smooth sauces or simple dressings (like olive oil or butter and cheese) or sauces in which the ingredients are small or cut into small pieces are most appropriate for long noodles like spaghetti and fettuccine. Chunky sauces, like those with pieces of sausage or cauliflower, tend to work better with short shapes like penne or farfalle. Of course, there are exceptions to this rule—like spaghetti with clams—but when I see angel hair pasta garnished with a pound of mixed seafood, as I often do on American menus, I suspect that the cook doesn't really understand the concept.

PASTA ALLA NORMA

SERVES 4 TO 6

Vincenzo Bellini's celebrated opera Norma, *which premiered at La Scala in Milan in 1831, has long been considered one of the masterpieces of the bel canto tradition. The usual story is that when the Sicilian writer and theatrical producer Nino Martoglio—who, like Bellini, was a native of Catania—first tasted pasta dressed with tomato sauce, fried eggplant, and ricotta salata, he thought it was as close to perfection as the opera was, and gave it this name. The dish is almost certainly older than the opera, though, and it must have had another name for some time, since Martoglio was not born until 1870. Whoever christened it, I'd like to think that he or she was conscious of the inherent wordplay: the role of Norma was created at La Scala by one of the great Italian sopranos of the nineteenth century, Giuditta Pasta.*

SALT

¼ CUP/60 MILLILITERS OLIVE OIL

2 EGGPLANTS/AUBERGINES, ABOUT 8 OUNCES/
250 GRAMS EACH, PEELED AND CUT INTO ¼-INCH/
6-MILLIMETER CUBES

2 CUPS/480 MILLILITERS TOMATO SAUCE,
HOMEMADE (PAGE 371) OR COMMERCIAL

1 POUND/500 GRAMS SHORT PASTA SUCH AS PENNE,
PENNE RIGATE, MACCHERONI, OR ZITI

PEPPER

3 OUNCES/90 GRAMS RICOTTA SALATA, GRATED

10 TO 15 BASIL LEAVES, COARSELY SHREDDED

Bring a large pot of salted water to a boil over high heat.

Meanwhile, heat the oil in a large frying pan over medium-high heat. Add the eggplants and stir quickly to coat all the pieces with oil. Cook, stirring frequently, until they start to brown, 5 to 6 minutes. Transfer to paper towels to drain.

At the same time, heat the tomato sauce over medium heat, then reduce the heat to low.

Add the pasta to the boiling water and cook until al dente, 8 to 12 minutes. Drain well, then return the pasta to the pot. Stir in the eggplant and tomato sauce and season generously with salt and pepper.

Transfer the pasta to a warmed serving bowl. Sprinkle the cheese, then the basil leaves over the pasta.

FUSILLI WITH SAUSAGE AND CABBAGE

SERVES 4 TO 6

The cruciform vegetables—including cabbage, broccoli and its relatives, and cauliflower—are greatly loved in southern Italy, and often end up in pasta (see Orecchiette with Broccoli Rabe, page 83, and Rigatoni with Cauliflower, page 87). This is a popular Calabrian variation on the theme.

¼ CUP/60 MILLILITERS EXTRA-VIRGIN OLIVE OIL

1 SMALL HEAD SAVOY CABBAGE, ABOUT 1 POUND/
500 GRAMS, SHREDDED

2 GARLIC CLOVES, CHOPPED

¼ TEASPOON PEPERONCINI

1 POUND/500 GRAMS MILD ITALIAN SAUSAGE,
CASING REMOVED, FINELY CHOPPED

SALT AND PEPPER

2 CUPS/480 MILLILITERS TOMATO SAUCE,
HOMEMADE (PAGE 371) OR COMMERCIAL

1 POUND/500 GRAMS FUSILLI

GRATED PECORINO ROMANO FOR SERVING

Heat the oil in a large frying pan over medium-low heat. Add the cabbage, garlic, and peperoncini and cook, stirring occasionally, until the cabbage softens, 10 to 12 minutes.

Raise the heat to medium and add the sausage. Continue cooking, stirring frequently, until browned, about 10 minutes more. Season with salt and pepper, then stir in the tomato sauce. Reduce the heat to low, cover, and cook for 12 to 15 minutes more to blend the flavors.

Meanwhile, bring a large pot of salted water to a boil over high heat. Add the pasta to the pot and cook until al dente, 8 to 12 minutes.

Drain the pasta well, return it to the pot, and stir in the sauce. Transfer to a warmed serving bowl. Pass the cheese at the table.

ORECCHIETTE WITH BROCCOLI RABE

SERVES 4 TO 6

Orecchiette—which means "little ears," a not inapt description of shape—are the heraldic pasta form of Puglia, but are found today all over central and southern Italy, from Abruzzo to Basilicata. In their home regions, orecchiette are usually homemade, shaped with a well-practiced thumb, but the dried version, widely available, is very good. When this dish is made outside Italy, the broccoli rabe often competes equally with the pasta for plate space, but in Italy it is usually just an accent. I've split the difference here. It is common in Puglia to shower the finished orecchiette not with cheese but with toasted bread crumbs—once a common substitute for cheese in poorer households.

½ POUND/250 GRAMS BROCCOLI RABE, FINELY CHOPPED

SALT

1 POUND/500 GRAMS ORECCHIETTE

½ CUP/120 MILLILITERS EXTRA-VIRGIN OLIVE OIL

6 ANCHOVY FILLETS, MINCED

PEPPER

GRATED RICOTTA SALATA OR TOASTED BREAD CRUMBS, HOMEMADE (PAGE 378) OR COMMERCIAL, FOR SERVING

Put the broccoli rabe into a large pot of salted cold water. Bring the water to a boil over medium-high heat. When it is boiling, raise the heat to high and add the orecchiette. Cook until the pasta is al dente, 8 to 12 minutes.

Meanwhile, heat together the oil and anchovy fillets in a small pan over medium heat.

When the pasta is ready, drain it and the greens and transfer them to a warmed serving bowl. Pour the anchovy oil over the top and season generously with pepper; if necessary, add a little salt. Pass the cheese at the table.

CAVATELLI WITH TURNIP GREENS AND SPICY TOMATO SAUCE

SERVES 4 TO 6

Cavatelli are made similarly to orecchiette (at left), but instead of being formed into "ears," they take a shape sometimes described as resembling little hats or caps. The word itself probably derives from cavato, *meaning "gouged out" or "pulled away" (concave comes from the same root), because cavatelli are made by "gouging" indentations in small pieces of dough. Like orecchiette, cavatelli are much favored in Puglia, where they are sometimes called* cavatieddi. *But, also like their auriculate cousin, they are eaten over much of central and southern Italy, in this case under a wide variety of names. In Puglia in earlier times, they were sometimes made with flour milled from fava/broad beans, which was cheaper than store-bought wheat flour. This is a typical Puglian recipe.*

¼ CUP/60 MILLILITERS EXTRA-VIRGIN OLIVE OIL

1 SMALL ONION, MINCED

2 GARLIC CLOVES, MINCED

4 TO 6 VERY RIPE TOMATOES, PEELED, SEEDED, AND CHOPPED, OR ONE-HALF 28-OUNCE/875-GRAM CAN SAN MARZANO TOMATOES, DRAINED AND CHOPPED

½ TEASPOON PEPERONCINI, OR MORE TO TASTE

SALT AND PEPPER

1 POUND/500 GRAMS CAVATELLI

½ POUND/250 GRAMS TURNIP GREENS, FINELY CHOPPED

GRATED RICOTTA SALATA FOR SERVING

Heat the oil in a medium saucepan over medium heat. Add the onion and garlic and cook, stirring frequently, until the onion softens, 6 to 8 minutes. Add the tomatoes and peperoncini and season with salt and pepper. Reduce the heat to low and simmer uncovered, stirring frequently, until the sauce is almost dry, about 20 minutes.

Meanwhile, bring a large pot of salted water to a boil over high heat. Add the pasta to the pot and cook for 3 to 4 minutes. Add the turnip greens and continue to cook until the pasta is al dente, 5 to 8 minutes more.

Drain the pasta and return it to the pot. Stir in the sauce and transfer to a warmed serving bowl. Pass the cheese at the table.

HOT STUFF

We don't think of Italian cuisine as being particularly spicy, but in the southern reaches of the country, both sweet peppers and chiles—the latter often dried and crushed or powdered—are a surprisingly frequent addition to pasta and other dishes. Peperoncini (dried chile flakes) also find their way into some modern-day Roman dishes, including two of the city's favorite pastas, spaghetti all'amatriciana and penne all'arrabiata (*arrabiata* means "angry," an obvious reference to the heat the flakes induce). A proverb in Basilicata says, *"Lu paprini e lu pupon ie' lu pranz r' lu cafun"* (The sweet pepper and the spicy pepper are the farmer's lunch). Such a lunch would be a pretty healthful one, too, full of vitamin C, carotene, potassium, and other good stuff, including capsaicin, thought to stimulate the release of endorphins—natural pain relievers said to promote an overall feeling of well-being.

Possibly the spiciest concoction in Italy is the 'nduja of Calabria—the name might be a dialect corruption of andouille, French for "tripe sausage"—a spreadable salami made from meat of the pig's head. (It is similar to the sobrasada of Majorca, and one theory suggests that emigrés from Calabria might have introduced it to the Spanish island centuries ago.) Sugna piccante, lard flavored with fennel seeds and chile powder, is a related condiment sometimes seen in Basilicata. Like 'nduja, it is typically slathered on grilled bread.

Dried sweet peppers are widely used, as well, and those from the town of Senise in Basilicata are famous (see page 310). One day in Bernalda, northeast of Senise, I had a remarkable pasta dish whose dialect name I believe was *segna rizz*: homemade fettuccine-like noodles, thick and with deckled edges, were absolutely buried in sweet red pepper powder—unusual and very good.

PENNE VALDOSTANA

SERVES 4 TO 6

This is "macaroni and cheese" as it is understood in the Valle d'Aosta, a region famous for its cheeses, above all fontina. It is the kind of dish you want to find waiting for you when you tramp through the snow on a windy winter day in the villages near the French border.

SALT

I POUND/500 GRAMS PENNE

2 TABLESPOONS BUTTER, PLUS MORE FOR GREASING

½ CUP/120 MILLILITERS HEAVY/DOUBLE CREAM

¼ POUND/125 GRAMS TALEGGIO, CUT INTO ½-INCH/125-CENTIMETER CUBES

6 OUNCES/175 GRAMS FONTINA, CUT INTO ½-INCH/1.25-CENTIMETER CUBES

I½ CUPS/150 GRAMS GRATED PARMIGIANO-REGGIANO

Bring a large pot of salted water to a boil over high heat. Add the pasta to the pot and cook until al dente, 8 to 12 minutes. Drain the pasta well and transfer it to a large warmed bowl.

Meanwhile, preheat the oven to 400°F/200°C/gas 6. Lightly butter a shallow baking dish just large enough to hold the sauced pasta.

At the same time, melt the butter in a medium saucepan over low heat. Add the cream, taleggio, fontina, and about two-thirds of the parmigiano and cook, stirring constantly, until the cheese melts into a rich, creamy sauce.

Add the cheese sauce to the pasta and toss well. Then transfer the mixture to the prepared baking dish. Sprinkle the remaining parmigiano over the top.

Bake until the cheese begins to brown, 4 to 6 minutes. Serve directly from the dish.

PENNE COOKED IN WHITE WINE

SERVES 4 TO 6

In earlier times, this simple but unusual preparation was traditional in the olive-growing towns of the western Italian Riviera, above Bordighera and Sanremo. It was made each autumn to celebrate the first pressing of the fruit for oil, and the oil stirred in at the end came straight from the press. The wine gives the pasta a sweet character, nicely offset by plenty of parmigiano.

I⅓ BOTTLES VERMENTINO OR OTHER DRY, UNOAKED ITALIAN WHITE WINE

SALT

I POUND/500 GRAMS PENNE, PREFERABLY PENNE RIGATE

⅓ CUP/80 MILLILITERS MILD EXTRA-VIRGIN OLIVE OIL

I CUP/100 GRAMS GRATED PARMIGIANO-REGGIANO

Put the wine and about 1 cup/240 milliliters water into a large pot, salt it generously, and bring to a boil over high heat.

Add the pasta and stir well so that it doesn't stick together. Reduce the heat to low and simmer uncovered, stirring frequently, until all the liquid is absorbed and the pasta is cooked through, 18 to 20 minutes.

Stir in the oil and parmigiano, then adjust the salt and transfer to a warmed bowl to serve.

RIGATONI WITH CAULIFLOWER

SERVES 4 TO 6

This is a classic Sicilian recipe. It can certainly be made with fresh tomatoes, but more than one Sicilian friend has told me that he or she prefers the canned ones.

½ CUP/120 MILLILITERS EXTRA-VIRGIN OLIVE OIL

1 CUP/60 GRAMS TOASTED BREAD CRUMBS, HOMEMADE (PAGE 378) OR COMMERCIAL

1 HEAD CAULIFLOWER, SEPARATED INTO FLORETS AND FINELY CHOPPED

6 TO 8 ANCHOVY FILLETS, FINELY CHOPPED

4 GARLIC CLOVES, MINCED

½ TEASPOON PEPERONCINI

SALT AND PEPPER

5 WHOLE CANNED SAN MARZANO TOMATOES, COARSELY CHOPPED

1 POUND/500 GRAMS RIGATONI OR PENNE RIGATE

Heat about 1 tablespoon of the oil in a large frying pan over medium heat. Add the bread crumbs, stir well, and cook, stirring frequently, until they are well toasted, about 15 minutes. Set them aside.

Add the remaining oil to the same frying pan over medium heat. Add the cauliflower and cook, stirring frequently, for about 10 minutes. Stir in the anchovies, garlic, and peperoncini and season with salt and pepper. Stir in ½ cup/120 milliliters water, cover, reduce the heat to low, and cook for about 20 minutes more.

Add the tomatoes to the cauliflower mixture, stir well, and continue to cook, uncovered, until the tomato liquid is absorbed, about 10 minutes.

Meanwhile, bring a large pot of salted water to a boil over high heat. Add the pasta to the pot and cook until al dente, 8 to 12 minutes. Drain the pasta well and return it to the pot. Stir in the cauliflower mixture and transfer to a warmed serving bowl. Pass the bread crumbs at the table.

LINGUINE WITH CRABMEAT

SERVES 4 TO 6

Pastas similar to this one are made all along the middle and upper Adriatic coast of Italy, from Venezia Giulia down through the Marche, usually with the meat of the Adriatic crabs called grancevole or granseole.

¼ CUP/60 MILLILITERS EXTRA-VIRGIN OLIVE OIL

2 GARLIC CLOVES, MINCED

6 TO 8 SPRIGS ITALIAN PARSLEY, MINCED

1 CUP/240 MILLILITERS TOMATO SAUCE, HOMEMADE (PAGE 371) OR COMMERCIAL, PUREED IN A BLENDER OR FOOD PROCESSOR

2 TABLESPOONS TOMATO PASTE, HOMEMADE (PAGE 371) OR COMMERCIAL

¼ TEASPOON PEPERONCINI

SALT AND PEPPER

1 POUND/500 GRAMS LINGUINE

½ POUND/250 GRAMS FRESH-PICKED CRABMEAT

Heat the oil in a large frying pan over medium-low heat. Add the garlic and parsley and cook, stirring occasionally, for 2 to 3 minutes. Add the tomato sauce, tomato paste, and peperoncini and season with salt and pepper. Stir well, then reduce the heat to low, cover, and let simmer for about 20 minutes.

Meanwhile, bring a large pot of salted water to a boil over high heat. Add the pasta to to the pot and cook until al dente, 8 to 12 minutes. Drain the pasta well and return it to the pot.

Stir the crabmeat into the sauce and heat through, 1 to 2 minutes. Add the sauce to the pasta and stir well. Transfer to a warmed serving bowl.

CUSCUS ALLA TRAPANESE

SERVES 6

Cuscus has long been considered one of the glories of Sicilian gastronomy, especially on the western end of the island, where the art of making the pasta itself, from two kinds of semolina flour, was historically much respected. There is, unfortunately, no good way to make cuscus (or couscous) without the two-part steamer—a perforated top pan set over a pan to hold the liquid—called a cuscusera (but more likely to be found in the United States under its French Moroccan or Tunisian name, couscoussière). The seal between the two parts of the vessel has to be airtight. Traditionally, a strip of bread dough was formed around the seam, but plastic wrap works just as well. (See page 382 for sources for couscoussières.)

1½ POUNDS/750 GRAMS READY-TO-COOK COUSCOUS

1 CUP/240 MILLILITERS EXTRA-VIRGIN OLIVE OIL

2 ONIONS, MINCED

4 GARLIC CLOVES, MINCED

8 SPRIGS ITALIAN PARSLEY, MINCED

SALT AND PEPPER

8 BAY LEAVES

3 CUPS/720 MILLILITERS TOMATO SAUCE, HOMEMADE (PAGE 371) OR COMMERCIAL

1 PINCH SAFFRON THREADS

2 TABLESPOONS BLANCHED ALMONDS, MINCED

2 POUNDS/1 KILOGRAM MIXED FIRM-FLESHED OCEAN FISH FILLETS OR STEAKS (AT LEAST TWO KINDS, SUCH AS JOHN DORY, COD, HALIBUT, OR MAHI MAHI) AND 1 POUND/500 GRAMS EEL, ALL CUT INTO LARGE PIECES, OR 3 POUNDS MIXED FIRM-FLESHED OCEAN FISH FILLETS AND STEAKS AND NO EEL

HARISSA (NORTH AFRICAN HOT CHILE PASTE) OR PEPERONCINI FOR SERVING (OPTIONAL)

Put the couscous into a large bowl. Drizzle in ½ cup/120 milliliters warm water, then sift the couscous with your fingers to break up any lumps. Stir in half the oil, half the onion, half the garlic, and half the parsley, and season with salt and pepper.

Lay the bay leaves on the bottom of the basket portion of the couscoussière, then spoon in the couscous, flattening it gently with the back of a spoon, but not packing it down. Fill the bottom portion of the couscoussière with water to within about 1½ inches/3.75 centimeters of the base of the basket. Wrap plastic wrap/cling film around the rim of the bottom portion, being careful not to let any hang down where it might ignite from the stove top. Fit the basket into the bottom portion. Wrap more plastic wrap/cling film around the rim of the basket, then put the lid on the basket. Bring the water to a boil over high heat, reduce the heat to low, and let the couscous steam for 1 hour.

Meanwhile, heat the remaining oil in a Dutch oven or other heavy pot over medium heat. Add the remaining onion, garlic, and parsley and cook, stirring frequently, until the onion softens and begins to color, 8 to 10 minutes. Stir in the tomato sauce, saffron, almonds, and 4 cups/1 liter water and bring to a boil over high heat. Reduce the heat to low and simmer, uncovered, for 30 minutes to create a flavorful broth.

Add the fish to the broth and continue simmering until the fish are cooked through, 10 to 15 minutes. Remove from the heat and keep warm.

Preheat the oven to 200°F/95°C.

Transfer the cooked couscous to a large ovenproof serving bowl. Remove 2 cups/480 milliliters of the broth from the Dutch oven. Strain out any solids and return them to the pot. Pour the strained broth over the couscous, then cover the bowl tightly with aluminum foil and put it into the oven for 20 minutes.

Using a slotted spoon, carefully remove the fish pieces from the Dutch oven and arrange them on a warmed serving platter. Strain the broth, discarding the solids, and transfer the broth to a warmed bowl or gravyboat. Serve the couscous, fish, and broth together. Serve the harissa on the side, if you like.

A DISH OF ARAB ORIGIN

Couscous is North African; cuscus (or cùscus, or cùscussù) is Italian. It *is* pasta, after all, made by pushing semolina pellets through a sieve. Some sources suggest that it was taken to Sicily by Arab conquerors as early as the late tenth century, but this cannot be proven. The sixteenth-century Vatican chef Bartolomeo Scappi describes what he identifies as a Moorish dish called *succussu*, eaten in Rome, but that wasn't until 1570. Scholars think cuscus probably arrived in the Tuscan port city of Livorno around the same time, introduced by Sephardic Jewish refugees from Spain, and it is still sometimes found there. Also in the sixteenth century, it found its way to Sardinia—where it remains popular particularly in the towns of Carloforte and Calasetta—most probably imported by Genoese traders who had an outpost at Tabarka on the Tunisian coast. (Sardinians also eat fregula, which is like a larger, toasted cuscus.)

Today, cuscus is eaten most often in western Sicily, notably around Trapani, which lies only about three hundred miles from Tunisia. Cuscus alla trapanese (see facing page) is typically made with fish and shellfish, but I've read about versions that also include chicken. In his 1891-vintage manual *La scienza in cucina e l'arte di mangiar bene* (*Science in the Kitchen and the Art of Eating Well*), Pellegrino Artusi gives a recipe for cuscussù made with veal brisket, boneless veal, a chicken liver, and a hard-boiled egg. He describes it as "a dish of Arab origin, which the descendants of Moses and Jacob, in their peregrinations, have carried around the world." He proceeds to give a complex recipe for it, then asks rhetorically at the end, "Is this dish worth all the maddening effort it requires?" His response: "To me, it is not a dish to make a great fuss over, but if prepared with great care, it can please even those whose palates are not used to such dishes."

BUCATINI CON LE SARDE

SERVES 4 TO 6

One of the most famous of all Sicilian primi piatti, pasta with sardines (pasta chi sardi in Sicilian dialect) was originally a seasonal dish, made only from March through September when sardines are running and wild fennel covers the hillsides. Today, it is likely to be found year-round. The pasta shape most often used for the dish is bucatini, a kind of thick spaghetti with a hole through the core, virtually identical to perciatelli. Wild fennel has a stronger flavor than its cultivated counterpart, with a flatter bulb and thinner fronds. If it doesn't grow wild where you live, you may sometimes find it at farmers' markets. In its absence, the smaller inner fronds of cultivated fennel may be substituted. Whichever kind you use, use plenty of it; it is almost as important to this dish as the sardines. Sicilian recipes typically call for two or three bunches. When fresh sardines are unavailable, I have made this dish with good-quality olive oil–packed sardines from Spain—unorthodox and more expensive than the fresh ones, but quite delicious. If using these, reduce the quantity of oil to ¼ cup/60 milliliters.

SALT

1 POUND/500 GRAMS BUCATINI OR PERCIATELLI

6 TABLESPOONS/90 MILLILITERS EXTRA-VIRGIN OLIVE OIL

1 ONION, FINELY CHOPPED

2 CUPS/30 GRAMS LOOSELY PACKED FINELY CHOPPED WILD OR CULTIVATED FENNEL FRONDS AND THIN STALKS

4 ANCHOVY FILLETS, MINCED

1 TABLESPOON PINE NUTS

2 TABLESPOONS GOLDEN RAISINS/SULTANAS

½ TEASPOON SAFFRON THREADS, CRUMBLED INTO ½ CUP/120 MILLILITERS WARM WATER

¾ POUND/375 GRAMS FRESH SARDINE FILLETS (ABOUT 1 POUND/500 GRAMS WHOLE SARDINES)

PEPPER

Bring a large pot of salted water to a boil over high heat. Add the pasta to the pot and cook until al dente, 8 to 12 minutes.

Meanwhile, heat the oil in a large frying pan over medium heat. Add the onion and cook, stirring frequently, until it softens, 6 to 8 minutes. Add the fennel and cook, stirring, for 2 to 3 minutes, then stir in the anchovies, pine nuts, raisins, and saffron water.

Stir well and cook for 2 for 3 minutes more, then stir in the sardine fillets, breaking them up into large pieces. Raise the heat to medium-high and cook until the sardines are cooked through, 3 to 4 minutes. Season with salt and pepper.

Drain the pasta well and return it to the pot. Add the sauce, stir well, and transfer to a warmed serving bowl.

SPAGHETTI WITH TOMATO SAUCE

SERVES 4 TO 6

"The angels in paradise," the mayor of Naples proposed in 1930, "eat nothing but vermicelli al pomodoro." (Vermicelli, "little worms," and spaghetti, "little strings," are synonymous.) Elsewhere in these recipes, when tomato sauce is an ingredient in other sauces or stews, I've given the option of using homemade or commercial sauce. Not so here. When tomato sauce is to stand on its own, it is well worth the effort of concocting it yourself.

SALT

1 POUND/500 GRAMS SPAGHETTI

3 CUPS/720 MILLILITERS TOMATO SAUCE (PAGE 371), HEATED

PEPPER

6 TO 8 BASIL LEAVES, JULIENNED

GRATED PARMIGIANO-REGGIANO FOR SERVING

Bring a large pot of salted water to a boil over high heat. Add the pasta to the pot and cook until al dente, 8 to 12 minutes.

Drain well, then transfer the pasta to a warmed serving bowl, add the sauce, and toss well. Top with a few grinds of pepper, and then scatter over the basil. Pass the parmigiano at the table.

THE PERFECT CHEESE

"The ideal Parmesan," British travel writer and journalist H. V. Morton felt he had to inform his readers as late as the 1960s, "is not the familiar and costly hard rock familiar to English kitchens, but a pale gold, close-textured cheese covered everywhere with innumerable pinpoint holes." He was talking, of course, about parmigiano-reggiano, Italy's most famous and versatile cheese. Parmigiano, commonly called Parmesan in English (and in French), has been made at least since the fifteenth century: Bartolomeo Sacchi, better known as Platina, mentioned *parmigiano* from the Cisalpine regions" in his pioneering gastronomic guide *De honesta voluptate et valetudine* (*On Honest Pleasure and Well-Being*), published in the latter part of the fifteenth century (sources disagree as to the exact date). An engraving from Rome dated 1646 depicts a cheesemonger with half a wheel of what is clearly parmigiano under one arm and a wedge of it in the other hand. Its fame spread beyond Italy: Molière reportedly asked for a morsel of parmigiano on his deathbed in 1673, and Diderot mentions it in his mid-eighteenth-century *Encyclopédie*.

Made from raw cow's milk, parmigiano is named for the province of Parma in Emilia-Romagna and made there and in the provinces of Reggio-Emilia and Modena and in parts of the provinces of Bologna and the Lombardian province of Mantua. Grana padano, a similar cheese that has its partisans (and is in any case almost always less expensive than parmigiano-reggiano), may be legally produced in specific parts of Emilia-Romagna, Lombardy, the Veneto, and Trentino–Alto Adige; that from the province of Trento is particularly prized. (Parmigiano, of course, is also widely imitated elsewhere; I won't even mention the salty sawdust that comes in those green cardboard canisters, but will note that the "imported" parmigiano often found in supermarkets may well come from Argentina, or even Australia.)

Parmigiano is full of vitamins and minerals, protein, and amino acids and is comparatively low in salt and cholesterol, but of course that's not why people buy it. It has a complex flavor, nutty, buttery, and fruity, accented by tiny salt crystals. Grated over pasta or risotto, it seems to meld with and accentuate the flavors of the dish. As a constituent of stuffings, it helps bind ingredients together even as it brightens the way they taste. And it is a superior table cheese, especially when it is less than three years old and still crumbly (or older than that but from an unbreached wheel). Many restaurants in Italy offer parmigiano-reggiano and only parmigiano-reggiano as an after-dinner cheese. Their attitude seems to be, if we can offer perfection, why bother with anything else?

The cheese has something else going for it, too. There has been much talk in recent years about unami, the mysterious "fifth taste," after bitterness, saltiness, sweetness, and sourness. In fact, discovered more than a century ago by Kikunae Ikeda, a physics professor at Tokyo Imperial University, umami—sometimes called "savoriness"—is the result of an amino acid called glutamate. (Ikeda made a fortune by isolating the compound and selling it as the seasoning known as MSG, for monosodium glutamate.) Parmigiano contains more free glutamate than any other natural substance on Earth.

SILK MERCHANT AND GOURMET

On January 25, 1851, a silk merchant named Pellegrino Artusi went to the theater with his younger sister in their hometown of Forlimpopoli, near Forli in Emilia-Romagna. The cream of local society was in the audience, and all were horrified when the curtain rose to reveal not a stage set but a band of armed brigands led by the notorious Stefano Pelloni, known as Il Passatore (the Smuggler). Pelloni demanded a large ransom from the crowd, instructing each to send a family member home to bring back money and valuables. The citizenry did as they were told, the bandits escaped with their loot, and no one was injured. Artusi's sister, however, was so traumatized that he soon moved with her to Florence to escape the unhappy memory, and it was there that he later began to devote himself to the pleasures of the table. Thus, it is possible that we have a famous bandit to thank for what might fairly be called the first real Italian cookbook.

Artusi may have been a merchant, but he was an educated one, and in his adoptive Tuscany he wrote a biography of writer and revolutionary Ugo Foscolo and a book of commentary on the letters of poet Giuseppe Giusti. He was also a serious gourmet, and began collecting recipes. In 1891, when he was seventy-one, he self-published a collection of 475 recipes, in an edition of one thousand, under the title *La scienza in cucina e l'arte di mangiar bene* (*Science in the Kitchen and the Art of Eating Well*). The book sold slowly at first, but eventually caught on, and a second edition appeared, this time from a real publisher. He continued adding recipes to subsequent printings—the thirteenth, the last to be published while he was still alive, had 790—and by the time of his death in 1911, more than 200,000 copies had been sold. (A glossary of nonstandard Italian words published in 1931 listed *artusi* as a synonym for "cookery book.")

It is sometimes said that *La scienza* was the first cookbook to include recipes from all over Italy. This is a bit of an exaggeration, as most of them seem to come (not surprisingly) from Tuscany and Emilia-Romagna. After the first few editions, readers in other parts of the country began to send Artusi recipes for inclusion, but there is very little that could be identified as coming from south of Rome (or north of Milan). Still, the book's appeal is easy to divine. For one thing, it eschews most of the French terminology that had filled earlier cookbooks in Italy. And Artusi writes clearly, with frequent personal observations, and cheerfully admits his amateur status. "Cooking is a troublesome sprite," he writes in his introductory material. "Often it may drive you to despair." Before offering a recipe for pappardelle all'arentina (with a sauce including duck and veal spleen), he explains, "I present this not as a refined dish, but as one suitable for family cooking." Of a formula for pasticcio di maccheroni, he reassures readers that "a *pasticcio* always comes out well no matter how it is prepared."

SPAGHETTI ALLA CALABRESE

✳

SERVES 4 TO 6

Ginger (zenzero in Italian) was widely used in savory dishes all over the peninsula in medieval times, but has disappeared from most regions today, apart from its use in pastry making. Experts of old-style Venetian food will sometimes tell you that it still has a place in the cooking of La Serenissima, but I've never encountered it there, in real life or in modern-day recipes. In the traditionally impoverished regions of Basilicata and Calabria, though, ginger is still used to spice up sauces, along with the ubiquitous peperoncini. Waverley Root writes that "pasta asciutta alla calabrese is spaghetti or macaroni with a thick tomato sauce and a fiery addition of ginger," similar to the maccheroni alla carrettiera of Basilicata. I've also encountered a ginger-spiced spaghetti without tomatoes, flavored instead with olives and anchovies.

¼ CUP/60 MILLILITERS EXTRA-VIRGIN OLIVE OIL

5 GARLIC CLOVES, MINCED

I PIECE FRESH GINGER, ABOUT 2 INCHES/
5 CENTIMETERS LONG, PEELED, HALVED CROSSWISE,
AND JULIENNED

½ TEASPOON PEPERONCINI, OR MORE TO TASTE

2 CUPS/480 MILLILITERS TOMATO SAUCE,
HOMEMADE (PAGE 371) OR COMMERCIAL

6 TO 8 MINT LEAVES, JULIENNED

SALT

I POUND/500 GRAMS SPAGHETTI

GRATED PECORINO SARDO FOR SERVING

Heat the oil in a large frying pan over medium heat. Add the garlic, ginger, and peperoncini and cook for 2 to 3 minutes. Add the tomato sauce and mint, stir well, and season with salt. Reduce the heat to low and simmer until the sauce is very thick, 15 to 18 minutes.

Meanwhile, bring a large pot of salted water to a boil over high heat. Add the pasta to the pot and cook until al dente, 8 to 12 minutes.

Drain the pasta well and return it to the pot, then add the sauce and toss well. Transfer to a warmed serving bowl. Pass the cheese at the table.

SPAGHETTI ALL'AMATRICIANA

✳

SERVES 4 TO 6

Although a standard of Roman cooking today, this dish is named for, and possibly originally comes from, the ancient town of Amatrice in far northeastern Lazio, near the borders of Umbria, the Marche, and Abruzzo. One explanation for its popularity in the Italian capital is that several of the chefs who served in the Vatican came from Amatrice. The sauce is often made with pancetta, but it is traditionally flavored with the milder cured pork jowl called guanciale. This used to be impossible to find outside of Italy, but has become increasingly common in specialty markets in the United States and Britain (see page 382 for a source). Pedants scoff at menu writers who render this preparation's name as spaghetti alla matriciana, as if it were in the style of someone from a place called Matrice. At it turns out, that's not wholly incorrect: in medieval times, Matrice was indeed the town's name.

2 TABLESPOONS EXTRA-VIRGIN OLIVE OIL

¼ POUND/125 GRAMS GUANCIALE, DICED

½ SMALL ONION, MINCED

I SMALL DRIED RED CHILE

4 OR 5 PLUM TOMATOES, PEELED, HALVED
LENGTHWISE, SEEDED, AND SLICED

SALT

I POUND/500 GRAMS SPAGHETTI

3 OUNCES/90 GRAMS PECORINO ROMANO, GRATED

Heat the oil in a medium frying pan over medium heat. Add the guanciale and cook, stirring frequently, until it begins to brown, 5 to 6 minutes. With a slotted spoon, remove the guanciale to paper towels to drain.

Add the onion and chile to the fat remaining in the pan and cook over medium heat, stirring frequently, until the onion begins to soften, 5 to 6 minutes. Add the tomatoes, season with salt, and continue cooking until the sauce thickens, 10 to 12 minutes. Remove and discard the chile, then stir in the guanciale and cook for 5 to 6 minutes more to blend the flavors.

Meanwhile, bring a large pot of salted water to a boil over high heat. Add the pasta to the pot and cook until al dente, 8 to 12 minutes.

Drain the pasta well, then transfer it to a warmed serving bowl. Sprinkle the pecorino over the pasta, spoon the sauce over the top, and toss well.

SPAGHETTI AL PESTO TRAPANESE

SERVES 4 TO 6

We quite rightly associate pesto with Genoa and the surrounding Ligurian countryside, but this interesting variation on that classic sauce of crushed basil, garlic, pine nuts, and cheese has been made for many generations in and around the ancient western Sicilian town of Trapani.

½ CUP/120 MILLILITERS EXTRA-VIRGIN OLIVE OIL

I CUP/60 GRAMS TOASTED BREAD CRUMBS, HOMEMADE (PAGE 378) OR COMMERCIAL

SALT

I POUND/500 GRAMS SPAGHETTI OR BUCATINI

4 GARLIC CLOVES, CHOPPED

LEAVES FROM I SMALL BUNCH BASIL

20 ROASTED ALMONDS

½ POUND/250 GRAMS RIPE CHERRY TOMATOES, PEELED AND QUARTERED

PEPPER

Heat about 2 tablespoons of the oil in a large frying pan over medium heat. Add the bread crumbs, stir well, and cook, stirring frequently, until they are well toasted, about 15 minutes. Set them aside.

Bring a large pot of salted water to a boil over high heat. Add the pasta to the pot and cook until al dente, 8 to 12 minutes.

Meanwhile, scatter a pinch or two of salt in the bottom of a large mortar. Add the garlic and crush it to a paste with a pestle. Add the basil leaves, almonds, and about 2 tablespoons of the oil and continue crushing until a coarse paste is formed. Add the tomatoes and carefully crush them into the pesto, then work in the remaining 4 tablespoons oil to form a thick sauce. Season generously with salt and pepper.

Drain the pasta well and transfer it to a warmed serving bowl. Add the pesto, toss well, and then scatter the toasted bread crumbs over the top.

SPAGHETTI ALLA CHITARRA WITH ABRUZZESE MEAT SAUCE

SERVES 4 TO 6

One of my prized possessions is a chitarra *(guitar) given to me as a birthday present by Marcella Hazan. I cannot play this guitar, though; nobody could, at least not musically. It isn't really a guitar at all, but a contraption for making the Abruzzese specialty spaghetti alla chitarra. It consists of a wooden frame laced with metal strings, thus its name (though it looks more like a zither than a guitar). The dough, rolled out fairly thick, is laid over the strings, then a rolling pin is passed firmly over it, pushing the pasta down onto a slanted board. It emerges with square-cut sides, which some-how make it seem particularly hearty and rustic, and well suited to this rough-hewn meat sauce. It is possible to buy a* chitarra *in the United States at some specialty stores (see page 382 for a source), but you can buy excellent-quality artisanal dry spaghetti alla chitarra (under the Latini label, among others).*

¼ CUP/60 MILLILITERS EXTRA-VIRGIN OLIVE OIL

I ONION, FINELY CHOPPED

¼ POUND/125 GRAMS LAMB STEW MEAT, CHOPPED

¼ POUND/125 GRAMS VEAL STEW MEAT, CHOPPED

¼ POUND/125 GRAMS BONELESS PORK RIBS, CHOPPED

4 TO 6 RIPE TOMATOES, SEEDED AND GRATED (SEE RAW TOMATO COULIS, PAGE 371), OR ONE-HALF 28-OUNCE/875-GRAM CAN SAN MARZANO TOMATOES, DRAINED AND CHOPPED

SALT

I POUND/500 GRAMS SPAGHETTI ALLA CHITARRA

I TEASPOON PEPERONCINI

½ CUP/50 GRAMS GRATED PECORINO ROMANO, PLUS MORE FOR SERVING

PEPPER

Heat the oil in a large frying pan over medium heat. Add the onion and cook, stirring frequently, until it softens, 6 to 8 minutes. Add the lamb, veal, and pork and continue cooking, stirring frequently, until the meats begin to brown, 6 to 8 minutes. Add the tomatoes and season with salt. Stir well, reduce the heat to low, cover, and simmer until the meats are very tender, about 1½ hours.

When the sauce is almost ready, bring a large pot of salted water to a boil over high heat. Add the pasta to the pot and cook until al dente, 8 to 12 minutes.

Drain the pasta well and transfer it to a warmed serving bowl. Stir the peperoncini and the cheese into the sauce, then spoon it over the spaghetti and toss well. Adjust the salt if necessary, and grind some pepper over the top. Serve with additional cheese.

SPAGHETTI WITH SALT COD AND BLACK OLIVES

SERVES 4 TO 6

At his delightful Luna Rossa in Terranova di Pollino, near Potenza in southern Basilicata, Federico Valicenti makes this dish with two unique products from the region: black Majatica olive al forno, or baked olives, from Ferrandina, which are toasted, dry-salted, then baked according to a technique dating back three hundred years, and the sun-dried semispicy peperoni di Senise, sweet red peppers that are all but essential to the cooking of the region (see page 310). Senise peppers are available in the United States (see page 382 for a source), but I have been unable to find Ferrandina olives, so use Kalamatas as an imperfect substitute. (Note that Italians typically cook with unpitted olives; pit yours if you wish.)

3 TABLESPOONS EXTRA-VIRGIN OLIVE OIL

1 SMALL ONION, HALVED AND VERY THINLY SLICED

5 LARGE, RIPE TOMATOES, SEEDED AND GRATED (SEE RAW TOMATO COULIS, PAGE 371)

1 CUP/150 GRAMS BLACK FERRANDINA BAKED OLIVES OR KALAMATA OLIVES

2 DRIED ITALIAN SWEET PEPPERS OR 1 LARGE ANCHO CHILE, FINELY CHOPPED

½ POUND/250 GRAMS SALT COD, PREPARED FOR COOKING (PAGE 378)

SALT

1 POUND/500 GRAMS SPAGHETTI

3 OR 4 SPRIGS ITALIAN PARSLEY, MINCED

Heat the oil in a large frying pan over medium heat. Add the onion and cook, stirring frequently, until very soft and beginning to brown, 6 to 8 minutes. Add the tomatoes, olives, and peppers, reduce the heat to low, stir well, and cook for about 3 minutes. Flake the salt cod into the frying pan with your fingers, stir well, season with salt, and continue cooking until the sauce reduces, 10 to 12 minutes.

Meanwhile, bring a large pot of salted water to a boil over high heat. Add the pasta to the pot and cook until al dente, 8 to 12 minutes.

Drain the pasta well and return it to the pot, then add the sauce and toss well. Transfer to a warmed serving bowl and sprinkle the parsley on top.

SPAGHETTI WITH SHRIMP AND PISTACHIO PESTO

SERVES 4 TO 6

I've had variations on this dish all over Sicily. Use fresh shrimp if possible. The best I have found for this purpose are tiny, sweet Maine shrimp, in season from December through March or April every year. See page 382 for a source.

SALT

1 POUND/500 GRAMS SPAGHETTI

1 POUND/500 GRAMS SMALL SHRIMP/PRAWNS, PEELED

1 CUP/240 MILLILITERS PESTO GENOVESE (PAGE 374), WITH ½ CUP/75 GRAMS PISTACHIO NUTS CRUSHED WITH THE OTHER INGREDIENTS

2 TABLESPOONS EXTRA-VIRGIN OLIVE OIL

Bring a large pot of salted water to a boil. Add the pasta to the pot and cook until almost done al dente, 7 to 9 minutes. Add the shrimp to the pot and cook for about 1 minute more.

Drain the pasta and shrimp, and put them into a warmed serving bowl. Add the pesto and oil, season with salt, and toss well.

BUSIATE WITH SWORDFISH AND EGGPLANT

SERVES 4 TO 6

Pasta alla Norma (page 81) is often called the most typical of Sicilian pastas, but to me this preparation of busiate—long, thick, twisted noodles—not only based on the island's most venerable pasta form but also using some of its celebrated typical raw materials, is the definitive Sicilian pasta. The recipe is an adaptation of one from the excellent Trattoria Cantina Siciliana, in the heart of Trapani's old town, near the historic church of San Pietro. See page 382 for a source for busiate.

4 TABLESPOONS/60 MILLILITERS OLIVE OIL

I SMALL EGGPLANT/AUBERGINE, ABOUT ¼ POUND/ 125 GRAMS, CUT INTO ¼-INCH/6-MILLIMETER CUBES

½ POUND/250 GRAMS SWORDFISH FILLET, CUT INTO ¼-INCH/6-MILLIMETER CUBES

16 MINT LEAVES, JULIENNED

3 TABLESPOONS SLIVERED BLANCHED ALMONDS

15 TO 20 SMALL CHERRY TOMATOES

SALT

I POUND/500 GRAMS BUSIATE OR SPAGHETTI

Heat 3 tablespoons of the oil in a large sauté pan over medium-high heat. Add the eggplant and stir quickly to coat all the the pieces with oil. Cook, stirring frequently, until they start to brown, 5 to 6 minutes. Transfer to paper towels to drain.

Adding the remaining 1 tablespoon oil to the same pan over medium-high heat. Add the swordfish and cook, stirring constantly, until just cooked through, 2 to 3 minutes. Reduce the heat to low, return the eggplant to the pan, and stir in the mint, almonds, and tomatoes. Stir well, season with salt, and let cook, stirring occasionally, until the eggplant is very soft, about 10 minutes more.

Meanwhile, bring a large pot of salted water to a boil over high heat. Add the pasta to the pot and cook until al dente, 8 to 12 minutes.

Drain the pasta well, then stir it into the pan with the sauce, turning it until it is thoroughly coated. Transfer to a warmed serving bowl.

NOODLE NAMES

More than five hundred varieties of pasta are made in Italy, but there are many more pasta names than that, since the same shapes often have many different monikers. Sometimes these describe the shape of the pasta (penne means "quills," spaghetti means "little strings," farfalle means "butterflies"), sometimes they refer to how the pasta is made (schiaffettoni, or "slaps"; corpu de diu, or "blows of the finger"), and occasionally they describe an imagined function (abbotta pezziende, meaning "feed the beggar"; strangolapreti, meaning "priest-stranglers"— apparently a suggestion that they are so good they would induce potentially fatal gluttony even in a man of God). Here is a random list of some other pasta names:

Avemarie—Hail Marys

Budelletti—very thin intestines

Cazzetti d'angeli—little angels' penises

Code di topo—mouse tails

Creste di gallo—cockscombs

Diavoletti—little devils

Dischi volanti—flying saucers

Eliche—propellers

Falloni—big phalluses

Folletti—elves

Garganelli—chickens' gullets

Gobbini—lame ones

Gomiti—elbows

Lenzolere e cuscenere—sheets and pillows

Lucciole—fireflies

Lumachelle—little snails

Nastrini—little ribbons

Occhi di passero—sparrow's eyes

Orecchie d'asino—donkey's ears

Pannicelli—swaddling clothes

Paglia e fieno—straw and hay

Picagge—dressmaker's ribbons

Racchette—tennis rackets

Radiatore—radiators

Scorze di mandorle—almond shells

Sedani—celeries

Semi d'avena— oat seeds

Sorcetti—little mice

Stortini—little twisted ones

Struncatura—sawdust

Tempestine—little storms

Trenette—train tracks

Vipere cieche—blind snakes

Zavardouni—slovenly women

Ziti—bridegrooms

PASTA FRESCA

HOMEMADE GOODNESS

Ridi, ridi, che la mamma ha fatto i gnocchi.
[Laugh, laugh, because Mamma is making gnocchi.]
—*Italian proverb*

She ordered tagliatelle. . . . So what if the tagliatelle hung in unruly
strands from the fork as she raised it to her mouth?
—*Marian Keyes*, Last Chance Saloon

Virtually any form of pasta you can name, egg or water, fresh or dried, can be bought commercially today. There is simply no need to make your own— not even gnocchi or stuffed pastas like ravioli and tortellini. On the other hand, once you learn the basics, it is not hard, and it is very satisfying. When most Italians do make pasta at home, they make egg pasta, which is to say pasta in which water plays no part, the only moisture being provided by eggs. In Italy,

commercial pasta all'uovo must contain 5½ percent egg solids by weight. If you make your own, it will likely be richer than that, which is not a bad thing. It will also be, at least theoretically, luminously golden. Water-dough pasta is worth making yourself, too, though, if you need gnocchi or some other particular shape—you can buy dried trofie, for instance, but they are not the same as homemade ones—or if you need eggless pasta for a lasagna or ravioli recipe (the commercial versions of flat pasta sheets tend to be too thick for my taste).

I've been unable to discover exactly when and where the idea of making pasta with eggs originated. The fortified medieval town of Campofilone in the Marche claims to have been its birthplace, but as far as I can tell the only evidence to back up that claim is a reference, in documents from the local Abbey of San Bartolomeo, to *macceroncini* in the fifteenth century. It seems more likely that pasta all'uovo would have developed in Emilia-Romagna, both because its cuisine is famously rich and because it encompasses much of the Po Valley, where the soft winter wheat—high in starch and low in protein—that makes the best egg-based pasta is grown. (In her invaluable *Encyclopedia of Pasta*, Oretta Zanini De Vita reports that an expert on grain mills named Pasquale Barracano liked to call pasta made from soft wheat "merely a pastification of bread.") A pasta factory was chartered in Bologna as early as 1586, but the region's most famous pasta, tagliatelle, was supposedly invented in Bologna in 1487, by a chef named Mastro Zafirano, in honor of the marriage of Lucrezia Borgia to the Duke of Ferrara ("supposedly" because the marriage is widely reported to have occurred in 1501). The egg-induced golden hue of the strands, it is said, was a tribute to Borgia's blonde hair. (The Bolognese take their tagliatelle seriously, in any case: it has been decreed that their width should correspond to ¹⁄₁₂,₂₇₀ of the height of the Torre degli Asinelli, one of the two landmark medieval towers in the city's historic center; there is a golden replica of a strand of the pasta, for comparison's sake, at the local Chamber of Commerce office.)

Another pasta maker reportedly modeled Bologna's famous meat-stuffed pasta, tortellini, after the navel of Venus (or of his mistress, depending on which version you believe). Tortellini, first described in the 1830s, and elsewhere known in slight variation as cappellacci or cappelletti, are labor-intensive to produce, but ultimately economical: in her excellent book on the cooking of Emilia-Romagna, *The Splendid Table*, Lynne Rossetto Kasper writes that ½ pound/250 grams of boiled meat fills enough tortellini to feed twelve—with the added advantage that the water in which the meat is boiled can be used as broth to cook the pasta. (I recommend Kasper's book to anyone who wants to tackle tortellini or the other filled pastas for which Emilia-Romagna is famous.)

BEYOND DURUM

Italians make their dry pasta, or *pasta secca*, exclusively with the flour, or semolina, produced from durum wheat (*Triticum durum*), a hard wheat high in gluten and in protein. Softer flour is used for the fresh egg-based pastas most common to Emilia-Romagna. Pasta made from unrefined flour (that is, whole-wheat/wholemeal flour), usually durum, is traditional in parts of the Veneto, Campania, and Puglia, and has gained popularity all over Italy in recent years, presumably for its perceived health benefits. But durum and soft flour are not the only possible constituents of Italy's most emblematic culinary creation. Two of modern-day wheat's ancestors or early relatives, emmer wheat and spelt, are sometimes used for pasta (and are also cooked as a kind of wheat berry in soup, the former in particular). Both grains are called *farro* in Italian. The term by itself almost always means emmer wheat, though most English-language cookbooks translate it as spelt. Theoretically, spelt should be described as farro grande or farro spelta (emmer wheat is farro medio). Just to confuse things, a third kind of farro, farro piccolo, is a wheat called einkorn, but I have never encountered it in Italy.

Buckwheat, called *grano saraceno*, or "Saracen grain," is sometimes used in the mountainous reaches of northern Italy, where it is favored because it has a comparatively short growing season and likes rocky soil. I've had buckwheat pasta in Liguria, but the most famous example is the pizzoccheri of the Valtellina in Lombardy (see page 116), earthy in both color and flavor. (Hans Christian Andersen once noted that the buckwheat plant has beautiful flowers and suggested that the dark shade of its grain comes from the plant having been singed by lightening as a punishment for its pride.) Chestnut flour goes into pasta in Liguria, Tuscany, parts of Piedmont, and a few other areas.

Then there is grano arso, or "burnt grain." This is durum wheat, but durum wheat like no other: After the harvest each year, it was common for farmers to set the stubble on fire, to fertilize the land for the next year's crop. Apparently, in earlier, poorer times, peasants in Puglia and to a lesser extent Basilicata and Molise would rake through the ashes and find burnt grain, which they would mill into flour. The result is dark and smoky tasting, and produces pasta with a memorable and not at all unpleasant flavor. Today, of course, like so much "poor food" of the past, grano arso is a specialty item sold in fine food shops.

TROFIE WITH PESTO

SERVES 4 TO 6

Watching an accomplished Ligurian home cook make this squiggly little gnocchi-like pasta is a humbling experience: it is done with remarkable speed and grace. For those of us who have not been making them for half a century or more, it takes some practice to turn out consistently sized and shaped trofie—but ill-formed, irregular ones will cook just as nicely and taste just as good. The trofie may also be served with tomato sauce (see page 371) or simply tossed with butter or extra-virgin olive oil and grated Parmigiano-Reggiano.

4 CUPS/500 GRAMS FLOUR, PLUS MORE FOR DUSTING

SALT

1 CUP/240 MILLILITERS PESTO GENOVESE (PAGE 374)

In a large bowl, mix together the flour and a generous pinch of salt. Whisk in about 2 cups/480 milliliters water, pouring it in a slow, steady stream. When the dough begins to form, flour your hands well and knead it to form a firm but pliant dough. (Add a bit more water if necessary.) When the dough is ready, cover it with a kitchen towel and let it sit for 30 minutes.

Generously dust a work surface with flour. Flour your hands again, then pinch off a piece of dough about the size of a small grape and roll it between your palms into a baton about 1½ inches/3.75 centimeters long. Grasp the ends of the baton and quickly twist them in opposite directions, then scoot it over onto the floured surface. Repeat the process until all the dough is used up. If you run out of space for the just-made trofie, lightly dust the ones you have made with flour and put the remaining ones on top. Let the trofie sit for about 30 minutes after the last one is made.

Bring a large pot of salted water to a boil. Add the trofie to the pot and cook until they have all risen to the top, 3 to 5 minutes.

Drain them well, then put them into a warmed serving bowl, add the pesto, and toss well.

MALLOREDDUS
(SARDINIAN GNOCCHI)

SERVES 4 TO 6

This saffron-scented gnocchi is a specialty of Sardinia. Its name is dialect for "little calves," from malloru *(bull), a fanciful description of their shape. The ridges in the gnocchi were originally made by pressing the dough against the side of a wicker basket. Store-bought dried malloreddus, without the saffron, is available (see page 382 for a source), but the pasta is much better freshly made. Here it is dressed simply with olive oil and cheese, but you can also toss it with tomato sauce (page 371).*

4 CUPS/500 GRAMS FLOUR, PLUS MORE FOR DUSTING

SALT

½ TEASPOON POWDERED SAFFRON OR LIGHTLY TOASTED AND CRUSHED SAFFRON THREADS

½ CUP/120 MILLILITERS EXTRA-VIRGIN OLIVE OIL

½ CUP/50 GRAMS GRATED PECORINO SARDO, PLUS MORE FOR SERVING

In a large bowl, mix together the flour, a pinch of salt, and the saffron, then make a well in the center. Pour 1½ cups/360 milliliters warm water into the well, then mix the water into the flour mixture with a wooden spoon. The dough should be firm but pliable. (Add a bit more water if necessary.)

Turn the dough out onto a floured work surface and knead until pliant, 1 to 2 minutes. Divide the dough into 20 equal pieces. Roll each piece between your palms into a strand about ½ inch/1.25 centimeters in diameter. Cut each strand into pieces about 1 inch/2.5 centimeters long. With your thumb, press both sides of each piece of dough against the tines of a fork. As the pieces are shaped, put them aside in a single layer on another floured surface. Let the gnocchi sit for about 15 minutes after the last one is made.

Meanwhile, bring a large pot of salted water to a boil over high heat. Add the gnocchi to the pot and cook until they have all risen to the top, 3 to 5 minutes.

Drain them well, then put them into a warmed serving bowl. Add the oil and cheese, toss well, and season with salt. Pass additional cheese at the table.

PESTO PRESTO

Some people make pesto (see page 374) by tossing basil, garlic, pine nuts, olive oil, parmigiano, and a little salt into a food processor and flipping a switch. The Genoese cringe at the thought (or at least say they do in public). The very name of this celebrated sauce, they point out, comes from the verb *pestare*, "to pound," which in turn is derived from the Latin *pistillium*, meaning "a pounder" or "a pestle." Isn't it obvious, then, that pesto should be made in a mortar? (Some Ligurian cooks claim that cutting the veins of basil leaves, whether with a knife or with the blades of a processor, stems the flow of the aromatic compounds that help make the sauce so wonderful. I suspect this is more folklore than science.)

I like making pesto with a mortar and pestle myself for several reasons: the sauce smells great as it comes together (you don't get much aroma out of a whirring Cuisinart, unless it's a faint hint of overheated metal); it's easy to adjust quantities as you go; and it's a great way to get out a little aggression. Here are a few suggestions for making particularly good pesto:

1. Smaller basil leaves are usually sweeter and not as aggressively minty as larger ones, and so make better pesto. To avoid bitterness, take the time to trim off the stems as well as the stalks (I can tell a stemmy pesto in an instant; it's a common fault).

2. Go easy on the garlic. Although what was apparently the first published reference to the sauce, in *La cuciniera genovese; ossia la vera maniera di cucinare alla genovese* by G. B. Ratto (originally published anonymously in 1864), calls it *battuto all'aglio (pesto)*—"beaten mixture with garlic (pesto)"—using too much of this pungent bulb thrusts the basil into the background, which is not the idea at all.

3. If possible, use Mediterranean, not Asian, pine nuts. The former are elongated, the latter teardrop shaped; the Mediterranean ones are more expensive and difficult to find in the United States, but they have better flavor and are worth looking for. Whatever you use, though, taste one first to make sure it is not rancid. Pine nuts are very oily and go bad quickly (always store them in the refrigerator to retard spoilage). It is better to make pesto with walnuts, which is common in some corners of Liguria, or with no nuts at all, than to give the sauce a rancid overtone.

4. For added complexity, use equal parts parmigiano-reggiano and pecorino sardo.

5. Use good olive oil, preferably a mild-flavored one from Liguria (or Catalonia).

6. Make your pesto no more than a day or so before you are going to use it. The homemade stuff always tastes best fresh.

WINTER SQUASH GNOCCHI WITH MEAT SAUCE

SERVES 4 TO 6

Pumpkin or other winter squashes are used as a filling for ravioli and other stuffed pastas all over Italy. In the frasche, *or informal farmhouse restaurants, of Friuli (see page 70), they are sometimes made into hearty gnocchi.*

I SMALL ACORN OR BUTTERNUT SQUASH, I TO
1½ POUNDS/500 TO 750 GRAMS, QUARTERED
AND SEEDED

2 EGGS

SALT

I CUP/125 GRAMS FLOUR, PLUS MORE FOR DUSTING

2 TABLESPOONS EXTRA-VIRGIN OLIVE OIL

I ONION, CHOPPED

½ POUND/250 GRAMS GROUND/MINCED PORK

½ POUND/250 GRAMS GROUND/MINCED VEAL

2 OR 3 CHICKEN LIVERS, TRIMMED AND MINCED

PEPPER

3 CUPS/720 MILLILITERS TOMATO SAUCE,
HOMEMADE (PAGE 371) OR COMMERCIAL

Preheat the oven to 350°F/175°C/gas 5.

Put the squash, cut side up, into a baking pan and cover the pan with aluminum foil. Bake until soft, about 1 hour.

Remove the squash from the oven. When it is cool enough to handle, scrape out the flesh into a sieve and, with the back of a wooden spoon, press out as much liquid as possible. Put the squash into a large bowl, add the eggs and plenty of salt, and mash with a fork or a potato masher. Add the flour and work it into the mixture to form a thick, soft dough. (Add a bit more flour if the dough doesn't stick together.)

Generously dust a work surface with flour. Using a tablespoon, form the dough into oval gnocchi, putting them on the floured surface as they are formed. Let them sit while you proceed to the next step.

Heat the oil in a large frying pan over medium heat. Add the onion, pork, veal, and chicken livers, break up the ground meats with a wooden spoon, and season generously with salt and pepper. Cook, stirring frequently, until the onions are very soft and the meats are browned, about 20 minutes.

Drain the onion mixture in a colander or sieve, then return it to the frying pan and add the tomato sauce. Reduce the heat to low and simmer uncovered, stirring occasionally, until slightly thickened, about 20 minutes more.

Meanwhile, bring a large pot of salted water to a boil over high heat. Working in batches, add the gnocchi to the pot and cook until they rise to the surface, 1 to 2 minutes. As the gnocchi are done, remove them from the pot with a slotted spoon and transfer them to a warmed serving bowl.

When all the gnocchi are cooked, spoon the sauce over them, but do not toss.

CHESTNUT GNOCCHI WITH PINE NUT PESTO

SERVES 4 TO 6

For centuries, chestnuts were a staple of the Ligurian entroterra *(see page 111), eaten by themselves but also made into flour for bread and pasta. These particular gnocchi are a specialty of the Valle Argentina, north of Sanremo. The "pesto" of pine nuts was a traditional substitute for real pesto in the winter months, when no basil was grown—before, that is, the advent of the first basil greenhouses in the early twentieth century, which made the herb available year-round. (See page 382 for a source for chestnut flour.)*

I CUP/125 GRAMS CHESTNUT FLOUR

3 CUPS/375 GRAMS ALL-PURPOSE/PLAIN FLOUR,
PLUS MORE FOR DUSTING

SALT

I CUP/150 GRAMS PINE NUTS

¼ CUP/60 MILLILITERS EXTRA-VIRGIN OLIVE OIL

2 TABLESPOONS GRATED PARMIGIANO-REGGIANO,
PLUS MORE FOR SERVING

In a large bowl, mix together the flours, then mix in about 1 teaspoon salt. Whisk in about 2 cups/480 milliliters water, pouring it in a slow, steady stream. When the dough begins to form, flour your hands well and knead it to form a firm but pliant dough. (Add a bit more water if necessary.) When the dough is ready, cover it with a kitchen towel and let it sit for 30 minutes.

Generously dust a work surface with all-purpose flour. Flour your hands again, then pinch off a piece of dough about the size of a small grape and roll it between your palms into a baton about 1½ inches/3.75 centimeters long, then gently form it into a C (don't worry if it doesn't completely hold its shape). Scoot each gnoccho over onto the floured surface. Repeat the process until all the dough is used up. If you run out of space for the just-made gnocchi, lightly dust the ones you have made with flour and put the remaining ones on top. Let the gnocchi sit for about 30 minutes after the last one is made.

Meanwhile, put the pine nuts and a pinch of salt in a mortar and crush into a coarse paste, then pour in the oil in a thin stream, stirring with the pestle to make a thick sauce. (You may need a little more oil.) Stir in the parmigiano, and adjust the seasoning with salt if necessary.

Bring a large pot of salted water to a boil. Add the gnocchi to the pot and cook until they have all risen to the top, 3 to 5 minutes.

Drain them well, then put them into a warmed serving bowl, add the pesto, and toss well. Pass additional cheese at the table.

CASUNZIEI
(VENETO-STYLE BEET AND TURNIP RAVIOLI)

SERVES 4 TO 6

These earthy ravioli are a specialty of the northern Veneto, the mountainous region between Belluno and the ski resort of Cortina d'Ampezzo. The filling is sometimes seasoned with chives, nettles, mint, or other herbs. The cheese traditionally grated over it is zigar, a dried or smoked chive-flavored cow's milk ricotta—not, as far as I can discover, exported.

SALT

4 BEETS/BEETROOT, PEELED AND QUARTERED

2 LARGE POTATOES, PEELED AND QUARTERED

2 TURNIPS, PEELED AND QUARTERED

¼ TO ½ CUP/15 TO 30 GRAMS TOASTED BREAD CRUMBS, HOMEMADE (PAGE 378) OR COMMERCIAL

PEPPER

FRESH PASTA NO. 2 (PAGE 369), IN SHEETS

FLOUR FOR DUSTING

6 TABLESPOONS/90 GRAMS BUTTER, MELTED AND KEPT WARM

2 TABLESPOONS POPPY SEEDS

GRATED PARMIGIANO-REGGIANO FOR SERVING

Bring a large pot of salted water to a boil over high heat. Add the beets and cook for about 10 minutes, then add the potatoes and turnips. Cook until all the vegetables are very soft, 20 to 30 minutes. Drain the vegetables, then pass them through a food mill or puree them in a food processor. Transfer the vegetable mixture to a medium bowl. If it is too moist to hold together, add enough bread crumbs to absorb the moisture and bind the mixture. Season the mixture generously with salt and pepper.

Dust a work surface with flour. Lay one sheet of pasta on the floured surface. Cut each sheet into 2½- to 3-inch/6.25- to 7.5-centimeter squares. Put about 1 teaspoon of the vegetable mixture in the center of each square. Fold each square over into a triangle, enclosing the filling, and press the edges together with your fingertips. Transfer the filled triangles to a floured baking sheet. Repeat with the remaining pasta sheets and filling (you might have some filling left over). Dust the triangles lightly with flour, and refrigerate them on the baking sheet(s) for 1 hour.

Bring a large pot of salted water to a boil over high heat. Add the triangles to the pot and cook until they have all risen to the top, 3 to 5 minutes.

Transfer the pasta to a warmed bowl with a slotted spoon, add the melted butter and poppy seeds, and toss well. Serve with the cheese passed at the table.

BREAD OF THE BACKCOUNTRY

Traveling in Italy in the late sixteenth century, the French essayist Michel de Montaigne reported that in Bagno a Corsena, near Lucca in Tuscany, "the people eat 'wooden bread': so they proverbially call the bread made of chestnuts, which is their principal crop. . . ." Peasants in Liguria called the chestnut tree *l'albero del pane*—"the tree of bread"—not only because they could make bread (and pasta) from chestnut flour, but because it was the daily source of nourishment in some particularly impoverished places. An old saying from Triora, in the Liguria *entroterra*, or "backcountry," probably was not much of an exaggeration: "A matin castagne, a megiudi pestümi, a sèira castagnòn" (In the morning, chestnuts; at midday, chestnut crumbs; in the evening, dried chestnuts). In times of privation, fresh chestnuts were eaten either boiled or roasted or stewed in milk or wine; dried ones went into soups or were reconstituted by boiling in water with fennel flowers and salt, or were just popped into the mouth and chewed, like caramels.

Preparing dried chestnuts was a difficult task, and was often tackled as a community project. In Liguria, for instance, a dozen pounds/six kilograms of chestnuts were put into heavy sacks on the floor, then beaten by two people at a time with (chestnut-wood) sticks to crack their shells. This reportedly required exactly forty blows; fewer wouldn't do the job and more would crush the meats as well as the shells. The hulled chestnuts were then taken to a *seccatoio*, or "drying place," spread out on elevated alder-wood grilles high above a slow fire, and smoke-dried for hours, as farmers and their friends and neighbors waited patiently, gossiping and eating. (That the process was frustratingly slow may be gleaned from the fact that the term for chestnut drying, *seccatura*, also means "nuisance" or "tedium.") When the chestnuts were ready, everyone would gather around to pick through them. The wormy or rotten ones became fodder for the pigs, and the good ones were milled into flour or stored dry.

CIALZÒNS
(TRIESTINO RAVIOLI)

SERVES 4 TO 6

Cialzòns (also spelled cjalsòns) are a kind of stuffed pasta from Trieste. The name is dialect for calzone, *which means "trouser" or "trouser leg," and, like the more familiar folded pizzas of that name, cialzòns are plump half-moons, though much smaller. (Their shape does not suggest that of a trouser leg any more than the shape of a calzone does, but never mind.) Like most labor-intensive pastas in Italy, they were traditionally associated with special-occasion holiday eating, like Christmas or Easter dinner. There are numerous regional variations: some are filled with polenta, some with bread-soaked milk, some with ricotta. Some versions are made with meat, and others are sweet, involving dried fruits and chocolate. I once had cialzòns in this style on a chilly afternoon at a little restaurant in Duino—a name that will be familiar to readers of Rainer Maria Rilke—on the so-called Triestino Riviera.*

½ CUP/125 GRAMS FRESH RICOTTA

I EGG YOLK, BEATEN

I GREEN/SPRING ONION, MINCED

2 SPRIGS ITALIAN PARSLEY, MINCED

6 MINT LEAVES, JULIENNED

SALT AND PEPPER

FLOUR FOR DUSTING

FRESH PASTA NO. I (PAGE 368), IN SHEETS

4 TABLESPOONS/60 GRAMS BUTTER, MELTED AND KEPT WARM

¼ POUND/125 GRAMS SMOKED RICOTTA, COARSELY GRATED

In a medium bowl, mix together the fresh ricotta, egg, onion, parsley, mint, a pinch of salt, and few grinds of pepper. Set aside.

Dust a work surface with flour. Lay one sheet of pasta on the floured surface. With a round cookie cutter or the rim of a glass 2½ to 3 inches/6.25 to 7.5 centimeters in diameter, cut out 6 disks from the sheet. (Discard the scraps.) Put about 1 scant teaspoon of the ricotta mixture on one-half of each disk, leaving a roughly ¼-inch/6-millimeter border around the edge. Fold each disk over into a half-moon, enclosing the filling, and gently but firmly crimp together the edges with your fingers. Transfer the filled half-moons to a floured baking sheet/tray. Repeat with the remaining pasta sheets and filling (you might have some filling left over). Dust the half-moons lightly with flour, and refrigerate them on the baking sheet(s) for 1 hour.

Bring a large pot of salted water to a boil over high heat. Add the half-moons to the pot and cook until they have all risen to the top, 3 to 5 minutes.

Transfer them to a warmed bowl with a slotted spoon, add the butter and smoked ricotta, toss well, and season with pepper before serving.

SARDINIAN POTATO RAVIOLI

SERVES 4 TO 6

*These distinctive ravioli—variously known in Sardinia as
cu'irigionis, culurzones, culurgionis, or culingionis, among
other things (I have been unable to divine an etymology for the
name)—are usually made with fiscidu, a pungent brined pecorino
sardo. I have never been able to find it in the United States, but
unbrined Sardinian pecorino (often labeled fiore sardo) may be
substituted.*

I POUND/500 GRAMS POTATOES, PEELED AND
QUARTERED

SALT

3 TABLESPOONS EXTRA-VIRGIN OLIVE OIL

I SMALL ONION, MINCED

2 GARLIC CLOVES, MINCED

¾ CUP/75 GRAMS GRATED YOUNG PECORINO SARDO

6 TO 8 MINT LEAVES, FINELY CHOPPED

I CUP/125 GRAMS ALL-PURPOSE/PLAIN FLOUR, PLUS
MORE FOR DUSTING

I CUP/125 GRAMS SEMOLINA PASTA FLOUR

2 CUPS/480 MILLILITERS TOMATO SAUCE,
HOMEMADE (PAGE 371) OR COMMERCIAL

8 TO IO BASIL LEAVES, TORN INTO PIECES

GRATED AGED PECORINO SARDO FOR SERVING

Put the potatoes into a large pot with salted cold water to
cover. Bring to a boil over medium-high heat and cook until
the potatoes are easily pierced with a fork, 20 to 30 minutes.

Meanwhile, heat 2 tablespoons of the oil in a small frying pan
over medium heat. Add the onion and garlic and cook, stirring
frequently, until the onion softens, 6 to 8 minutes.

When the potatoes are ready, drain them, reserving about ¼ cup/
60 milliliters of the cooking water. Pass the potatoes through
a ricer directly into the pot. Stir in the reserved cooking water
and the onion mixture with its oil and mix together well. Stir in
the young pecorino and the mint, season generously with salt,
and set aside.

In a large bowl, mix together both flours and a pinch of salt,
then make a well in the center. Pour the remaining 1 tablespoon
oil into the well, then slowly pour in about ⅔ cup/160 milliliters
warm water, mixing it into the flour with a wooden spoon as you
do. Use just enough water to obtain a firm but pliable dough;
add a little more if necessary.

Turn the dough out onto a floured work surface and knead
until pliable, 8 to 10 minutes. Cover the dough with a damp
kitchen towel and let it rest for about 30 minutes.

On a lightly floured work surface, roll out the dough ¹⁄₁₆ inch/
2 millimeters thick. With a round cookie cutter or the rim of a
glass about 3½ inches/8.5 centimeters in diameter, cut out as
many disks as possible from the sheet. Gather the scraps and
reroll once to cut out more disks.

Put about 1 teaspoon of the potato mixture in the center of
each disk, then gather up the edges of the disk and press them
together over the filling in a purselike shape (one traditional
recipe specifies the shape of a fig), crimping the seam. Transfer
the raviolo to a floured baking sheet/tray. Repeat the process
with the remaining disks and filling (you might have some filling left over). Dust the ravioli lightly with flour, and refrigerate
them on the baking sheet(s) for 1 hour.

Heat the tomato sauce in a small pot over low heat.

Bring a large pot of salted water to a boil over high heat. Add
the ravioli to the pot and cook until they have all risen to the
top, 3 to 5 minutes.

Transfer them to a warmed serving bowl with a slotted spoon.
Stir the basil into the hot tomato sauce, then spoon the sauce
over the ravioli. Pass the cheese at the table.

RED MULLET RAVIOLI

SERVES 4 TO 6

Ravioli filled with fish is a comparative rarity in Italy, and a comparatively recent innovation—the earliest recipe I could find dates only from 1880—but it has become increasingly popular in recent years in Liguria, arguably the birthplace of ravioli. This is the version I discovered almost twenty years ago at the lamented Cà Peo in Leivi, in the hills overlooking Chiavari.

I WHOLE RED MULLET OR FARMED STRIPED BASS, ABOUT 1½ POUNDS/750 GRAMS, CLEANED, FILLETED, AND SKINNED, WITH BONES, HEAD, AND TAIL RESERVED

½ CUP/120 MILLILITERS DRY WHITE WINE

I ONION, HALVED CROSSWISE

I CARROT, HALVED CROSSWISE

BOUQUET GARNI OF 2 SPRIGS EACH ITALIAN PARSLEY, MARJORAM OR OREGANO, AND MINT AND I BAY LEAF, TIED TOGETHER SECURELY WITH KITCHEN TWINE

3 TABLESPOONS BUTTER

I TABLESPOON EXTRA-VIRGIN OLIVE OIL

I EGG, LIGHTLY BEATEN

I CUP/250 GRAMS FRESH RICOTTA

SALT AND PEPPER

FLOUR FOR DUSTING

FRESH PASTA NO. I (PAGE 368), IN SHEETS

2 GARLIC CLOVES, MINCED

2 RIPE TOMATOES, SEEDED AND GRATED (SEE RAW TOMATO COULIS, PAGE 371)

Put the fish bones, head, and tail in a medium pot. Add the wine, onion, carrot, and bouquet garni, and then add water just to cover the ingredients. Bring to a boil over high heat, reduce the heat to low, cover, and simmer for 1 hour.

Meanwhile, cut the fish fillets into large pieces. Melt half the butter with the oil in a medium frying pan over low heat. Add about two-thirds of the fish pieces and cook, stirring frequently, until just cooked through, 3 to 4 minutes. Transfer the fish and cooking juices to a medium bowl and mash thoroughly with a fork, removing any errant bones. Mix in the egg and ricotta, then season with salt and pepper.

Dust a work surface with flour. Put one sheet of pasta on the floured surface, and halve it lengthwise with a sharp knife. Center about ½ teaspoon of the fish mixture about ¾ inch/ 2 centimeters from the top of 1 sheet, and flatten it slightly with the back the spoon. Repeat the process at 1½-inch/ 3.75-centimeter intervals down the center of the sheet, ending about ¾ inch/2 centimeters from the bottom of the sheet. You should have six mounds of fish mixture in all. Carefully fold the other half of the sheet over the half with the fish mixture, then press down on the dough around the mounds of filling and lightly but firmly crimp the edges with your fingers. Cut the ravioli into squares with a pastry or pizza cutter or a long-bladed knife. Press the edges of each raviolo together well. Transfer the ravioli to a floured baking sheet/tray. Repeat the process with the remaining pasta sheets and filling (you might have some filling left over). Dust the ravioli lightly with flour and refrigerate them on the baking sheet(s) for 1 hour.

Melt the remaining butter in a medium saucepan over low heat. Add the garlic and cook, stirring frequently, until the garlic softens, about 5 minutes. Add the tomatoes, then strain the fish broth into the pan. Add the uncooked fish, raise the heat to medium-high, and cook at a slow boil until the liquid has thickened and reduced by half, 10 to 15 minutes. Reduce the heat to low, break up the fish with a fork, and season with salt and pepper.

Meanwhile, bring a large pot of salted water to a boil over high heat. Add the ravioli and cook until they have all risen to the top, 3 to 5 minutes.

Transfer them to a warmed bowl with a slotted spoon and spoon the fish sauce over them before serving.

PIZZOCCHERI

(BUCKWHEAT PASTA WITH CABBAGE AND POTATOES)

SERVES 4 TO 6

*This is the classic pasta of the Valtellina region of Lombardy,
where it is taken so seriously that it has spawned not one but two
annual festivals in its honor in the municipality of Teglio, and has
its integrity protected by an Accademia del Pizzocchero di Teglio.
Its name (also spelled pizzocheri and pinzocheri) seems to derive
from bizzo, a dialect variation of bigio, which is a word for "gray"
in Italian, and presumably refers to the color of the noodles. Oretta
Zanini De Vita, in her essential Encyclopedia of Pasta, further
relates it to a group of gray-clad heretic monks called bizzochi.
The cheese most often used for pizzoccheri is bitto, a Valtellinese
variety—it is so identified with the dish that in Teglio it is sometimes called pizzoccherino—but a firm fontina may be substituted
if necessary. See page 382 for a source for bitto. If you choose not to
make your own pasta, use 1 pound/500 grams dried pizzoccheri.*

½ CUP/65 GRAMS ALL-PURPOSE/PLAIN FLOUR, PLUS
MORE FOR DUSTING

1¼ CUPS/220 GRAMS BUCKWHEAT FLOUR

SALT

1 LARGE POTATO, PEELED AND CUT INTO 1-INCH/
2.5-CENTIMETER CUBES

1 ONION, CHOPPED

6 TABLESPOONS/90 GRAMS BUTTER

1 SMALL HEAD SAVOY CABBAGE, ABOUT 1 POUND/
500 GRAMS, SHREDDED

1 CUP/100 GRAMS GRATED BITTO OR AGED FONTINA

Mix together both flours in a large bowl, then mix in about
1 teaspoon salt. Make a well in the center of the flour mixture.
Pour ¾ cup/180 milliliters warm water into the well, then
mix the water into the flour mixture with a wooden spoon.
The dough should be firm but pliable. (Add a bit more water
if necessary.)

Turn the dough out onto a floured work surface and knead
until pliable, 1 to 2 minutes. Divde the dough in half. Roll out
half of the dough about ⅛ inch/3 millimeters thick. Cut by
hand into strips about ½ inch/1.25 centimeters wide and 2½ to
3½ inches/6.25 to 8.75 centimeters long. Set the strips aside on
a floured surface. Repeat with the remaining dough. Let sit for
about 30 minutes after the last strips are cut.

Bring a large pot of salted water to a boil over high heat. Add
the potato and onion and cook for about 5 minutes, then
add the pasta and cook until just done, about 10 minutes more.
(If using dried commercial pasta, cook the potato and onion
for about 10 minutes, then add the pasta and cook for about
15 minutes more.)

Meanwhile, preheat the oven to 350°F/175°C/gas 5. Melt
the butter in a large frying pan over medium heat. Add the
cabbage and cook, stirring frequently, until cooked but still
a little crunchy, 6 to 8 minutes.

Drain the pasta and potatoes and transfer them to a warmed
serving bowl. With a slotted spoon, transfer the cabbage to the
pasta, stir well, and then stir in the cheese. Transfer the mixture to a shallow baking dish just large enough to hold it, and
drizzle the cooking butter from the frying pan over the top.

Bake until the top begins to brown, 5 to 6 minutes. Serve
directly from the dish.

TAGLIERINI WITH PESTO OF BASIL, PARSLEY, AND MARJORAM

SERVES 4 TO 6

Pestos made from herbs other than basil—among them parsley, marjoram, borage, even arugula/rocket—were common in Liguria until the early twentieth century. Basil has a comparatively short growing season in the region, withering in the autumnal cold before other herbs—and no self-respecting Ligurian connoisseur of this emblematic sauce would deign to use basil from the hotter south, scorned around Genoa for its bitter, minty character. Even after commercial greenhouses began supplying Genoese basil year-round in the early 1900s, many locals continued to consider traditional pesto genovese to be exclusively a warm-weather pleasure (not least because the greenhouse basil was more expensive than that grown outdoors, and the Genoese are notoriously thrifty). Today, basil has become such big business in the area that it is available at reasonable prices all year to almost everybody, and nonbasil pestos are rare. Even though it also uses basil, this version keeps alive the memory of earlier alternative recipes and is still sometimes encountered in the region of Castelnuovo Magra, near La Spezia, on Liguria's far southeastern end.

I GARLIC CLOVE, MINCED

6 TO 8 WALNUT HALVES, CHOPPED

COARSE SEA SALT

I CUP/15 GRAMS TIGHTLY PACKED BASIL LEAVES

I CUP/15 GRAMS TIGHTLY PACKED ITALIAN PARSLEY LEAVES

I TABLESPOON MARJORAM LEAVES

½ CUP/50 GRAMS GRATED PARMIGIANO-REGGIANO

6 TABLESPOONS/90 MILLILITERS EXTRA-VIRGIN OLIVE OIL

I POUND/500 GRAMS TAGLIERINI OR LINGUINE, HOMEMADE WITH FRESH PASTA NO. 2 (PAGE 369) OR COMMERCIAL (FRESH OR DRIED)

Put the garlic, walnuts, and a pinch of salt into a large mortar and crush them to a paste with a pestle.

Add the basil to the mortar a little at a time and crush to a coarse paste, grinding the leaves against the side of the mortar. Add another pinch of salt, then repeat the process with the parsley and finally the marjoram.

Add the cheese to the mortar and crush it into the pesto, then drizzle in the oil, continuing to work the mixture with the pestle until it forms a paste that is not quite smooth. Set aside to mellow for 20 to 30 minutes.

Meanwhile, bring a large pot of salted water to a boil. Add the pasta to the pot and cook until just done, 3 to 4 minutes for fresh pasta and 8 to 12 minutes for dried.

Drain the pasta, transfer to a warmed serving bowl, add the pesto, and toss well.

TAGLIATELLE WITH PROSCIUTTO

✳

SERVES 4 TO 6

Tagliatelle (which, like taglierini and tagliolini, takes its name from the verb tagliare, *"to cut") exists all over Italy, often under some local dialect name, but is the definitive pasta of Emilia-Romagna, and especially of Bologna. The classic sauce for tagliatelle is ragù bolognese, but in and around Parma, northwest of Bologna, it is often eaten this way, as well.*

3 TABLESPOONS BUTTER

½ POUND/250 GRAMS PROSCIUTTO (NOT SLICED), DICED

I SMALL ONION, MINCED

½ CUP/120 MILLILITERS HEAVY/DOUBLE CREAM

½ CUP/120 MILLILITERS WHOLE MILK

SALT AND PEPPER

I POUND/500 GRAMS TAGLIATELLE, HOMEMADE WITH FRESH PASTA NO. 2 (PAGE 369) OR COMMERCIAL (FRESH OR DRIED)

2 TO 3 TABLESPOONS GRATED PARMIGIANO-REGGIANO, PLUS MORE FOR SERVING

Melt the butter in a medium frying pan over medium-high heat. Add the prosciutto and cook, stirring constantly, until it begins to brown, 2 to 3 minutes. Reduce the heat to medium-low, add the onion, and cook, stirring frequently, until it begins to soften, 6 to 8 minutes. Add the cream and milk and season with salt and pepper.

Meanwhile, bring a large pot of salted water to a boil. Add the pasta to the pot and cook until just done, 3 to 4 minutes for fresh pasta, 8 to 12 minutes for dried.

Drain the pasta and transfer to a warmed serving bowl. Stir the cheese into the sauce, then add the sauce to the pasta and toss well. Serve with additional cheese on the side.

LASAGNETTE WITH ARTICHOKES

✳

SERVES 6 TO 8

Ristorante Cocchi is in an unpromising location, in an ordinary-looking hotel in a drab part of Parma, but it is quite possibly that city's best restaurant. In fact, it is the kind of place that made me fall in love with restaurants in Italy in the first place: warm, comfortable, and well run, with an ample menu of superbly prepared dishes, full of flavor but lacking in any pretension. This simple pasta dish is one of Cocchi's quiet triumphs.

JUICE OF 2 LEMONS

8 TO 10 ARTICHOKES

4 TABLESPOONS EXTRA-VIRGIN OLIVE OIL

I GARLIC CLOVE, MINCED

½ CUP/120 MILLILITERS DRY WHITE WINE

SALT AND PEPPER

FRESH PASTA NO. 2 (PAGE 369), IN SHEETS 9 BY 13 INCHES/23 BY 33 CENTIMETERS (4 SHEETS), OR ONE 9-OUNCE/255-GRAM PACKAGE BARILLA (NO BOILING REQUIRED) LASAGNA

2½ CUPS/600 MILLILITERS SALSA BESCIAMELLA (PAGE 374)

6 OUNCES/175 GRAMS FONTINA, CUT INTO ½-INCH/ I.25-CENTIMETER CUBES

I CUP/100 GRAMS GRATED PARMIGIANO-REGGIANO, PLUS MORE FOR SERVING

2 TABLESPOONS COLD BUTTER, CUT INTO SMALL PIECES

Put the lemon juice into a medium bowl with 2 to 3 cups/ 480 to 720 milliliters water.

Cut the stems off the artichokes. Follow this whole process with one artichoke at a time: Pull off the tough outer leaves by hand, then trim off more layers of leaves with a sharp knife until only the tenderest leaves, or heart, remain. Scoop out and discard the choke, then cut the artichoke lengthwise into slices about ¼ inch/6 millimeters thick. Immediately put the slices into the acidulated water to stop them from turning black.

Heat the oil in a large frying pan over medium-low heat. Drain the artichokes and add to the pan with the garlic. Cook the artichoke slices, stirring frequently, until they are soft, 10 to 12 minutes. Add the wine, reduce the heat to low, and cook until the artichoke slices are very tender, about 10 minutes more. Season generously with salt and pepper.

Meanwhile, bring a large pot of salted water to a boil over high heat. Cut the pasta sheets in half crosswise, then add the halved sheets to the pot two or three at a time and cook until just done, 3 to 4 minutes. Drain the pasta and lay the sheets in a single layer on nonlinty dish towels. Skip this cooking step if using commercial pasta.

Meanwhile, preheat the oven to 400°F/200°C/gas 6.

Spread a thin layer of besciamella on the bottom of a 9-by-13-inch/23-by-33-centimeter baking dish. Lay two sheets of pasta over the sauce, slightly overlapping them if necessary to cover the bottom of the dish. Top that with another thin layer of besciamella, then spread about one-third of the artichoke mixture over the sauce. Cover the artichokes with about one-third of the fontina cubes and one-fourth of the parmigiano. Lay two more pasta sheets on top of the cheeses and repeat the process: besciamella, artichokes, cheeses. Repeat the entire process one more time, then lay the final two pasta sheets over the last layer of cheeses. Dust the top layer of pasta with the remaining parmigiano and dot it with the butter.

Bake until the top is golden and bubbly, about 45 minutes. Serve immediately.

PAPPARDELLE WITH HARE SAUCE

SERVES 4 TO 6

This is one of the most famous of Tuscan pasta forms, its name deriving from the verb pappare, *"to gobble," presumably on the theory that its goodness will encourage the eater to do just that. Recipes for the dish published in America typically call for rabbit instead of hare, which has never made any sense to me. There's nothing wrong with rabbit, certainly, but it is fairly bland compared to its wild cousin, and is no more an apt substitute than, say, chicken would be in a recipe for roast partridge. Real wild-shot Scottish hare is available in this country, fresh in season (roughly August through February) and frozen otherwise (see page 382 for a source); it is expensive, but essential to this preparation. Around Arezzo, which claims pappardelle with hare sauce as a local recipe, the hare is supposed to be hung for at least two days before it is cooked, but this probably isn't necessary. (The "Belgian hare" sometimes kept as a house pet, incidentally, has nothing to worry about: it is really a rabbit bred to look like a hare, and probably wouldn't make great eating.)*

½ CUP/120 MILLILITERS RED WINE VINEGAR

2 CUPS/480 MILLILITERS DRY RED WINE

5 TABLESPOONS/75 MILLILITERS EXTRA-VIRGIN OLIVE OIL

2 GARLIC CLOVES, CRUSHED

1 SPRIG ROSEMARY

2 BAY LEAVES

1 WILD HARE, 3 TO 4 POUNDS/1.5 TO 2 KILOGRAMS, CUT INTO 6 OR 8 PIECES

1 ONION, MINCED

1 CARROT, FINELY CHOPPED

1 STALK CELERY, FINELY CHOPPED

6 TO 8 SAGE LEAVES, JULIENNED

SALT AND PEPPER

1 CUP/240 MILLILITERS TOMATO SAUCE, HOMEMADE (PAGE 371) OR COMMERCIAL

2 TABLESPOONS TOMATO PASTE, HOMEMADE (PAGE 371) OR COMMERCIAL

1 POUND/500 GRAMS PAPPARDELLE, HOMEMADE WITH FRESH PASTA NO. 2 (PAGE 369) OR COMMERCIAL (FRESH OR DRIED)

GRATED PARMIGIANO-REGGIANO FOR SERVING

Combine the vinegar, half the wine, and 2 tablespoons of the oil in a baking dish large enough to hold the hare. Add the garlic, rosemary, and bay. Cover the baking dish and set aside for 2 hours.

After 2 hours, add the hare and marinate it for 2 hours at room temperature, turning it after the first hour.

When the hare is almost ready to come out of the marinade, heat the remaining 3 tablespoons oil in a large frying pan over medium-high heat. Add the onion, carrot, celery, and sage, sprinkle with salt and pepper, and cook, stirring frequently, until the vegetables soften and begin to brown, 10 to 12 minutes. Remove the hare pieces from the marinade (discard the marinade), blot them dry, and add them to the frying pan. Continue cooking, turning the hare frequently, until the hare is lightly browned and the vegetables are caramelized, 10 to 12 minutes.

Deglaze the pan with the remaining wine, scraping up the browned bits on the bottom. Continue cooking until the wine has evaporated, then stir in the tomato sauce and tomato paste. Reduce the heat to low, cover, and cook, stirring and turning the hare occasionally, until the hare is very tender, about 1 hour.

Remove the hare from the frying pan, turning off the heat but leaving the sauce in the covered frying pan. Set the hare aside to cool. When it is cool enough to handle, pick the meat from the bones with your hands, shred it, and return it to the frying pan. Stir it in well, then cover the frying pan and keep the sauce warm over very low heat, stirring occasionally.

Bring a large pot of salted water to a boil over high heat. Add the pasta to the pot and cook until just done, 3 to 4 minutes for fresh pasta and 8 to 12 minutes for dried.

Drain the pasta, then transfer to a warmed serving bowl, add the sauce, and toss well. Pass the cheese at the table.

VINCISGRASSI

SERVES 6 TO 8

According to legend, this unusual variation on lasagna—a specialty of the Marche, and particularly the area around Macerata, south of Ancona—was invented in 1799 by a local chef who, attempting to curry favor with Austrian occupation forces, named it in misspelled honor of the Austrian prince Alfred I of Windisch-Grätz. Unfortunately for this fanciful etymology, Alfred would have been only twelve years old at the time; in any case, the same dish is known as pincegrassi *in neighboring Abruzzo, and a Maceratese chef named Antonio Nebbia published a recipe for a similar dish called* princigras *in 1779, before Alfred was born. Traditional recipes often called for the addition of sweetbreads, bone marrow, or calf's brains.*

4 TABLESPOONS/60 GRAMS BUTTER, PLUS MORE FOR GREASING

2 TABLESPOONS EXTRA-VIRGIN OLIVE OIL

1 ONION, FINELY CHOPPED

4 SPRIGS ITALIAN PARSLEY, MINCED

¼ POUND/125 GRAMS PANCETTA, DICED

½ POUND/250 GRAMS FRESH PORCINI OR OTHER WILD MUSHROOMS, FINELY CHOPPED

1 POUND/500 GRAMS CHICKEN LIVERS, TRIMMED AND CHOPPED

1 CUP/240 MILLILITERS DRY WHITE WINE

1 CUP/240 MILLILITERS TOMATO SAUCE, HOMEMADE (PAGE 371) OR COMMERCIAL

SALT AND PEPPER

2½ CUPS/600 MILLILITERS SALSA BESCIAMELLA (PAGE 374)

FRESH PASTA NO. 2 (PAGE 369), WITH 2 TABLESPOONS MARSALA ADDED TO THE DOUGH, IN SHEETS ABOUT 9 BY 13 INCHES/23 BY 33 CENTIMETERS (3 SHEETS)

1 CUP/100 GRAMS GRATED PARMIGIANO-REGGIANO, PLUS MORE FOR SERVING

Melt half the butter with the oil in a large frying pan over medium heat. Add the onion and parsley and cook, stirring occasionally, until the onion softens, 8 to 10 minutes. Add the pancetta, mushrooms, and chicken livers, stir well, and continue cooking until the livers are beginning to brown, 8 to 10 minutes. Add the wine, raise the heat to high, and cook, stirring constantly, until most of the alcohol burns off and the liquid has reduced slightly, 2 to 3 minutes. Reduce the heat to low and stir in the tomato sauce. Season with salt and pepper, then cook uncovered, stirring frequently, until the sauce is very thick, 30 to 45 minutes.

Remove from the heat and let cool to room temperature, then stir in the besciamella.

Meanwhile, bring a large pot of salted water to a boil over high heat. Add the pasta sheets to the pot one at a time and cook until al dente, 3 to 4 minutes. Drain the pasta and lay the sheets in a single layer on nonlinty kitchen towels.

Preheat the oven to 350°F/175°C/gas 5. Lightly butter a 9-by-13-inch/23-by-33-centimeter baking dish.

Lay one pasta sheet on the bottom of the prepared dish, then spread about one-third of the sauce over the sheet. Sprinkle about one-third of the parmigiano over the sauce. Cover the cheese with another pasta sheet. Dot the pasta with some of the remaining butter, then spread half the remaining sauce over the pasta sheet and cover it with half the remaining cheese. Again cover the cheese with a pasta sheet, dot it with butter, and spread on the remaining sauce. Dot the top of the sauce with any remaining butter, and sprinkle the remaining cheese over the top.

Bake until the top is golden brown, 25 to 30 minutes. Serve with more parmigiano.

THE HEARTLAND OF ITALIAN FOOD

Ladies and gentlemen, I give you Emilia-Romagna. Every region of Italy has its own foodstuffs and defining dishes, but this particular one, which stretches across Italy, nearly coast to coast, seems almost indecently endowed with gastronomic treasures. Raw materials first: Within this region of a little over 7,700 square miles/20,000 square kilometers are found rice, corn, and wheat; a cornucopia of fruit and vegetables; dairy animals including the rare Vacche Rosse cattle; championship pigs of the Large White, Landrance, and Duroc breeds; an abundance of wild game; trout and frogs and eels from fresh waters; and excellent seafood from the Adriatic coast.

What the culinary artisans of Emilia-Romagna do with their natural bounty is the real wealth here, though. This is the home of parmigiano-reggiano (the finest of it made from the milk of those Vacche Rosse cows), arguably the best cheese in the world (see page 92). It is the birthplace of aceto balsamico (balsamic vinegar), which in its artisanal form is a condiment of the utmost elegance and complexity. It is the source of much of Italy's best commercial pasta, and also of one of the country's most underrated red wines, the Sangiovese of Albana (and of Lambrusco, a wine of great charm, the soda-pop reputation earned by the most banal, mass-produced examples of the stuff aside). Above all, Emilia-Romagna is the capital of Italian pork butchery. Travelers in the region as early as the seventeenth century remarked on its cured meats. From Emilia-Romagna come prosciutto di Parma, probably the world's most famous ham and certainly one of the best, and its super-refined cousin, culatello di Zibello; mortadella, the original "baloney," among the most subtle of salumi; the stuffed pig's foot called zampone; cotechino sausage, essential (with lentils) to welcome the New Year; and endless salamis and sausages and prosciutto variations (like the cured spalla, or shoulder, of Parma).

The cuisines of Emilia-Romagna—I use the plural because it is really two very different regions, Emilia and Romagna, linked politically more than gastronomically—are as rich and varied as the region's artisanal creations. Bordered by more regions than any other region in Italy—Liguria, Piedmont, Lombardy, Tuscany, Veneto, and the Marche—Emilia-Romagna draws influences from all of them. And it has itself developed some of the greatest glories of Italian cuisine, especially in and around Bologna—the region's capital, variously called La Turrita ("The Towered," a nickname that a glance at its skyline will explain), La Dotta ("The Learned"; it is home to the oldest university in the Western world, founded in 1088), La Rossa ("The Red," a reference both to its terra-cotta tile roofs and its penchant for leftist governments), and La Grassa ("The Fat," courtesy of the aforementioned salumi).

The people of Emilia-Romagna are said to be the best pasta cooks in Italy (though other regions would doubtless disagree). At the very least, we must admit that the region's tortellini in brodo, tagliatelle al ragù (or alla bolognese, the same thing), and lasagne al forno are among the absolute triumphs of the genre. Add to that creations like the epic boiled dinner called bollito misto, the superior trippa alla bolognese, the unlikely but irresistible pork cooked in milk (see page 233), the ubiquitous naanlike flatbread called piadina (see page 152), and the local landbound version of fritto misto, which may include calf's brains, sweetbreads, baby lamb chops, cubes of mortadella, small balls of mozzarella, zucchini/courgettes, artichokes, potato croquettes, squash blossoms, eggplant/aubergine, mushrooms, apples, thick cream, and amarettini (tiny almond macaroons), among many other things. If for some reason I had to limit my Italian dining to a single region for the rest of my life, I might very well have to choose this one.

ANTI-PASTA

In his *Futurist Cookbook*, published in 1932—a book that was more parody and provocation than culinary manual—the idealogue and poet Filippo Tommaso Marinetti asked Italians to give up pasta. "*Pastasciutta*, however grateful to the palate," he wrote, "is an obsolete food; it is heavy, brutalizing, and gross; its nutritive qualities are deceptive; it induces skepticism, sloth, and pessimism." What he didn't say, but was surely thinking, was that a large portion of the wheat used to make pasta in Italy was imported from Russia and North America. One of Mussolini's goals was to reduce or eliminate his country's dependence on foreign trade, so Marinetti—who was to become active in Fascist causes—would have been espousing a politically expedient position.

The second most prominent anti-pasta personality in Italy, half a century later, was the esteemed chef Gualtiero Marchesi, considered the founder of *nuova cucina*, Italy's adaptation of French nouvelle cuisine. In the early 1980s, at his eponymous restaurant in Milan—which was to become Italy's first Michelin three-star establishment in 1985—Marchesi stunned the Italian food community by eliminating pasta from his menu. He found traditional Italian food to be vulgar and common, he said, and was quoted in *Time* magazine as asking rhetorically, "Why should I make pasta like the others?" He changed his mind a few years later, and there is pasta aplenty on the menu now at his current restaurant in Erbusco, near Brescia—including a dish of cold spaghetti with caviar.

RICE AND POLENTA

GRAINS OF SATISFACTION

Every risotto is only one risotto [that is,
risotto is never the same twice].
—*Lele Masiol, Murano restaurateur, in conversation with the author*

[Polenta] is obviously one of those dishes to which
one must become attached in infancy.
—*Sean O'Faolain, An Autumn in Italy*

Rice was known to the Romans, but they used it medicinally for the most part, and never cultivated it in any quantity. It first made an impact in Italy when the Moors imported rice itself—though probably not its cultivation—to Sicily in the eighth or ninth century. Most early Italian rice recipes were Middle Eastern in style, using the grain primarily as a thickening agent, often combined with almond milk, in the category of dishes, both sweet and savory,

known as *biancomangiare* (related to the French *blancmange*). By the tenth century, when Moorish hegemony over Sicily was more or less complete and extensive irrigation systems had been built, some rice was exported from there. The first important rice plantations, though, were in the plains of the Po Valley in the mid-fifteenth century, and the region today is Italy's undisputed rice capital—and the largest rice-growing area in Europe. In its broadest definition, the Po River basin includes portions of Valle d'Aosta, Piedmont, Liguria, Lombardy, Emilia-Romagna, Trentino, the Veneto, and Friuli–Venezia Giulia, but 90 percent of Italy's rice is grown in the narrow wedge of land defined by the provinces of Novara, Vercelli, and Pavia, southwest of Milan in Lombardy and Piedmont. This is one of the corners of Europe most suitable for rice cultivation, for its mild climate and abundance of water—harnessed by extensive irrigation systems installed in the mid-nineteenth century.

Apart from a fairy tale involving a disgruntled worker on Milan's Duomo in the sixteenth century, it's hard to find any information on the history of Italy's most famous rice dish, risotto, and it's equally difficult to divine why and when the starchy short-grained varieties essential for making risotto were first developed. There are said to be as many as 145 rice cultivars grown in

Italy today (one source says 172), though the only ones most of us will need to be concerned about in cooking Italian food are the common risotto varieties: Arborio, Vialone Nano, and Carnaroli (which is the most expensive and produces the creamiest risottos). I was surprised to learn that these appeared only after the first successful intervarietal crossbreeding experiments were conducted at the agricultural station in Borsano, near Varese in Lombardy, in 1925. Fairy tales aside, it seems quite possible that risotto as we know it today wasn't around much before then, either, though rice dishes under the same name are recorded in the late nineteenth century. A lot of mystique is attached to risotto making, but it is a simple process once you have the knack—and no, you don't have to stir it constantly, just fairly often. Most Italian home cooks, incidentally, use stock cubes (usually Knorr brand), not homemade broth, for their risotto.

We know polenta today as a kind of cornmeal mush, but it wasn't always that. It derives its name from *puls*, the Latin word for varieties of gruel eaten by the ancient Romans as much as two millennia before corn arrived in Europe. (The same word gives us "pulse," as in lentil or chickpea.) In its earliest forms, polenta was made from ground dried chestnuts, farro, and possibly even acorns, among other things. Corn (maize) was being grown in Italy as early as 1554, near Verona and Rovigo, and by the late sixteenth century, it was widely cultivated in the Veneto. At first, it was eaten mostly in that region, but by the eighteenth century, it had begun to find popularity in Friuli, Lombardy, and elsewhere. In Lombardy, reported the Irish writer Sean O'Faolian in the mid-twentieth century, "every family has a special polenta pot and a big wooden spoon, or a stick, to stir the meal." Eating it with quail in Bergamo, he found it "stodgy and uninteresting."

Cornmeal was plentiful and cheap, though, and polenta was filling, so it became an integral part of Italian home cooking, especially (though not exclusively) in the north. My friend Bepi D'Este, from Burano in the Venetian lagoon, remembers that when his family was lucky enough to have risotto instead of polenta, his grandfather would always stick three grains of rice—"never more, never less"—to his shoe, then go down to the local bar for a drink, where the rice would be sure to be noticed. This was his way of bragging that his family was doing well.

BASIC POLENTA

❄

SERVES 4 TO 6

There's a lot of conflicting advice out there about how to cook polenta. The water should be boiling, or maybe simmering, or, no, at room temperature. The cornmeal should be added in a thin stream, or just poured steadily from a bowl. The polenta should be stirred constantly for an hour, or maybe an hour and a half . . . unless, of course, twenty minutes is sufficient. Or, hey, just forget about all that work and buy instant polenta. In the dozen years or so that I was at Saveur, the test kitchen must have made polenta thirty or forty times, using every different method imaginable. This technique, which is basically Marcella Hazan's, gave the best results for the least amount of work—but it is still reasonably labor-intensive.

SALT

2 CUPS/320 GRAMS COARSE-GRIND WHITE
OR YELLOW POLENTA

Put 6½ cups/1.5 liters water into a large, heavy-bottomed pot and bring to a boil over high heat. Stir in 1 tablespoon salt and reduce the heat to medium-low. When the water slows to a simmer, start adding the polenta in a very slow, steady stream, stirring it constantly with a long, strong wooden spoon. ("The stream of cornmeal must be so thin that you can see the individual grains," counsels Hazan. "A good way to do it is to let a fistful of cornmeal run through nearly closed fingers.") Continue adding the polenta and stirring until it is used up and then stir the polenta until it is thick and beginning to pull away from the sides of the pan, about 20 minutes.

Serve the polenta immediately, or pour it out onto a wooden board or platter to cool for later use, shaping it into a rectangle about 1 inch/2.5 centimeters thick as it cools if you are going to fry it later.

CORNMEAL AND
BUCKWHEAT POLENTA

❄

SERVES 6 TO 8

When the Moors invaded southern Italy in the late seventh century, one of the many plants they brought with them was buckwheat, known to this day in Italian as grano saraceno, *or "Saracen grain"—and, like rice, it eventually migrated north. In making their early versions of polenta, residents of rural Piedmont would have mixed two or more varieties of grain for purely practical reasons, using up whatever they had. Today, buckwheat is sometimes added to cornmeal for variety of flavor and texture. The result is a particularly hearty polenta, perfect for accompanying robust stews or braised meat or game dishes.*

SALT

2½ CUPS/400 GRAMS FINE-GRIND YELLOW POLENTA

⅔ CUP/120 GRAMS BUCKWHEAT FLOUR

Put 10 cups/2.5 liters of water and 2 tablespoons of salt into a large, heavy-bottomed pot and bring to a boil over high heat.

Meanwhile, mix together the polenta and buckwheat flour in a medium bowl.

When the water is boiling, pour in the polenta mixture in a slow, steady stream, whisking constantly. Reduce the heat to medium-low and cook, stirring frequently with a wooden spoon, until the mixture is very thick, about 45 minutes.

Serve the polenta immediately, or pour it out onto a wooden board or platter to cool for later use, shaping it into a rectangle about 1 inch/2.5 centimeters thick as it cools if you are going to fry it later.

TASTY MEMORIES

I've got petto di faraona al crescione (breast of guinea hen with watercress) from Vecchio Molino in Certosa di Pavia, cappon magro (an elaborate Ligurian arrangement of room-temperature vegetables and seafood in green sauce) from Manuelina in Recco, pastissada de caval (a sort of lasagna with a sauce of . . . horsemeat) from 12 Apostoli in Verona, and both risotto con lumache (risotto with snails) and anguilla marinata (marinated eel) from Al Bersagliere in Goito. (I used to have some others, but they've been lost to time, or maybe to divorce.) I'm not talking about food, exactly; I'm talking about *piatti del buon ricordo*, "good-memory plates," which commemorate food.

In 1964, the Touring Club Italiano—which is more or less the AAA of Italy—organized what they called the Unione Ristoranti del Buon Ricordo, an invitation-only association of a dozen eating places around the country that served local, traditional dishes. Each restaurant was asked to choose one typical offering to be designated as a piatto del buon ricordo on the menu. If the diner ordered it, he or she would receive,

at the end of the meal, a complimentary hand-painted ceramic plate, roughly nine inches/twenty-three centimeters in diameter, bearing the name of the restaurant, the name of the dish, and an evocative folk-artish image. Many more restaurants have been added over the years, and some have been subtracted. There are now more than 120 of them, representing all of Italy's twenty regions (there are also one each—all Italian, of course—in Austria, Luxembourg, France, and Hong Kong, and 12 in Japan). Some of the restaurants have changed their choice of dishes, and thus their plates, over the years, so more than 200 different designs have been issued. Not surprisingly, the plates, made by the Fratelli Solimene Ceramica Vietri Mare on the Amalfi Coast, have become collectors' items. There's even an enthusiasts' club in Turin. I've ordered many good-memory plates around Italy over the years, and most—if not all—of the food I've gotten as a result has been pretty good. Even the disappointing ones have an upside, though: if you don't walk away with a good memory, at least you still walk away with a nice plate.

POLENTA WITH PORCINI

SERVES 4 TO 6

Funghi porcini (little pig mushrooms)—Boletus edulis, or ceps— or just plain porcini, as they are commonly called, are arguably the most flavorful of all mushroom varieties, and in Lombardy they are frequently employed to dress up polenta.

¼ CUP/60 MILLIMETERS EXTRA-VIRGIN OLIVE OIL, PLUS MORE FOR BRUSHING AND GREASING

15 TO 20 SMALL FRESH PORCINI MUSHROOMS (ABOUT 2 INCHES/5 CENTIMETERS LONG), QUARTERED LENGTHWISE

I GARLIC CLOVE, MINCED

SALT AND PEPPER

BASIC POLENTA (PAGE 131), COOLED IN A RECTANGLE I INCH/2.5 CENTIMETERS THICK

½ CUP/120 MILLILITERS VEAL BROTH (PAGE 373) OR COMMERCIAL BEEF BROTH

½ CUP/50 GRAMS GRATED PARMIGIANO-REGGIANO

Heat the oil in a large frying pan over medium-high heat. Add the porcini and garlic and cook, stirring frequently, until the porcini are golden brown, about 5 minutes. Season with salt and pepper and set aside.

Cut the polenta into four to six rectangles, each about 3 by 5 inches/7.5 by 12.5 centimeters. Brush the rectangles well with oil.

Lightly grease a large grill pan (preferably) or cast-iron frying pan and heat over high heat until very hot. Working in batches if necessary, sear the polenta rectangles, turning once, until crisp and slightly charred on both sides, 2 to 3 minutes per side.

Meanwhile, return the frying pan with the porcini to high heat, pour in the broth, and deglaze the pan, scraping up the browned bits on the bottom and cooking, stirring constantly, until almost all of the liquid has evaporated.

Put the polenta rectangles on 4 to 6 warmed plates and spoon the mushrooms and their juices over the top, dividing them equally. Sprinkle evenly with the cheese and serve.

POLENTA WITH WHITE BEANS AND KALE

SERVES 4 TO 6

This unusual preparation of polenta is a specialty of northwestern Tuscany, where it is called polenta incatenata, *"enchained polenta" (probably a reference to the shreds of kale it contains, perhaps thought to suggest chains or ropes), or, curiously,* infarinata—*which would seem to mean "floured," though no flour is involved.*

¾ CUP/175 GRAMS DRIED CANNELLINI BEANS, SOAKED OVERNIGHT IN WATER TO COVER

SALT

6 LARGE LEAVES KALE, STALKS REMOVED AND LEAVES JULIENNED

½ CUP/120 MILLILITERS EXTRA-VIRGIN OLIVE OIL

2¼ CUPS/360 GRAMS COARSE-GRIND YELLOW POLENTA

½ CUP/50 GRAMS GRATED PARMIGIANO-REGGIANO

Drain the beans and put them into a large pot. Add 6 cups/ 1.5 liters water, cover, and bring just to a simmer over medium heat (do not boil). Continue cooking for about 1 hour. Reduce the heat to low and continue cooking until the beans are tender but the skins have not begun to crack, 45 minutes to 1½ hours more, depending on the age of the beans. Salt the beans generously.

Add the kale and the oil to the pot and stir well. Continue cooking, uncovered, for about 10 minutes, then start adding the polenta in a very slow, steady stream, stirring it constantly with a long, strong wooden spoon. Continue adding the polenta and stirring until it is used up and the polenta is thick and the mixture is beginning to pull away from the edges of the pan, about 20 minutes.

Adjust the seasoning if necessary, and dust with the parmigiano before serving.

POLENTA WITH SNAILS

SERVES 4 TO 6

In the so-called citte delle lumache, *or "snail towns," of Italy—among them Nonantola, Bobbio, and Casumaro in Emilia-Romagna, Molini di Triora in Liguria, Cherasco and Borgo San Dalmazzo in Piedmont, Cantalupo di Bevagna in Umbria, Cannole in Puglia, and Gesico in Sardinia—snails are typically eaten not just by themselves but in sauce for pasta or polenta. A key flavoring in this particular recipe is mentuccia, also called nepitella, a pungent, minty herb known in English as lesser calamint (Calamintha nepeta). Some sources incorrectly identify it as pennyroyal (Mentha pulegium), an herb used by the ancient Romans, but one whose oil is toxic in large doses. I've never seen lesser calamint sold as an herb in shops or at farmers' markets in the United States, but if you have a garden (or even a windowsill), you can grow it. A half-and-half combination of oregano and mint makes an acceptable substitute. See page 382 for sources for canned snails and for mentuccia plants.*

¼ CUP/60 MILLILITERS EXTRA-VIRGIN OLIVE OIL

I ONION, MINCED

I STALK CELERY, MINCED

2 GARLIC CLOVES, MINCED

4 SPRIGS ITALIAN PARSLEY, MINCED

I TEASPOON MENTUCCIA LEAVES, OR I TEASPOON EACH WHOLE OREGANO LEAVES AND JULIENNED MINT LEAVES

½ CUP/120 MILLILITERS DRY WHITE WINE

3 CUPS/720 MILLILITERS TOMATO SAUCE, HOMEMADE (PAGE 371) OR COMMERCIAL

I TEASPOON PEPERONCINI, OR MORE OR LESS TO TASTE

70 TO 80 WELL-DRAINED CANNED SNAILS, HALVED

BASIC POLENTA (PAGE 131), SOFT AND WARM

Heat the oil in a large frying pan over medium heat. Add the onion, celery, garlic, parsley, and mentuccia and cook, stirring frequently, until the onion softens, 6 to 8 minutes. Add the wine, tomato sauce, and peperoncini, season with salt and pepper, and cook, stirring frequently, until the sauce thickens slightly, 12 to 15 minutes.

Stir in the snails and cook until just heated through, 2 to 3 minutes.

Divide the polenta equally between 4 to 6 warmed plates and spoon the sauce over the top to serve.

POLENTA WITH GORGONZOLA

SERVES 4 TO 6

When I was writing regularly about wine, I used to make an annual pilgrimage to Verona to attend Vinitaly, the massive international wine trade show. Almost every night during my stay, if there wasn't an organized banquet somewhere that I had to attend, I would end up (along with many of my colleagues) at a place called Antica Bottega del Vino, on a little side street in the middle of town. (It is said that a century ago, there were literally hundreds of such places in the city.) As its name suggests, wine is the specialty; every available surface seems to be crowded with bottles—supposedly one hundred thousand of them in all—and scores of good wines are available by the glass. I rarely had a complete dinner (I had usually been snacking all day), but one dish I always looked forward to, sitting at a little wooden table out in the front part of the place, was a big slab of slightly charred fried polenta topped generously with just-melting gorgonzola. This is approximately how it was made.

BASIC POLENTA (PAGE 131), COOLED IN A RECTANGLE I INCH/2.5 CENTIMETERS THICK

2 TABLESPOONS EXTRA-VIRGIN OLIVE OIL, PLUS MORE FOR BRUSHING AND GREASING

I POUND/500 GRAMS GORGONZOLA DOLCE (YOUNG GORGONZOLA), CHILLED, THEN CUT INTO SLICES ¼ INCH/6 MILLIMETERS THICK

Preheat the broiler/grill.

Cut the polenta into four to six rectangles, each about 3 by 5 inches/7.5 by 12.5 centimeters. Brush the rectangles well with oil. Lightly grease a shallow, flameproof baking pan or dish large enough to hold the polenta rectangles in a single layer and set aside.

Lightly grease a large grill pan (preferably) or cast-iron frying pan and heat over high heat until very hot. Working in batches if necessary, sear the polenta rectangles, turning once, until crisp and slightly charred on both sides, 2 to 3 minutes per side. As the polenta pieces are done, transfer them to the prepared baking pan, and immediately cover each slice generously with slices of gorgonzola so the cheese begins to melt from the heat of the polenta.

When all the slices are cooked and covered with gorgonzola, put the baking pan under the broiler until the cheese turns golden, 1 to 2 minutes. Serve immediately.

THE LIEUTENANT-COLONEL
DINES IN ITALY

*The food-loving English journalist and man-about-town who signed himself Lieut.-Col.
Newnham-Davis (his first name was Nathaniel, a fact he rarely revealed), traveled all over
Europe and to the fringes of Asia in the late nineteenth and early twentieth centuries, eating
and drinking and recording what he consumed. A veteran of the East Kent Regiment who
had fought in the so-called Zulu War of 1879 and later served in India and China, Newnham-
Davis published his most famous work,* The Gourmet's Guide to Europe, *in 1903 (with
one Algernon Bastard as coauthor). This is an excerpt from his enlightening, if not always
accurate (or correctly spelled), remarks on "Italian Cookery" in that book.*

There is no cookery in Europe so often maligned without cause as that of Italy. People who are not sure of their facts often dismiss it contemptuously as being "all garlic and oil," whereas very little oil is used except at Genoa, where oil, and very good oil as a rule, takes the place of butter, and no more garlic than is necessary to give a slight flavour to the dishes in which it plays a part.... An Italian cook frys better than one of any other nationality. In the north very good meat is obtainable.... Farther and farther south, as the climate becomes hotter, the meat becomes less and less the food of the people, various dishes of paste and fish taking its place, and as a compensation the fruit and the wine become more delicious. The fowls and figs of Tuscany, the white truffles of Piedmont, the artichokes of Rome, the walnuts and grapes of Sorrento, might well stir a gourmet to poetic flights. The Italians are very fond of their *Risotto*, the rice which

they eat with various seasonings—with sauce, with butter, and with more elaborate preparations. They also eat their *Paste asciutte* in various forms. It is *Maccheroni* generally in Naples, *Spaghetti* in Rome, *Trinetti* in Genoa. *Alla Siciliana* and *con Vongole* are but two of the many ways of seasoning the *Spaghetti*....

There are many minor differences in the components of similarly named dishes at different towns; the *Minestrone* of Milan and Genoa differ, and so does the *Fritto Misto* of Rome and Turin....

The "Zabajone," the sweet, frothing drink beaten up with eggs and sugar, is made differently in different towns.... It is a splendidly sustaining drink, whether drunk hot or iced, and Italian doctors order it in cases of depression, and it might well find a place in the household recipes of English and American households.

POLENTA PASTIZZADA

SERVES 6

This dish, also called polenta pasticciata *(both spellings can be translated loosely as "polenta in pie form"), is typical of Lombardy, and a version popular in Milan is dressed up with layers of* bescia-mella *(béchamel sauce). But Waverley Root reported also having found a version in the Veneto, in which the meat sauce was enhanced with cockscombs.*

5 TABLESPOONS BUTTER, PLUS MORE FOR GREASING

2 TABLESPOONS EXTRA-VIRGIN OLIVE OIL

I POUND/500 GRAMS GROUND/MINCED VEAL

½ POUND/250 GRAMS MILD ITALIAN SAUSAGE, CASING REMOVED, FINELY CHOPPED

SALT AND PEPPER

I ONION, MINCED

I CARROT, FINELY CHOPPED

I GARLIC CLOVE, MINCED

I CUP/240 MILLILITERS DRY RED WINE

¼ CUP/60 MILLILITERS TOMATO PASTE, HOMEMADE (PAGE 371) OR COMMERCIAL

I PINCH FRESHLY GRATED NUTMEG

BASIC POLENTA (PAGE 131), COOLED IN A RECTANGLE I INCH/2.5 CENTIMETERS THICK AND CUT INTO THIN SLICES

2 CUPS/200 GRAMS GRATED PARMIGIANO-REGGIANO

Heat 2 tablespoons of the butter and 1 tablespoon of the oil in a large frying pan over medium-low heat. Add the veal and sausage, breaking them up with a wooden spoon, and season generously with salt and pepper. Cook, stirring frequently, until the meats are cooked through but not browned, 12 to 15 minutes.

Remove the meats from the frying pan with a slotted spoon and drain on paper towels. Chop as finely as possible and reserve.

Add 2 tablespoons of the butter and the remaining 1 tablespoon oil to the same pan over medium-high heat. Add the onion, carrot, and garlic and cook, stirring often, until the vegetables are browned, 10 to 12 minutes.

Return the meats to the pan, stir well, and deglaze the pan with the wine, scraping up the browned bits on the bottom. Reduce the heat to low and stir in the tomato paste and nutmeg. Simmer uncovered, stirring frequently, until the sauce thickens, about 20 minutes. Remove from the heat and let cool in the pan for about 10 minutes.

Meanwhile, preheat the oven to 375°F/190°C/gas 5. Lightly butter a deep baking dish at least 7 by 11 inches/18 by 28 centimeters.

Line the bottom of the prepared dish with polenta slices, fitting them tightly in a single layer and covering the entire bottom. Spoon about one-third of the sauce over the polenta. Sprinkle about one-third of the parmigiano over the sauce. Arrange another layer of polenta slices over the parmigiano, then add half of the remaining meat sauce, followed by half of the remaining parmigiano. Lay the last layer of polenta over the parmigiano, and top with the remaining meat sauce. Dot the top of the sauce with the remaining butter.

Bake until the top has browned, 20 to 30 minutes. Sprinkle the remaining parmigiano over the finished dish before serving.

LEMON RISOTTO

This unusual risotto recipe comes from around Lake Garda, between Venice and Milan, where—unexpectedly for so northern an area—commercial lemon groves have been cultivated for centuries. Wash the lemons well before zesting them.

8 CUPS/2 LITERS CHICKEN BROTH, HOMEMADE (PAGE 372) OR COMMERCIAL

4 TABLESPOON/60 GRAMS BUTTER

I SMALL ONION, MINCED

2½ CUPS/500 GRAMS CARNAROLI OR OTHER RISOTTO RICE

I CUP/240 MILLILITERS SOAVE OR OTHER DRY WHITE WINE

FINELY GRATED ZEST FROM 3 LEMONS AND JULIENNED ZEST FROM I LEMON, PREFERABLY ORGANIC

I CUP/100 GRAMS GRATED PARMIGIANO-REGGIANO

SALT

Bring the broth to a simmer over low heat.

Melt the butter in a large pot over low heat. Add the onion and cook, stirring frequently, until it begins to soften, 2 to 3 minutes. Add the rice and cook, stirring constantly to coat it thoroughly in butter, for about 4 minutes. Add the wine and cook, stirring frequently, until it has evaporated.

Ladle about 1 cup/240 milliliters of the simmering broth into the rice and stir it frequently until the liquid has been absorbed, 2 to 3 minutes. Repeat the process several times, adding broth only when the previous broth has been absorbed, until the rice is cooked through but al dente, 20 to 25 minutes total. (You may have some broth left over.)

Stir in the grated lemon zest and the parmigiano and season with salt. Divide the risotto equally between 4 to 6 warmed plates or shallow bowls and garnish with the julienned lemon zest and serve.

RISOTTO WITH LEEKS AND SQUASH

Lori De Mori and Jason Lowe, the Tuscan-based authors of Beaneaters & Bread Soup: Portraits and Recipes from Tuscany, *had this elegant risotto at the Bonacossi family's Villa di Capezzana winery in Carmignano. Family chef Patrizio Cirri gave them the recipe, which I've adapted slightly.*

6 CUPS/I.5 LITERS CHICKEN BROTH, HOMEMADE (PAGE 372) OR COMMERCIAL

3 TABLESPOONS EXTRA-VIRGIN OLIVE OIL

2 LEEKS, WHITE PART ONLY, JULIENNED

I POUND/500 GRAMS BUTTERNUT OR ACORN SQUASH, PEELED, SEEDED, AND CUBED

2 SPRIGS ITALIAN PARSLEY, MINCED

4 TABLESPOONS/60 GRAMS BUTTER

I SMALL ONION, MINCED

2½ CUPS/500 GRAMS CARNAROLI OR OTHER RISOTTO RICE

¼ CUP/60 MILLILITERS DRY WHITE WINE

½ CUP/50 GRAMS GRATED PARMIGIANO-REGGIANO

SALT

Bring the broth to a simmer over low heat.

Heat the oil in a medium frying pan over low heat. Add the leeks and cook, stirring frequently, until soft but not browned, 10 to 12 minutes. Add 1 or 2 tablespoons of the broth if they begin to brown. Add the squash and continue cooking, stirring occasionally, until the vegetables have the consistency of thick marmalade, about 30 minutes, adding several tablespoons of the broth from time to time to keep the vegetables moist. Stir in the parsley, then set the pan aside off the heat.

Melt the butter in a large pot over low heat. Add the onion and cook, stirring frequently, until it begins to soften, 2 to 3 minutes. Add the rice and cook, stirring constantly to coat it thoroughly in butter, for about 4 minutes. Add the wine and cook, stirring frequently, until it has evaporated.

THE LEMONS OF LAKE GARDA

In 1912, D. H. Lawrence and Frieda Weekley (who was to become his wife two years later) embarked on a walking tour of Italy. This is part of Lawrence's account, from his Twilight in Italy, of a visit to the centuries-old lemon greenhouses around the appropriately named town of Limone, on the Lombardian side of Lake Garda.

I went into the lemon-house, where the poor trees seem to mope in the darkness. It is an immense, dark, cold place. Tall lemon trees, heavy with half-visible fruit, crowd together, and rise in the gloom. They look like ghosts in the darkness of the underworld, stately, and as if in life, but only grand shadows of themselves. . . . There is a subtle, exquisite scent of lemon flowers. . . .

We went out of the shadow of the lemon-house on to the roof of the section below us. When we came to the brink of the roof I sat down. The padrone stood behind me, a shabby, shaky little figure on his roof in the sky, a little figure of dilapidation, dilapidated as the lemon-houses themselves. . . .

"*Voyez*," said the padrone, with distant, perfect melancholy. "There was once a lemon garden also there—you see the short pillars, cut off to make a pergola for the vine. Once there were twice as many lemons as now. Now we must have vine instead. From that piece of land I had two hundred lire a year, in lemons. From the vine I have only eighty."

"But wine is a valuable crop," I said. "Ah—*così-così!* For a man who grows much. For me—*poco, poco—peu.*" Suddenly his face broke into a smile of profound melancholy, almost a grin, like a gargoyle. . . .

"*Vous voyez, monsieur*—the lemon, it is all the year, all the year. But the vine—one crop—?"

Lemon trees in a "lemon-house," Limone sul Garda, Lombardy, circa 1900.

Ladle about 1 cup/240 milliliters of the broth into the rice and stir it frequently until the liquid has been absorbed, 2 to 3 minutes. Repeat the process several times, adding broth only when the previous broth has been absorbed, for about 15 minutes, then stir in the squash and leeks. Continue cooking until the rice is cooked through but al dente, another 5 to 10 minutes, adding more broth as necessary. (You may have some broth left over.)

Season with salt, stir in the parmigiano, then divide the risotto equally between 4 to 6 warmed plates or shallow bowls to serve.

RISOTTO WITH WHITE TRUFFLES

SERVES 4 TO 6

White truffles are one of the rarest and most expensive luxury ingredients in the world, so what are they doing in a book on "country cooking"? They are here because they are in some ways the quintessential rural ingredient, foraged in the forest, with the help of dogs, and eaten all over their home region of Piedmont and beyond, even today, in restaurants both rustic and sophisticated. If you love white truffles, in fact, and happen to be in northern Italy while they are in season, it's worth seeking out trattorias outside the cities and large towns, where you're apt to find simply but perfectly cooked risotto or pasta with shavings of tartufi bianchi offered at a comparatively moderate price. The best way to shave truffles over risotto or pasta is with a small handheld mandoline made specifically for that purpose. See page 382 for sources for the mandoline and for white truffles themselves.

8 CUPS/2 LITERS CHICKEN BROTH, HOMEMADE (PAGE 372) OR COMMERCIAL

4 TABLESPOONS/60 GRAMS BUTTER

1 SMALL ONION, MINCED

2½ CUPS/500 GRAMS CARNAROLI OR OTHER RISOTTO RICE

1 CUP/240 MILLILITERS SOAVE OR OTHER DRY WHITE WINE

1 CUP/100 GRAMS GRATED PARMIGIANO-REGGIANO

SALT

AS LARGE A FRESH WHITE TRUFFLE AS YOU CAN AFFORD, GENTLY RUBBED CLEAN

Bring the broth to a simmer over low heat.

Melt the butter in a large pot over low heat. Add the onion and cook, stirring frequently, until it begins to soften, 2 to 3 minutes. Add the rice and cook, stirring constantly to coat it thoroughly in butter, for about 4 minutes. Add the wine and cook, stirring frequently, until it has evaporated.

Ladle about 1 cup/240 milliliters of the broth into the rice and stir it frequently until the liquid has been absorbed, 2 to 3 minutes. Repeat the process several times, adding broth only when the previous broth has been absorbed, until the rice is cooked through but al dente, 20 to 25 minutes. (You may have some broth left over.)

Stir in the parmigiano and season with salt. Divide the risotto between 4 to 6 warmed plates or shallow bowls, and shave the truffle over the top, dividing it equally. Serve immediately.

SWORDFISH AND FENNEL RISOTTO

SERVES 4 TO 6

I first had this dish at a restaurant in Ansedonia, in far southern Tuscany, near the border with Lazio in Grossetto Province. But it is a typical Sicilian dish, as its main ingredients suggest.

6 CUPS/1.5 LITERS SEAFOOD BROTH, HOMEMADE (PAGE 372) OR COMMERCIAL

6 TABLESPOONS/90 GRAMS BUTTER

1 ONION, MINCED

1 SMALL BULB FENNEL, INCLUDING STALKS AND FRONDS, FINELY CHOPPED

½ POUND/250 GRAMS SWORDFISH STEAK, CUT INTO ½-INCH/1.25-CENTIMETER CUBES

2½ CUPS/500 GRAMS CARNAROLI OR OTHER RISOTTO RICE

¼ CUP/60 MILLILITERS DRY WHITE WINE

SALT AND PEPPER

Bring the broth to a simmer over low heat.

Melt half the butter in a medium frying pan over low heat. Add the onion, fennel, and 2 to 3 tablespoons of the broth and cook, stirring frequently, until the fennel is very soft and the broth has evaporated, 12 to 15 minutes. Add the swordfish and continue cooking, stirring frequently, until the swordfish is cooked through, 5 to 6 minutes more, then set the pan aside off the heat.

Meanwhile, melt the remaining butter in a large pot over low heat. Add the rice and cook, stirring constantly to coat it thoroughly in butter, for about 4 minutes. Add the wine and cook, stirring frequently, until it has evaporated.

Ladle about 1 cup/240 milliliters of the broth into the rice and stir it frequently until the liquid has been absorbed, 2 to 3 minutes. Repeat the process several times, adding broth only when the previous broth has been absorbed, for about 20 minutes, then stir in the fennel and swordfish. Continue cooking until the rice is cooked through but al dente, another 5 to 10 minutes, adding more broth as necessary. (You may have some broth left over.)

Season the risotto generously with salt and pepper, then divide between 4 to 6 warmed plates or shallow bowls to serve.

RIPIDDU NIVICATU

SERVES 4 TO 6

The name of this dramatic-looking specialty of Catania in Sicily means something like snow-covered volcanic ash (ripiddu is probably most accurately defined as "lapillus"; look it up). In his comic novel Sicilian Tragedi *(that's the title in Italy; it was published in English as* Sicilian Tragedee—*go figure), Ottavio Cappellani says of one character, the unpleasant seventy-year-old Contessa Salieri, "From the makeup she is wearing it looks as if she has fallen face down in a plate of ripiddu nivicatu. . . ." This dish is an exception to the usual Italian aversion to combining cheese and seafood. Fresh cuttlefish is difficult to find in the United States, and when it does end up in fish markets, it has usually lost its ink sac. Squid makes an adequate substitute for cuttlefish, though its flavor and texture are different. See page 382 for a source for packets of cuttlefish ink.*

6 CUPS/1.5 LITERS SEAFOOD BROTH, HOMEMADE (PAGE 372) OR COMMERCIAL

6 TABLESPOONS/90 GRAMS BUTTER

1 ONION, MINCED

2½ CUPS/500 GRAMS CARNAROLI OR OTHER RISOTTO RICE

¼ CUP/60 MILLILITERS DRY WHITE WINE

TWO 0.14-OUNCE/4-GRAM PACKETS CUTTLEFISH INK

1 POUND/500 GRAMS CUTTLEFISH OR SQUID, PREFERABLY FRESH, CLEANED AND CUT INTO RINGS ABOUT 1 INCH/2.5 CENTIMETERS WIDE

SALT AND PEPPER

2 CUPS/480 MILLILITERS TOMATO SAUCE, HOMEMADE (PAGE 371) OR COMMERCIAL

1 TABLESPOON PEPERONCINI

SCANT 1 CUP/200 GRAMS FRESH RICOTTA

Bring the broth to a simmer over low heat.

Melt the butter in a large pot over low heat. Add the onion and cook, stirring frequently, until it softens, 6 to 8 minutes. Add the rice and cook, stirring constantly to coat it thoroughly in butter, for about 4 minutes. Add the wine and cook, stirring frequently, until it has evaporated. Stir in the cuttlefish ink.

Ladle about 1 cup/240 milliliters of the broth into the rice and stir it frequently until the liquid has been absorbed, 2 to 3 minutes. Repeat the process several times, continuing to stir constantly and adding broth only when the previous broth has been absorbed. Cook until the rice is cooked through but al dente, 5 to 10 minutes more, adding more broth as necessary. When you add the last portion of broth, add the cuttlefish and stir in well. (You may have some broth left over.) Cook for 2 minutes, then season generously with salt and pepper.

While the risotto is cooking, heat the tomato sauce in a small saucepan over medium heat. Stir in the peperoncini, then reduce heat to low to keep warm.

To serve, divide the risotto between 4 to 6 warmed plates or shallow bowls, then top with the tomato sauce, dividing it equally. Crumble the ricotta on top, again dividing it equally.

SAVORY PIES, FOCACCIA, AND THEIR KIN

❋

FROM THE BAKER'S OVEN

Cui scippa timpuna, mancia cudduruna.
[He who weeds the difficult terrain gets to eat the focaccia.]
—*Sicilian proverb*

"Pizza alla Pizzaiola" [is] a kind of Yorkshire pudding eaten either with cheese
or anchovies and tomatoes flavoured with thyme.
—*Lieut.-Col. Newnham-Davis*, The Gourmet's Guide to Europe (*1903*)

I t takes roughly one pound/five hundred grams of flour to make enough noodles to serve four to six people. When the same quantity of flour is turned into dough for a savory pie—*torta* in Italian—or pizza, it yields forms of food that will feed twice that number. It's probably not coincidental, then, that these two Italian specialties—one not very well-known or seen much outside Italy and the other so well-known in every corner of the globe that it almost

doesn't seem Italian anymore—were invented, at least in their present-day forms, in two of the poorest parts of Italy: Liguria and Campania, respectively. And unlike pasta, which is almost always eaten as part of a larger repast, savory pies and pizzas are usually served as *piatti unici*, "one-dish meals"—another economy.

The ancient Egyptians and later the Greeks and Romans ate savory ingredients enclosed in dough, and elaborate variations on the theme were popular in medieval court cooking (remember "Four and twenty blackbirds baked in a pie," that "dainty dish to set before a king"). The first written recipe for a *torta* in Italy dates from circa 1300; this is a pie whose origins are ascribed to Lavagna, in Liguria, filled with chicken, mussels, bacon, eggs, and cheese, flavored with saffron, sage, and parsley. Italy's most famous savory pie today is probably the Genoese specialty torta pasqualina (see page 161), or Eastertide torta, filled with Swiss chard and (traditionally) the cheeselike clabbered cream called prescinsêua, and in earlier times always made with thirty-three layers of dough—one for each year of Jesus's life. Today, simpler pies remain common fare in the Ligurian backcountry, where they are typically filled with assorted greens, potatoes, or wild mushrooms.

Pizza is, of course, basically an open-face savory pie. Early uses of the term, in fact (as by the papal chef Bartolomeo Scappi in 1570),

clearly refer to closed pies that have nothing to do with pizza in the modern sense. Pizza as we know it today, both in pure form and in infinite variation, apparently developed as a popular street food in and around Naples only in the nineteenth century. At first, it was appreciated mostly in Campania and elsewhere in the south. When nineteenth-century Florentine writer Carlo Collodi (né Carlo Lorenzini), best known as the author of *The Adventures of Pinocchio*, visited Naples, he was unimpressed. "The charred look of the toasted crust," he wrote, "the pale sheen of garlic and anchovy, the green-and-yellow color of the oil and fried herbs, and the scattered red pieces of tomato give pizza the appearance of elaborate filthiness that matches that of its seller."

Focaccia is, to use the trendy term, a flatbread. The first time I encountered it, in Rome, it was called *pizza bianca*, and it would not be entirely incorrect to describe the most common varieties of focaccia as pizza crust without the toppings (or with the simplest of them, like just salt, olive oil, and/or rosemary or other herbs). The word *focaccia* derives from the Latin word *focus*, "hearth," and like flatbreads the world over it would have originally been cooked on the hearth's hot stones.

OPPOSITE, BOTTOM: *Italian bakers, circa 1900.*

PANELLE
(CHICKPEA FLOUR FRITTERS)

✹

SERVES 6 TO 8

Panelle are the Sicilian equivalent of the panisses of Nice and vicinity, essentially fritters made from chickpea flour that has been cooked like polenta. One of the island's great gastronomic delights, they are street food, found in markets like the famous Vucciria or larger but less famous Il Capo in Palermo, and sold all over the island in the frigitterie, or fry shops. Sicilians often eat them as an unlikely sandwich filling, much as the Spanish fill sandwiches with slabs of potato omelet. See page 382 for a source for chickpea flour.

1½ CUPS/360 MILLILITERS EXTRA-VIRGIN OLIVE OIL,
PLUS MORE FOR GREASING

COARSE SEA SALT

2 CUPS/250 GRAMS CHICKPEA FLOUR

PEPPER

Lightly oil a shallow 9-by-13-inch/23-by-33-centimeter baking pan.

In a large pot, combine ½ cup/120 milliliters of the oil, 1 teaspoon salt, and 3 cups/720 milliliters water. Turn the heat to medium and immediately begin pouring in the flour in a very slow, steady stream, whisking constantly until it is well combined. Add a little more water if necessary to obtain a thick but still fluid consistency. Continue cooking and stirring constantly, switching to a long, strong wooden spoon when the mixture becomes too thick for the whisk, until it is thick and beginning to pull away from the sides of the pan, about 20 minutes.

When the mixture is ready, pour it into the prepared pan and smooth the top with a rubber spatula. Cover with plastic wrap/cling film and refrigerate for at least 2 hours or up to 3 days.

To serve, cut into 3- or 4-inch/7.5- or 10-centimeter squares or into triangles of the same length. Pour the remaining 1 cup/240 milliliters oil into a large frying pan over high heat and heat to 375°F/190°C. Working in batches, fry the pieces until crisp and golden brown, 3 to 4 minutes. As they are done, drain the panelle on paper towels.

Dust generously with pepper before serving.

FARINATA
(CHICKPEA FLOUR CRÊPE)

✹

SERVES 6

This Ligurian specialty, virtually identical to the socca of Nice, is basically a kind of crêpe or pancake made with chickpea flour. Chickpeas are an abundant crop everywhere, and the flour made by drying and grinding them was cheap around Genoa in earlier times—while wheat flour, which had to be imported from elsewhere in Italy or from abroad, was expensive. Although it now makes its appearance, with various refinements, on restaurant menus, farinata was originally street food, and around the port of Genoa and in towns all along the Ligurian coast, it is still sold out of stalls and other take-out places. That said, some of the best farinata I've ever eaten was at a place called Luchin in Chiavari, where immense fire-blackened trays of it come out of a wood-burning oven all day long.

2¼ CUPS/280 GRAMS CHICKPEA FLOUR

¼ CUP/60 MILLILITERS EXTRA-VIRGIN OLIVE OIL,
PLUS MORE FOR GREASING AND DRIZZLING

SALT

1 TABLESPOON ROSEMARY LEAVES (OPTIONAL)

VERY FINELY GROUND PEPPER

Pour 2 cups/480 milliliters room-temperature water into a large bowl, then sift in the flour very slowly, whisking it into a smooth batter. Whisk in the oil and 1 tablespoon salt, then cover the bowl with a kitchen towel and set it aside to rest for 1 hour.

Preheat the broiler/grill. Lightly oil a pizza or paella pan 12 to 15 inches/30 to 38 centimeters in diameter.

Pour the batter into the prepared pan, shaking the pan gently to distribute the batter evenly. Broil/grill for about 4 minutes, then reduce the heat to 450°F/230°C/gas 8 and bake until dark brown around the edges, 6 to 8 minutes more. If using the rosemary, scatter it over the top before the final baking.

To serve, dust with pepper and cut into irregular pieces.

PIADINA

MAKES 6

The piadina is the flour tortilla or the naan of the Romagna portion of Emilia-Romagna, the ubiquitous flatbread, as simple as can be, ancient in origin, versatile. (A Michigan-based importer who brings commercially produced piadina from Italy, under the PiadaMe! label, brags that his product may be used as a "Bread substitute at restaurants, Sandwich bread [folded or cut wedges], Sandwich roll, Accompanying ingredient for many recipes and plates, Dipping wedges, Pizza base, Base for sweet spreads.") The piadina is a little bland by itself, but served warm, folded over some shards of stracchino or other semisoft cheese, or good prosciutto, or even sautéed greens, it is extraordinarily good.

3½ CUPS/435 GRAMS FLOUR, PLUS MORE FOR DUSTING

½ TEASPOON BAKING SODA/BICARBONATE OF SODA

SALT

2 TABLESPOONS LARD

Sift the flour and baking soda together into a mound on a large, lightly floured surface, and make a well in the center. Dissolve 1 teaspoon salt in ⅓ cup/80 milliliters warm water. Put the lard and about half the water into the well, then flour your hands and work the wet ingredients into the flour until a firm dough forms, adding more water if necessary.

Knead the dough until smooth and elastic, about 10 minutes. Divide the dough into six balls of roughly equal size. Still working on the floured surface, flatten and stretch each ball into a disk 7 to 8 inches/18 to 20 centimeters in diameter. Let the disks rest for 10 minutes.

Heat a cast-iron griddle or frying pan over medium heat until hot but not smoking. Prick the tops of the disks lightly with a fork, then slip a disk onto the hot surface and cook, turning once, for 2 to 3 minutes per side. The disk is ready to turn when tiny bubbles appear on the raw surface. The finished disk should be speckled with little black burn marks from the griddle.

Repeat with the remaining disks, stacking them as they are done to keep them warm for serving.

LIGURIAN-STYLE FOCACCIA

SERVES 4 TO 6

This may be hard to believe when every sandwich shop and super-market in the land now seems to offer "focaccia" alongside white, wheat, and rye, but when I started going to Italy in the 1960s, this simple flatbread was virtually unknown in America, at least outside hardcore Italian neighborhoods. There are different versions of focaccia all over Italy, but this is the crisp, if admittedly oily, variation preferred in Liguria.

½ CUP/120 MILLILITERS EXTRA-VIRGIN OLIVE OIL, PLUS MORE FOR GREASING AND BRUSHING

ONE ¼-OUNCE/7-GRAM PACKET ACTIVE DRY YEAST

3 CUPS/375 GRAMS FLOUR, PLUS MORE FOR DUSTING

SALT

Oil a large bowl and set it aside. Pour 1 cup/240 milliliters warm water into a medium bowl, dissolve the yeast in the water, and let stand until foamy, about 5 minutes. Stir in the oil.

Mix together the flour and 1 teaspoon salt in a large bowl, and make a well in the center. Pour the yeast mixture into the well, then stir the yeast mixture into the flour with a wooden spoon until a slightly sticky dough forms. Add a little more water if necessary to achieve the correct consistency.

Turn the dough out onto a floured work surface. Coat your hands with flour, then knead the dough until it is smooth and elastic, 2 to 3 minutes. Shape the dough into a ball, put it into the oiled bowl, and roll it in the bowl to coat it lightly with oil on all sides. Cover the bowl with a kitchen towel and set it in a warm spot until the dough roughly doubles in size, about 2 hours.

Lightly oil a 7-by-11-inch/18-by-28-centimeter baking pan. Turn the dough out onto a floured work surface and shape it into a rectangle to fit the baking pan. Put it in the oiled pan and pat the top down gently so it is even. Using the handle end of a wooden spoon, make regular rows of slight indentations across the entire surface, spacing the indentations about 2 inches/5 centimeters apart. Cover the pan with a kitchen towel and allow the dough to rise for another hour at room temperature.

Preheat the oven to 450°F/230°C/gas 8.

Brush the top of the dough lightly with oil, then sprinkle with salt. Bake until golden brown, 20 to 25 minutes.

Serve warm or at room temperature, cut into wedges or squares.

Variation: Sprinkle 2 tablespoons rosemary or thyme leaves over the top of the focaccia after it has been in the oven for about 10 minutes.

FOCACCIA COL FORMAGGIO
(CHEESE-STUFFED FLATBREAD)

SERVES 4

The Consorzio Focaccia col Formaggio di Recco, which is dedicated to the "protection" of this irresistible dish, lists as members some fifteen restaurants, seven bakeries, and two take-out places in Recco itself and three neighboring towns. It also publishes what locals consider the official recipe for the specialty. This is a slight adaptation of it. See "The Pride of Recco," facing page, for more on focaccia col formaggio, and page 382 for a source for crescenza cheese.

3 CUPS/375 GRAMS FLOUR, PLUS MORE FOR DUSTING

SALT

3 TABLESPOONS EXTRA-VIRGIN OLIVE OIL, PLUS
MORE FOR GREASING

½ POUND/250 GRAMS CRESCENZA, STRACCHINO,
OR TELEME

Mix together the flour and 2 teaspoons salt in a large bowl, and make a well in the center. Pour 1 cup/240 milliliters warm water and 2 tablespoons of the oil into the well, then stir the wet ingredients into the flour with a wooden spoon to form a smooth, firm dough.

Turn the dough out onto a floured work surface. Coat your hands with flour, then knead the dough until smooth and elastic, 2 to 3 minutes. Divide the dough in half, and form each half into a ball. Roll out each ball as thinly as possible into a 12- to 15-inch/24- to 38-centimeter disk.

Preheat the oven to 450°F/230°C/gas 8. Lightly oil a pizza or paella pan 12 to 15 inches/30 to 38 centimeters in diameter.

Carefully lay one disk on the prepared pan. Grate the cheese over the surface; if it is too moist to grate, pinch little bits off the cheese and position them all around the dough. Leave a

¾-inch/2-centimeter border of dough uncovered. Carefully place the second dough disk over the cheese, and press down lightly on the edges of the dough to seal. Poke a few series of holes in the top with a fork. Drizzle the remaining 1 tablespoon oil over the top, then season with salt.

Bake until the surface is golden brown, 15 to 20 minutes. Serve hot, cut into squares or wedges.

SCACCIATA
(SICILIAN STUFFED BREAD)

SERVES 4 TO 6

It is entirely possible that the world capital of scacciata, which in Sicily is a kind of bread stuffed with cheese and vegetables and sometimes meat, isn't Catania—the city in eastern Sicily with which it is most often identified—but Middletown, Connecticut. Sicilian immigrants settled in Middletown, better known as the home of Wesleyan University, in the late nineteenth and early twentieth centuries, and some were obviously Catanese, because today most of the city's twenty-five or so Italian restaurants and pizzerias, as well as some of its bakeries and delis, offer scacciata in various forms. It wouldn't be an exaggeration to call it Middletown's civic dish. Of course, it is hardly forgotten in Catania, either, where it is usually filled with the local purple cauliflower called bastardu. *(A version of scacciata found in the province of Caltanissetta, in central Sicily, the home of the famous digestivo Amaro Averna, combines eel with the cauliflower.) To the best of my knowledge, nobody grows bastardu commercially in the United States, but conventional cauliflower makes an adequate substitute.*

6 TABLESPOONS/90 MILLILITERS EXTRA-VIRGIN
OLIVE OIL, PLUS MORE FOR GREASING AND BRUSHING

3¼ CUPS/400 GRAMS SEMOLINA PASTA FLOUR

ONE ¼-OUNCE/7-GRAM PACKET ACTIVE DRY YEAST

SALT

ALL-PURPOSE/PLAIN FLOUR FOR DUSTING

6 GREEN/SPRING ONIONS, FINELY CHOPPED

1 SMALL CAULIFLOWER, SEPARATED INTO SMALL
FLORETS

12 ANCHOVY FILLETS, FINELY CHOPPED

½ POUND/250 GRAMS YOUNG CACIOCAVALLO, CUT
INTO ¼-INCH/6-MILLIMETER CUBES

THE PRIDE OF RECCO

Every town in Italy seems to have its own proprietary dish and/or signal foodstuff. In Recco, a municipality of about ten thousand inhabitants twenty miles/thirty-five kilometers or so southeast of Genoa on Italy's Ligurian coast, that specialty is a highly addictive arrangement of bread dough and cheese called *focaccia col formaggio*—"focaccia with cheese" (see facing page). This is not conventional focaccia, not even the usual Ligurian kind (see page 152). It consists of two thin layers of crispy dough enclosing a sea of molten cheese—an Italian version of the grilled cheese sandwich or the quesadilla, if you will, but better. The dough is salty, rich with olive oil, and simultaneously flaky and a little chewy (in a good way), with enough little oven-darkened bits to make it interesting. The cheese—originally a local variety called formagetta but now crescenza or stracchino—is runny, almost like clotted cream, but pleasantly sour, and becomes slightly grainy as it cools. The overall effect is wonderful.

One Manuelina Capurro, who had a trattoria in Recco in the late nineteenth and early twentieth centuries, claimed to have invented focaccia col formaggio.

In fact, Cato the Elder (234–149 BC) described something that sounds very much like it, called *scribilita*, made by enclosing slices of cheese in sheets of dough; and legend has it that villagers fleeing the Saracens in early medieval times retreated to the mountains where they ate cheese and flatbread cooked on hot stones. Capurro, though, may well have codified the preparation of the thing as we know it today, and it was almost certainly Capurro who popularized it to visitors from Genoa as a specialty of Recco. Her original trattoria did not survive World War II, but in 1960, Capurro's grandniece, Maria Rosa, and her husband, Gianni Carbone, opened a new restaurant in Recco, dubbing it Manuelina in her honor, and featuring, well, you know what. Good focaccia col formaggio is also served nearby at a place called Da Ö Vittorio, and at a restaurant named Vitturin 1860, where the house specialty is brought up from the downstairs kitchen on a kind of oversize vertical lazy Susan that covers one whole wall of the dining room.

Oil a large bowl and set it aside. Put the semolina pasta flour, yeast, half the oil, and 1 teaspoon salt into the bowl of a stand mixer fitted with a dough hook and mix on low until well combined. Increase the speed to medium-low and gradually drizzle in 1¼ cups/300 milliliters cold water until the dough begins to form, 1 to 2 minutes. Increase the speed to medium-high and mix until the dough begins to pull away from the sides of the bowl, about 2 minutes. Turn the dough out onto a lightly floured board and knead until smooth and elastic, 3 to 4 minutes.

Shape the dough into a ball, put it into the oiled bowl, and roll it in the bowl to coat it lightly with oil on all sides. Cover the bowl with a kitchen towel and set it aside in a warm spot until the dough doubles in size, about 2 hours.

Meanwhile, heat the remaining oil in a large frying pan over medium heat. Add the green onions and cauliflower and cook, stirring frequently, until the vegetables are soft, 12 to 15 minutes. Stir in the anchovies and season with salt.

Preheat the oven to 375°F/190°C/gas 5. Lightly grease a 9-by-13-inch/23-by-33-centimeter baking sheet/tray.

Turn the dough out onto a work surface dusted with all-purpose flour. Divide the dough in half and shape each half into a ball. Then very lightly roll out each half into a rectangle with about the same dimensions as the baking sheet, shaping it with your hands after it is roughly the correct shape. Transfer one rectangle to the prepared baking sheet. Flatten the dough with your hands, extending it to the edges of the pan. Let the dough rest for about 10 minutes. It will shrink back from the edges a little, so stretch it out again.

Spoon the cauliflower mixture over the dough, spreading and flattening it with the back of a wooden spoon and leaving about 1 inch/2.5 centimeters uncovered around the edges of the pan. Distribute the caciocavallo evenly over the filling, the lay the other dough rectangle on top, stretching it to the edges. Crimp the edges of the rectangles together, sealing them well. Make three or four diagonal slits in the top crust.

Bake until golden brown, 35 to 45 minutes. To serve, cut into squares or rectangles.

PIZZA RUSTICA
(ROMAN POTATO PIZZA)

SERVES 6 TO 10

The word pizza *(which may or may not derive from the Greek* pitta, *"pie" or "cake") is used in a number of contexts in traditional Italian cooking. It is by no means always the familiar flat round of dough topped with mozzarella and tomato sauce. It is not surprising, then, that the term* pizza rustica *can also have different meanings. Around central Italy, it appears in several variations in which it is a kind of* torta, *filled with some combination of meats and cheeses, often with eggs included. Waverley Root reports having encountered a sweet version in Basilicata that was made with puff pastry enclosing grapes, ricotta, and sweet salami. The* pizza rustica *I came to know in the bakeries of the Lazio and Abruzzo, though, was something much simpler: a rectangular pizza with a slightly puffy crust, topped with thinly sliced potatoes. When my Roman friends and I would take day trips out into the countryside, we always seemed to manage to pass a bakery with a well-used blackened tray of* pizza rustica *in the window just before lunchtime, and often ended up eating our "first course" walking around with a slab of it in our hands.*

½ CUP/120 MILLILITERS EXTRA-VIRGIN OLIVE OIL

3¼ CUPS/400 GRAMS FLOUR, PLUS MORE FOR DUSTING

ONE ¼-OUNCE/7-GRAM PACKET ACTIVE DRY YEAST

SALT

2 TO 3 WAXY POTATOES (ABOUT ¾ POUND/375 GRAMS TOTAL), VERY THINLY SLICED WITH A MANDOLINE, THEN SLICES IMMERSED IN ICE WATER

2 TABLESPOONS ROSEMARY LEAVES

Oil a large bowl with 1 tablespoon of the oil and set it aside. Put the flour, yeast, and 1 teaspoon salt into the bowl of a stand mixer fitted with a dough hook, and mix on low speed until well combined. Increase the speed to medium-low and gradually drizzle in 1½ cups/360 milliliters cold water until the dough begins to form, 1 to 2 minutes. Increase the speed to medium-high and mix until the dough is smooth and elastic and begins to pull away from the sides of the bowl, 10 to 12 minutes.

Shape the dough into a ball, put it into the oiled bowl, and roll it in the bowl to coat it lightly with oil on all sides. Cover the bowl with a kitchen towel and set it in a warm spot until the dough roughly doubles in size, about 2 hours.

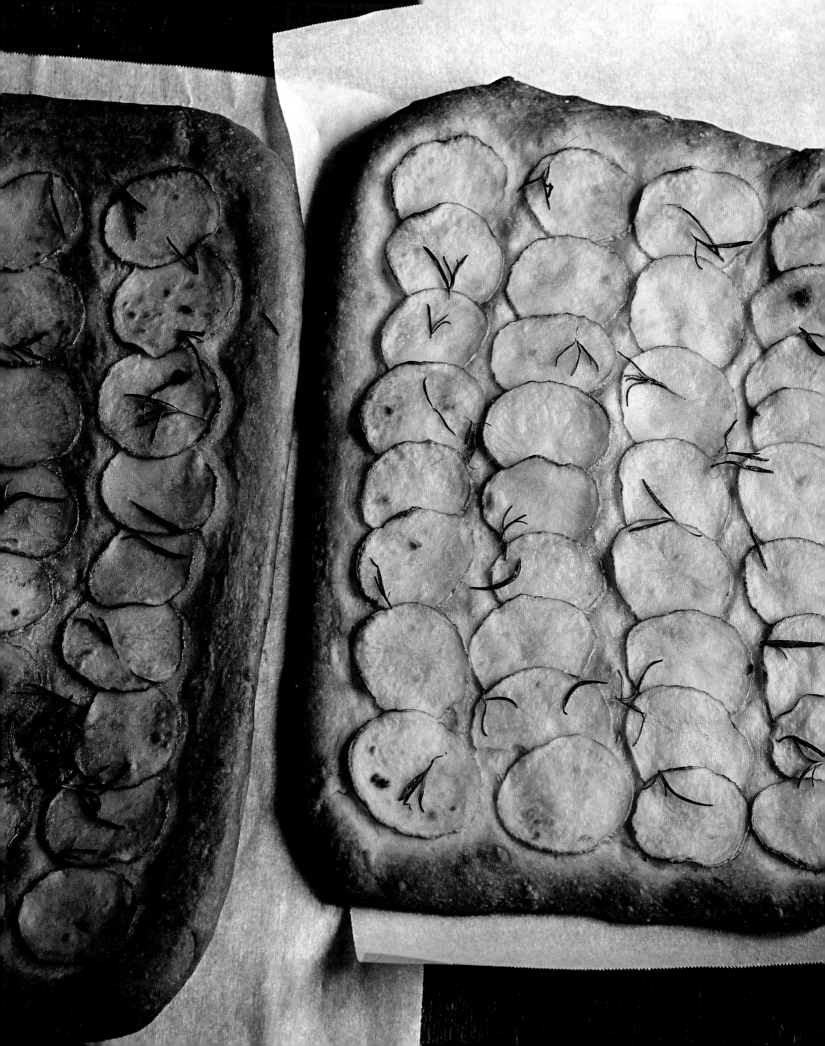

Drain the potato slices and pat them dry with paper towels, pressing out as much moisture as you can. Toss them with 2 tablespoons of the oil and season them generously with salt, then set them aside.

Preheat the oven to 475°F/240°C/gas 9. Oil a large baking sheet/tray, about 13 by 18 inches/33 by 45 centimeters, with 1 tablespoon of the oil.

Turn the dough out onto a floured work surface and shape into a ball. Then very lightly roll out into a rectangle about 12 by 15 inches/30 by 38 centimeters, shaping it with your hands after it is roughly the correct shape. Transfer the dough to the prepared baking sheet. Flatten the dough with your hands, extending it to the edges of the pan. Let the dough rest for about 10 minutes. It will shrink back from the edges a little, so stretch it out again.

Brush the surface of the dough with 2 tablespoons of the oil, then arrange the potato slices in an overlapping pattern on top of the dough, leaving about 1 inch/2.5 centimeters uncovered around the edge of the pan. Sprinkle the rosemary over the potatoes, then drizzle the remaining 2 tablespoons oil over the potatoes. Salt the pizza generously.

Bake until crisp and golden brown, about 25 minutes. To serve, cut into squares or rectangles. Serve hot or at room temperature.

TARANTESE POTATO TART

❋

SERVES 4

Taranto, on the Adriatic coast of Puglia, was once the Greek city-state of Taras, one of the great powers of so-called Magna Graecia (see page 42), along with Sybaris—modern-day Sibari—down the coast in Calabria, so famous for its residents' indulgent lifestyle that it gave us the word sybaritic. In later centuries, the region grew poor, however, and the use of potatoes (which could be grown) to extend flour (which had to be purchased) was typical.

2 TABLESPOONS EXTRA-VIRGIN OLIVE OIL, PLUS MORE FOR GREASING

½ RECIPE POTATOES PUREED WITH OLIVE OIL (PAGE 331), AT ROOM TEMPERATURE

1 CUP/125 GRAMS FLOUR

2 TABLESPOONS BUTTER, SOFTENED

1 EGG, LIGHTLY BEATEN

1 TEASPOON OREGANO LEAVES

12 ANCHOVY FILLETS

½ POUND/250 GRAMS FRESH MOZZARELLA, CUT INTO ½-INCH/1.25-CENTIMETER CUBES

SALT AND PEPPER

Preheat the oven to 425°F/220°C/gas 7. Lightly oil a 7-by-11-inch/18-by-28-centimeter oval baking dish.

Put the potatoes into a large bowl, add the flour, butter, and egg, and mix well with a wooden spoon until a thick dough forms.

Transfer the dough to the prepared dish, patting it down gently with your hands so that the surface is flat. Sprinkle the oregano evenly over the surface. Arrange the anchovies in a spoke pattern radiating out from the center of the dough, then scatter the mozzarella cubes evenly between the spokes. Season with salt and pepper.

Bake until the top is lightly browned, 20 to 25 minutes. Cut into wedges to serve.

POTATO TORTA

SERVES 6 TO 8

I learned how to make this unusual torta—which may be served in thin wedges as an appetizer or cut more generously, with a green salad on the side, as a light but satisfying meal—from Mara Allavena at her Osteria del Portico in the Ligurian mountain village of Castelvittorio.

2 CUPS/250 GRAMS FLOUR, PLUS MORE FOR DUSTING

SALT

3 EGGS, 2 LIGHTLY BEATEN

½ POUND/250 GRAMS BUTTER, SOFTENED

4 RUSSET OR OTHER FLOURY POTATOES

1 TABLESPOON GRATED PARMIGIANO-REGGIANO

¼ CUP/60 GRAMS FRESH RICOTTA

1 CUP/240 MILLILITERS WHOLE MILK

PEPPER

2 TABLESPOONS EXTRA-VIRGIN OLIVE OIL, PLUS MORE FOR GREASING

Sift the flour and 1 teaspoon salt together into a large bowl. Stir the beaten eggs into the flour, then work in the butter, mixing with a fork until a crumbly mixture forms. Gather the mixture together into a ball, place on a floured work surface, and knead until smooth and elastic, about 5 minutes.

Return the dough to the bowl, cover the bowl with a kitchen towel, and refrigerate for 2 hours.

Meanwhile, bring a large pot of salted water to a boil over high heat. Reduce the heat to medium-high, add the potatoes, and cook until tender when pierced with a fork, 25 to 35 minutes, depending on their size. Drain the potatoes and set them aside to cool. When they are cool enough to handle, peel them and put them into a large bowl. Mash them with a potato masher, then mix in the remaining egg, the parmigiano, the ricotta, and the milk and season with salt and pepper. Continue mixing until a smooth paste forms, then set aside.

Preheat the oven to 375°F/190°C/gas 5. Lightly oil a pizza or paella pan 12 to 15 inches/30 to 38 centimeters in diameter, then dust it very lightly with flour.

Roll out the dough on a floured work surface into a disk 18 to 20 inches/45 to 50 centimeters in diameter. Transfer the dough to the prepared pan, positioning it so that it extends evenly over the rim on all sides. Spread the potato mixture evenly over the dough covering the bottom of the pan, leaving 1-inch/2.5-centimeter border uncovered around the edges of the pan. Gently pat the filling down flat with a spatula. Carefully pull the overhanging dough toward the middle of the torta from all sides until it almost covers all the filling. Leave a small hole at the center. Brush the top with the oil.

Bake until lightly browned on top, 30 to 40 minutes. Cut into wedges to serve.

TAKING IT EASY

In a roundabout way, McDonald's has done a lot for traditional food, in Italy and elsewhere. In the 1980s, Carlo Petrini, a native of Bra in Piedmont, was a communist and a gastronome—the two are not mutually exclusive in Italy—who wrote about food for the communist dailies *L'Unità* and *Il Manifesto*, eventually co-editing a pullout wine section for the latter called *Gambero Rosso, or Red Shrimp*. (I don't know if Petrini has ever read the late English critic Kenneth Tynan, who was himself a socialist with a taste for fine French food, but he would have understand what Tynan meant when he wrote, "Socialism that denies the pleasures of the gullet is socialism disfigured by the English puritan tradition.") In 1986, when McDonald's opened its first outpost in Rome, near the historic Spanish Steps, Petrini, in common with many of his fellow Italians, was outraged. (This was not, incidentally, the first McDonald's in Italy, most reports to the contrary; that dubious honor goes to Bolzano, in Trentino–Alto Adige, where a unit of the chain appeared on the Waltherplatz in 1985.) Petrini responded by launching a protest organization called ARCIGOLA, a name linking that of a left-leaning cultural and social club called the Associazione Ricreativa e Culturale Italiana, or ARCI, with the Italian word for (*pace* Kenneth Tynan) gullet, *gola*. He used the pages of *Gambero Rosso* to express the organization's views, which initially were basically that we should refuse to eat fast food, and instead should relax and enjoy what we eat and drink. In other words, he said, we should celebrate slow food—and Slow Food became the name of an organization with increasingly ambitious goals.

Today, Slow Food is said to have more than 100,000 members in 130-plus countries around the world, organized into not cells but *convivia*. The goals of the group include education, lobbying, preserving heirloom plant and animal varieties, recognizing regional food products and traditions (and saving them in an Ark of Taste), and organizing events in which a good deal of food and drink, at least theoretically locally and organically produced, is consumed with pleasure. Since 1996, Slow Food has run a gigantic biennial food and wine fair called Salone del Gusto (Salon of Taste) in Turin. An adjunct to Slow Food, Terra Madre (Mother Earth) was founded in 2004. This is a network of food communities in every corner of the globe, from wine producers in Chã das Caldeiras in Cape Verde to the Huehuetenango hibiscus tea producers of Guatemala to the Herdwick sheep breeders of England. Terra Madre also convenes every two years in Turin, with satellite events in other countries (I attended the first one in Ireland, in Waterford, in 2009). Slow Food has inspired numerous other likeminded movements that have nothing to do with gastronomy, among them Slow Shopping, Slow Travel, Slow Parenting, Slow Art, and Slow Money—the last of which I feel I know only too well.

TORTA PASQUALINA

SERVES 8

This savory Eastertide specialty, typical of Liguria, was tradition-
ally made with thirty-three layers of dough, ten on the bottom and
twenty-three on the top, one for each year of Christ's life on Earth.
With that association in mind, it is interesting to note that Friedrich
Nietzsche, who famously and on more than one occasion declared
that "God is dead," convinced his landlady, when he lived in Genoa
in the 1880s, to teach him how to make this specialty.

6 CUPS/750 GRAMS FLOUR, PLUS MORE FOR DUSTING

¾ CUP/180 MILLILITERS EXTRA-VIRGIN OLIVE OIL

SALT

4 POUNDS/2 KILOGRAMS SWISS CHARD, THICK
STEMS REMOVED

1 CUP/100 GRAMS GRATED PARMIGIANO-REGGIANO

1 CUP/250 GRAMS FRESH RICOTTA

2 TABLESPOONS FINELY CHOPPED MARJORAM

2 TABLESPOONS HEAVY/DOUBLE CREAM

5 EGGS

2½ TABLESPOONS BUTTER

Put the flour into a large bowl, and make a well in the center.
Pour 6 tablespoons/90 milliliters of the oil, 2 teaspoons salt,
and 2 cups/480 milliliters cold water into the well, then stir
the wet ingredients into the flour with a wooden spoon until
a smooth dough forms.

Turn the dough out onto a floured work surface. Coat your
hands with flour, then knead the dough until smooth, about
20 minutes. (The dough will remain sticky.) Divide the dough
into six balls of equal size, wrap them individually in plastic
wrap/cling film, and refrigerate for 2 to 3 hours.

Meanwhile, bring a large pot of salted water to a boil over high
heat, add the chard, and cook until thoroughly wilted, 4 to
5 minutes. Drain the chard and refresh it under cold running
water. Drain again and squeeze out as much moisture as possible. Chop the chard finely.

Heat about 3 tablespoons of the remaining oil in a large frying
pan over medium heat. Add the chard and cook, stirring occasionally, until tender, about 3 minutes. Transfer the chard to
a large bowl and let cool for about 10 minutes. Stir in the parmigiano, ricotta, marjoram, and cream. Season with salt and
set aside.

Preheat the oven to 400°F/200°C/gas 6. Lightly oil a round
glass or ceramic baking dish at least 13 inches/33 centimeters
in diameter and 3 inches/7.5 centimeters deep.

Roll out one chilled dough ball on a floured work surface into
a thin disk 13 to 14 inches/32 to 35 centimeters in diameter.
Gently lay the disk in the prepared dish, then lightly brush the
surface with some of the remaining 3 tablespoons oil. Repeat
the process with two more dough balls.

Spread the Swiss chard mixture evenly over the layered dough,
then make five evenly spaced indentations in the chard with the
back of a large spoon. Break 1 egg into each of the indentations.
Top each egg with ½ tablespoon butter. Season generously
with salt.

Roll out the remaining dough balls the same way, laying the
first one on top of the filling and the next two on top of that
one, brushing each layer with oil. Crimp the rims of the dough
sheets together to seal.

Bake until golden, about 45 minutes. Serve warm or at room
temperature, cut into wedges or squares.

SARDINIAN FLATBREAD "LASAGNA"

✳

SERVES 6 TO 8

Pane carasau, also called carta *(or* fogli*)* di musica, *meaning "music paper," is found on nearly every Sardinian table. Said to have been first made many centuries ago in the harsh, mountainous Barbagia region in east-central Sardinia—it keeps well, so shepherds would pack it when they went off with their flocks for long periods—it is unleavened and crisp and parchment thin, hence its name. It can be eaten as a kind of cracker, with shards broken off from the large irregular rounds in which it is baked, but it is often moistened before eating. I remember vividly a meal in a farmhouse near Borutta, in the northern part of the island, where a huge platter was lined with pane carasau and a roast baby lamb was set down on top of it—its juices soaking into the bread in the most delicious way. A common way of eating pane carasau, however, is like this, in the form of* pani frattàu—*almost a kind of lasagna. See page 382 for a source for the bread.*

4 CUPS/1 LITER LAMB BROTH (PAGE 373), HEATED

SALT

6 SHEETS PANE CARASAU

2 CUPS/200 GRAMS GRATED YOUNG PECORINO SARDO

6 CUPS/1.5 LITERS TOMATO SAUCE, HOMEMADE (PAGE 371) OR COMMERCIAL, HEATED

6 TO 8 EGGS

Season the broth with salt.

Line the bottom of a wide, deep bowl with one sheet of the bread, breaking it into large pieces to fit and covering the entire bottom. Drizzle about ¼ cup/60 milliliters of the broth over the bread, then sprinkle with a few spoonfuls of the cheese. Spread about 1 cup/240 milliliters of the tomato sauce over the cheese and bread.

Put another sheet of the bread on top of the tomato sauce, again breaking it into pieces to fit and covering the entire surface of the tomato sauce. Press it down lightly but firmly into the tomato sauce. Repeat the process with the broth, cheese, and tomato sauce, then add another sheet of bread, again breaking it to fit and pressing it down lightly. Repeat the process until you have used up all the bread, ending with a layer of tomato sauce. Sprinkle the remaining cheese over the final layer of sauce. Set the bowl aside to let the bread soak in the broth and sauce until it is completely soft, about 5 minutes.

Bring the remaining broth to a gentle simmer in a medium frying pan over medium heat. Working in batches, break 2 or 3 eggs into the broth, cover the frying pan, and poach the eggs until the whites are just firm, about 3 minutes. Remove the eggs with a slotted spatula and blot on paper towels to absorb the excess moisture. Season the eggs with salt and keep warm. Repeat with the remaining eggs.

To serve, scoop portions of the lasagna out of the bowl with a large serving spoon onto individual plates. Top each serving with a poached egg.

FISH

GIFT OF THE WATERS

The Holy Church has designated fish as a Lenten food, knowing its
ability to repress the pangs of human weakness.
—*Antonio Latini, Scalco alla moderna (circa 1692)*

The best fish, called *pesce nobile*, are *sturione* [sturgeon], *triglia* [red mullet],
sfoglia [sole?], *spigola dentale* [sea bass? dentex?], *pesce-spada* [swordfish],
calamaretti [baby squid], *cernia* [grouper], etc. . . .
—*Mariana Starke, Travels in Italy, between the Years 1792 and 1798*

Italy has about 4,600 miles/7,600 kilometers of coastline, and no point in the country is more than 150 miles/250 kilometers from saltwater. Not surprisingly, then, seafood has been popular in Italy, especially near the coast, for as long as humans have known how to reap the bounty of the Mediterranean. The range of what's available is immense, from tiny threads of fish flesh like Liguria's *bianchetti* (anchovy spawn) and Venice's *gô* (goby) to the glorious (and endangered) bluefin tuna caught off Sicily and Sardinia, which commonly weigh almost 300 pounds/150 kilograms and have been recorded at more than six times that.

It is hardly surprising, then, that Italy has developed a complex and varied seafood cuisine. Simply roasted or grilled fish is common everywhere (on the glass-blowing island of Murano in the Venetian lagoon, eel was sometimes cooked in the glass-cooling ovens), and some areas, especially Liguria and Venice, are known for the skill with which local cooks fry fish in bread crumbs or batter. Arrigo Cipriani, the patriarch of the Venice-based Harry's Bar empire, told me about a traditional method of frying fish once used by the women of the Venetian lagoon island of Burano, where his family comes from: They would heat a deep pan, like a wok, on a wood fire, with oil on one side and a small fish on the other, and then spoon the oil over the fish until it was cooked. This was a way of conserving oil. Another Buranese I know, Bepi D'Este, adds that after this was done, the blackened bits of flour (called *murcia*) would be strained out of the oil (*ia*), and some oil would be poured on top of the fish. "That gave it some moisture so we could eat more polenta with it," he says. Waverley Root describes a very different way of cooking fish, the freshwater variety, around Lake Piediluco, near Terni in Umbria: The whole fish was placed directly in the flames and allowed to char—carbonize—completely. When its black crust was slipped off, Roots says, the flesh was perfectly done.

There are also countless recipes for fish-based pasta and risotto, and no coastal region of Italy is without its own fish soup or stew. Other complex fish preparations exist, too. For instance, Inspector Montalbano, Andrea Camilleri's fictional Sicilian detective and gourmand, encounters a stuffed bass in saffron sauce at one trattoria that leaves him "breathless, almost frightened." Later he devours remarkable polpettone (meatballs) made of unspecified fish with onion, hot chile, whisked eggs, salt, pepper, and bread crumbs, as well as "two other flavors, hiding under the taste of the butter used in the frying . . . [which] he recognized [as] cumin and coriander."

The emblematic fish of Sicily are the swordfish and the bluefin tuna. Scottish novelist Tobias Smollett noted in the 1760s that "the emperor [another name for swordfish] associates with the tunny fish, and is always taken in their company." He called the meat of swordfish "white as the finest veal, and extremely delicate." Bluefin tuna was prized even more. Theresa Maggio, who wrote an evocative book about *mattanza*, the ancient Sicilian tuna-fishing ritual now all but vanished, proposes that for the ancient peoples of the Mediterranean, tuna was what the buffalo were to the Plains Indians, "a yearly miracle." (Bluefin is clearly depicted in a four-thousand-year-old cave painting on the island of Levanzo, off Trapani.) The Sicilians, among others, preserved tuna by sun-drying it into *mosciamme*, or curing it with spices—like the ficassa di tonno, or "tuna salami," still eaten in Trapani. Vincenzo Florio, a Calabrian-born Sicilian millionaire (his enterprises included a shipping line and a Marsala wine company) is credited with having first canned tuna with olive oil instead of simply salting it, some time in the mid-nineteenth century. American canneries took up the idea as early as 1903, and the next thing you knew we were all eating Chicken of the Sea with mayonnaise for lunch. I doubt, in fact, that anybody aside from the odd fisherman consumed fresh tuna in America or Great Britain until the 1970s at the earliest. (The first time I had tuna that didn't come in a can was in the late 1960s, at a cheap students' trattoria on an obscure *campo* in Venice, in the form of a griddled tuna steak. It was very thoroughly cooked—none of this "charred-rare" stuff—but, while a bit chewy, pretty good.) Canning isn't the only means of preserving fish, and—while this may seem surprising, considering the plentitude of fresh fish available to them—the Italians in many regions are also fond of cod that has been dried or salted, the majority of which is imported from Scandinavia. The taste for these items developed for reasons both religious and logistical, and persisted simply because people grew to like them.

In the fifteenth century, Bartolomeo Sacchi, better known as Platina, author of the first printed cookbook in history, expressed a surprising disdain for saltwater fish, writing that "it is not in fact good food, and it creates a great thirst." Later Italian gastronomes definitely don't share his opinion.

Unfortunately, though much of Italian freshwater fish cookery is superb, it is almost unknown outside Italy. The traditional recipes of the northern Veneto for risottos based on pike, trout, perch, bleak, and sturgeon alone could reanimate many a tired Italian restaurant menu.

A septuagenarian fisherman in Palermo harbor, 1943.

FRIED TROUT WITH SAGE BUTTER

SERVES 4

This is a favorite way of cooking trout in alpine Piemonte, in some of whose streams trout still thrive.

6 TABLESPOONS/90 GRAMS BUTTER

JUICE OF ½ LEMON

15 TO 20 SAGE LEAVES, 3 JULIENNED, THE REST COARSELY CHOPPED

4 WHOLE TROUT, 10 TO 12 OUNCES/315 TO 375 GRAMS EACH, CLEANED, HEADS AND TAILS ON

½ CUP/65 GRAMS FLOUR

SALT

Melt the butter in a small pan over low heat, then stir in the lemon juice and the chopped sage. Let simmer until the butter starts to brown, 6 to 8 minutes. Remove from the heat and strain the butter through a sieve into a large frying pan, pressing down on the sage leaves with the back of a wooden spoon.

Heat the butter in the frying pan over medium-high heat. Dust the trout with the flour, then fry them (in two batches if necessary), turning once, until golden brown and just cooked through, about 6 minutes per side.

Transfer the trout to 4 warmed plates, then add the julienned sage leaves and salt to the butter in the pan. Cook for about 30 seconds, then drizzle the butter and sage over the trout and serve.

COLD MARINATED CATFISH, GRAMIGNAZZO STYLE

SERVES 4

We tend to think of the catfish as a creature of the American South, and maybe of China and Southeast Asia, but the wels catfish (Silurus glanis)—there are countless varieties around the world—has been an important food source in various parts of Europe, including Italy, for centuries. Today it is widely fished in, among other places, the tributaries of the Po, and is found on restaurant menus from Cremona down through towns like Stagno Lombardo and Isola Pescaroli in Lombardy and into Zibello (whose main gastronomic fame is as the source of culatello di Zibello, arguably Italy's finest prosciutto) and Gramignazzo in Emilia-Romagna. This is a common preparation in the area.

6 TABLESPOONS/90 MILLILITERS EXTRA-VIRGIN OLIVE OIL

4 CATFISH FILLETS, ½ POUND/250 GRAMS EACH, SKIN ON

2 ONIONS, VERY THINLY SLICED

½ CUP/50 GRAMS GOLDEN RAISINS/SULTANAS

6 WHOLE CLOVES

1 TEASPOON SUGAR

SALT

1 CUP/240 MILLILITERS DRY WHITE WINE

½ CUP/120 MILLILITERS WHITE WINE VINEGAR

Heat 2 tablespoons of the oil in a large frying pan over medium heat. Add the catfish, skin side down, and fry until cooked through, 6 to 8 minutes. Drain the fish on paper towels.

Let the frying pan cool for a few minutes, then wipe it out with paper towels. Add the remaining 4 tablespoons oil to the same pan over medium heat. Add the onions and cook, stirring frequently, until they soften, 6 to 8 minutes. Add the raisins, cloves, sugar, and 2 teaspoons salt, stir well, and then add the wine and vinegar. Reduce the heat to low, cover, and simmer for 20 minutes.

Put the catfish into a glass or ceramic dish just large enough to hold them in a single layer, then pour the marinade over them. Let cool to room temperature, cover, and refrigerate for 2 to 3 days.

Bring to room temperature before serving.

EEL, BOLSENA STYLE

SERVES 4

Lake Bolsena, in the province of Viterbo in northern Lazio, was formed hundreds of thousands of years ago in the crater of an immense volcano, known to the Romans as Mount Vulsini. It is unusually clean for a body of freshwater near major urban centers, and its piscatorial life thrives with such fish as perch, lake pike, whitefish, tench, and smelts. The most famous swimming creature in the lake, though, is its eel, prized since Roman times, and even mentioned by Dante in his Inferno *as one of the foods consumed by the gluttonous Pope Martin IV. Larger eels are usually marinated, then brushed with olive oil and grilled; smaller eels are typically cut into little pieces, floured, and deep-fried—or cooked like this. Asian markets are a good source for eel.*

¼ CUP/60 MILLILITERS EXTRA-VIRGIN OLIVE OIL

2 GARLIC CLOVES, CRUSHED

2 POUNDS/1 KILOGRAM SMALL EELS, SKINNED, HEADS DISCARDED, CLEANED, AND CUT INTO 2-INCH/5-CENTIMETER PIECES

1 TEASPOON ROSEMARY LEAVES

2 BAY LEAVES

1 TEASPOON PEPERONCINI

3 OR 4 RIPE TOMATOES, SEEDED AND GRATED (SEE RAW TOMATO COULIS, PAGE 371)

1 CUP/240 MILLILITERS WHITE WINE VINEGAR

SALT AND PEPPER

Heat the oil in a pot over medium heat. Add the garlic and cook, stirring occasionally, until lightly browned, 5 to 6 minutes. Press down firmly on the cloves with a fork, then remove and discard them.

Add the eels, rosemary, bay leaves, peperoncini, tomatoes, and vinegar and season with salt and pepper. Stir well, reduce the heat to low, and simmer, uncovered, until the eels are cooked through and sauce is very thick, 25 to 30 minutes.

EEL, FRIULI STYLE

SERVES 6

This is a version of brodetto, the fish stew ubiquitous along Italy's Adriatic coastline. The recipe is adapted from one by Lidia Bastianich.

1 WHOLE EEL, 3 TO 4 POUNDS/1.5 TO 2 KILOGRAMS, SKINNED, HEAD DISCARDED, AND CLEANED

1½ CUPS/185 GRAMS FLOUR

¾ CUP/180 MILLILITERS RED WINE VINEGAR

¾ CUP/180 MILLILITERS EXTRA-VIRGIN OLIVE OIL

SALT AND WHITE PEPPER

1 ONION, CHOPPED

¼ CUP/60 MILLILITERS TOMATO PASTE, HOMEMADE (PAGE 371) OR COMMERCIAL

1 LARGE BUNCH GREEN/SPRING ONIONS, CHOPPED

BASIC POLENTA (PAGE 131), SOFT AND WARM

Cut the eel crosswise into pieces 1½ to 2 inches/3.75 to 5 centimeters thick. Dredge the pieces in the flour, shaking off the excess.

In a medium pot, combine the vinegar and 4 cups/1 liter water and bring to a simmer over medium heat.

Meanwhile, heat the oil in a Dutch oven or large, deep frying pan over medium-high heat. Working in batches if necessary, add the eel pieces and cook, turning once, until they are cooked through, about 5 minutes per side. As they are ready, drain them on paper towels. Season generously with salt and pepper.

Reduce the heat to medium and add the onion to the pot. Cook, stirring frequently, for about 5 minutes. Add about ½ cup/120 milliliters of the vinegar-water, stirring well and scraping up the browned bits on the bottom, then stir in the tomato paste. Add 1 cup/240 milliliters of the vinegar-water, stir well, bring to a boil over high heat, and then reduce the heat to medium.

Carefully place the eel pieces in the pot in a single layer. Add about half the remaining vinegar-water and cook for about 5 minutes. Add the rest of the vinegar-water and the green onions and cook until the onions soften, about 10 minutes more. Adjust the seasoning.

Serve the stew with the polenta on the side.

THE TROUBLE WITH
ZUPPA DI PESCE

In Siren Land, *one of several travel books he wrote about Italy, Norman Douglas (best known as the author of* South Wind, *a rather scandalous account of the goings-on on an island clearly modeled on Capri) devotes a number of paragraphs to excoriating fish soup as it is prepared around Naples. This is an abridged version of his remarks.*

Take breath, gentle maiden; the while I explain to the patient reader the ingredients of the diabolical preparation known as *zuppa di pesce*. The *guarracino*, for instance, is a pitch-black marine monstrosity, 1 to 2 inches/2.5 to 5 centimeters long, a mere blot, with an Old Red Sandstone profile and insufferable manners . . . whose sole recommendation is that its name is derived from *korakinos* (*korax* = a raven; but who can live on Greek roots?). As to the *scorfano*, its name is unquestionably onomato-poetic, to suggest the spitting-out of bones; the only difference, from a culinary point of view, between the *scorfano* and a toad being that the latter has twice as much meat on it. The *aguglia*, again, is all tail and proboscis; the very nightmare of a fish—as thin as a lead pencil. Who would believe that for this miserable sea-worm with verdigris-tinted spine, which an ordinary person would thank you for not setting on his table, the inhabitants of Siren land fought like fiends. . . . And everybody knows the *totero* or squid, an animated ink-bag of perverse leanings, which swims backward because all other creatures go forward and whose india-rubber flesh might be useful for deluding hunger on desert islands, since, like American gum, you can chew it for months, but never get it down. . . . The fact is, there is hardly a fish in the Mediterranean worth eating. . . .

SEVEN DISHES, SEVEN FISHES

Since around the seventh century, many Italians, especially in central and southern Italy, have celebrated Christmas Eve with a cena della Vigilia, or "dinner of The Vigil," celebrating the impending arrival of the Christ Child on Christmas morning. The meal was always as lavish as circumstances would permit, but because good Catholics would abstain from meat during Advent, the weeks leading up to Christmas, it was a feast based on seafood. It became known, in fact, as the Festa dei Sette Pesci (Feast of the Seven Fish). Why seven? In honor of (depending on whom you ask) the seven days of the week, the seven cardinal virtues, or the seven sacraments. (Some versions of the feast expand the menu to twelve or thirteen dishes, for the twelve apostles or the twelve plus Jesus.) The composition of the menu varies greatly, but eel (the big kind, called *capitone*) and salt cod are traditional for the occasion, in both cases usually either stewed (in umido) or fried. Today, observance of The Vigil with a feast of seven fish is comparatively rare in Italy, but remains popular in traditional Italian American households.

SBROSCIA
(FRESHWATER FISH STEW)

❋

SERVES 4

This old-style fisherman's stew from Lake Bolsena, in the northern part of Lazio, takes its name from a local dialect word for "soft snow," presumably a reference to the dissolving flesh of the freshwater fish it contains. It is properly made with mentuccia, a pungent, minty relative of oregano much prized in Lazio and known in English as lesser calamint (see page 136). A half-and-half combination of mint and oregano can be substituted.

2 POUNDS/1 KILOGRAM SMALL TO MEDIUM FRESHWATER FISH SUCH AS PERCH, TROUT, OR SMELTS, CLEANED AND CUT INTO LARGE PIECES OR LEFT WHOLE IF SMALL

1 TEASPOON MENTUCCIA LEAVES, OR 1 TEASPOON EACH OREGANO AND JULIENNED MINT LEAVES

1 ONION, FINELY CHOPPED

2 GARLIC CLOVES, MINCED

2 RIPE TOMATOES, SEEDED AND GRATED (SEE RAW TOMATO COULIS, PAGE 371)

½ TEASPOON PEPERONCINI

2 TABLESPOONS EXTRA-VIRGIN OLIVE OIL

SALT

4 THICK SLICES DAY-OLD OR LIGHTLY TOASTED COUNTRY-STYLE BREAD

Combine the fish, mentuccia, onion, garlic, tomatoes, peperoncini, and oil in a medium pot. Add 4 cups/1 liter water and season generously with salt. Bring to a boil over high heat, then reduce the heat to low, cover partially, and cook, stirring occasionally, until fish is beginning to fall apart, about 30 minutes.

Put a slice of bread in each of 4 warmed bowls just large enough to hold it. Ladle the soup over the bread and serve.

CACCIUCCO
(LIVORNESE FISH STEW)

❋

SERVES 6 TO 8

This is a specialty of the Tuscan port town of Livorno—called Leghorn in English, for reasons I've never quite understood. (Leghorn chickens, today one of the most widely raised varieties worldwide, were developed near here and named for the city.) Cacciucco seems to me to be the most ebullient, and certainly the most abundant, of the many fish stews cooked in various parts of Italy. This one-pot celebration of the fisherman's bounty is traditionally made with precisely five varieties of fish—one, it is said, for each c in its name.

½ CUP/120 MILLILITERS EXTRA-VIRGIN OLIVE OIL

1 ONION, CHOPPED

1 CARROT, CHOPPED

1 STALK CELERY, CHOPPED

4 GARLIC CLOVES, 2 MINCED, 2 WHOLE

4 SPRIGS ITALIAN PARSLEY, MINCED

½ FRESH CAYENNE OR SERRANO CHILE, MINCED

4 SAGE LEAVES, JULIENNED

½ TEASPOON FENNEL SEEDS

1 POUND/500 GRAMS CUTTLEFISH OR SQUID, CLEANED AND CUT INTO LARGE PIECES

1 CUP/240 MILLILITERS RED WINE

2 RIPE TOMATOES, SEEDED AND GRATED (SEE RAW TOMATO COULIS, PAGE 371)

SALT AND PEPPER

8 CUPS/2 LITERS SEAFOOD BROTH, HOMEMADE (PAGE 372) OR COMMERCIAL

2 POUNDS/1 KILOGRAM ASSORTED OCEAN FISH FILLETS SUCH AS JOHN DORY, HALIBUT, COD, MAHI MAHI, AND RED MULLET, CUT INTO LARGE PIECES

8 SHRIMP/PRAWNS IN THE SHELL, PREFERABLY FRESH

8 THICK SLICES COUNTRY-STYLE BREAD, GRILLED OR TOASTED

Heat the oil in a Dutch oven or other large, heavy pot over medium heat. Add the onion, carrot, celery, minced garlic, parsley, chile, sage, and fennel seeds and cook, stirring frequently, until the vegetables soften, 6 to 8 minutes.

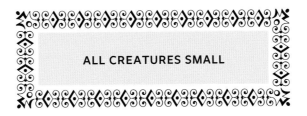

ALL CREATURES SMALL

Venice is hardly the country: It's a marvelous, utterly unique city with canals instead of streets, once the capital of a comparatively small but very wealthy mercantile and military empire. But the Venetian lagoon, into which the city extends, is shaped a bit like a pudgy cartoon version of the Italian boot itself and is surprisingly rural in places. It is a vast wetland, the largest in the Mediterranean basin, covering about 136,000 acres/336,000 hectares of mud flats, salt marshes, and open water. Several of the islands in the lagoon are agricultural, yielding vegetables of extraordinary quality (the Prosecco producer Bisol has recently planted a thousand grapevines on the island of Mazzorbo, and plans to make wine there), and the lagoon's marshy fringes harbor wild ducks and other game birds that are an unexpectedly important part of traditional Venetian cooking.

The real bounty of the lagoon, and the Adriatic Sea beyond, of course, is a meager but immensely varied array of top-quality seafood, some of it found only here and much of it diminutive in size. It is hard to imagine a good, typically Venetian meal without these tiny treasures. They include not just scampi but also beverasse and malgarotte (thumbnail-size clams), soft-shell crabs (moleche) no larger than a silver dollar, bovoletti (tiny sea snails), moscardini (octopuses with bodies no bigger than golf balls), folpetti (even smaller octopuses), calamaretti (small squid), seppietti (baby cuttlefish), canestrelli (bay scallops), peoci (little thick-bearded mussels), and passerini, literally "little sparrows," a kind of undersize lagoon sole.

I was in Venice itself in early June 2010 and was awakened one morning by a chorus of dissonant horns echoing up from the canals; I wondered for a moment if I had somehow been transported to the Holland Tunnel at rush hour on a Friday afternoon. Looking out my window, I saw at least a hundred fishing boats zigzagging among the vaporetti and the water taxis and the gondolas, their pilots clearly angry. It turns out that they were protesting the belated implementation by the Italian government of new European Union fishing rules. These would, among other things, mandate the use of nets with mesh large enough to let many of those small sea creatures slip through. "Look," my Venetian friend Luca di Vita, co-owner of the city's splendid little Alle Testiere restaurant, later told me, "the Adriatic isn't deep, maybe 35 meters at the most, and shallower water means smaller fish and shellfish. This isn't about conservation. The things we fish aren't babies; they're full grown. They don't get any bigger. The new law is perfect for the southern Mediterranean, but not for here. These little creatures are our treasure, the base of our cuisine."

As I write this, no one seems to know for sure what's going to happen to these culinary essentials. There is apparently a possibility that the Italian government will be able to negotiate some exceptions for traditional fishing practices; there is also a possibility that Venetians won't pay any more attention to the new rules than Parisians do to the smoking ban in cafés.

Reduce the heat to low, add the cuttlefish, and cook for about 10 minutes. Add the wine and tomatoes, season with salt and pepper, and cook for 15 minutes more. Add the broth, cook for 10 minutes, then add the fish and the shrimp and cook until the fish is just cooked through, about 10 minutes more.

Have ready 8 warmed wide, deep bowls. Rub the bread slices on one side with the whole garlic cloves, and put a slice in each bowl. Ladle some liquid from the pot over the bread. Distribute the fish and shrimp evenly on top of the bread and then moisten with more liquid before serving.

BRODETTO
(ADRIATIC SEAFOOD STEW)

SERVES 8

This dense stew is served along the coast of the Marche and Abruzzo. Porto Recanati, San Benedetto del Tronto, Ancona, and Fano in the former region and Pescara and Vasto in the latter are particularly famous for their versions. "The only element about brodetto that is always the same," Waverley Root once observed, "is that it is never the same." This recipe, then, is an amalgam of several styles.

¾ CUP/180 MILLILITERS EXTRA-VIRGIN OLIVE OIL

I ONION, CHOPPED

3 GARLIC CLOVES, 2 MINCED, I WHOLE

6 TO 8 SPRIGS ITALIAN PARSLEY, MINCED

½ CUP/120 MILLILITERS WHITE WINE VINEGAR

2 RIPE TOMATOES, SEEDED AND GRATED (SEE RAW TOMATO COULIS, PAGE 371)

¼ TEASPOON PEPERONCINI

SALT AND PEPPER

2 POUNDS/I KILOGRAM MONKFISH OR I POUND/ 500 GRAMS EACH MONKFISH AND SEA BASS, CUT INTO LARGE PIECES

8 FRESH SARDINES, HEAD AND TAIL ON, CLEANED AND HALVED CROSSWISE

16 SMALL TO MEDIUM MUSSELS (NOT LARGE GREEN-LIP MUSSELS), THOROUGHLY SCRUBBED AND DEBEARDED

I CUP/240 MILLILITERS DRY WHITE WINE

8 THICK SLICES COUNTRY-STYLE BREAD

Heat ½ cup/120 milliliters of the oil in a Dutch oven or other other large, heavy pot over medium heat. Add the onion, minced garlic, and parsley and cook, stirring frequently, until the onion begins to soften, about 5 minutes. Add the vinegar and cook for 3 minutes more. Add the tomatoes and peperoncini, season with salt and pepper, and cook for about 5 minutes more.

Add the monkfish (and the sea bass, if using), cover, and cook for about 5 minutes. Add the sardines, mussels, and wine, then re-cover the pot and cook until the mussels open, about 5 minutes more. Discard any mussels that failed to open.

While the stew is cooking, preheat the broiler/grill. Brush the bread slices on both sides with the remaining ¼ cup/60 milliliters oil, and season with salt on one side. Arrange on a baking sheet/tray and slip in the broiler. Broil/grill, turning once, until toasted on both sides. Remove from the broiler, and rub both sides of each slice with the whole garlic clove.

Put a bread slice in each of 8 warmed bowls. Ladle the stew over the bread, dividing the fish and shellfish evenly to serve.

GRILLED SARDINES
WITH FENNEL

SERVES 4

When I started cooking Italian food in California many years ago, fresh sardines were unheard of, unless you lived in a fishing community. Today they are common at fish shops and even in supermarkets. This simple method of cooking them is found in many regions of Italy's west coast.

4 TABLESPOONS/60 MILLILITERS EXTRA-VIRGIN OLIVE OIL

I LARGE BULB FENNEL, SLICED PAPER-THIN WITH A MANDOLINE

I ONION, VERY THINLY SLICED

I TEASPOON GRATED LEMON ZEST

16 FRESH SARDINES, CLEANED, HEAD AND TAIL ON

SALT AND PEPPER

JUICE OF ½ LEMON

Light a grill/barbecue and let the coals or wood get very hot (if using a gas grill, preheat to about 600°F/315°C).

Meanwhile, heat 2 tablespoons of the oil in a small frying pan over low heat. Add the fennel, onion, and lemon zest and cook, stirring frequently, until the vegetables are soft but have not begun to brown, 8 to 10 minutes.

Brush the sardines on both sides with about 1 tablespoon of the oil and season them generously with salt and pepper. Grill the sardines, turning once, until cooked through, 2 to 3 minutes per side.

Divide the sardines between 4 plates, drizzle them with the remaining oil and then the lemon juice. Scatter the cooked fennel and onions over the top and serve.

SCAPECE DI VASTO

✳

SERVES 4 TO 6

The word scapece, *according to the Web site of the Academia Barilla, the educational culinary organization run by the big Barilla food company, "comes from the Latin 'Esca Apicie': sauce from Apicio." No it doesn't. It comes from the Spanish* escabeche *or Catalan* escabetx, *words derived ultimately from the Perso-Arabic word* sikbaj, *meaning "vinegar stew." The term, in whatever language, describes food that is cooked (usually fried) and then preserved in a vinegar-based marinade. This technique efficiently keeps food safe from spoilage, and fish and vegetables and sometimes poultry have long been prepared in this manner all over Italy. This version comes from the ancient town of Vasto, in Chieti Province, on the Adriatic coast of Abruzzo. One curiosity of the recipe is its use of saffron: even though Abruzzo produces Italy's best example of that spice. It is so valuable that almost all of it is sold, and it is rarely used in the local cooking (there is a saying that at Christmas Mass, you'll know who had a good year by the smell of his clothes). When I first encountered this dish (not in Vasto, but inland), it was made with skate, which I thought worked particularly well.*

2 POUNDS/1 KILOGRAM SKATE WINGS OR SHARK OR SWORDFISH STEAKS, SKIN AND BONES REMOVED

½ CUP/65 GRAMS FLOUR

6 TABLESPOONS/90 MILLILITERS EXTRA-VIRGIN OLIVE OIL

SALT

1 SMALL ONION, FINELY CHOPPED

2 CUPS/480 MILLILITERS WHITE WINE VINEGAR

1 TEASPOON SAFFRON THREADS

Cut the fish into pieces about 2 by 3 inches/5 by 7.5 centimeters. Dredge the pieces in the flour, shaking off the excess.

Heat 4 tablespoons/60 milliliters of the oil in a large frying pan over medium-high heat. Add the fish and fry, turning once, until cooked through, 2 to 3 minutes per side, depending on the thickness. Drain the fish pieces on paper towels and season generously with salt.

Heat the remaining 2 tablespoons oil in a small frying pan over medium heat. Add the onion and cook, stirring frequently, until it softens, 6 to 8 minutes.

Meanwhile, heat the vinegar in a small pot over low heat until it simmers, then crumble the saffron into it. Cook for about 2 minutes.

Rinse a 1-quart/1-liter Mason or other hermetic jar with boiling water, then dry it with a clean kitchen towel. Put about one-fourth of the fish into the jar, and spoon about one-third of the onion and its oil over the fish. Repeat the process with three more layers of fish and two more additions of onion and oil, ending with fish. Pour the vinegar slowly over the top layer of fish. If it doesn't completely cover the fish, heat a little more vinegar and add it. Cover tightly.

Marinate in the refrigerator for at least 3 days before serving. It will keep for up to 3 weeks.

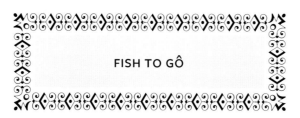

FISH TO GÔ

One of the classic dishes of Venetian cooking is risotto di gô. Gô, or gò (*ghiozzo* in Italian) is a small, very bony fish (*Zosterisessor ophiocephalus*)—we'd call it goby—found all over the Mediterranean, but actively fished only in the Venetian lagoon. Its bones make it all but impossible to eat, but it is used for flavoring rice, an effect many cooks manage by putting the poached gô in a linen bag and squeezing the juices out into the pot. My friend Bepi D'Este, a native of Burano in the lagoon, says that his wife can bone it with a knife—but then, he adds, she's a fisherman's daughter, after all. (He also says that when she eats a sole "the cats are sad. The skeleton is so clean, you could comb your hair with it.")

According to Bepi, in winter, when the water gets cold, most of the fish in the lagoon swim out into the sea, which is deeper and thus stays warm beneath the surface. The gô, on the other hand, remains, burrowing into the mud for warmth. "You can find their holes in the shallows," he says. "There are always two, so you block one and then put your hand into the other to grab the fish. If you're really good at it, you know how to grab only the full-grown ones, leaving the babies to mature." Luca di Vita, who serves some of the best seafood in Venice (which is saying something) at his little osteria Alle Testiere, says, "The truth is gô is a fish with no flavor. Risotto di gô is a legend. But it's important to preserve our legends."

MIXED GRILL OF FISH WITH ANCHOVY SAUCE

SERVES 6

Some variation on this simple preparation is made in virtually every coastal region of Italy.

3 TABLESPOONS EXTRA-VIRGIN OLIVE OIL, PLUS MORE FOR GREASING AND BRUSHING

JUICE OF 1 LEMON

4 TABLESPOONS/60 GRAMS ANCHOVY PASTE

PEPPER

3 POUNDS/1.5 KILOGRAMS ASSORTED MEDIUM-SIZE WHOLE OCEAN FISH, CLEANED, HEADS AND TAILS (OR AT LEAST TAILS) ON

SALT

2 LARGE BRANCHES ROSEMARY

Whisk together the oil, lemon juice, and anchovy paste in a small bowl. Season the sauce with pepper and set it aside.

Meanwhile, light a grill/barbecue and let the coals or wood burn down to medium-hot (if using a gas grill, preheat to about 500°F/260°C). Season the cavity of each fish lightly with salt. Oil a hinged grilling basket, then lay the fish in it and fasten it securely.

Brush the fish on both sides with oil, using the rosemary branches as brushes. Grill/barbecue the fish, turning once, until the skin is crisp and lightly browned and the fish is just cooked through, 6 to 10 minutes, depending on thickness.

Divide the fish evenly into six portions and place on individual plates. Whisk the sauce again, then drizzle it over the fish to serve.

PESCE ALL'ACQUA PAZZA

SERVES 2 TO 4

Fish "in crazy water" is a classic Neapolitan fishermens' dish, typically made with spigola (sea bass) or orata (sea bream).

¼ CUP/60 MILLILITERS EXTRA-VIRGIN OLIVE OIL

16 TO 20 RIPE CHERRY TOMATOES, HALVED

4 GARLIC CLOVES, EACH SLICED LENGTHWISE INTO 3 OR 4 SLICES

6 SPRIGS ITALIAN PARSLEY, MINCED

½ TEASPOON PEPERONCINI

SALT

1 SEA BASS, SEA BREAM, RED SNAPPER OR OTHER FLAKY-FLESHED WHITE OCEAN FISH, 1½ TO 2 POUNDS/750 GRAMS TO 1 KILOGRAM, FILLETED WITH SKIN ON

Put the oil into a large frying pan with a cover and swirl it around to coat the bottom. Add the tomatoes, garlic, parsley, peperoncini, and 3 cups/720 milliliters water and season with salt.

Cover the frying pan and bring the mixture almost to a boil over medium-high heat. Reduce the heat to low and simmer covered, stirring occasionally, for 45 minutes.

Uncover the pan, raise the heat to high, and cook, stirring frequently, until the liquid has reduced by about half. Reduce the heat to medium and add the fillets side by side, skin side up. Cook for about 5 minutes, then carefully turn the fillets with a spatula and cook until cooked through, about 5 minutes more. Serve immediately.

RED SNAPPER, LIVORNO STYLE

✳

SERVES 4

People so often think of Tuscany in terms of Florence or Siena, or of the hill towns of Chianti, that they sometimes forget that it has a long and varied seacoast, stretching between Liguria and Lazio. The most important Tuscan port city—the third largest on Italy's western coast—is Livorno. It is famous for its once-prosperous Jewish community and as the birthplace of artist Amedeo Modigliani. It is also noted in some circles for the liqueurs produced here—Tuaca and Galliano—and in other circles for its proximity to Bolgheri, now one of the most prestigious wine regions in Italy. Locals cite French influences in the city's cuisine, but it is known primarily for the quality and diversity of its fish. This is a typical dish.

2 TABLESPOONS EXTRA-VIRGIN OLIVE OIL, OR MORE IF NEEDED

4 RED SNAPPER, BRANZINI, STRIPED BASS, OR OTHER FIRM-FLESHED WHITE OCEAN FISH FILLETS 6 OUNCES/175 GRAMS EACH

1 ONION, THINLY SLICED

1 GARLIC CLOVE, MINCED

¼ CUP/60 MILLILITERS DRY RED WINE

2 RIPE TOMATOES, SEEDED AND GRATED (SEE RAW TOMATO COULIS, PAGE 371)

½ CUP/75 GRAMS PITTED BLACK OLIVES, QUARTERED LENGTHWISE

½ TEASPOON OREGANO OR MARJORAM LEAVES

SALT

Heat the oil in a large frying pan over medium heat. Add the fish fillets and sauté, turning once, for 2 minutes per side. Remove the fillets with a spatula and set them aside on a warm plate.

Add the onion and garlic to the oil remaining in the pan, adding a bit more oil if necessary to prevent scorching, and cook, stirring frequently, until the onion softens, 6 to 8 minutes. Add the wine, tomatoes, olives, and oregano, stir well, and season with salt.

Reduce the heat to low, return the fillets to the pan, and spoon some of the sauce over them. Cover the pan and cook until the fillets are cooked through, about 10 minutes.

Transfer the fillets to a warmed platter. Raise the heat to high and cook, stirring constantly, until the sauce thickens, 1 to 2 minutes. Spoon the sauce onto 4 warmed plates, dividing it equally. Place a fish fillet on each sauced plate and serve.

ROAST SEA BASS WITH CHANTERELLES

✳

SERVES 4

Wild mushrooms are a favorite food in the countryside of Friuli and the Venezia Giulia. This recipe is adapted from one used by the Trattoria Risorta in the fishing village of Muggia, across the bay from Trieste.

2 WHOLE BRANZINI OR STRIPED BASS, 2 TO 3 POUNDS/1 TO 1.5 KILOGRAMS EACH, CLEANED AND FILLETED WITH SKIN ON, WITH HEAD AND BONES RESERVED

1 CUP/240 MILLILITERS EXTRA-VIRGIN OLIVE OIL

2 ONIONS, CHOPPED

2 CARROTS, CHOPPED

2 STALKS CELERY, CHOPPED

6 BAY LEAVES

1½ CUPS/360 MILLILITERS DRY WHITE WINE

2 TABLESPOONS TOMATO PASTE, HOMEMADE (PAGE 371) OR COMMERCIAL

2 TABLESPOONS FLOUR, WHISKED INTO 2 CUPS/480 MILLILITERS WATER

SALT AND PEPPER

¾ POUND/375 GRAMS CHANTERELLES, QUARTERED

Preheat the oven to 350°F/175°C/gas 5.

Halve the fish fillets crosswise, then score the skin with a cross-hatch pattern and set aside. Chop the fish head and bones into large pieces and set aside.

Heat ¼ cup/60 milliliters of the oil in a medium roasting pan/tray on the stove top over medium-high heat. Add the onions, carrots, celery, and bay leaves and cook, stirring frequently, for 5 to 6 minutes. Add the fish head and bones and continue cooking, stirring frequently, until the bones begin to brown, 5 to 6 minutes more. Deglaze the pan with the wine, scraping up the browned bits on the bottom. Stir in the tomato paste and cook for about 2 minutes, then stir in the flour water.

Put the roasting pan in the oven and roast until the liquid has reduced by about half, 20 to 25 minutes. Strain the liquid through a fine-mesh sieve into a medium bowl, pushing on the solids with the back of a wooden spoon. You should have about 1½ cups/360 milliliters liquid.

Set half the liquid aside and put the rest into a blender. Start the motor running at slow speed and slowly pour 3 tablespoons of the oil through the hole in the blender lid. Process until the sauce is emulsified, then transfer it to a small saucepan, season with salt and pepper, and keep it warm over low heat.

Heat 2 tablespoons of the oil in a medium frying pan over medium heat. Add the chanterelles and cook, stirring frequently, until they begin to brown, 3 to 5 minutes. Add the reserved liquid, season with salt and pepper, then remove from the heat, cover, and set aside.

Heat 3 tablespoons of the oil in a large frying pan over high heat. Season the fish fillets generously with salt and pepper and sear them, skin side down, until the skin is crisp and golden, about 1 minute. Turn them over, reduce the heat to medium, and cook until fish is cooked through, 3 to 5 minutes.

To serve, place the fish pieces on 4 warmed plates, and top with the mushrooms, dividing them evenly. Spoon the warm sauce over the mushrooms and around the fish. Drizzle the remaining ¼ cup/60 milliliters oil evenly over the mushrooms.

ROAST WHOLE SEA BASS

SERVES 2 TO 4

I spent a week one recent winter on the Ligurian coast just east of Genoa, researching an article about a local specialty, the highly addictive focaccia col formaggio (see page 154). One evening, though, I decided to have dinner in a place where no focaccia is served (not easy in the region), and, with a couple of friends, ended up at a tiny seafood-only restaurant called Da Paolo, in Camogli's medieval quarter. After we had devoured plates of local anchovies, big juicy mussels, and an unusual pâté of cuttlefish, the chef-proprietor's wife came out hefting a huge metal tray on which were arrayed five or six kinds of fish so fresh they were practically winking at us. After some debate—the porgy? the turbot?—we settled on a beautiful, plump, wild-caught branzino, which is often described as Mediterranean sea bass. It turned out to be wonderful. This is how it was cooked. (I prefer to cook the fish with its head on—I just like the way it looks—but you may remove it if you're squeamish.)

I WHOLE BRANZINO OR OTHER SEA BASS, 2 POUNDS/ I KILOGRAM, PREFERABLY WILD-CAUGHT, CLEANED

SALT

2 SMALL BUNCHES THYME

2 SMALL LEMONS, I HALVED, I QUARTERED

¼ CUP/60 MILLILITERS EXTRA-VIRGIN OLIVE OIL, PLUS MORE FOR GREASING

I GARLIC CLOVE, MINCED

Preheat the oven to 425°F/220°C/gas 7.

Rinse the fish in cold water and pat it thoroughly dry with paper towels. Salt it generously inside and out, then cut three diagonal slashes, spaced equally, in the top side of the fish. Push the thyme bunches and the lemon halves into the cavity, and set the fish aside.

Heat the oil in a small pan over medium heat. Add the garlic and cook, stirring occasionally, until it softens, about 2 minutes. Remove from the heat.

Lightly oil a roasting pan/tray just large enough to hold the fish. Lay the fish in it, slashed side up, and pour the oil and garlic evenly over the top.

Roast until the skin is slightly crisp and fish is cooked through, about 20 minutes. Serve with the lemon wedges.

RAW DEAL

These days, the menus at nearly every sophisticated Italian restaurant in the United States, and an increasing number in Italy itself, offer at least one example of something called *crudo*, literally "raw," and meaning some kind of raw fish or shellfish served as sashimi or in the form of tartare or carpaccio, often dressed with Mediterranean condiments like olive oil, balsamic vinegar, or fresh herbs. (The excellent Marea in New York City is probably not the only restaurant that has a whole crudo bar.) I find this amusing, because until pretty recently, few Italians would have been caught dead eating slivers of uncooked pesce. Raw seafood is not completely unknown in Italy. My Venetian friend Luca di Vita remembers eating raw razor clams and baby mussels as a child. "We'd spend summers with a cabana on the Lido," he once told me, "and dig them out of the sand. We'd take them back to the cabana, squeeze lemon on them, and when they'd open, just pop them into our mouths."

More recently, sushi bars have attracted an Italian following, especially in the larger cities like Rome and Milan (the Venetian bacaro called Naranzaria serves sushi, too). There's even a chef from the Marche, Moreno Cedroni, who has developed a whole repertoire of imaginative raw seafood dishes that he calls "susci" (pronounced sushi in Italian) at his Il Clandestino and Madonnina del Pescatore restaurants. But crudo as it is served today? There may have been an odd antecedent here and there, but I'm almost certain that the entire genre was invented in New York City in the 2000s, by one of two chefs, either David Pasternack at Esca or Scott Conant at the now-defunct L'Impero.

SALT COD, NEAPOLITAN STYLE

SERVES 4

A similar dish in Basilicata uses abundant Senise peppers (see page 382 for sources), sweet and only slightly spicy, in place of the bell peppers and peperoncini.

1½ POUNDS/750 GRAMS SALT COD, PREPARED FOR COOKING (SEE PAGE 378)

I CUP/125 GRAMS FLOUR

½ CUP/120 MILLILITERS EXTRA-VIRGIN OLIVE OIL

2 LARGE ONIONS, SLICED

3 OR 4 RIPE TOMATOES, SEEDED AND GRATED (SEE RAW TOMATO COULIS, PAGE 371)

SALT

1½ POUNDS/750 GRAMS RED BELL PEPPERS/ CAPSICUMS, CHARRED AND PEELED (PAGE 376), THEN CUT INTO NARROW STRIPS

I TEASPOON PEPERONCINI

4 TO 6 SPRIGS ITALIAN PARSLEY, MINCED

Cut the salt cod into 1½- to 2-inch/3.75- to 5-centimeter cubes. Dredge the cubes in the flour, shaking off the excess.

Heat half the oil in a large frying pan over medium-high heat. Working in batches if necessary, add the salt cod cubes and fry, turning them several times, until golden brown on all sides, 3 to 4 minutes. As they are ready, drain them on paper towels.

Let the frying pan cool for a few minutes, then wipe it out with paper towels. Add the remaining oil to the same pan over medium heat. Add the onions and cook, stirring frequently, until they soften, 6 to 8 minutes. Add the tomatoes, season with salt, and cook, stirring frequently, until the sauce is very thick, 8 to 10 minutes.

Reduce the heat to low and stir in the bell peppers, peperoncini, and parsley. Cook, stirring frequently, until the peppers soften, 6 to 8 minutes. Stir in the salt cod, mixing well to coat it evenly with the sauce, and cook until the salt cod is heated through and sauce thickens slightly, about 10 minutes more. Serve immediately.

BAKED CALABRESE SALT COD

SERVES 4

In Calabria, this dish is often made not with salt cod but with stockfish. The former, however, is much easier to deal with.

3 TABLESPOONS EXTRA-VIRGIN OLIVE OIL

I ONION, MINCED

I STALK CELERY, FINELY CHOPPED

2 GARLIC CLOVES, MINCED

2 RIPE TOMATOES, SEEDED AND GRATED (SEE RAW TOMATO COULIS, PAGE 371)

IO TO 15 KALAMATA OLIVES, PITTED AND COARSELY CHOPPED

IO TO 12 BASIL LEAVES, COARSELY CHOPPED

2 TABLESPOONS PINE NUTS

1½ POUNDS/750 GRAMS SALT COD, PREPARED FOR COOKING (SEE PAGE 378)

2 POTATOES, PEELED AND CUBED

SALT

Heat the oil in a large frying pan over medium heat. Add the onion, celery, and garlic and cook, stirring frequently, until the vegetables soften, 6 to 8 minutes. Add the tomatoes, olives, basil, and pine nuts, then cook for about 10 minutes longer, stirring frequently.

Meanwhile, preheat the oven to 375°F/190°C/gas 5.

Flake the salt cod into the frying pan with your hands, then stir in the potatoes and season with salt. Transfer the mixture to a shallow baking dish just large enough to accommodate it.

Bake until the potatoes are cooked and the top is starting to brown, about 20 minutes. Serve immediately.

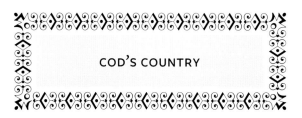

COD'S COUNTRY

The most important non-Mediterranean seafood eaten in Italy isn't Scottish salmon or shrimp from Thailand, though both are readily available in the country's fish markets. It is North Atlantic cod, which for many centuries has come into Italy in two distinct forms: salt cod and stockfish. The trade in preserved fish between Scandinavia and the Mediterranean dates from as early as about AD 1000. The northern countries needed salt, wine, and olive oil, which they could not produce themselves. In return, they offered meaty cod processed in ways (some of them using Mediterranean salt) that allowed it to be kept for many months, even years, before consumption—a valuable quality in the days before refrigeration and rapid transport.

According to one theory, stockfish first appeared in Italian cuisine after the Council of Trent, a series of Catholic doctrinal conferences in the mid-sixteenth century. The council reinforced and expanded rules about abstinence from meat during periods of the liturgical calendar. Since fish was the principal alternative source of protein, and since fresh fish was accessible only to those who lived in coastal regions, the availability of preserved fish would help the faithful to avoid animal flesh. Some suspect that a Swedish cleric at the meetings, one Olof Mansoon, or Olao Magno, may have promoted the idea. The official

entry of dried cod into the Italian culinary canon came in 1570, when the papal chef Bartolomeo Scappi published several recipes for it. One called for it to be floured and fried, then served with orange sauce and pepper; another stewed it with olive oil, white wine, verjuice, ground almonds, various herbs, pepper, cinnamon, and cloves. I once ate stockfish at a sagra in Badalucco, in the Ligurian backcountry, prepared in what was said to be a medieval style: it was simmered in wine, water, and veal broth for hours with dried mushrooms, onions, olive paste, and pine nuts, then crushed with a large wooden dowel and served as almost a mush. (It was actually pretty good.)

Today, both stockfish and salt cod are eaten pureed or stewed, and the latter is sometimes floured and fried or even grilled or roasted like fresh fish. Most of the salt cod and stockfish eaten in Italy now comes from Norway, Iceland, or (a comparative newcomer to the trade) Newfoundland. Both products begin with fresh-caught cod. Depending on its size and shape, a decision is made whether to preserve it through drying or salting. The best fish is cleaned, decapitated, and hung otherwise whole on wooden racks to dessicate in cold, dry wind (the most famous location for this process is Norway's Lofoten Islands). The resulting stockfish is as hard as wood (it is believed to take its name from the Dutch word *stoc* or *stok*, meaning a "stick" or "cane")—you could hurt somebody with it—and must be tenderized and/or soaked for a week or more to render it edible. (During the latter process, it emits a pungent odor that would likely scare some people away from ever eating it.) Arrigo Cipriani of Harry's Bar, a great aficionado of stockfish, told me that people used to soften it by beating it with wooden sticks on marble slabs on the sidewalk. He once bought an old-fashioned machine for working it himself, he added, which involved the kind of rollers you used to see on old washing machines.

Cod not destined for air-drying, after itself being cleaned and decapitated, is splayed open and buried in salt until some but not all of its moisture is absorbed. Italians call salted cod *baccalà* and dried cod *stoccafisso* or *pesce stocco* (or just *stocche* in Genoa)— except in the Veneto and Friuli, where stockfish is called . . . *baccalà*, as well. (Elizabeth David may be forgiven, then, for having written that *baccalà* and *stoccafisso* were one and the same.) A "baccalà," in Italian American usage, incidentally, is what another culture might call a mensch: an admirable person with good qualities.

INVOLTINI OF SWORDFISH

This is a traditional but unexpectedly elegant dish from the north-eastern Sicilian agricultural capital of Messina, founded by the Greeks about a thousand years ago.

I CENTER-CUT PIECE SWORDFISH, 2 POUNDS/
I KILOGRAM, CUT INTO 18 VERY THIN SLICES

6 TABLESPOONS/90 MILLILITERS EXTRA-VIRGIN
OLIVE OIL, PLUS MORE FOR GREASING

I ONION, FINELY CHOPPED

I STALK CELERY, FINELY CHOPPED

2 GARLIC CLOVES, MINCED

½ CUP/30 GRAMS TOASTED BREAD CRUMBS,
HOMEMADE (PAGE 378) OR COMMERCIAL

I TABLESPOON CAPERS

4 ANCHOVY FILLETS, FINELY CHOPPED

6 TO 8 BASIL LEAVES, COARSELY TORN

2 OUNCES/60 GRAMS AGED PROVOLONE, CUT INTO
¼-INCH/6-MILLIMETER CUBES

¼ CUP/25 GRAMS GRATED PECORINO SARDO

2 EGGS, LIGHTLY BEATEN

SALT AND PEPPER

6 TO 8 SPRIGS ITALIAN PARSLEY, MINCED

Trim off and discard any skin from the swordfish, then trim off any irregular edges from the fish. Finely chop the trimmings and set them aside.

Cut two pieces of waxed/greaseproof paper, each about 24 inches/60 centimeters long. Lightly oil one side of each sheet. Place as many swordfish pieces as will fit, with about 2 inches/5 centimeters between them (and 2 inches/5 centimeters from the edge of the paper) on the oiled side of one sheet. Place the other sheet, oiled side down, on top. Using a meat mallet or clean, flat-bottomed wine bottle, gently but firmly pound the swordfish pieces, flattening them until they nearly touch one another. Set the swordfish aside, still sandwiched between the waxed-paper sheets. Repeat the process as needed to flatten all the swordfish.

Heat 4 tablespoons/60 milliliters of the oil in a large frying pan over medium heat. Add the onion, celery, garlic, and swordfish trimmings and cook, stirring frequently, until the vegetables soften, 6 to 8 minutes. Stir in the bread crumbs, capers, and anchovies and cook, stirring often, for 2 to 3 minutes more.

Set the frying pan aside off the heat, and let the mixture cool to room temperature. Then stir in the basil, provolone, pecorino, and eggs, and season generously with salt and pepper, mixing well to combine thoroughly.

Preheat the oven to 425°F/220°C/gas 7. Soak 36 wooden toothpicks in water.

Gently lift the top sheet of waxed paper off one of the swordfish "sandwiches," and put a heaping tablespoon of the filling in the middle of each piece, flattening it slightly with your fingers. Roll the swordfish around it, tucking in the ends, as if you were making stuffed grape leaves. Secure both ends of each roll with a toothpick. Lightly oil a baking dish large enough to hold all the swordfish rolls side by side, and arrange the rolls in it.

Bake until the swordfish is cooked through and beginning to brown, about 15 minutes.

To serve, arrange the rolls on a warmed platter, drizzle the remaining 2 tablespoons oil over the top, and sprinkle with the parsley.

SWORDFISH WITH PINE NUTS AND RAISINS

SERVES 4

First appearing in Libre del Coch—*literally, Cook's Book—
in Barcelona in 1520, this is a very old recipe. The author, who
signed himself alternately Mestre Robert (Master Robert, suggesting that he was a master chef) or Robert de Nola, was the royal
chef to Ferdinand III (1452–1516), the Aragonese king of Naples.
Nola was an important town about twenty miles northeast of
Naples, though there is some speculation that Robert may have
been a Catalan. Whatever he was, he obviously knew his seafood:
he gives recipes for about thirty varieties of fish and shellfish, of
which this is among the most appealing to modern palates.*

1½ POUNDS/750 GRAMS SWORDFISH STEAKS

I CUP/125 GRAMS FLOUR

3 TABLESPOONS EXTRA-VIRGIN OLIVE OIL

I CUP/240 MILLILITERS DRY WHITE WINE

½ CUP/120 MILLILITERS FRESH ORANGE JUICE

JUICE OF ½ LEMON

20 ROASTED ALMONDS

I TEASPOON MINCED ITALIAN PARSLEY

I TEASPOON MINCED MINT

I TEASPOON MINCED MARJORAM

½ CUP/50 GRAMS GOLDEN RAISINS/SULTANAS,
PLUMPED IN WARM WATER FOR 10 MINUTES AND
DRAINED

½ CUP/75 GRAMS PINE NUTS, LIGHTLY TOASTED
IN A SMALL, DRY FRYING PAN

SALT AND PEPPER

Cut the swordfish into strips about 1 inch/2.5 centimeters
thick, 2 inches/5 centimeters wide, and 4 inches/10 centimeters
long. Dredge the strips in the flour, shaking off the excess.

Heat the oil in a large frying pan over medium-high heat.
Working in batches, add the swordfish pieces and cook lightly,
turning them frequently with tongs, until they begin to take
on a light golden color on all sides, 6 to 8 minutes. As they are
ready, drain them on paper towels.

Deglaze the pan with the wine, orange juice, and lemon juice,
scraping up the browned bits on the bottom. Continue cooking
until liquid is reduced by half, 3 to 4 minutes.

Meanwhile, using a mortar and pestle, crush together the
almonds, parsley, mint, and marjoram until a coarse paste forms.
Add a teaspoon or two of liquid from the pan if the mixture is
too dry.

Stir the crushed almond mixture into the liquid in the frying
pan, and add the raisins and pine nuts. Return the swordfish to
the frying pan and stir together all the ingredients well. Cook
for about 1 minute, then season with salt and pepper. Serve
immediately.

SWORDFISH
AL SALMORIGANO

SERVES 4

Salmorigano sauce, found in Sicily and elsewhere in southern Italy, takes its name from one of its primary ingredients, oregano. It works well on any flavorful grilled or baked fish.

I CUP/240 MILLILITERS EXTRA-VIRGIN OLIVE OIL

4 SWORDFISH STEAKS, 6 OUNCES/175 GRAMS EACH

SALT AND PEPPER

JUICE OF I LEMON

2 GARLIC CLOVES, MINCED

6 TO 8 SPRIGS ITALIAN PARSLEY, MINCED

I TABLESPOON OREGANO LEAVES

Heat 3 tablespoons of the oil in a large frying pan over medium-high heat. Season the swordfish generously with salt and pepper, add it to the pan, and fry for about 4 minutes on the first side.

Meanwhile, vigorously whisk together the remaining oil and lemon juice, then stir in the garlic, parsley, oregano, and a bit of salt.

Turn the swordfish steaks, spoon the sauce over them, and continuing cooking until they are just cooked through, about 4 minutes more. Transfer the swordfish to a warmed serving platter and continue cooking the sauce for about 2 minutes, then spoon it over the fish. Serve immediately.

TUNA FRITTERS
WITH TOMATO SAUCE

SERVES 4

This preparation, sometimes made with sardines, is typical of western Sicily. I've adapted this recipe from one given by Mary Taylor Simeti in her excellent book Pomp and Sustenance: Twenty-Five Centuries of Sicilian Food.

I CUP/60 GRAMS TOASTED BREAD CRUMBS, HOMEMADE (PAGE 378) OR COMMERCIAL, SOAKED IN ¾ CUP/180 MILLILITERS WHOLE MILK

I POUND/500 GRAMS SKINLESS, BONELESS TUNA STEAKS, FINELY CHOPPED

2 TABLESPOONS GRATED PECORINO SARDO

2 TABLESPOONS GOLDEN RAISINS/SULTANAS

2 TABLESPOONS PINE NUTS

4 OR 5 SPRIGS ITALIAN PARSLEY, MINCED

4 OR 5 MINT LEAVES, MINCED

SALT AND PEPPER

I EGG, LIGHTLY BEATEN

3 OR 4 TABLESPOONS FLOUR

¼ CUP/60 MILLILITERS EXTRA-VIRGIN OLIVE OIL

2 CUPS/480 MILLILITERS TOMATO SAUCE, HOMEMADE (PAGE 371) OR COMMERCIAL

Squeeze the moisture out of the bread crumbs, then combine them in a large bowl with the tuna, cheese, raisins, pine nuts, parsley, and mint, and season with salt and pepper. Stir in the egg, mixing it in thoroughly, then work the mixture well with your hands until it is a coarse paste. Form the mixture into about 16 patties, each about 2 to 3 inches/5 to 7.5 centimeters in diameter. Dust them on both sides with flour, shaking off any excess, and set them aside.

Select a frying pan large enough to hold all the patties side by side, add the oil, and heat over medium-high heat. Add the patties and fry, turning once, until golden brown on both sides, about 3 minutes per side. Reduce the heat to low, pour the tomato sauce over the patties, and cook, turning the patties several times until they are cooked through and the sauce is slightly reduced, 12 to 15 minutes. Serve immediately.

CRUSTACEANS, CEPHALOPODS, AND BIVALVES

TREASURES OF THE SEA AND SHORE

Quand a manca al pess e' bon anch i gambar.
[When you don't have fish, even shrimp are good.]
—*Romagnola proverb*

Calamari? Trenta oppure trenta.
[Squid? Thirty or else thirty (that is, cook it
for thirty seconds or thirty minutes).]
—*A fishmonger in the Marche, in conversation with the author, 1975*

The shells of limpets, mussels, scallops, and razor clams have been found in Etruscan archeological sites, but there is no evidence that these ancient inhabitants of the Italian peninsula had found a way to farm them. The Romans, on the other hand, were masters at the art. Roughly a century before the beginning of the Christian era, a Roman hydraulic engineer named Sergius Orata became famous for breeding (and selling) oysters—a joke at the time was that he was so skilled in ostraculture that he could raise the bivalves on the roof of his house—and by the first century, oysters, mussels, and sea dates (*Lithophaga lithophaga*) were being cultivated in the Gulf of Lerici, in Liguria, among other places. (Now a protected species, the sea date was so prized for flavor that in the twelfth century, the Holy Roman Emperor Frederick Barbarossa demanded a tribute of upturned shields filled with them from the lords of Vezzano, near La Spezia.) Oysters are rare in traditional Italian cooking, but mussels and clams are common, the latter existing in several forms—including vongole, which are like littlenecks; vongole veraci, "true clams," which are carpet shells; tiny telline or arselle clams; and razor clams. Like all bivalves in Italy—at least outside of sushi bars or modern Italian restaurants influenced by same—these are all nearly always served cooked.

Shrimp/prawns are greatly appreciated in Italy, but not as much as the famous scampi of Venice and vicinity—which are actually small lobsters (*Nephrops norvegicus*), found mostly in the Adriatic, but identical to Dublin Bay prawns. Spider crabs (*Maja squinado*) and related species are consumed, but often end up in seafood soups and stews instead of being eaten on their own. The soft-shell version of the common Mediterranean crab (*Carcinus aestuarii*) is eaten in the Veneto. A traditional method of preparing these, an old-school Venetian bartender once told me, was to break eggs into a large bowl, then add the live crabs and let them crawl around, eating the egg and coating themselves in it. They'd then be plucked out, rolled in flour, and thrown live into the bubbling oil. This sounds barbaric but delicious. There is a little true lobster (genus *Homarus*) in the Mediterranean, the kind with big claws more often found in the North Atlantic—these are called *astice* in Italian—but much more common is *langosta*, a spiny lobster (*Palinurus elephas*), sometimes called saltwater crayfish, which exists in several forms, all with thin pincers but none with claws. In my opinion, it is more flavorful than its clawed cousin.

Cephalods are eaten so widely in Italy that in English, we usually call the most popular of them, the squid, by its Italian name, *calamari*. A stroll through one of Italy's great fish markets—whether it's the Rialto in Venice or La Peschiera in Catania or anything in between—will quickly reveal that there are many sizes and shapes of squid, cuttleish, and octopus in the sea. Those most common on Italian tables are squid (*Loligo vulgaris*) and baby squid, called *calamaretti*, which are usually stewed or fried; cuttlefish or inkfish (*Sepia officianalis*), cooked likewise; and *totani* (*Todarodes sagittatus*), or flying squid, larger than calamari and usually grilled or stuffed. So-called squid-ink pasta or risotto, incidentally, is nearly always made with cuttlefish ink (a pigment used by cephalopods as a kind of smoke screen to protect them from their enemies); squid have ink, too, but very little of it. The little purple octopuses called *moscardini*, especially favored in Venice (where they are known as *folpetti*), can be delicious. Some connoisseurs claim that the longer the tentacles, the better the flavor.

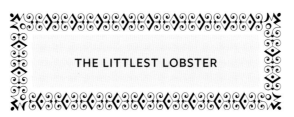
The miniature lobsters the Italians call *scampi* are delicious cooked in olive oil, garlic, and white wine. They are even better lightly floured and deep-fried, however, or in risotto, and the larger ones grill superbly. Scampi have a sweet flavor with a tinge of salt; I find them addictive. Although they are comparatively scarce in most of the Mediterranean, they are fished with some regularity in the Adriatic, and are thus most often seen in the Veneto (any fritto misto in Venice or the islands of the lagoon worthy of the name includes them) and in coastal Emilia-Romagna and the Marche.

The word *scampo* in Italian also means "escaped." The American chef Lydia Shire plays on the homonymic relationship in the name of her Italianate Scampo restaurant in Boston, which is lodged in a hotel built around a former jail. The seafood called *scampo*, though, seems to have borrowed its name from the Greek word *kampe*, meaning a "bending" or "winding"—presumably a reference to the way it curls up when stripped of its shell and cooked.

GRILLED SHRIMP
WITH ROSEMARY

✳

SERVES 6

The best shrimp I've ever had in Italy come from the Gulf of Tigullio, an indentation in the Ligurian coastline between Portofino to the west and Chiavari and Lavagna to the east. They are plump, red shrimp, full of flavor, and are best when they are cooked very simply, preferably without a sauce. In the early 1990s, I rented an apartment for a week on the far side of the Portofino peninsula, in Recco. The apartment had a small balcony with a little grill on it. I bought Tigullio shrimp two days in a row from the Recco market and cooked them like this.

6 STRAIGHT ROSEMARY BRANCHES, 6 TO
8 INCHES/15 TO 20 CENTIMETERS LONG, SOAKED
OVERNIGHT IN WATER

2 TO 3 TABLESPOONS EXTRA-VIRGIN OLIVE OIL

24 LARGE SHELL-ON FRESH SHRIMP/PRAWNS

SALT

Light a grill/barbecue and let the coals or wood get very hot (if using a gas grill, preheat to about 600°F/315°C).

Drain and dry the rosemary branches, then pull off a few leaves from each one, producing about 2 tablespoons of leaves in all. Mince the leaves, and in a small bowl, combine them with the oil.

Skewer 4 shrimp on each rosemary branch, then brush them on both sides with the oil and season them generously with salt.

Grill/barbecue the shrimp, turning once, until just done, about 3 minutes per side. Serve hot or at room temperature.

STUFFED SQUID

✳

SERVES 4

My Genoese friends Giorgio Bergami and Maria Deidda made this dish for me one night with the large squid called totani. *These are sometimes available in the United States, especially at Asian markets. Smaller squid work just as well, but they are a little more work.*

4 LARGE SQUID (ABOUT 6 INCHES/15 CENTIMETERS
LONG AND 3 INCHES/7.5 CENTIMETERS WIDE)
OR 8 OR 12 SMALLER SQUID, PREFERABLY FRESH,
CLEANED

1 GARLIC CLOVE, MINCED

4 SPRIGS ITALIAN PARSLEY, MINCED

½ TEASPOON MARJORAM OR OREGANO LEAVES

½ CUP/50 GRAMS GRATED PARMIGIANO-REGGIANO

1 THICK SLICE COUNTRY-STYLE BREAD, CRUST
TRIMMED AND SOAKED IN WHOLE MILK

2 EGGS, LIGHTLY BEATEN

SALT AND PEPPER

3 TABLESPOONS EXTRA-VIRGIN OLIVE OIL

6 LARGE, RIPE TOMATOES, SEEDED AND GRATED
(SEE RAW TOMATO COULIS, PAGE 371)

½ CUP/75 GRAMS PINE NUTS

Cut the tentacles from the squid bodies. Set the squid bodies aside. Mince the tentacles. Mix them with the garlic, parsley, marjoram, and cheese in a small bowl. Lightly squeeze the moisture out of the bread, tear it into small pieces, and add to the mixture. Stir in the eggs and season generously with salt and pepper.

Stuff the squid bodies with the mixture, and close the open end securely with a toothpick.

Heat the oil in a large frying pan over medium heat. Add the squid and cook, turning several times, until lightly browned on both sides, 6 to 8 minutes. Add the tomatoes and 1 cup/ 240 milliliters water to the pan, cover, and cook for 30 minutes. Add the pine nuts and continue cooking, uncovered, until the sauce thickens, 10 to 15 minutes.

Remove the squid from the sauce and cut into slices about 1½ inches/3.75 centimeters thick for large squid and 1 inch/ 2.5 centimeters thick for smaller ones. Divide the squid slices evenly between 4 plates. Season the tomato sauce with salt and pepper, then spoon over the squid. Serve immediately.

GRILLED SQUID

SERVES 4 TO 6

In America in the 1970s, calamari was breaded and fried, period. I don't know that it had ever dawned on me that it could be cooked in other ways. I still remember vividly the first time I saw small squid—not the miniature calamaretti, but regular ones, maybe 3 to 4 inches/ 7.5 to 10 centimeters long (plus tentacles)—simply grilled: it was on the impressive self-service antipasto table at a restaurant in Verona called Nuovo Marconi, and I liked it so much that I went back for seconds—which I believe was frowned on.

1½ TO 2 POUNDS/750 GRAMS TO 1 KILOGRAM SMALL SQUID BODIES (10 TO 15 SQUID IN ALL), PREFERABLY FRESH, CLEANED

¼ CUP/60 MILLILITERS EXTRA-VIRGIN OLIVE OIL

SALT AND PEPPER

JUICE OF 1 LEMON

Light a grill/barbecue and let the coals or wood get very hot (if using a gas grill, preheat to about 600°F/315°C).

Score the whole squid bodies in two or three places on each side with a sharp knife. Toss them in a medium bowl with about half the oil and plenty of salt and pepper.

Grill/barbecue the squid, turning once, until just cooked through, about 1 minute per side. Transfer them to a platter and drizzle the remaining oil and the lemon juice over them. Serve hot or at room temperature.

OCTOPUS ALLA LUCIANA

❋

SERVES 4

This is the most celebrated preparation of the octopus in and around Naples. It is named for the city's Santa Lucia neighborhood, once home to the fishermen who brought the octopuses in. Though it is traditionally made with whole fresh octopus, I've had the best results using thawed frozen tentacles: the freezing process tenderizes the meat.

1½ TO 2 POUNDS/750 GRAMS TO 1 KILOGRAM FROZEN OCTOPUS TENTACLES, THAWED AND CUT INTO PIECES ABOUT 2 INCHES/5 CENTIMETERS LONG

SALT AND PEPPER

½ CUP/120 MILLILITERS EXTRA-VIRGIN OLIVE OIL

2 RIPE TOMATOES, SEEDED AND GRATED (SEE RAW TOMATO COULIS, PAGE 371)

2 GARLIC CLOVES, MINCED

4 SPRIGS ITALIAN PARSLEY, MINCED

Preheat the oven to 325°F/160°C/gas 3.

Season the tentacles generously all over with salt and pepper. Put the oil into an earthenware or glass baking dish with a lid. Add the tentacles and turn them to coat with the oil. Add the tomatoes, garlic, and parsley and mix together well.

Cover the baking dish with aluminum foil, pressing down the edges as tightly as possible, then cover the dish with its lid. Bake the octopus, shaking the dish occasionally so that the pieces don't stick to the bottom, until tender, about 2 hours. Serve hot or at room temperature.

POLPI IN PURGATORIO
(SPICY OCTOPUS, MOLISE STYLE)

SERVES 4

In southern Italy, dried red chile flakes—peperoncini—are sometimes called la droga di poveri—"the drug of the poor"—because, unlike black pepper, grown in tropical climes and imported into Italy, chile plants grow in every yard. "Octopus in purgatory," is a specialty of Molise, a small, largely bucolic region on the Adriatic, and the "newest" region of Italy, having been administratively separated from Abruzzo only in 1963. Called i pulepe 'npregatorie in the local dialect, it is one of the spiciest Italian dishes I've encountered.

½ CUP/120 MILLILITERS EXTRA-VIRGIN OLIVE OIL

2 ONIONS, FINELY CHOPPED

2 GARLIC CLOVES, MINCED

8 TO 10 SPRIGS ITALIAN PARSLEY, MINCED

2 TEASPOONS PEPERONCINI, OR MORE TO TASTE

1½ TO 2 POUNDS/750 GRAMS TO 1 KILOGRAM FROZEN OCTOPUS TENTACLES, THAWED AND CUT INTO PIECES ABOUT 2 INCHES/5 CENTIMETERS LONG

SALT

Heat half the oil in a medium frying pan over medium heat. Add the onions, garlic, parsley, and peperoncini and cook, stirring frequently, until the onions soften, 6 to 8 minutes.

Put the tentacles in a pot and add the onion mixture and the remaining oil. Add enough water just to cover the tentacles, then bring it to a boil over high heat. Reduce the heat to low, season generously with salt, cover, and cook, stirring occasionally, until the liquid has evaporated, about 2 hours. Serve immediately.

CLAMS IN GARLIC AND WHITE WINE

SERVES 2 TO 4

This dish is best made with small, sweet carpet-shell clams (Tapes decussatus), which the Italians call vongole veraci, "true clams," as if all related bivalves are imposters. Manila clams, littlenecks, or small cherrystones may be substituted if necessary. This dish, with slight regional variation, is served up and down Italy's Adriatic coast.

6 TABLESPOONS/90 MILLILITERS EXTRA-VIRGIN OLIVE OIL

1 TO 2 GARLIC CLOVES, MINCED

2 TABLESPOONS MINCED ITALIAN PARSLEY

48 CARPET-SHELL OR MANILA CLAMS (ABOUT 4 POUNDS/2 KILOGRAMS), SCRUBBED

1 CUP/240 MILLILITERS DRY WHITE WINE

2 TABLESPOONS ITALIAN BRANDY

SALT

TOASTED COUNTRY-STYLE BREAD SLICES FOR SERVING

Select a large, deep frying pan with a lid big enough to hold the clams. Add the oil to the pan and place over medium-high heat. Add the garlic and parsley and cook for about 1 minute. Add the clams, cover the pan, and cook for about 1 minute more, shaking the pan once or twice. Add the wine and brandy and cook, uncovered, until the alcohol has burned off, 2 to 3 minutes. Cover the pan again and continue cooking, shaking the pan once or twice, until the clams have opened, about 3 minutes more. Discard any that failed to open.

Season the clams generously with salt and serve with the toasted bread.

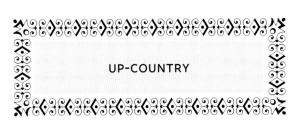

UP-COUNTRY

Until late 2008, when he closed Gambero Rosso, his restaurant in San Vincenzo on the Tuscan coast, just northwest of Grosseto, Fulvio Pierangelini was considered one of the best chefs in Italy, possibly the best. I would have argued that, despite the refinement of his cooking (and his prices), he was also one of the most eloquent exponents of the virtues of Italian country cooking. Born in Rome but brought up in this part of Tuscany, Pierangelini learned to cook from his mother, and as a teenager enjoyed making dinner for his friends. Although his mother's food was traditional, he had an inventive streak himself; he remembers adding smoked salmon to spaghetti alla carbonara on one occasion, and another time he flavored a risotto with Campari. His first professional cooking job came at a bar and disco called Casa Rossa, in Baratti, just south of San Vincenzo. He liked the work well enough that in 1980, he and his wife, Emanuela, bought a derelict summer seafood restaurant in San Vincenzo, already called Gambero Rosso.

His food was very simple at first, and it remained simple, even as it grew more sophisticated in execution. His first creation to make critics sit up and take notice was a puree of chickpeas with shrimp, rustic but exquisite. In the years before he shut his restaurant down—for "a pause," he told me, adding that "I'm full of ideas and projects"—he had developed a style of cooking that I think might be described as elegance reduced to its core. It occurred to me one evening that it was the kind of food a farm wife might have cooked if she could have made her wildest fantasies come true. I remember Pierangelini's silky baccalà mantecato—the Italian version of brandade—topped with a few thin slices of sandalwood-hued white Tuscan truffles and drops of olive oil; his minestrone asciutto (dry minestrone) composed of very flavorful, very tiny vegetables—carrots the size of roof nails, turnips not much bigger than peas—with two rosy, little ingot-shaped pieces of fresh tuna marinated in ginger and other spices; his slightly chewy agnolotti, with a rich golden dough filled with intense, cooked-down fresh tomatoes and topped with a "little salad" of tiny squid, scampi, and shrimp, all barely cooked; his round, deckle-edge sweet onion ravioli, glistening in butter and striped with excellent aceto balsamico; his moscardini (baby octopuses), almost Nantucket red, squeaky and sweet, atop sauces of almond and red pepper that tasted vividly of exactly what they were made of; his paper-thin slices of moist, herb-flavored suckling pig, from a herd of heritage Cinta Senese pigs raised by his son, on a bed of potatoes puréed with olive oil and of sliced sautéed porcini. . . .

"The first step in my cuisine," Pierangelini explained, "is to find the best materials. Then, it's a matter of how I work with them. One must know them, feel them; one must decide all that one can do with them and still remain natural." It is a measure of the trust that Pierangelini inspires that when he offered me a dessert one day of licorice ice cream with beet/beetroot puree and white truffles, I actually sampled it—and liked it. "This is not dessert," he assured me. "You take licorice, beets, and three slices of truffle, and you have the earth."

EIGHT-LEGGED DINNER

Because the octopus is an unusual-looking creature, it is frequently depicted in ancient frescoes and mosaics. Because it is also delicious, in a surprisingly mild way (given its fearsome aspect), it is also widely eaten all over the Mediterranean—generally just the tentacles in the case of the larger creatures, but the whole thing if they are small (meaning with heads not much bigger than golf balls). The latter are typically stewed with tomatoes and/or onions (or added to fish stews or soups), or, if they are small enough, fried whole. The tentacles of a larger octopus are often grilled and eaten hot or cold. Waverley Root describes a dish from the coast of Romagna in which a small octopus is stuffed with the roe and livers of hake and the flesh of various fish and roasted on a spit; he notes that the preparation is "highly tasty and nearly indigestible (which is probably why it has almost disappeared from circulation)." He also describes huge boiled octopuses in Sicily, weighing eight to ten pounds/four to five kilograms and having tentacles "as thick and fleshy as a baby's leg." Octopus that lives along the shore, hiding in the rocks, is more prized for flavor than the paler octopus that inhabits the seabed, and some authorities maintain that the larger the thing, the better its flavor (I'm not sure I agree).

In Liguria, the area around Lerici in the Gulf of La Spezia—also called the Golfo dei Poeti, or Gulf of the Poets (because both Dante and Petrarch are known to have spent time in the area, Byron swam in its waters, and Shelley drowned in a boating accident there)—is particularly known for its octopus. D. H. Lawrence recounts a tale from Tellaro, a town not quite three miles/five kilometers south of Lerici, where the local church stands close to the water: One night, it seems, the citizenry was awakened by the frantic tolling of the church bell, the signal of an impending pirate raid. When they assembled at the church, however, they found a huge octopus, on the rocks below the belfry, pulling on the bell cord.

MUSSELS, ALGHERO STYLE

SERVES 4

Alghero, a fortified port town in northwestern Sardinia, has a Catalan past (see page 207), and to this day, a small percentage of (mostly older) Alghero residents still speak a dialect of Catalan and streets and some shops bear Catalan names. Even the local name for mussels employs a Catalan spelling, cotzes, instead of the Italian cozze. This is, in any case, the way fishermen around Alghero traditionally prepare this popular bivalve.

3 TABLESPOONS EXTRA-VIRGIN OLIVE OIL

2 GARLIC CLOVES, MINCED

4 SPRIGS ITALIAN PARSLEY, MINCED

8 TO 10 BASIL LEAVES, JULIENNED

4 ANCHOVY FILLETS, MASHED WITH A FORK

½ CUP/120 MILLILITERS DRY WHITE WINE

¼ CUP/60 MILLILITERS WHITE WINE VINEGAR

2 POUNDS/1 KILOGRAM SMALL TO MEDIUM MUSSELS (NOT LARGE GREEN-LIP MUSSELS), THOROUGHLY SCRUBBED AND DEBEARDED

SALT AND PEPPER

Heat the oil in a pot large enough to hold the mussels over medium heat. Add the garlic, parsley, and basil and cook, stirring frequently, for 1 to 2 minutes.

Mix the anchovies, wine, and vinegar together in a small bowl, then add the mixture to the pot and stir well. Add the mussels, cover the pot, and cook, shaking the pot once or twice, until the mussels open, 2 to 3 minutes. Discard any that failed to open.

Toss the mussels quickly in the sauce, then divide them equally between 4 bowls. Season the liquid remaining in the pot with salt and pepper and serve on the side for dipping.

TIELLA
(MUSSEL AND POTATO CASSEROLE)

SERVES 4

One of those food words that can mean a number of different things in Italian, tiella is the name of a kind of glazed earthenware dish—like the cazuela of Spain—but it can also refer to a number of different things cooked in such a vessel: a kind of double-crust bread-dough torta filled with octopus or other seafood that is a specialty of Gaeta in Lazio; an eggplant and potato casserole from the Abruzzo; a baked stew of lamb with potatoes, onions, and wild mushrooms in Puglia; and a specialty in parts of Calabria and some parts of Puglia involving mussels, potatoes, and rice. Waverley Root calls tiella "one of the few Spanish dishes which have been taken into the Italian repertory" and says that "tiella . . . [is] distantly related to paella." Whether he means the name or the food it describes is unclear, and his attempt to give it a Spanish origin is unconvincing (at least to this student of paella and other Spanish dishes). This, in any case, is the kind of tiella I've eaten on the Calabrian coast.

2 POUNDS/1 KILOGRAM SMALL TO MEDIUM MUSSELS (NOT LARGE GREEN-LIP MUSSELS), THOROUGHLY SCRUBBED AND DEBEARDED

½ CUP/120 MILLILITERS DRY WHITE WINE

2 GARLIC CLOVES, MINCED

4 SPRIGS ITALIAN PARSLEY, MINCED

1 TABLESPOON EXTRA-VIRGIN OLIVE OIL, PLUS MORE FOR GREASING

1 ONION, VERY THINLY SLICED

1 LARGE, RIPE TOMATO, FINELY CHOPPED

½ CUP/50 GRAMS GRATED PECORINO ROMANO

1 POUND/500 GRAMS POTATOES, PEELED AND THINLY SLICED

1 CUP/200 GRAMS ABORIO OR OTHER SHORT-GRAIN RICE

SALT AND PEPPER

½ CUP/30 GRAMS TOASTED BREAD CRUMBS, HOMEMADE (PAGE 378) OR COMMERCIAL

Preheat the oven to 350°F/175°C/gas 5.

Put the mussels and the wine into a pot just large enough to hold them, place over medium heat, cover, and steam until they open, 2 to 3 minutes. Discard any that fail to open.

Drain the mussels in a colander set over a bowl, reserving the cooking liquid. When the mussels are cool enough to handle, remove the top shells, leaving the meats sitting in the bottom shells. Strain the cooking liquid through several layers of cheesecloth/muslin, then set it and the mussels aside separately.

Mix the garlic and parsley together in a small bowl. Lightly oil a deep earthenware, glass, or ceramic baking dish large enough to hold the mussels side by side in a single layer. Cover the bottom with the onion. Sprinkle half the garlic-parsley mixture over the onion, then scatter about half the tomato over it. Sprinkle half the cheese over the tomato. Lay half the potato slices over the cheese, then sprinkle the rice evenly over the potato slices. Season the mussels with salt, then sprinkle with the remaining garlic-parsley mixture. Arrange them in the baking dish, meat side up. Top with the remaining tomato, then the remaining potato slices. Season the potato slices generously with salt and pepper, then sprinkle the bread crumbs over them, followed by the rest of the cheese. Drizzle the oil over the cheese.

Add enough water to the reserved cooking liquid to make 2 cups/480 milliliters, then slowly pour it down the insides of the baking dish. Bake until the rice is cooked and cheese is golden brown, 45 to 50 minutes. Serve immediately.

GRILLED SPINY LOBSTER

SERVES 4

When I wasn't grilling fresh shrimp (see page 197) on the balcony of my (all too briefly) rented apartment in Recco, roughly twenty years ago, I sometimes splurged on an aragosta, *or spiny lobster—a clawless creature that, as noted earlier, I find more flavorful than its pincered Atlantic cousin. A related variety of spiny lobster is fished off the coast of California and western Mexico and in the Gulf of Mexico; it makes a good substitute for the Mediterranean kind. Italian cooks often split the lobsters lengthwise before cooking, and then grill them meat side down. Cooking them whole as I do here takes a little longer but leaves the flesh attractively moist.*

2 SPINY LOBSTERS, 1½ TO 2 POUNDS/750 GRAMS TO 1 KILOGRAM EACH, RINSED AND DRIED BUT LEFT WHOLE

2 TO 3 TABLESPOONS EXTRA-VIRGIN OLIVE OIL

1 LEMON, QUARTERED LENGTHWISE

SALT

Light a grill/barbecue and let the coals or wood get very hot (if using a gas grill, preheat to at least 500°F/260°C).

Put the lobsters on the grill, stomach side down, and cook for 10 minutes, or until the stomachs are lightly browned but not burned (if they brown too quickly, move them so that they're not directly over the flame). Using tongs, turn the lobsters onto their backs and grill for 10 minutes longer.

Remove the lobsters from the grill and set them on a cutting board on their stomachs. Using a large, heavy, sharp knife, carefully halve them lengthwise. Turn them cut sides up, drizzle with the olive oil, squeeze a lemon quarter over each half, and season generously with salt.

Serve hot or at room temperature.

CATALAN COUNTRY

The town of Alghero, in the province of Sassari on Sardinia's northwestern coast, was founded almost a thousand years ago by the powerful Doria family from Genoa, a city with which Sardinia in general has long and complex historical and cultural connections. It was taken over in the mid-fourteenth century by the combined forces of two Iberian powers, the Kingdom of Aragón and the County of Barcelona, and subsequently colonized by Catalan fishermen, farmers, and merchants. A fortified port town serving an important agricultural area (many of the island's best wineries are nearby), Alghero was ceded to Piedmont's House of Savoy 350 years later, but Catalan influence remained strong. Today, Catalanists in Spain consider Alghero—which they call l'Alguer—to be one of the *països catalans*, or "Catalan lands" (the others being Catalonia itself, the Balearic Islands, the region of Valencia, and the Roussillon in France).

About a quarter of Alghero's population speaks Catalan as a first language today, and a revival of interest in the Catalan aspects of the city's heritage is under way. (Franca Masu, who writes and sings songs in Algherese Catalan, has had success all over Italy as well as in Catalonia.) Disappointingly to me, the one dish that Italians associate with Alghero's Catalan traditions, a preparation of spiny lobster in tomato sauce called *aragosta alla catalana*, turns out not to be traditional at all: the owner of a big, popular restaurant near the waterfront told me that he had invented it to satisfy customers who asked for something Catalan.

"SCAMPI" WITH GARLIC AND PARSLEY

SERVES 4

Unlike a lot of my colleagues in the culinary pontification game, I don't get particularly upset by the term shrimp scampi *on a menu. Italian scampi, of course, aren't shrimp. The scampo, as noted on page 195, is a kind of tiny lobster, as a close inspection of it in its native state will verify. But I read "shrimp scampi" as meaning shrimp in the style in which scampi are often cooked along the Adriatic coast (where they prosper)—which, in its simplest form, is quickly sautéed in olive oil with garlic and parsley. Scampi have a limited season, from late winter through late spring, but during that period may sometimes be found in fish shops in the United Kingdom, sometimes identified as Dublin Bay prawns. To the best of my knowledge, however, they are not imported into the United States—certainly not fresh, in any case. The closest substitute I've found are Alaskan spot prawns (see page 382 for a source), though this recipe works well with any smaller fresh shrimp, too.*

¼ CUP/60 MILLILITERS EXTRA-VIRGIN OLIVE OIL

COARSE SALT

1½ POUNDS/750 GRAMS FRESH SHELL-ON SPOT PRAWNS

4 GARLIC CLOVES, MINCED

4 SPRIGS ITALIAN PARSLEY, MINCED

Heat the oil in a large frying pan over high heat until it is almost smoking. Scatter in plenty of salt, then add the prawns and cook them quickly, stirring and tossing to cook on all sides, for about 1 minute. Add the garlic and parsley and continue cooking, stirring constantly, until just done, about 30 seconds more. Serve hot or at room temperature.

FRITTO MISTO DI MARE

SERVES 4 TO 6

I encountered my first fritto misto di mare—"mixed fried seafood"— when I was barely twenty, at a small portside restaurant in Muggia, a Venetian-looking town across the bay from Trieste, near the Slovenian border. Before ordering it, I asked my more worldly English girlfriend if it would be like the fried shrimp I knew from back home. "Exactly," she said, in the sarcastic tone she did so well. Various small fish, like whitebait, fresh anchovies, or small fresh sardines, are often included in the mix. And in Venice, where fritto misto di mare is an art form, tiny soft-shell crabs and/or Adriatic scampi are common ingredients.

¾ POUND/375 GRAMS CLEANED SMALL SQUID BODIES, CUT INTO RINGS ½-INCH/1.25 CENTIMETERS WIDE, WITH TENTACLES HALVED LENGTHWISE

½ POUND/250 GRAMS CLEANED SMALL CUTTLEFISH OR OCTOPUSES, HALVED OR QUARTERED, DEPENDING ON SIZE

½ POUND/250 GRAMS SMALL SHRIMP/PRAWNS, PREFERABLY FRESH, PEELED AND DEVEINED

½ POUND/250 GRAMS BAY SCALLOPS

1 OR 2 TRAYS ICE CUBES

2 CUPS/250 GRAMS FLOUR

SALT

4 CUPS/1 LITER OLIVE OIL OR CANOLA OIL

4 TO 6 LEMON WEDGES

Put the squid, cuttlefish, shrimp, and scallops into a large bowl and add water to cover and the ice cubes. Set aside for 1 hour.

Put the flour in a large bowl and season it generously with salt. Heat the oil in a deep fryer or a deep saucepan fitted with a frying basket to 375°F/190°C.

Drain the shellfish. Working as quickly as you can (if possible, ask somebody to help), shake the excess water off the squid, cuttlefish, and shrimp, then dredge them in the flour, shaking off the excess. Add them to the hot oil in batches and fry until golden brown and just cooked through, 30 to 45 seconds. As they are done, drain them on paper towels. Repeat the process with the bay scallops, frying them for 30 to 45 seconds.

Pile on a platter, season with salt, and serve with lemon wedges.

POULTRY AND RABBIT

✳

FOOD FROM THE FARMYARD

Chicken . . . is so widely available today that we are losing sight of its historic
role—as invalid food, or as an important part of a vanished rural economy.
—*Gillian Riley*, The Oxford Companion to Italian Food

The bridge from wild to domestic meat is provided by rabbit. . . .
—*Waverley Root*, The Food of Italy

hicken, the most common of barnyard fowl, was first domesticated perhaps as long as ten thousand years ago in Asia, and is believed to have been introduced to the Mediterranean by the Phoenicians around the start of the first millennium BC. (Greek pottery from around 700 BC includes images of the bird.) Because it is a reasonably hardy fowl and doesn't require much space to fatten—and because it could provide eggs, a valuable source of protein

(and an essential ingredient in one whole category of pasta), almost endlessly until it was ready for the stew pot, and even then leave nourishing broth behind after it had been eaten—it became extremely popular throughout Italy. And because its flesh is comparatively bland, for centuries Italian doctors recommended its consumption not only for invalids but also for pregnant women and the aged. (Clifford Wright, a specialist in Mediterranean food history, notes that, curiously, one region where it is not much eaten is Sicily; the shortest recipe section in any Sicilian cookbook, he says, will be that for chicken.)

Perhaps because wild ducks were abundant in many parts of the world, the duck was not domesticated until about 4000 BC, probably in China. The Greeks and Romans ate domestic duck, and it was a favorite fowl in Renaissance Tuscany. Geese may have been domesticated even later, but were known to the ancient Egyptians—and have a place in Roman legend: loud squawks of a flock in the temple of Juno on the Capitoline Hill reportedly alerted soldiers to a night attack by the Gauls, circa 390 BC. Traditional goose recipes are relatively rare in Italy today, but the bird has long fulfilled an important function: in some parts of Italy, especially around Pavia in Lombardy and in parts of Friuli, goose is used as a substitute for pork (the bird

is very fatty, like the pig) in making prosciutto, salami, and the like. (Goose salumi is important, for obvious reasons, in Italian Jewish cuisine.)

Turkey reached Italy in the sixteenth century, almost certainly by way of Spain, and became surprisingly popular, eventually supplanting peacock as the centerpiece for festive banquets and much later giving competition to capon as a holiday treat. In the late nineteenth century, Pellegrino Artusi wrote that turkey broth is "very tasty," and recommended serving it as soup with malfattini ("badly made little ones," that is, irregular gnocchetti) or with "rice with cabbage or turnips [or] spelt or cornmeal made more flavorful with two sausages crumbled up in it."

Like ducks, rabbits were so plentiful in the wild (to the point that they were, and still are, pests, decimating crops with great enthusiasm) that there was little reason for farmers to raise them. The Romans may have been the first to do so in Europe (there is an image in a mural in Pompeii of a rabbit eating figs, though it is unclear whether or not the fruit was being fed to him to improve the flavor of his flesh). The food historian Gillian Riley describes a painting listed in a 1618 inventory of the property of Grand Duke Cosimo II de' Medici of Florence that shows an idealized farmyard in which not only rabbits but guinea pigs, a porcupine, and a hedgehog are being fattened for the table.

TUSCAN FRIED CHICKEN

✳

SERVES 4

Fried bread dough with stracchino cheese, fried vegetables, fried chicken, fried rabbit, fried calf's brains—ah, Tuscan food at its finest. We tend to have a particular idea of the cooking of fabled Tuscany: crostini, ribollita, white beans, pappardelle, meats grilled or roasted in a hot oven (above all the famous bistecca alla fiorentina, or T-bone steak). But olive oil is a vital constituent of Tuscan cuisine, and one of the best uses to which it may be put is as a medium for deep-frying. Not surprisingly, then, Tuscan cooks are often masters of the fryer's art. I first learned this decades ago at a country trattoria called I Ricchi, in the hillside town of Cercina above Florence (you can see the city in the distance from the restaurant's terrace), whose menu includes all the above-named dishes. This recipe is adapted from theirs.

4 EGGS

I CUP/125 GRAMS FLOUR

I CHICKEN, 2½ TO 3½ POUNDS/1.25 TO
1.75 KILOGRAMS, CUT INTO 8 TO 12 PIECES

SALT AND PEPPER

3 TO 4 CUPS/720 MILLILITERS TO I LITER EXTRA-
VIRGIN OLIVE OIL

Lightly beat the eggs in a wide, shallow bowl. Put the flour in a second wide, shallow bowl. Season the chicken pieces generously with salt and pepper. Dip each piece in the beaten eggs, then the flour, then the eggs again, shaking off the excess egg and flour each time. As they are coated, set the chicken pieces aside.

Pour the oil to a depth of about 2 inches/5 centimeters into a deep frying pan and heat over high heat to 375°F/190°C. Reduce the heat to medium-high. Working in batches, fry the chicken pieces until they turn golden brown, 8 to 10 minutes. (Reduce the temperature if the oil begins to smoke.) As they are done, transfer to paper towels to drain before serving.

Variation: Substitute 1 rabbit, 2½ to 3½ pounds/1.25 to 1.75 kilograms, cut into 8 to 12 pieces, for the chicken. Proceed as directed.

POLLO ALLA CACCIATORA

✳

SERVES 4

Variations on this dish of chicken stewed with tomatoes are served all over Italy. It is, of course, the same dish that American cooks know under the name "chicken cacciatore." If you know that a cacciatore is a hunter, you might well wonder why a hunter would be cooking a barnyard bird. In fact, the dish is properly named not for the hunter but for his wife, the cacciatora. One story is that this was a traditional hearty evening meal served to men before they went out on their early morning chase. I think it is more likely that this is what the signora cooked for dinner when the signore came home with no wild birds in his game bag.

¼ CUP/60 MILLILITERS EXTRA-VIRGIN OLIVE OIL

I CHICKEN, 3 POUNDS/1.5 KILOGRAMS, CUT INTO
8 PIECES

2 GARLIC CLOVES, MINCED

2 ONIONS, CHOPPED

I CUP/240 MILLILITERS DRY WHITE WINE

4 TO 6 RIPE TOMATOES, PEELED, SEEDED, AND
CHOPPED, OR ONE 28-OUNCE/875-GRAM CAN WHOLE
SAN MARZANO TOMATOES, DRAINED AND CHOPPED

I BAY LEAF

I TEASPOON MARJORAM LEAVES

SALT AND PEPPER

I CUP/240 MILLILITERS CHICKEN BROTH,
HOMEMADE (PAGE 372) OR COMMERCIAL

Heat the oil in a large frying pan with a cover over medium-high heat. Add the chicken pieces and cook, turning once, until browned on both sides, 8 to 10 minutes. Transfer the chicken to a plate and set it aside.

Reduce the heat to medium-low, add the garlic and onions, and cook, stirring frequently, until the onions soften, 6 to 8 minutes. Deglaze the pan with the wine, scraping up the browned bits on the bottom. Return the chicken to the pan. Add the tomatoes and their juices, the bay leaf, and the marjoram and season with salt and pepper.

Reduce the heat to low, cover, and cook, adding the broth gradually as the tomato juices evaporate and turning the chicken occasionally, until the chicken is tender, about 45 minutes. Adjust the seasoning with salt and pepper before serving.

POLLO ALLA DIAVOLA

※

SERVES 4

There is some disagreement around Italy as to just what chicken "devil's style" really is. Some chefs "devil" it by marinating it in vinegar; others sprinkle it liberally with peperoncini. In his landmark (if not always accurate) tome The Food of Italy, *Waverley Root mentions a Florentine interpretation that involves a ginger sauce (he also alludes to a version of the dish from the Veneto). According to Artusi (see page 94), the dish earned its name "because it is supposed to be seasoned with strong cayenne pepper and served with a very spicy sauce, so that whoever eats it feels his mouth on fire and is tempted to send both the chicken and whoever cooked it to the devil." In the Tuscan town of Impruneta, just south of Florence, which calls itself the birthplace of the dish (it is featured at Impruneta's annual civic festival every spring), it is spiced with nothing more than lots of black pepper. (The town is also famous for a very peppery stew called* peposo; *see page 260.) I came to know and love the dish not in Tuscany but in the hill towns of the Castelli Romani in the Lazio, where it likewise earns its sobriquet from nothing more than an abundance of black pepper. Because it is butterflied/spatchcocked and flattened, pollo alla diavola is often confused with—or considered synonymous with—pollo al mattone, "with the brick," a preparation said to date from Etruscan times, so-named because a brick is traditionally used to hold it flat during cooking. As far as I can tell, pollo al mattone is just pollo alla diavola without all the pepper. Either one, incidentally, is a dish for the grill, not the frying pan or the oven.*

I CHICKEN, 3 TO 4 POUNDS/1.5 TO 2 KILOGRAMS

½ CUP/120 MILLILITERS EXTRA-VIRGIN OLIVE OIL

JUICE OF 2 LEMONS

SALT AND PEPPER

To butterfly/spatchcock the chicken, place it breast side down. Using a sharp knife or poultry shears and working from the tail end toward the neck, cut along both sides of the backbone and remove it. Turn the chicken breast side up and roll a rolling pin over it, pressing down hard to flatten the bird as much as possible.

Put the bird in a dish large enough to hold it flat, then drizzle about half the oil and half the lemon juice over it. Season it generously with salt and pepper and set it aside at room temperature to marinate for 1 hour.

Combine the remaining oil and lemon juice in a small bowl and add more pepper to taste (remember that the finished bird should be spicy).

Meanwhile, light a grill/barbecue and let the coals or wood burn down to medium-hot (if using a gas grill, preheat to about 500°F/260°C).

Grill/barbecue the chicken, basting it occasionally with oil and lemon juice and turning it occasionally, until it is dark brown and crusty on both sides, about 45 minutes.

Let the chicken rest for about 10 minutes off the grill, then cut into quarters to serve.

ROAST GUINEA HEN

SERVES 4

Guinea hen or guinea fowl, faraona *in Italian, is a delicious, meaty bird, both hunted (it is a relative of the partridge) and raised domestically. It is particularly popular in northern Italy. Artusi (see page 94) writes that* faraona *was "a symbol of brotherly love in ancient times." See page 382 for a source.*

2 GUINEA HENS, 2 TO 3 POUNDS/1 TO 1.5 KILOGRAMS EACH

SALT AND PEPPER

4 ONIONS; 2 WHOLE, 2 CHOPPED

2 SMALL BUNCHES THYME

OLIVE OIL FOR GREASING

2 GARLIC CLOVES, CHOPPED

1½ CUPS/360 MILLILITERS DRY WHITE WINE

3 TABLESPOONS FLOUR

1½ CUPS/360 MILLILITERS CHICKEN BROTH, HOMEMADE (PAGE 372) OR COMMERCIAL

Preheat the oven to 450°F/230°C/gas 8.

Season the guinea hens generously inside and out with salt and pepper, then put a whole onion and one bunch of thyme into the cavity of each hen. Tie the legs of each bird together with kitchen twine.

Lightly oil a roasting pan/tray just large enough to hold both hens side by side. Mix the garlic into the chopped onions, then put the onions into the roasting pan, flattening them down with a spatula. Place the birds on top of the onions.

Roast the birds until they are browned, 15 to 20 minutes. Reduce the temperature to 375°F/190°C/gas 5, pour the wine into the pan, and continue to roast until an instant-read thermometer inserted into the thigh without touching bone registers 170°F/75°C, about 45 minutes more.

Transfer the hens to a platter, snip and remove the twine, and remove and discard the onions and thyme bunches from the cavities. Tent loosely with aluminum foil.

With a slotted spoon, transfer the onions in the roasting pan to a small bowl. Stir the flour into the pan drippings. Place the roasting pan over two burners on the stove top over medium heat, and cook, stirring, for 2 to 3 minutes. Pour in the broth, stirring constantly and scraping up any browned bits on the bottom. Raise the heat to high and cook, stirring constantly, until the liquid has reduced by about half, 4 to 5 minutes.

Carve the guinea hens and serve with the sauce on the side.

ROAST GUINEA HEN WITH PEVERADA SAUCE

SERVES 4

There are numerous variations on this sauce, said to be of medieval origin. It is a specialty of the Veneto, and is sometimes served with roast duck, goose, rabbit, or hare, as well as guinea hen. I first had something similar to this version in Verona, where it is called peara.

2 GUINEA HENS, 2 TO 3 POUNDS/1 TO 1.5 KILOGRAMS EACH

SALT AND PEPPER

3 TABLESPOONS EXTRA-VIRGIN OLIVE OIL, PLUS MORE FOR GREASING

1 GARLIC CLOVE, CRUSHED

2 OUNCES/60 GRAMS SOPRESSATA OR OTHER DRY-CURED ITALIAN SALAMI, MINCED

4 CHICKEN LIVERS, TRIMMED AND CHOPPED

4 ANCHOVY FILLETS, CHOPPED

6 TO 8 SPRIGS ITALIAN PARSLEY, MINCED

GRATED ZEST OF ½ LEMON

2 TABLESPOONS POMEGRANATE JUICE

1 TABLESPOON RED WINE VINEGAR

2 TABLESPOONS TOASTED BREAD CRUMBS, HOMEMADE (PAGE 378) OR COMMERCIAL

Preheat the oven to 450°F/230°C/gas 8.

Season the guinea hens generously inside and out with salt and pepper, then tie the legs of each bird together with kitchen twine.

Lightly oil a roasting pan/tray just large enough to hold both hens side by side. Roast the birds until they have browned, 15 to 20 minutes. Reduce the heat to 375°F/190°C/gas 5 and continue to roast

MR. DICKENS EATS ITALIAN

The fare a traveler might have expected to find on the road in Italy in the mid-nineteenth century was apparently both simple and abundant, at least judging from an account left by Charles Dickens of a meal he enjoyed one night at an inn in Stradella, not quite twenty-five miles/forty kilometers west of Piacenza, in Emilia-Romagna. The inn itself, he writes, "was a series of strange galleries surrounding a yard; where our coach, and a wagon or two, and a lot of fowls, and firewood, were all heaped up together, higgledy-piggledy; so that you didn't know, and couldn't have taken your oath, which was a fowl and which was a cart." The evening meal, served in the room of "a very old priest," was as follows: "The first dish is a cabbage, boiled with a great quantity of rice in a tureen full of water, and flavored with cheese. It is so hot, and we are so cold, that it appears almost jolly. The second dish is some bits of pork, fried with pigs' kidneys. The third, two red fowls. The fourth, two little red turkeys. The fifth, a huge stew of garlic and truffles, and I don't know what else; and this concludes the entertainment."

until an instant-read thermometer inserted into the thigh without touching bone registers 170°F/75°C, about 45 minutes more.

Meanwhile, heat the oil in a frying pan over medium heat. Add the garlic, sopressata, chicken livers, anchovy fillets, parsley, and lemon zest and cook, stirring constantly, until the livers have begun to color, 3 to 4 minutes. Reduce the heat to low, add the pomegranate juice and vinegar, stir well, and cook until sauce has thickened, about 10 minutes more. Stir in the bread crumbs and season with salt and plenty of pepper. Pass the sauce through a food mill, or process in a food processor to a coarse puree.

Transfer the hens to a platter, snip the twine, and carve them. Pass the sauce at the table when serving.

SOPA COÀDA
(TREVISO SQUAB "SOUP")

SERVES 6

Despite its name, which means "hatched [or simmered] soup" in the local dialect, this specialty of Treviso, a dozen miles or so north of Venice, isn't a soup at all, but a dish of layered bread and squab. Waverley Root speculates (not very convincingly) that "though the bread is less subtle than the delicate pastry leaves of the Moroccan pastilla, [sopa coàda] is reminiscent of this famous dish, so that one wonders whether it did not enter Veneto when this area was the chief window on the Moslem world." In earlier times, sopa coàda was often made a day before serving and reheated.

4 TABLESPOONS/60 GRAMS BUTTER, PLUS MORE FOR GREASING

I SMALL ONION, FINELY CHOPPED

I STALK CELERY, FINELY CHOPPED

I CARROT, FINELY CHOPPED

6 SQUABS/PIGEONS, I POUND/500 GRAMS EACH, QUARTERED

SALT AND PEPPER

I½ CUPS/360 MILLILITERS SOAVE OR OTHER DRY WHITE WINE

4 CUPS/I LITER VEAL BROTH (PAGE 373) OR COMMERCIAL BEEF BROTH

6 LARGE SLICES DAY-OLD COUNTRY-STYLE BREAD

⅔ CUP/65 GRAMS GRATED PARMIGIANO-REGGIANO

Melt the butter in a large, deep frying pan over medium heat. Add the onion, celery, and carrot and cook, stirring frequently, until the vegetables begin to brown, 8 to 10 minutes. Add the squab pieces and cook, turning frequently, until they are lightly browned on all sides, 8 to 10 minutes.

Season the squab generously with salt and pepper, then pour the wine into the frying pan. Cook, uncovered, until most of the wine has evaporated, 6 to 8 minutes. Add the broth, reduce the heat to low, cover the pan, and cook until the squab pieces are tender, about 40 minutes.

Remove the squabs from the pan and set them aside until cool enough to handle. Meanwhile, strain the broth, discarding the vegetables.

Pick the meat from the squab quarters (reserve the bones for stock), leaving it in medium to large pieces.

Preheat the oven to 325°F/160°C/gas 3. Lightly butter a baking dish just large enough to hold two slices of the bread side by side.

Lay two bread slices in the baking dish, then sprinkle them with about one-third of the cheese. Lay half the squab meat on top of the cheese, then top it with two more bread slices. Sprinkle the bread with half the remaining cheese, then lay the remaining squab meat on top of the cheese. Cover the squab meat with the remaining bread slices, then drizzle about half the broth over the bread. Finally, sprinkle the top with the remaining cheese.

Bake until the cheese is golden brown and some of the broth has been absorbed, about 40 minutes. Serve in shallow bowls or dinner plates with rims. Heat the remaining broth and pass it at the table.

DUCK WITH
BITTER ORANGE SAUCE

SERVES 4

*Duck à l'orange has always made my teeth ache. The combina-
tion of the bird's unctuous fat and the cloying citrus glaze just
doesn't seem pleasant to me. It was a revelation, then, when I first
encountered the ancient Italian preparation—especially popular in
Tuscany—of duck in a sauce of* bitter oranges. *Now, this made
sense to me—using acidity and sharpness as a foil to the duck's
inbred richness. Bitter (Seville) oranges are intermittently available at Whole Foods Markets and other specialty food stores from
November through April.*

2 LARGE SEVILLE (BIGARADE) OR OTHER BITTER
ORANGES

1 DUCK, 4 TO 5 POUNDS/2 TO 2.5 KILOGRAMS

¼ CUP/60 MILLILITERS EXTRA-VIRGIN OLIVE OIL

SALT AND PEPPER

1 SMALL ONION

2 GARLIC CLOVES

1 SMALL BUNDLE THYME

½ CUP /120 MILLILITERS VIN SANTO OR MARSALA

1 CUP/240 MILLILITERS CHICKEN BROTH

Preheat the oven to 500°F/260°C/gas 10.

Zest the oranges with a vegetable peeler or zester, then halve
them both and squeeze out and reserve the juice from three
of the halves.

Brush the skin of the duck all over with the oil, then season
the duck generously inside and out with salt and pepper. Stuff
the cavity with the onion, garlic, thyme, and the remaining
orange half. Tie the legs together with kitchen twine and tuck
the wings under the back.

Put the duck, breast side up, into a roasting pan/tray just large
enough to hold it. Roast until the skin is brown and crisp,
25 to 30 minutes. Reduce the heat to 350°F/175°C/gas 5 and
continue roasting until an instant-read thermometer inserted
into the thigh without touching bone registers 170°F/75°C,
about 1 hour more.

Transfer the duck to a cutting board, tent it loosely in aluminum foil, and let it rest for about 10 minutes before carving.

Meanwhile, place the roasting pan over two burners on the stove
top over medium-high heat and cook until the juices begin to
caramelize. Skim the fat off the top of the juices, then pour in
the vin santo, broth, and reserved orange juice and deglaze the
pan, scraping up the browned bits on the bottom. Stir in the
reserved orange zest and continue cooking until the liquid is
reduced by about one-third.

Carve the duck into serving pieces, discarding the vegetables
in the cavity, and arrange on a platter. Moisten the meat with
some of the sauce, then serve. Pass the remaining sauce in a
sauceboat or small pitcher at the table when serving.

ROAST HOLIDAY CAPON

SERVES 6

*The ancient Romans apparently invented capon—that is, they
figured out that a neutered rooster (which is what a capon is) would
grow fatter than a chicken—and ever since then, the bird has been
a symbol of gourmandise in Italy. Until the twentieth century, in
fact, it was the common centerpiece of the Christmas Day feast,
at least from Rome northward. (Turkey has since edged it out.)
Usually available only around the holidays, it makes an impressive
main course for any serious dinner. This is a Piedmontese-style
preparation of the bird.*

1 CAPON, 7 TO 8 POUNDS/3.5 KILOGRAMS

6 TABLESPOONS/90 GRAMS BUTTER, SOFTENED

1 LARGE ONION, WHOLE, AND 1 MEDIUM ONION,
CHOPPED

1 BUNCH THYME

1 BUNCH MARJORAM OR OREGANO

SALT AND PEPPER

3 STALKS CELERY, CHOPPED

2 CARROTS, CHOPPED

½ CUP/120 MILLILITERS MARSALA

1 TO 2 CUPS/240 TO 480 MILLILITERS CHICKEN
BROTH, HOMEMADE (PAGE 372) OR COMMERCIAL

Preheat the oven to 350°F/175°C/gas 5.

Place the capon breast side up. Starting from the neck, slide
your fingers carefully under the skin to loosen it from the flesh.
Rub 2 tablespoons of the butter between the skin and flesh.

Stuff the cavity with the whole onion, the thyme, and the marjoram, then rub the remaining butter all over the skin of the bird. Season the capon generously all over with salt and pepper, then tie the legs together with kitchen twine and tuck the wings under the back. Put the capon, breast side up, on a rack set in a roasting pan/tray.

Scatter the chopped onion, the celery, and the carrots in the bottom of the roasting pan, then pour in the Marsala and 1 cup/240 milliliters of the broth.

Roast until an instant-read thermometer inserted into the thigh without touching bone registers 170°F/75°C, about 2½ hours. As the capon roasts, baste it every 30 minutes with the pan liquid, adding more broth if necessary so that there is always about 1 cup/240 milliliters liquid in the pan.

Transfer the capon to a platter, snip the twine, and remove and discard the onion, thyme, and marjoram from the cavity. Tent loosely with aluminum foil and let rest for about 10 minutes before carving.

Meanwhile, strain the pan juices into a small saucepan, discarding the vegetables. Reduce the juices over medium-high heat to about ¾ cup/180 milliliters. Carve the capon and drizzle the juices over the flesh before serving.

COUNTRY-STYLE TURKEY

SERVES 6

I don't know the provenance of this dish—the recipe appears, in a slightly different form, in Savina Roggero's 1973 cookbook Come scegliere e cucinare le carni (How to Select and Cook Meat)—*but it appealed to me as an unusual presentation of a bird that tends to otherwise be cooked in predictable ways, and I have served it to dinner guests with considerable success. Roggero calls for a turkey weighing 4 to 5 pounds/2 to 2.5 kilograms, a bird that is virtually unobtainable in the United States, where a "small" Thanksgiving turkey usually weighs at least 14 pounds/7 kilograms, and the smallest one I've ever seen came in at slightly more than 9 pounds/4.5 kilograms. To solve the problem, as the winter holidays approach, I ask my butcher to save me 5 pounds/2.5 kilograms of fresh turkey thighs, wings, and legs.*

4 TABLESPOONS/60 GRAMS BUTTER

3 TABLESPOONS EXTRA-VIRGIN OLIVE OIL

5 POUNDS/2.5 KILOGRAMS TURKEY THIGHS, WINGS, AND LEGS

2 ONIONS, FINELY CHOPPED

1 STALK CELERY, FINELY CHOPPED

1 CARROT, FINELY CHOPPED

SALT AND PEPPER

1 TABLESPOON FLOUR

½ CUP/120 MILLILITERS DRY WHITE WINE

8 TO 12 CUPS/2 TO 3 LITERS CHICKEN BROTH, HOMEMADE (PAGE 372) OR COMMERCIAL

3 TABLESPOONS TOMATO PASTE/PUREE, HOMEMADE (PAGE 371) OR COMMERCIAL, DILUTED WITH ½ CUP/120 MILLILITERS OF THE CHICKEN BROTH

1½ POUNDS/750 GRAMS POTATOES, PEELED AND CUT INTO 1-INCH/2.5-CENTIMETER CUBES

6 TO 8 BASIL LEAVES, FINELY CHOPPED

1 GARLIC CLOVE, MINCED

Melt the butter with the oil in a large, heavy pot over medium-high heat. Add the turkey pieces and cook, turning frequently, until browned on all sides, 6 to 8 minutes. Reduce the heat to medium, add the onions, celery, and carrot, and cook, stirring frequently, until the vegetables soften, 6 to 8 minutes. Season with salt and pepper, then stir in the flour. Add the wine and continue cooking until it evaporates, 4 to 6 minutes. Add enough broth to cover the ingredients, then add the diluted tomato paste and stir well. Reduce the heat to low, cover, and continue cooking, stirring occasionally, until the turkey pieces are very tender, about 30 minutes.

Add the potatoes, re-cover the pot, and cook until the potatoes are tender, about 30 minutes more. Stir in the basil and garlic and cook for 5 minutes. Serve immediately.

INDIAN ROOSTER

When the large, strange bird we know as the turkey first arrived in Italy from the Americas in the early sixteenth century (there is a mention of it in Rome in 1525), apparently brought by Spanish merchants, it was dubbed *pavone d'India*, "Indian peacock," or, more commonly, *gallo d'India*, "rooster of India," later shortened to *dindio* or *dindo*. This was probably a reference to its perceived exotic nature, not a misapprehension of its origin in either India or the so-called West Indies. It is now called *tacchino*, from *tacca*, "notch" or "nick," perhaps a reference to its wattles.

Large birds had long been considered appropriate fare for festive occasions in Italy. In medieval and Renaissance times, roasted swans and peacocks graced the tables of the upper classes, while the poor made do with coot or bustard. This plump nonflying newcomer quickly became popular for its size and the succulence of its flesh. (Salvador Dalí once wrote that birds in general "[awaken] in man the flight of the cannibal angels of his cruelty," using as an example the fact that "Della Porta in his *Natural Magic* [published in 1558] gives the recipe for cooking turkey without killing it, so as to achieve that supreme refinement: to make it possible to eat it cooked and living." Della Porta, incidentally, was a Neapolitan.) In 1561, the government of Vicenza, in the Veneto, banned the serving of turkey at official banquets because it was considered too extravagant.

Today, turkey is found commonly all over Italy, whole for serious dinners and in the form of cutlets and the like for more casual meals. Harry's Bar in Venice even serves tacchino tonnato, using turkey as a substitute for veal in this famous dish of cold sliced meat in tuna mayonnaise. What may well be the best-known "Italian" turkey dish internationally, turkey Tetrazzini, isn't really Italian at all, incidentally. Probably originally made with chicken, it was apparently invented by the chef at the Palace Hotel in San Francisco in the early years of the twentieth century, and was named for the Italian opera star Luisa Tetrazzini.

OVEN-BRAISED GOOSE, FRIULI STYLE

SERVES 8 TO 10

Though the goose has been raised in Italy since Roman times—somebody once said that the bird "embodies the flavor of the past"—it isn't seen much on Italian tables today. One region where it does seem to be esteemed, though, is Friuli. This is a typical way of preparing it there. Goose made in this fashion is sometimes served with simply cooked peas.

6 TABLESPOONS/90 MILLIMETERS EXTRA-VIRGIN OLIVE OIL

I GOOSE, 7 TO 9 POUNDS/3.5 TO 4.5 KILOGRAMS, CUT INTO 12 TO 16 PIECES (ASK YOUR BUTCHER)

I ONION, CHOPPED

I STALK CELERY, CHOPPED

2 GARLIC CLOVES, MINCED

I SMALL BUNCH ITALIAN PARSLEY, MINCED

6 SAGE LEAVES, COARSELY CHOPPED

I SPRIG ROSEMARY

I STICK CINNAMON

I CUP/240 MILLILITERS FRIULIAN PINOT GRIGIO, PINOT BLANC, OR OTHER DRY WHITE WINE

SALT AND PEPPER

I TO 2 CUPS/240 TO 480 MILLILITERS CHICKEN BROTH, HOMEMADE (PAGE 372) OR COMMERCIAL, HEATED

Heat the oil in a large Dutch oven or other heavy ovenproof pot over medium-high heat. Working in batches if necessary, add the goose pieces and cook, turning them frequently, until browned on all sides, 8 to 10 minutes. Transfer to a platter and set aside.

Preheat the oven to 300°F/150°C/gas 2.

Return the pot to medium heat and add the onion, celery, garlic, parsley, sage, rosemary, and cinnamon. Cook, stirring frequently, until the onion softens, 6 to 8 minutes. Raise the heat to high, add the wine, and deglaze the pot, scraping up the browned bits on the bottom. Return the goose pieces to the pot and stir to coat them with the vegetables. Season generously with salt and pepper, then pour in 1 cup/240 milliliters of the broth.

Place in the oven and cook uncovered, basting frequently with the cooking juices and adding more broth as needed if the pot begins to dry out, until the goose is thoroughly cooked and the skin has turned dark golden brown, about 2 hours. Serve immediately.

LAZIO-STYLE RABBIT STEW

SERVES 4

This is a typical rabbit recipe all over central Italy. I used to eat it with my Roman friends at casual restaurants when we would take weekend drives down toward historic towns like Fondi, on the Via Appia, or Cassino, near the border with Campania.

I RABBIT, 2½ TO 3 POUNDS/1.25 TO 1.5 KILOGRAMS, CUT INTO 6 SERVING PIECES

SALT AND PEPPER

¼ CUP/60 MILLILITERS EXTRA-VIRGIN OLIVE OIL

3 GARLIC CLOVES, CRUSHED

2 OUNCES/60 GRAMS PROSCIUTTO (NOT SLICED), FINELY CHOPPED

6 TO 8 MINT LEAVES, JULIENNED

I CUP/240 MILLILITERS ORVIETO OR OTHER DRY WHITE WINE

4 TOMATOES, CUT INTO 6 TO 8 WEDGES EACH

Season the rabbit generously with salt and pepper. Heat the oil in a Dutch oven or other heavy pot over medium-high heat. Add the garlic, then add the rabbit pieces and fry, turning them frequently with tongs, until golden brown on all sides, 8 to 10 minutes.

Remove and discard the garlic. Add the prosciutto and mint, stir well, then add the wine. Continue cooking until the wine has almost evaporated, 4 to 6 minutes. Add the tomatoes, reduce the heat to low, cover, and cook, stirring occasionally, until the rabbit is tender, about 40 minutes. If the tomatoes don't give off enough liquid, add a little water to the pot to keep the ingredients from sticking to the bottom. Adjust the seasoning with salt and pepper before serving.

RABBIT AND POTATO CASSEROLE

SERVES 4

I had this dish in a private home near Prato, in Tuscany, many years ago, cooked by a couple who were friends of an old friend of mine, and begged the recipe at the time. I've lost touch with the latter and can't recall the couple's name, but I still make the dish.

½ CUP/65 GRAMS FLOUR

SALT AND PEPPER

2 TABLESPOONS LARD OR RENDERED BACON FAT

¼ CUP/120 MILLILITERS EXTRA-VIRGIN OLIVE OIL

I ONION, FINELY CHOPPED

I RABBIT, 2½ TO 3 POUNDS/1.25 TO 1.5 KILOGRAMS, CUT INTO 6 SERVING PIECES

1½ POUNDS/750 GRAMS POTATOES, PEELED AND CUT INTO 2-INCH/5-CENTIMETER CUBES

2½ CUPS/600 MILLILITERS CHICKEN BROTH, HOMEMADE (PAGE 372) OR COMMERCIAL

Preheat the oven to 375°F/190°C/gas 5.

Put the flour into a large bowl, then season it generously with salt and pepper.

Melt the lard with the olive oil in a deep, flameproof baking dish with a lid or a Dutch oven or other heavy ovenproof pot with a lid over medium heat. Add the onion and cook, stirring frequently, until it softens, 6 to 8 minutes. Add the rabbit pieces and fry, turning them frequently with tongs, until golden brown on all sides, 8 to 10 minutes. Stir in the potatoes, then pour in the broth.

Cover the dish and bake for 1 hour. Uncover, raise the oven temperature to 450°F/230°C/gas 8, and continue to cook until the exposed rabbit pieces and potatoes are nicely browned, about 30 minutes more. Adjust the seasoning with salt and pepper before serving.

RABBIT BRAISED WITH HERBS

SERVES 4

In the inland reaches of the Veneto, from Belluno and Valdobbiadene to as far south as Vicenza, wild hare has long been a staple of traditional winter cooking. Closer to the coastline, and to the city of Venice itself, around Padua, Treviso, and Rovigo, domestic rabbit usually takes its place. This is a typical recipe of the latter area.

2 TABLESPOONS EXTRA-VIRGIN OLIVE OIL

I ONION, FINELY CHOPPED

2 GARLIC CLOVES, MINCED

I RABBIT, 2½ TO 3 POUNDS/1.25 TO 1.5 KILOGRAMS, CUT INTO 6 SERVING PIECES

I TABLESPOON FLOUR

2 CUPS/480 MILLILITERS SOAVE OR OTHER DRY WHITE WINE

I LARGE SPRIG ROSEMARY

6 TO 8 SAGE LEAVES

GRATED ZEST OF ½ LEMON

SALT AND PEPPER

Heat the oil in a Dutch oven or other heavy pot over medium heat. Add the onion and garlic and cook, stirring frequently, until they soften slightly, 2 to 3 minutes. Add the rabbit pieces and fry, turning them frequently with tongs and stirring the onion and garlic, until the rabbit is lightly browned on all sides and the vegetables are very soft and golden brown, about 10 minutes. Stir in the flour until well mixed.

Remove the rabbit pieces from the pot and set them aside. Raise the heat under the pot, add the wine, and deglaze the pot, stirring well and scraping up the browned bits on the bottom. Bring the wine to a boil, then reduce the heat to low. Add the rosemary, sage, and lemon zest, and season generously with salt and pepper.

Return the rabbit to the pot and cook, uncovered, over low heat until the liquid is reduced by about half, about 20 minutes. Cover and cook, turning the rabbit pieces in the liquid occasionally, until meat begins to fall off the bones, about 1 hour more. Adjust the seasoning with salt and pepper before serving.

THE FARMHOUSE TABLE

I am eating dinner at one of eight or nine tables in the garden of the farmhouse on the three-and-a-half-acre/eight-and-a-half-hectare farm called Le Garzette. Most of what I am enjoying was grown a short stroll from where I sit: a zucchini/courgette frittata, deep-fried baby artichokes and zucchini flowers, zucchini in sweet-and-sour sauce (you may sense a certain theme here), lasagna of peas and artichokes, penne with eggplant/aubergine and tomatoes, a salad of mixed lettuces, and finally, not from the farm but from local waters, some sole and gilthead bream, simply grilled. It is an excellent meal, made all the more delicious by the fact that I'm devouring it on the Lido, one of the barrier islands protecting Venice from the tides of the Adriatic. Le Garzette is the only agriturismo in Venice.

Farmers all over the world today have begun to think and talk about "value added," that is, ways to increase their income, beyond what they can earn from simply selling their crops, by turning those crops into finished food products (olive oil and cheese are classic examples), or by devising ways to convince nonfarmers to pay for a taste of the farm experience. Italy is ahead of the pack in this regard. As family farming in Italy became less profitable after World War II, through competition from agribusiness, the rise of convenience foods, and other factors, agricultural properties all over the country began to be abandoned. In 1985, though, inspired by informal efforts by some prescient farm owners, the Italian government formally established the *agriturismo* program, allowing (and encouraging) farm owners to offer guest accommodations and meals, the latter created primarily from foodstuffs grown or made on the farm, with a maximum of 35 percent of the materials brought in. Agriturismi—a portmanteau word combining *agriculutura* and *turismo*, "agriculture" and "tourism"—have developed over the years, some of them becoming almost luxurious in facilities (swimming pools are not unknown, and I've encountered linen sheets and luxury bath products in at least a few of them). And their restaurants often offer some of the best food in their region, not only largely farm grown but also reflecting local gastronomic traditions. The cooking is always fairly simple, but I have had some of my most memorable meals in Italy in such places. Agriturismo restaurants may or may not be open to nonguests, but it is always worth asking. A good source for information is www.en.agriturismo.it.

PORK, LAMB, AND GOAT

THE MEAT OF THE MATTER

Youthful lambs are delicacies to be met with in Italy,
and, despite their over-richness, they are delicious.
—*Dorothy Daly*, Italian Cooking

In agricultural areas where communications are sporadic,
the pig figures as the winter saviour of mankind.
—*Patience Gray*, Honey from a Weed

The pig is an animal to be reckoned with. In earlier times, in some rural parts of Italy, it was called *signore*, "the mister," an expression of respect. In the Abruzzo, it was said that the man who slaughtered the beast needed a chair and a glass of wine after he killed it, so heartbroken would he be. One common word for both the animal and its meat is *maiale*, a reference to the mythological character Maia, the goddess of spring and namesake of the month of May—perhaps because the animal was sometimes sacrificed in her honor.

At first glance, a pig would seem to be less useful than a cow or sheep, because it yields no usable milk (as mammals, sows do produce it, but it lacks the short-chain fatty acids that give the milk of other animals its agreeable "dairy" flavor, and it doesn't coagulate, so it is useless for making cheese). In the pig's favor, though, is the fact that it doesn't require pasturage and will feed quite happily on mast (acorns and the like from the forest floor) and table scraps. (I knew one farmer who fattened some piglets for months from barrels of sun-dried tomatoes that were *just* past their sell-by date.) Even more to the point, once it is dispatched, the pig yields not just generous helpings of delicious fresh meat—typically grilled/barbecued, oven roasted, or slow cooked in stews—but also vast quantities of flesh that lend themselves superbly to curing, smoking, and other means of preservation. The meat from one hefty porcine, turned into hams and sausages and the like, could provide protein for a family for a year.

In Catholicism, the predominant religion and cultural power in Italy, the lamb is a symbol of Christ—and the goat is sometimes identified with Satan. On the Italian table, both—when they are young—represent spring, because in the years before modern husbandry practices came into use, they reproduced only early in the year. The Roman term for very young lamb, generally not more than four weeks old, is *abbacchio*—a word derived, I'm sorry to report,

from the verb *abbacchiare*, which one old Italian dictionary describes as "to beat something violently against the ground, a wall, or suchlike," presumably a description of the means by which the animal was originally slaughtered. (A gentler etymology links the word to another meaning of *abbacchiare*, "to lower prices," supposedly because the glut of baby lambs on the market in April every year drove down their cost. Yeah, sure.) *Agnello*, as most lamb is labeled on menus, is the approximate equivalent to what we call spring lamb—no older than six months. *Castrato* is castrated, fattened male sheep, up to eighteen months old—what we would consider mutton. It is particularly popular in Abruzzo, a major lamb-consuming region, and is usually stewed. The cuisine of the Veneto isn't usually associated with lamb, but there is a famous traditional preparation, seldom made anymore, called *castelladina*, which is smoked mutton flavored with spices, usually served with gnocchi. The ancient specialty is made annually for the Feast of Santa Maria della Salute, November 21.

Goat was one of the first animals to be domesticated, and Neolithic farmers apparently kept herds for their milk, their hair (used for clothing), and their dung (dried and burned for fuel), and not only ate their meat but also used their hide for shelter and clothing and their bones for fertilizer. Young goat—kid, called *capretto*—is preferred for the table, and like lamb is often roasted whole.

PORK COOKED IN MILK

SERVES 6

I'm not sure where the idea of cooking pork with milk first came from—other than that it was presumably not a kosher Jewish community. I've seen the dish variously credited to Tuscany (possible), the Veneto (unlikely), and Emilia-Romagna (quite possible). I've also heard rumors that something very similar is prepared in the Spanish Basque country, though I've never found it there, and there's definitely a related Filipino recipe for pork cooked in coconut milk. I first encountered the dish myself, in recipe form, more than thirty years ago in The Classic Italian Cookbook *by Marcella Hazan—and first tasted it, in the version made by Ruth Rogers and Rose Gray at their River Café in London, a dozen years or so after that. Trying to make it myself at home, I always ended up with delicious pork, but could never achieve that dark brown, caramelized glazing that characterized the versions I had at the River Café and various restaurants in Italy where I later tried the dish. The photographer of this book, Christopher Hirsheimer, who is also a cookbook writer and one of the best natural cooks I've met, worked on the technique until she figured out how to do it right. This is an adaptation of her recipe.*

I BONELESS PORK LOIN, 3½ TO 4 POUNDS/
1.5 TO 2 KILOGRAMS

SALT AND PEPPER

2 TABLESPOONS EXTRA-VIRGIN OLIVE OIL

4 TABLESPOONS/60 GRAMS BUTTER

LEAVES FROM I BUNCH SAGE, HALF WHOLE,
HALF COARSELY CHOPPED

2 CUPS/480 MILLILITERS WHOLE MILK

2 CUPS/480 MILLILITERS HEAVY CREAM

4 TO 6 WIDE STRIPS LEMON ZEST

Season the pork generously all over with salt and pepper. Heat the oil and half the butter in a Dutch oven or other heavy pot or flameproof baking dish over medium-high heat, then add the pork, fat side down, and cook until browned, 2 to 3 minutes. Turn the pork and brown on each of the other three sides for 2 to 3 minutes.

Pour the fat off from the pan, then add the remaining butter. Add the whole sage leaves and fry for about 1 minute, then slowly pour in the milk and cream. Add the lemon zest, season with salt, and bring the liquid to a simmer (do not boil). Reduce the heat to low, partially cover the pot, and simmer for 1 hour, turning the pork after 30 minutes.

Add the chopped sage leaves and continue simmering for another hour, again turning the pork after 30 minutes. Uncover the pot and continue to simmer, turning the pork every 30 minutes, until the pork is very tender and the sauce has reduced by about three-fourths and turned golden brown, another 1½ to 2 hours. (Small curds of caramelized milk will form.)

Transfer the pork to a cutting board and let rest for 10 minutes. Carve into slices ½ inch/1.25 centimeters thick, arrange on a platter, and pour the curds and meat juices over the slices before serving.

STEWED PORK RIBS AND SAUSAGE

SERVES 4

This is a simplified version of the Lombardian pork stew called cassoeula, *which often includes pig's feet and sometimes ears and tail. It is traditionally served with polenta (see page 131).*

- 4 TABLESPOONS/60 GRAMS BUTTER
- 2 TABLESPOONS EXTRA-VIRGIN OLIVE OIL
- 1 POUND BABY BACK PORK RIBS, CUT INTO INDIVIDUAL RIBS
- 1 POUND/500 GRAMS MILD ITALIAN SAUSAGE, CASING REMOVED, COARSELY CHOPPED
- 1 ONION, FINELY CHOPPED
- 2 CARROTS, DICED
- 2 STALKS CELERY, DICED
- 4 LARGE TOMATOES, CHOPPED
- SALT AND PEPPER
- 1 LARGE HEAD SAVOY CABBAGE, ABOUT 2 POUNDS/1 KILOGRAMS, CORED AND SHREDDED

Melt the butter with the oil in a Dutch oven or other heavy pot over medium-high heat. Add the ribs and sausage and cook, stirring frequently, until well browned, 8 to 10 minutes.

Reduce the heat to low and add the onion, carrots, celery, and tomatoes. Stir well, season with salt and pepper, and then cover and cook for 20 minutes, stirring occasionally.

Stir in the cabbage and 1 cup/240 milliliters warm water. Re-cover and continue cooking for about 45 minutes, stirring occasionally. The ribs should be tender and the stew should be very thick. If it dries out too much, add a little more water as needed. Serve immediately.

GRILLED PORK CHOPS WITH GARLIC AND ROSEMARY

SERVES 4

This preparation is similar to that for the thin lamb chops called scottadito, *literally "finger burner." I've had both lamb and pork cooked this way around Tuscany, Umbria, and Lazio.*

- 12 TO 16 THIN-CUT PORK CHOPS, ABOUT 2 POUNDS/1 KILOGRAM TOTAL
- 4 GARLIC CLOVES, 2 CRUSHED, 2 MINCED
- ½ CUP/120 MILLILITERS EXTRA-VIRGIN OLIVE OIL
- SALT AND PEPPER
- 2 TABLESPOONS ROSEMARY LEAVES

Light a grill/barbecue and let the coals or wood get very hot (if using a gas grill, preheat to at least 600°F/315°C).

Rub the pork chops on both sides with the crushed garlic, then brush them on both sides with some of the oil and season them generously on both sides with salt and pepper. Stir the minced garlic and the rosemary into the remaining oil.

Grill/barbecue the pork chops for 2 minutes on one side, 1 minute with the grill cover on and 1 minute with it off. Turn the chops and repeat the process. The chops should be lightly charred on both sides and slightly pink inside.

Serve immediately, with the garlic and rosemary oil spooned over them.

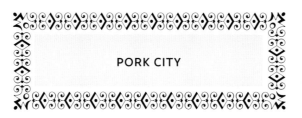

PORK CITY

I remember walking down the street in Norcia, a handsome little town near Perugia, in southeastern Umbria, for the first time and stopping in front of one of its many salumerie and just standing there staring. I had seen amazing arrays of cured pork products before, of course, most notably in Parma and Bologna. But this was a display of uncommon variety, and everything looked wonderful. I saw bastardone, a pale, soft salami meant to be spread on bread; prosciutto di Norcia, the local ham; ruddy, rough-textured salsiccia rustica di prosciutto, a rustic sausage in which that ham was included; horseshoe-shaped salamella norcina, a blend of shoulder meat and pancetta; pancetta itself; capocollo seasoned with wild fennel seeds; coppa di testa, a local version of the dry Italian head cheese; salsiccette appassite, fine-grained small sausages; the local specialty coglion di mulo (an impolite name that I won't translate here), made from very lean pork with a core of lardo (salt-cured pig fat); salami flavored with red wine; and salami made with the meat of wild boar (hunted in great number in the nearby Sibilline Mountains), with and without the black truffles that are another local treasure.

The pork specialists of Norcia have become probably the most respected in Italy, which is why in many parts of the country *norcino* has become a synonym for butcher. It hardly seems fair, but this small municipality boasts not only these meaty wonderments, and those black truffles, but also a particularly good pecorino cheese and a proximity to Casteluccio, which grows Italy's best lentils. No lover of real Italian food should miss it.

ROAST PORK LOIN, SICILIAN STYLE

SERVES 6

Pork loin is cooked in a similar manner all over central and southern Italy. This recipe comes from the Sicilian countryside, around Palermo.

1 BONELESS PORK LOIN, ABOUT 3 POUNDS/1.5 KILOGRAMS

SALT

1 TABLESPOON COARSELY CRUSHED PEPPERCORNS

1 SMALL ONION, MINCED

6 POTATOES, PEELED AND CUT INTO 2-INCH/ 5-CENTIMETER CUBES

3 TABLESPOON EXTRA-VIRGIN OLIVE OIL

1 CUP/240 MILLILITERS DRY WHITE WINE

Preheat the oven to 400°F/200°C/gas 6. Season the pork generously all over with salt, lightly pressing the salt into the surface of the meat. Put the roast on a rack in a medium roasting pan/tray. Scatter the peppercorns and the minced onion over the top of the pork, lightly pressing them into the surface of the meat.

Put the potatoes into a medium bowl, add the oil, season generously with salt, and toss the potatoes until well coated. Put the potatoes into the roasting pan around the roast.

Roast the pork and potatoes for 45 minutes, then pour the wine gently over the top of the pork. Stir the potatoes, then continue to roast the pork and potatoes, basting the meat with the pan juices several times, until the pork is cooked and has turned dark golden brown, another 45 minutes.

Transfer the pork to a cutting board and let it rest for 10 minutes. Leave the potatoes in the roasting pan and cover them lightly with aluminum foil to keep them warm.

Transfer the potatoes to a serving platter. Carve the pork into thick slices and arrange the slices over the potatoes. Pour any remaining pan juices over the pork before serving.

SALAMI AND SALUMI

The collective term for preserved pork products in Italian—the equivalent of the French word *charcuterie*—is *salumi*. (Salami, then, is a type—or rather a whole lot of types—of salumi. *Salama*, just to confuse things, is a large, coarse, offal-based sausage served hot, in a sauce, in Ferrara.) The variety of such things is dazzling. We know only a handful of types in America, and what we know is (with the exception of prosciutto) almost all made in this country or Canada, the importation of most pork products being prohibited by law. In Italy, every region has its specialties, as do many towns within those regions. (I once naively asked a salumiere in Bologna if he had any spalla cotta, which is cured and cooked pork shoulder. "Where do you think you are?" he replied. "*Parma?*" Silly me. Parma was sixty miles/one hundred kilometers away.) Patience Gray, in her book *Honey from a Weed*, describes a typical array, this from a shop in Mantua, in Lombardy: ". . . gigantic hams; every kind of smoked and fresh sausage; *coppa*, smoked loin of pork in the form of a large sausage closely bound with string; *bondiola*, a smoked boiling sausage round in shape; *musetti con lingua*, made from pig's snout and tongue; *lardo*, salted pig's fat cut from its rump; *capelli dei preti*, also called *triangoli*, small triangles of stitched pork skin stuffed with sausage meat, then smoked, for boiling; and nuggets of pork strung together to be flung into the soup."

Elsewhere in Italy, she might have found the conical, cotechino-like musèt of Friuli, seasoned with nutmeg, cinnamon, coriander, and cayenne; the pork-liver mazzafegati (liver killer) from Umbria; Basilicatas rough-textured, offal-filled, chile-spiced pezzente (beggar); the salam'd la duja from Po Valley rice country, flavored with red wine and encased in fat; the similarly named but completely different 'nduja of Calabria, spicy and spreadable; the also spreadable smoked ciauscolo from the Marche, seasoned with garlic and juniper berries; the ventricina found in Abruzzo and Molise, made with comparatively large pieces of pork seasoned with sweet paprika and (traditionally, at least) packed into a pig's bladder; and on and on—not to mention the prosciutto of Parma and San Daniele but also of Carpegna, Cormons, Sauris (where it is smoked as well as salt cured), and more. The Tuscan-born journalist and author Curzio Malaparte once claimed that the prosciutto on the table in front of him in Castel Gondolfo, near Rome, its origin unspecified, came from sacred pigs that rooted in the vicinity of village churches, and whose "flesh has the perfume of incense, and their lard is as soft as virgin wax."

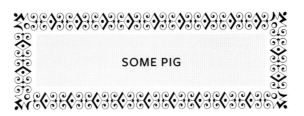

SOME PIG

You can usually smell porchetta before you see it: a perfume of roasting meat, earthy and sweet, with a faint overtone of herbs. Porchetta is sometimes described simply as "suckling pig" but it's a lot more than that: It's suckling pig that has been boned, stuffed with its own innards and herbs (theoretically wild), fennel chief among them, then sewn up, seasoned with salt and plenty of pepper, and roasted on a spit or in a wood-burning oven. In cross section, it looks somewhat like a kind of rough-hewn ballotine.

Though porchetta can be fancied up as sit-down fare, it is primarily outdoor food, street food. Indeed, I first encountered it myself on the streets of Trastevere in Rome, during the district's annual summertime Festa de Noantri (Festival of the Rest of Us—meaning those of us who live in bohemian Trastevere and not in the stodgier quarters of Rome), rotating above the embers of a wood fire in a wrought-iron cart that reminded me of a smaller version of the black metal

smokers American barbecue pit masters haul around to suburban parking lots. As we walked along, we ate slabs of it, cut from the roast, on big doughy rolls, and I thought it was one of the most delicious things I had ever tasted.

Porchetta is a specialty of Rome and of Lazio in general (Ariccia, in the Alban Hills, is said to have its own secret recipe), but it is also found in parts of Tuscany and in Umbria and the Marche. Visiting the town of Ascoli Piceno in the last of those regions, Waverley Root was once given a pamphlet full of local boosterism, including the statement that, "Only the [Marche]—since medieval times—[has] known how to give *porchetta* a golden color and a delicate taste by the skillful proportions of wild herbs." Root also suggests that, since porchetta seems most popular in areas where the Etruscans once lived, it is probably a dish of Etruscan origin.

SAUSAGE WITH GRAPES

SERVES 4 TO 6

"This is a trivial and ordinary dish," Pellegrino Artusi writes
of *salsiccia coll'uva,* "sausage with grapes," in his classic Science
in the Kitchen and the Art of Eating Well, *"but I mention
it because sausages, combined with the bittersweet taste of grapes,
might tickle someone's taste buds."* The only time I've had this
dish, in fact, wasn't exactly in Italy at all—but at a trattoria in
Mendrisio, in the wine country of Ticino, Italian-speaking Switzerland. There, as anywhere in Italy where a dish like this might be
made, the grapes would have seeds, making the eating of them
slightly messy. Feel free to substitute seedless grapes.

- 4 TABLESPOONS/60 GRAMS BUTTER
- 2 POUNDS/I KILOGRAM MILD ITALIAN SAUSAGES,
  EACH SCORED 3 OR 4 TIMES ON THE DIAGONAL
- I POUND/500 GRAMS RIPE TABLE GRAPES
- I CUP/240 MILLILITERS DRY WHITE WINE

Melt the butter in a Dutch oven or other heavy pot over low
heat. Add the sausages, cover, and cook, turning occasionally,
for 12 to 15 minutes. Add the grapes and wine, raise the heat to
medium-high, and bring the wine to a boil. Reduce the heat to
low and simmer uncovered, turning the sausages occasionally,
until the sausages are cooked through and the wine has evaporated, 10 to 12 minutes longer. Serve immediately.

LAMB SPIEDINI WITH PROSCIUTTO AND SAGE

SERVES 4

*This dish is typical of the casual rural trattoria fare served in the
little hill town restaurants of the Castelli Romani outside Rome. A
spiedo is a "spit" in Italian; a spiedino is a "skewer." (Curiously,
spiedo in Italian, like spit in English, means both a rod or stick on
which food is cooked and the saliva that well-cooked food presumably stimulates.)*

- I½ POUNDS/750 GRAMS BONELESS LEAN LAMB LOIN
  OR SHOULDER, CUT INTO I½-INCH/3.75-CENTIMETER
  CUBES
- 12 LARGE FRESH SAGE LEAVES
- ½ POUND/250 GRAMS PROSCIUTTO (NOT SLICED),
  CUT INTO I½-INCH/3.75-CENTIMETER CUBES
- 2 TO 3 TABLESPOONS EXTRA-VIRGIN OLIVE OIL
- SALT AND PEPPER

Light a grill/barbecue and let the coals or wood get very hot (if
using a gas grill, preheat to at least 600°F/315°C).

Thread the lamb, sage, and prosciutto alternately onto four
metal skewers each 6 to 8 inches/15 to 20 centimeters long,
beginning and ending with a piece of lamb and placing a sage
leaf between the pieces of lamb and prosciutto, making sure
that it touches both. (If using wooden skewers, soak them in
water for 30 minutes first.) Brush the skewers on all sides with
the oil, then season them generously with salt and pepper.

Grill/barbecue the skewers, turning them once (grill on two
sides only, top and bottom), until the edges of the sage leaves
have just begun to blacken, about 7 minutes per side. (Alternatively, place the skewers on a lightly oiled baking sheet/tray and
roast, turning them once, for the same amount of time in a pre-
heated 500°F/260°C/gas 10 oven.) Serve immediately.

LAMB WITH OLIVES AND ARTICHOKES

SERVES 4

This is a typical Ligurian preparation of lamb. I based this recipe on a version of the dish I once ate at the farm of Ca' Ertè, an agriturismo property (see page 228) in San Bernardino, above Sestri Levante. When you serve this dish, warn your guests that the olives are not pitted.

> JUICE OF 2 LEMONS
>
> 12 BABY ARTICHOKES
>
> 1½ POUNDS/750 GRAMS SHOULDER LAMB CHOPS, EACH CUT INTO 2 OR 3 PIECES
>
> 3 TABLESPOONS EXTRA-VIRGIN OLIVE OIL
>
> 2 SPRIGS ITALIAN PARSLEY, MINCED
>
> 2 GARLIC CLOVES, MINCED
>
> 1½ CUPS/360 MILLILITERS LIGURIAN VERMENTINO OR OTHER DRY WHITE WINE
>
> 30 TO 40 NIÇOISE OLIVES
>
> SALT AND PEPPER

Mix the lemon juice with 2 to 3 cups/480 to 720 milliliters water in a medium bowl.

Cut the stems off the artichokes. Follow this whole process with 1 artichoke at a time: Pull off the tough outer leaves by hand, then trim off more layers of leaves with a sharp knife until only the tenderest leaves, or heart, remain. Halve the artichoke lengthwise, then cut or scrape out and discard the choke and immediately put the halves in the acidulated water to stop them from turning black. Set aside.

Heat the oil in a large frying pan over medium-high heat. Working in batches, add the lamb and cook, turning the pieces frequently so they brown on all sides, 4 to 6 minutes. As the lamb pieces are ready, transfer them to paper towels to drain.

When all the lamb is cooked, add the parsley and garlic to the same pan, reduce the heat to low, and, adding a bit more oil if necessary, cook over very low heat for about 5 minutes. Raise the heat to high and deglaze the pan with the wine, scraping up the browned bits on the bottom. Reduce the heat to low again, and cover the pan.

Drain the artichoke halves and pat them dry, then halve each half lengthwise. Add them to the pan immediately, re-cover it, and cook for 10 minutes, stirring occasionally.

Return the lamb to the pan, add the olives, and season with salt and pepper. Re-cover the pan and cook, stirring often, until lamb is cooked through, about 15 minutes more. Serve immediately.

ABRUZZESE LAMB STEW

SERVES 6

Long before I had ever visited the region, I had read that Abruzzo, a mountainous, densely forested region on the Adriatic side of central Italy, was famous for its lamb. I learned the hard way that it was also famous for its herbs—over many a long night (followed by many a blurry morning) drinking after-dinner Centerba with my Rome-based Abruzzese friend Gianfranco. Centerba means "a hundred herbs," and though this fiery digestivo—think Green Chartreuse spiked with Everclear and steeped with pine needles— may or may not be infused with quite that many, it is undeniably herbaceous. This stew is infinitely safer. It was originally a shepherd's dish, cooked over an open fire in a cast-iron pot, flavored with whatever wild herbs were handy.

> 2 POUNDS/1 KILOGRAM LAMB STEW MEAT
>
> 2 WHOLE ONIONS
>
> 2 TABLESPOONS EXTRA-VIRGIN OLIVE OIL
>
> 1 TABLESPOON ROSEMARY LEAVES
>
> 1 TABLESPOON THYME LEAVES
>
> SALT
>
> 6 SLICES COUNTRY-STYLE BREAD, DAY OLD OR LIGHTLY TOASTED

Combine the lamb, onions, oil, rosemary, thyme, and a little salt in a pot with a tight-fitting lid. Cover and cook over medium heat, occasionally lifting the lid and shaking the pot so that nothing sticks to the bottom, for about 1¼ hours.

Uncover the pot. The meat should be damp, with a few tablespoons of juices around it. If it is too dry, add a little water, re-cover the pot, and cook for 10 to 15 minutes more. If there is too much liquid, cook uncovered for 10 to 15 minutes. If it is just right, it is ready to serve. Adjust the seasoning with salt.

Put a bread slice on each of 6 plates, then spoon an equal amount of the lamb and its juices over it. Discard the onions, or transfer them to a board, cut them into wedges, and distribute them equally between the plates to serve.

ROASTED LAMB BREAST

Lamb breast isn't a common cut of meat—you'll probably have to ask your butcher to order it for you—but it is delicious, and is a favorite in Lazio and Abruzzo, where it is often cooked this way.

I LAMB BREAST, 4 TO 5 POUNDS/2 TO 2.5 KILOGRAMS, CUT BETWEEN THE RIBS INTO PIECES 2 TO 3 INCHES/ 5 TO 7.5 CENTIMETERS WIDE

SALT AND PEPPER

4 GARLIC CLOVES, MINCED

IO TO 12 JUNIPER BERRIES, CRUSHED

2 TEASPOONS ROSEMARY LEAVES

2 TEASPOONS THYME LEAVES

2 TABLESPOONS EXTRA-VIRGIN OLIVE OIL

Preheat the oven to 350°F/175°C/gas 5.

Season the lamb generously with salt and especially pepper. Put the pieces, fatty side up, into a heavy roasting pan/tray large enough to hold them all in a single layer. Press the garlic and juniper berries into the top of the pieces, then scatter the rosemary and thyme over the pieces. Drizzle the oil over the top, then pour about ½ cup/120 milliliters water down the side of the pan.

Roast for about 45 minutes, then increase heat to 500°F/ 260°C/gas 10 and roast until the lamb is dark brown, 10 to 15 minutes more.

ROAST BABY LAMB

Abbacchio arrosto, as the Italians call roast baby lamb, is a springtime tradition throughout the country, especially from the center of the peninsula southward. It is particularly associated with Easter.

I WHOLE BABY LAMB, 12 TO 15 POUNDS/6 TO 7.5 KILOGRAMS, QUARTERED, WITH JOINTS CRACKED (ASK YOUR BUTCHER), AND TRIMMED OF EXCESS FAT

I CUP/240 MILLILITERS EXTRA-VIRGIN OLIVE OIL

CLOVES FROM 2 HEADS GARLIC, HALVED CROSSWISE

I½ CUPS/30 GRAMS FRESH ROSEMARY LEAVES

SALT AND PEPPER

4 POUNDS/2 KILOGRAMS FINGERLING POTATOES, HALVED OR QUARTERED

2 CUPS/480 MILLILITERS FRASCATI, ORVIETO, OR OTHER DRY WHITE WINE

Preheat the oven to 375°F/190°C/gas 5.

Make small incisions all over the meat with the tip of a paring knife. Rub the surfaces of the meat with 2 to 3 tablespoons of the oil, then push a piece of garlic and a few rosemary leaves into each incision. Season the lamb generously all over with salt and pepper.

Put the lamb, bone side down, into a large, heavy roasting pan/ tray. Crush any remaining garlic pieces and scatter them over the lamb. Roast for 30 minutes.

Meanwhile, in a large bowl, toss the potatoes with the remaining oil and rosemary.

When the lamb has roasted for 30 minutes, scatter the potatoes around it and stir to coat them with the pan juices. Pour the wine over the lamb, then continue roasting for about 1 hour more, basting occasionally with the pan juices. The lamb should be well done.

Remove the pan from the oven, transfer the lamb to a large warmed platter, and let rest for 15 to 20 minutes. Cover the potatoes and pan juices with aluminum foil to keep them warm.

Cut the lamb into pieces at the cracked joints. Add the potatoes to the platter with the lamb. Skim the fat from the pan juices, if any, and spoon the juices over the meat and potatoes to serve.

VEAL AND BEEF

SAVORY SUBSTANCE

My . . . recommendation is to put veal into your body in any way you can, since,
with all its good properties, you will find no healthier form of food.
—*Lorenzo Sassoli*, Lettera a Francesco Datini *(circa 1410)*

The only really good, tender meat to be found is *vitellone*, that is to say young beef.
—*Elizabeth David*, Italian Food, *quoting "an Italian friend"*

When you realize that many of Italy's greatest cheeses—including parmigiano-reggiano, fontina, taleggio, and most gorgonzola and mozzarella—are made from the milk of cows, and stop to think about how much pasturage beef cattle need (or at least needed in pre-feedlot days), it isn't really surprising that bovines have long been more valued in Italy as dairy animals than as a source of meat. Italian beef, in fact, has never had a very good reputation. I remember being taken aback to find, on my early trips to Italy, that the better restaurants often advertised on their menus that their steaks had come from Scotland or the United States. An exception is the fabled Chianina breed from Tuscany, massive and white, famous for producing the succulent meat most typically served in the region as bistecca alla fiorentina, Florentine-style grilled or oven-roasted T-bone. Interestingly, the Dante-spouting Tuscan celebrity butcher Dario Cecchini, from Panzano-in-Chianti, makes a point of not selling Chianina beef. He doesn't like it because he thinks it is being bred too lean. "In Italy, there is a phobia of fat [and] cholesterol," he writes on his Web site. "I do not use Chianina because I am not racist ["breedist" would be a better translation]." Instead, he buys beef raised by "a family of farmers in Catalonia [who are] butchers in the ancient tradition, giving me good meat with the right fat."

Veal is a different story. Veal might be called Italy's meat, being certainly the animal flesh most often associated with Italian cooking.

(Waverley Root even mentions a theory that the very name of Italy derived from the Latin word for it, *vitellus*, noting that this is "a theory not shared by modern etymologists." I should think not.) Why veal more than beef? Veal calves take much less time to raise than full-size beef cattle, obviously, and culling the calves is advantageous to the dairy industry. The line between veal and beef, however, was traditionally nowhere near as easily drawn in Italy as it usually is in other countries. Veal, at least theoretically milk-fed (though commercially raised today on formula), is called *vitello*; *vittelone*, "big veal," is slightly older (Federico Fellini adapted the term for his 1953 classic *I Vitelloni*, translating the term as young layabouts or mama's boys); *manzo* is young beef; *bue* is mature beef. The Romans, and probably later Italians as well, particularly prized the youngest veal of all: the meat of unborn calves cut from their mothers. You will be happy to hear that the consumption of such meat, called slink veal in English, is today banned in most countries, Italy included.

LIGURIAN VEAL ROLLS

✳

SERVES 4

Thin slices of veal wrapped around forcemeat or even just bread crumbs and herbs are popular along the French and Italian rivieras. The French sometimes call them oiseaux sans têtes, *"birds without heads," for their shape; the Italian version of the name is* uccellini *(or* osei*)* scappati, *"escaped birds," presumably because that's what they would be standing in for on the unsuccessful hunter's table. (The Sicilians eat* sarde a beccafico, *sardines similarly stuffed and rolled so that they are thought to resemble the "figpecker," that is, the common warbler.) In Liguria, on the other hand, veal rolls are called* tomaxelle, *which apparently comes from* tomaculum, *a Latin word for a kind of sausage. There is a story told that, when the Austrians and English besieged French-occupied Genoa in 1800, a group of captured Austrian officers was fed on tomaxelle and then released, so that they could report back that the city was in no danger of running out of food. (In fact, famine within the city's walls eventually led the French to surrender.) This recipe comes from the now-defunct Cà Peo restaurant in Leivi, above Chiavari.*

I TABLESPOON WHITE WINE VINEGAR

¼ POUND/125 GRAMS VEAL SWEETBREADS

5 TABLESPOONS/75 MILLILITERS EXTRA-VIRGIN OLIVE OIL

½ POUND/250 GRAMS LEAN VEAL, FINELY CHOPPED (NOT GROUND/MINCED)

I BAY LEAF

⅓ CUP/50 GRAMS PINE NUTS, MINCED

2 GARLIC CLOVES, MINCED

6 SPRIGS ITALIAN PARSLEY, MINCED

LEAVES FROM 3 SPRIGS MARJORAM OR OREGANO

I SLICE COUNTRY-STYLE BREAD, WITH CRUST, SOAKED IN I CUP/240 MILLILITERS VEAL BROTH (PAGE 373) OR COMMERCIAL BEEF BROTH

½ CUP/50 GRAMS GRATED PARMIGIANO-REGGIANO

5 EGGS

SALT AND PEPPER

FLOUR FOR DUSTING

12 VERY THIN SLICES VEAL, ABOUT 3 BY 4 INCHES/ 7.5 BY 10 CENTIMETERS (½ TO ¾ POUND/250 TO 375 GRAMS TOTAL WEIGHT)

Put the vinegar and 2 cups/480 milliliters water into a medium pot and bring to a boil over high heat. Reduce the heat to medium, add the sweetbreads, and blanch for 3 minutes. Drain the sweetbreads, peel them, cut out any veins or sinew, and cut the sweetbreads into three or four large pieces.

Heat half the oil in a large frying pan over medium heat. Add the sweetbreads, veal, and bay leaf and cook, stirring frequently, until the meats are lightly browned on all sides, 4 to 6 minutes. Add the pine nuts, garlic, parsley, and marjoram and mix them in thoroughly. Cook for 2 to 3 minutes more.

Gently squeeze the liquid out of the soaked bread, discarding the liquid. Finely chop the soaked bread. Remove and discard the bay leaf from the pan, then stir the chopped bread into the meat mixture, mixing well. Transfer the meat mixture to a food processor and process until smooth. Then transfer the meat mixture to a large bowl and stir in the cheese and eggs. Season generously with salt and pepper.

On a floured work surface, divide the meat mixture into 12 mounds of equal size. Put a slice of veal on the board, and put a mound of meat mixture in the middle of it. Smooth it down with your hand so that it extends to within about ¾ inch/ 2 centimeters of the edges on each side. Roll up each piece of veal to cover the mixture, then secure both ends of the roll with toothpicks, inserting them just beyond the filling.

Heat the remaining oil in a large frying pan over high heat. Working in batches if necessary, add the rolls and sauté them, turning them frequently, until golden brown on all sides, 4 to 6 minutes. Serve immediately.

VEAL STEW WITH RED PEPPERS AND BLACK OLIVES

Olives aren't typical in Abruzzese cooking, but I first encountered a dish like this, many decades ago, at a roadside trattoria in the region's southwestern corner, near Avezzano. I've reconstructed it from memory, fairly accurately I believe.

3 TABLESPOONS EXTRA-VIRGIN OLIVE OIL

2 POUNDS/1 KILOGRAM VEAL STEW MEAT OR RUMP ROAST, CUT INTO IRREGULAR PIECES, LARGER THAN BITE SIZE

1 ONION, VERY THINLY SLICED

1 GARLIC CLOVE, MINCED

¼ TEASPOON PEPERONCINI, OR TO TASTE

1 BAY LEAF

2 RED BELL PEPPERS, SEEDED, HALVED LENGTHWISE, AND VERY THINLY SLICED CROSSWISE

1 CUP/240 MILLILITERS DRY WHITE WINE

20 TO 24 BLACK ITALIAN OLIVES, PITTED AND HALVED

3 CUPS/720 MILLILITERS VEAL BROTH (PAGE 373) OR COMMERCIAL BEEF BROTH

SALT

Heat 2 tablespoons of the oil in a Dutch oven or other heavy pot over medium-high heat. Working in batches, add the veal and cook, turning the pieces frequently, until browned on all sides, 4 to 5 minutes. Transfer the veal to a plate and set aside.

Add the remaining 1 tablespoon oil to the pot, then add the onion, garlic, peperoncini, bay leaf, and peppers and stir well. Cook, stirring frequently, for about 3 minutes. Add the wine and continue cooking, stirring frequently, until the wine evaporates completely.

Return the veal to the pot, add the olives, broth, and about 1 teaspoon salt. Raise the heat to high and bring the broth to a boil. Immediately reduce the heat to low, cover, and let the stew simmer until the veal is tender but not disintegrating, about 1 hour. Adjust the seasoning before serving.

VEAL BREAST STUFFED WITH PARMIGIANO MOUSSE

This dish is a specialty at Ristorante Cocchi, my favorite restaurant in Parma, and involves a particularly interesting and delicious use of parmigiano-reggiano. (Please use the real thing, not a substitute.) Cocchi was kind enough to share its recipe with me.

1 CUP/60 GRAMS TOASTED BREAD CRUMBS, HOMEMADE (PAGE 378) OR COMMERCIAL

1 CUP/240 MILLILITERS VEAL BROTH (PAGE 373) OR COMMERCIAL BEEF BROTH

3 EGGS, LIGHTLY BEATEN

2 CUPS/200 GRAMS GRATED PARMIGIANO-REGGIANO

SALT

1 VEAL BREAST, 2½ TO 3 POUNDS/1.25 TO 1.5 KILOGRAMS, WITH A POCKET CUT INTO IT (ASK YOU BUTCHER)

⅔ BOTTLE DRY WHITE WINE

½ CUP/120 MILLILITERS EXTRA-VIRGIN OLIVE OIL

2 SPRIGS ROSEMARY

2 GARLIC CLOVES, CRUSHED

Put the bread crumbs into a large heatproof bowl. Heat the broth in a small pan just to a simmer over medium heat, then pour into the bread crumbs and mix well. Let the mixture cool for about 10 minutes, then mix in the eggs, cheese, and a pinch or two of salt.

Meanwhile, preheat the oven to 400°F/200°C/gas 6.

Fill the pocket in the veal breast with the stuffing and tie it shut in several places with kitchen twine. Put the veal breast into a baking dish large enough to hold it with a little room around the sides. Pour the wine and then the oil over the veal. Season the liquid generously with salt, then add the rosemary and garlic. Add water to cover the veal breast by about ½ inch/ 1.25 centimeters, then cover the baking dish and bake until exterior is dark golden brown, about 1½ hours.

Transfer the veal breast to a cutting board and let rest for 10 minutes. Snip the twine and carve into slices between the rib bones. Serve warm or at room temperature.

VEAL CHOPS VALDOSTANA

❋

SERVES 4

Fontina—the real thing, which has been made from raw cow's milk in the alpine reaches of the Valle d'Aosta for eight or nine hundred years—is one of Italy's great cheeses: aromatic, herbaceous, a little sweet. It also melts extremely well, and is used frequently in cooking, in its home region and beyond. I first encountered this classic preparation one October almost forty years ago at a little restaurant in the countryside near Saint-Vincent—I've long since forgotten its name— where slices of white truffle were added to the filling.

> 4 BONE-IN VEAL LOIN CHOPS, 6 TO 8 OUNCES/
> 175 TO 250 GRAMS EACH AND ABOUT 1 INCH/
> 2.5 CENTIMETERS THICK
>
> ¼ POUND /125 GRAMS MATURE (FIRM) FONTINA,
> THINLY SLICED
>
> SALT AND PEPPER
>
> 2 EGGS
>
> ½ CUP/65 GRAMS FLOUR
>
> 1 CUP/60 GRAMS TOASTED BREAD CRUMBS,
> HOMEMADE (PAGE 378) OR COMMERCIAL
>
> 6 TO 8 TABLESPOONS/90 TO 120 MILLIMETERS
> CLARIFIED BUTTER (PAGE 376)

With a sharp knife, carefully slice each veal chop in half horizontally to within ½ inch/1.25 centimeters of the bone. Divide the cheese slices evenly between the chops, slipping them in between the halves. With a meat mallet or the bottom of a clean, flat-bottomed wine bottle, gently pound the edges of each chop together.

Season the chops generously on both sides with salt and pepper. Lightly beat the eggs in a shallow bowl, put the flour into a second shallow bowl, and put the bread crumbs into a third bowl. Melt the butter in a frying pan large enough to hold all the chops over medium-high heat. One at a time, dredge the chops in the flour, dip them in the eggs, and then dredge them in the bread crumbs, shaking off the excess each time. Add to the hot butter and fry, turning once, until golden brown on both sides, 2 to 3 minutes per side.

Reduce the heat to low and cook, turning once, until tender and the cheese has melted, about 20 minutes more. Serve immediately.

ROAST VEAL LOIN

❋

SERVES 6

This simple preparation is a standard all over Italy, but especially from Rome north.

> 3 TABLESPOONS BUTTER
>
> 3 TABLESPOONS EXTRA-VIRGIN OLIVE OIL
>
> 1 BONELESS VEAL LOIN OR ROUND ROAST,
> 3 POUNDS/1.5 KILOGRAMS, TIED
>
> SALT AND PEPPER
>
> 1 GARLIC CLOVE, CRUSHED
>
> 1 ONION, CHOPPED
>
> 1 BAY LEAF
>
> 1 TABLESPOON ROSEMARY LEAVES
>
> ½ CUP/120 MILLILITERS VEAL BROTH (PAGE 373)
> OR COMMERCIAL BEEF BROTH
>
> 1 CUP/240 MILLILITERS DRY WHITE WINE

Preheat the oven to 325°F/160°C/gas 3.

Melt the butter with the oil in a heavy roasting pan/tray just large enough to hold the veal over medium-high heat. Season the veal generously with salt and pepper, add to the pan and cook, turning it frequently, until well browned on all sides, 6 to 8 minutes.

Add the garlic, onion, bay leaf, and rosemary to the pan, then add the broth. Roast the veal, turning it several times and basting it three or four times with the pan juices, until tender, about 1½ hours.

Transfer the veal to a cutting board and let rest for about 10 minutes before carving.

Meanwhile, transfer the roasting pan to the stove top and deglaze it with the wine over high heat, scraping up the browned bits on the bottom. Cook until the liquid has reduced by half, 2 to 3 minutes. Strain the sauce into a small bowl.

Snip the twine, carve the veal, and arrange the slices on a warmed platter. Spoon the sauce over the slices before serving.

SAY NEIGH

I stopped to eat at a nondescript trattoria outside Ferrara, in Emilia-Romagna, one day and saw something on the menu called *tagliatelle al sugo di somarino*. I didn't recognize that last word and asked the waiter what it was. *"Carne,"* he replied. Meat. I ordered the dish and enjoyed it very much; the *sugo* (sauce) was indeed meaty, with a faint sweetness and plenty of flavor. Back in my hotel later, I looked up the word *somarino* and discovered that what I had eaten was young donkey. It occurred to me that the waiter might well have thought it was funny (or have been trying to protect my sensibilities) by not telling me exactly what somarino was—but I wouldn't have minded a bit. I take care never to mention this around my elder daughter, who is an equestrian, but I quite like horsemeat and donkey meat and have eaten plenty of both over the years in various parts of Europe. (I even remember a horsemeat butcher years ago across from Seattle's Pike Place Market. This must have been one of the last ones in America, and it has been gone for decades; the sale and consumption of horsemeat is illegal in some states today and strongly frowned on just about everywhere in America and the United Kingdom.) Both donkey and horse seem to be popular around Ferrara, and donkey is eaten grilled and in pasta sauce in Sardinia, especially around Sassari.

Donkey also finds favor in Piedmont, where not only the beast itself but also a sausage and a stew made from it are called *tapulon*. Tapulon even figures in a kind of creation myth for the town of Borgomanero, in the mountains of Novara: According to the story, a group of pilgrims were returning from the Sacro Monte (a devotional complex) of San Francesco, near Orta San Giulio, and found themselves low on provisions when they stopped for the night. They decided to slaughter their pack donkey and stew its flesh with some wine they were carrying. They ate their dinner, washed down with more wine, and fell asleep. Awakening at their campsite in the morning, they realized how beautiful the spot was and decided to found a town there. Rather more recently, resistance fighters hiding from the Germans in the mountains of Piedmont during World War II, reportedly forced to eat donkey meat out of necessity, came to genuinely enjoy it, and brought a taste for it into postwar society.

Horsemeat is particularly popular in Trentino, Friuli, and the Veneto. The Veronese likely started eating it in the fifth century, to take advantage of the slain animals that littered the landscape after Visigoths came through. (The meat is said to be two to three times higher in lactic acid than other kinds of animal flesh, so is slower to spoil.) I think the first time I ate horsemeat in Italy—I had already had it in Belgium—was probably at 12 Apostoli in Verona, where one of the specialties used to be pastissada de caval, a kind of lasagna with horsemeat ragout, a dish to which early medieval origins are imputed. The town of Saonara, near Padua, is noted for its horsemeat salumi, and for a kind of bresaola (air-dried meat) made from horseflesh. I also remember an excellent horsemeat tartare at a bustling trattoria in the Tuscan city of Lucca. Italians in other parts of the country eat equines too, of course. Patience Gray once wrote that the horse butchers on the Salentine Peninsula in Calabria were more skilled than regular ones.

ROAST VEAL WITH CHESTNUTS

SERVES 4 TO 6

I'm not sure where I got this recipe, though it is possibly from Emilia-Romagna. I found it in a folder of notes from a drive I took in the early 1980s from Milan down to Piacenza and then to Parma. I have no recollection of having eaten this dish, and I never tried to cook it until recently. But I liked the results when I did, and it's an unusual preparation, so I pass it along herewith. See page 382 for a source for roasted peeled chestnuts.

3 TABLESPOONS BUTTER

I TABLESPOON EXTRA-VIRGIN OLIVE OIL

I BONELESS VEAL LOIN ROAST, ABOUT 2 POUNDS/
I KILOGRAM, TIED

I ONION, FINELY CHOPPED

I GARLIC CLOVE, MINCED

I BAY LEAF

I CUP/240 MILLILITERS DRY WHITE WINE

I CUP/240 MILLILITERS WHOLE MILK

I CUP/240 MILLILITERS VEAL BROTH (PAGE 373)
OR COMMERCIAL BEEF BROTH

SALT

16 TO 20 BOILED OR ROASTED AND PEELED
CHESTNUTS, COARSELY CHOPPED

Melt the butter with the oil in a Dutch oven or other heavy pot over medium-high heat. Add the veal and cook, turning frequently, until browned on all sides, 6 to 8 minutes. Reduce the heat to medium and add the onion, garlic, and bay leaf. Cook, stirring occasionally, until the onion softens, 6 to 8 minutes.

Add the wine and cook, stirring frequently and turning the veal several times, until the wine evaporates, 8 to 10 minutes. Add the milk and broth and season generously with salt. Cover the pot, reduce the heat to low, and cook the veal, turning it several times, until tender, about 1½ hours.

Transfer the veal to a cutting board, tent lightly with aluminum foil, and let rest while you prepare the chestnuts.

Add the chestnuts to the cooking liquid in the pot, raise the heat to medium-high, and cook, uncovered, until the sauce thickens and the chestnuts are heated through, 6 to 8 minutes.

Snip the twine, carve the veal, and arrange the slices on a warmed platter. Spoon the chestnuts and sauce over the slices to serve.

BRASATO

SERVES 6 TO 8

Brasato is basically Italian pot roast; the name means "braised," and, this being Italy, the braising liquid is always wine. When the term is used as a noun, it always means that beef will be the main ingredient; as an adjective, it can be applied to pork, lamb, chicken, rabbit, fish, even vegetables. I've had wonderful examples of brasato—beef—all over northern Italy, and though the recipes vary somewhat, I'm tempted to say that the main difference between them is the variety of wine that is used. I had one very good interpretation, at a little trattoria in Valpolicella in the Veneto, based on that region's famous high-proof Amarone. But brasato is really a dish of Piedmont and Liguria (in the latter place, dried porcini mushrooms, the secret ingredient of Genoese cuisine, are typically added), and in those places the wine is traditionally Barolo, though a good regional Nebbiolo or Barbera is likely to be employed these days. I had a particularly good brasato in the Ligurian backcountry, at the surprisingly elegant Manuel in Camporosso; this is my approximation of their recipe. Serve with fried polenta (see Polenta with Porcini, page 135, for a basic method), if you like.

I BOTTLE NEBBIOLO D'ALBA, BARBERA D'ALBA,
OR BARBERA D'ASTI

2 ONIONS, FINELY CHOPPED

2 CARROTS, FINELY CHOPPED

2 STALKS CELERY, FINELY CHOPPED

2 GARLIC CLOVES, MINCED

2 SPRIGS ROSEMARY

6 TO 8 SPRIGS MARJORAM OR OREGANO

2 BAY LEAVES

3 CUPS/720 MILLILITER VEAL BROTH (PAGE 373)
OR COMMERCIAL BEEF BROTH

¾ CUP/180 MILLILITERS EXTRA-VIRGIN OLIVE OIL

I BONELESS CROSS-RIB BEEF ROAST, 4 POUNDS/
2 KILOGRAMS

SALT AND PEPPER

Put the wine, onions, carrots, celery, garlic, rosemary, marjoram, bay leaves, broth, and ¼ cup/60 milliliters of the oil into a Dutch oven or other heavy pot. Season the roast generously all over with salt and pepper and add it to the pot. Bring the liquid to a boil over high heat, then immediately reduce the heat to low, cover, and simmer, turning the meat about every 30 minutes, until the meat is tender, about 4 hours.

Remove the meat from the pot and set it aside, loosely tented with aluminum foil. Remove and discard the rosemary and marjoram sprigs and bay leaves from the pot. Strain the broth into a bowl and set the broth and the vegetables aside separately.

Heat ¼ cup/60 milliliters of the oil in a large frying pan over medium-high heat. Add the vegetables and 1 cup/240 milliliters of the broth (reserve the rest for another use), mash the vegetables with a potato masher, and cook, stirring frequently, until the liquid evaporates, 6 to 8 minutes. Add the remaining ¼ cup/60 milliliters oil and cook until the mixture begins to fry, 5 to 6 minutes. Season with salt and pepper.

Carve the meat and arrange the slices on a platter. Spoon the sauce over the slices to serve.

PEPOSO
(TUSCAN PEPPERY BEEF STEW)

SERVES 4

Credit for the invention of this legendary dish is claimed by almost every Tuscan town that has a tile-making factory, with Impruneta, a dozen miles/twenty kilometers or so south of Florence, making the most vociferous case for itself. One thing everybody seems to agree on is that it was a dish originally slow cooked in a cooling kiln; indeed, it was sometimes called peposo notturno, *"nocturnal peposo," because it stewed overnight. (Some dishes on the glass-blowing Venetian island of Murano were similarly cooked in the furnaces as they cooled.) One story is that it was first made by craftsmen installing tiles on Brunelleschi's dome for the Florentine cathedral of Santa Maria del Fiore. They were supposedly paid at least partially in peppercorns, and so put them to good use. Peposo almost always has tomato paste or tomato sauce in it today, but if we are to honor its supposed (pre-Columbian) Brunelleschian beginnings, we should leave it out. Authentic peposo is unusual, too, because it is one Italian stew that doesn't begin with a soffritto (see page 64), and so contains no olive oil. A variation on the dish is made with pork.*

2 POUNDS/1 KILOGRAM BEEF STEW MEAT

12 GARLIC CLOVES

2 TABLESPOONS CRUSHED (NOT GROUND) PEPPERCORNS

SALT

1 CUP/240 MILLILITERS TOMATO SAUCE, HOMEMADE (PAGE 371) OR COMMERCIAL (OPTIONAL)

1 BOTTLE CHIANTI

BRUSCHETTA (PAGE 37), OPTIONAL

Preheat the oven to 275°F/135°C/gas ½.

Put the beef and garlic into a Dutch oven or other heavy oven-proof pot, sprinkle with the peppercorns, and season generously with salt. Spoon the tomato sauce over the top (if using), then pour in the Chianti just to cover all the ingredients. You may not need all of it.

Bake for 6 hours without opening the Dutch oven. The meat should be very tender and the sauce very thick. Continue baking for 1 to 2 hours more if neccesary.

Serve over bruschetta, if you like.

PARTY TIME

A *sagra* (from the Latin *sacer*, "dedicated" or "holy") is a festival staged in honor of some local foodstuff or food product or dish. Almost every town and village in Italy seems to have an annual sagra (some have more than one), lasting for a day or more, and usually involving speeches, dancing, food-themed competitions, parades and/or fireworks, and the like, along with the ritual consumption of the comestible being feted. Organizers often claim some ancient provenance for their sagra, and it's not unlikely that agricultural fairs or harvest celebrations have been around for centuries. The modern-style sagra, though, with its elements of small-town boosterism and often some commercial tie-in, is a comparatively recent invention. I doubt that there were very many, if any, until the late 1950s. Today, they are ubiquitous, a kind of fad; it's as if no municipality expects to be taken seriously in food-loving Italy if it doesn't have something edible to acknowledge.

Sagre are usually staged on weekends, and are sometimes attached to civic or religious holidays. There are sagre devoted to cherries, lemons, chestnuts, strawberries, peaches, grapes (and also wine— a lot of those); peas, artichokes, beans, peas, new potatoes, eggplants/aubergines, zucchini/courgettes, hot chiles, snails, wild boar, cuttlefish, tuna, olive oil (a lot of those, too), tripe, honey, nougat. Every July, Tresigallo, in Emilia-Romagna, holds its Sagra del Somarino, honoring young donkey (for eating). Many sagre hail specific dishes—ravioli, gnocchi, bollito misto, polenta and sausage, minestrone. Agliano Terme in Piedmont has one for trout cooked on a stone; San Marco dei Cavoti in Campania celebrates a "festa of the oven" and a sagra of homestyle bread and white pizza simultaneously (the distinction between a festa and a sagra is not clear). Follo, in Liguria, even stages a sagra dedicated to a non-Italian dish: its Sagra dell'Asado revolves around Argentinean-style roasted meats, the technique for which was brought home by Ligurian emigrants who had ventured to South America for employment. Sagre can be crowded tourist spectacles, but they can also be great fun—opportunities to taste authentic regional cooking in colorful, vibrant surroundings.

OPPOSITE: *The Festa degli Gnocchi, Guastalla, Emilia-Romagna, 1921.*

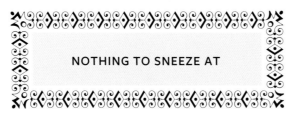

NOTHING TO SNEEZE AT

Some sources credit Alexander the Great with having brought black pepper (the berry of the vine called *Piper nigrum*) back to Greece from its native India, and it seems to have traveled from Greece to Rome, where it quickly found an enthusiastic following. (The majority of the recipes in *De re coquinaria* [see page 39] employ it.) Because it came from so far away and could not be successfully cultivated around the Mediterranean, pepper was an expensive commodity. Pliny the Elder mentions it in the first century, but he failed to see its culinary appeal and made a snide remark about the wisdom of trading gold for weeds. When the Visigoths and Huns besieged Rome in the fifth century, both demanded the spice as a part of their tribute. After Vasco da Gama sailed around the Horn of Africa in 1498, establishing a direct sea route to India, the Portuguese became Europe's pepper sellers, briefly maintaining a monopoly on the trade until the Venetians, and later the Dutch and the English, began to take over. Medieval cooking in Italy is full of pepper, and of preparations with names that announce its presence, like *peperata*, *peverada*, and *peposo* (see pages 217 and 260), and it remains a common spice in Italy today, as elsewhere around the world.

One thing pepper was probably never used for, some sources to the contrary, was to cover up the smell or taste of rotten meat. To begin with, it was too expensive to use on a large scale, and anyone who could have afforded a lot of it would surely have been able to afford fresh meat as well. More to the point, though, it simply wouldn't have worked. My friend Charles Perry pointed this out to me many years ago: "The next time you have a piece of meat that's gone bad," he said, "pour all the pepper you want on it. I guarantee you it will still smell the same."

GAME

THE FLAVORS OF THE HUNT

Italians fancy themselves as hunters. In Carrara there were 15,000 men
with gun permits and about six small birds.
—*Patience Gray*, Honey from a Weed

Chi va a caccia senza cani, torna a casa senza lepri.
[Those who hunt without dogs come home without hares.]
—*Tuscan proverb*

One wintry afternoon, twenty years ago or so, tramping across a hilltop in Togliano, near Cividale del Friuli, I came upon an eerie deserted parthenon of trees with a vacant two-story shack at one end. Was this the playing field for some obscure Friulian ball game? The site of some pre-Christian ritual? No, I later learned, it was an *uccellanda*, an elaborate setup for trapping game birds. A ceiling of nets would be hung between the trees, covering the clearing,

and caged birds would be set down in the middle of the field. Other birds, drawn by the singing of the unwilling Judases, would flock under the nets to join them, at which point someone would fire a single shot from the shack and the birds, scared, would fly blindly up into the nets above and be captured. A thousand or more little birds—ortolans, starlings—could be captured in a single day by this method. We think of hunting as shooting, but when the purpose of capturing wild birds and hooved animals was sustenance, not sport, anything was fair. I remember vividly an Italian Renaissance painting, hanging in the Palais des Papes in Avignon, depicting servants brushing tree branches with glue—to capture any birds unfortunate enough to land on them. Waverley Root mentions that medieval records from a bank in Perugia record a loan of "40 pieces" for a machine for catching thrushes, technique unspecified.

Even after all the usual creatures had been domesticated in Italy—ducks, chickens, geese, goats, sheep, pigs, cattle—wild game, known collectively in Italian as *caccia* (the word, which means hunting as well as what's caught, derives from the Latin *captiare*, "to chase"), remained extremely popular. In their book *Italian Cuisine: A Cultural History*, Alberto Capatti and Massimo Montanari quote a sixteenth-century work by Cristoforo Messisbugo, steward to the Ferrarese-born cardinal Ippolito d'Este, in which he catalogs the meats that should be made available to a noble table: "wild and domestic boar, stag, deer, roe buck, lamb, kid, wether, suckling pig, hares, rabbits, dormice, peacocks, wild and domestic pheasants, partridge, rock partridge, francolin [a relative of the pheasant], thrush, gray partridge, woodcock, ortolans, . . . herons, snipe, wild and domestic duck, large, medium, and small-sized teal, plover and other fowl." Fox and badger were also eaten (in *Honey from a Weed*, Patience Gray gives a recipe for braised fox in the Tuscan manner from "an old anarchist in Carrara"). In the Po delta wetlands around Codigoro in Emilia-Romagna, there was an old specialty of risotto with folaga (coot), a fish-eating aquatic bird that is said to have a fishy, muddy flavor. The Venetians say it must be skinned and soaked for at least a day in wine and water to render it edible.

Hare is hunted all over Italy, and there is some deer hunting in Tuscany and elsewhere. Ibex and chamois are shot in the Valle d'Aosta, and sometimes find their way onto local menus. Wild boar is practically a religion in the Maremma, in southwestern Tuscany, and is hunted and consumed with great enthusiasm in Sardinia. The town of Gemmano, near San Marino in far southeastern Emilia-Romagna, celebrates the beast with an annual festival dedicated to pappardelle with boar meat.

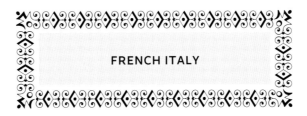

FRENCH ITALY

When I first pulled off the road leading up to the tunnel of Gran San Bernardo (or Grand-Saint-Bernard), which burrows through the Alps connecting Italy with Switzerland, and drove slowly, in heavy snow, through the town of Étroubles, I thought I was in France. The name of the place sounded French, to begin with, and the names of businesses were all in French. The restaurant I pulled up in front of looked like a mountain house on the outskirts of Chamonix or in French-speaking Switzerland (both of which are nearby), with tall, slanted roofs reaching almost down into the snowbanks. The menu was in French and Italian, and my lunch, a dense pork stew, was as Gallic as could be. I wasn't in France, of course: I was in the Valle d'Aosta, the smallest of Italy's twenty regions. Surely, I thought, the area must have belonged to France (or Switzerland) at one time, just as the Trentino–Alto Adige region belonged to Austria until politics redrew the borders.

But as I spent more time in this beautiful, if not well-known, corner of Italy, eating its hearty stews and game dishes and sampling its excellent wines—made from familiar grapes like Pinot Noir, Gamay, and Muscat, as well as less familiar ones like Petit Rouge, Blanc de Morgex, and Vien de Nus—I learned that this wasn't true. The French occupied the Valle d'Aosta for a period of only about twenty-five years, in the mid-sixteenth century. It was, however, conquered successively by the Burgundians and the Franks, before being given to the House of Savoy in 1031. It remained in Savoyard hands, becoming part of the Kingdom of Sardinia (along with Piedmont and Liguria) until 1861, when it became part of the newly consolidated Kingdom of Italy. The Savoyards, whose capital was Turin, were largely French speaking, and the language was widely used in the Valle d'Aosta while they were in charge. The region has its own language, though, Valdôtain, a relative of Provençal, and you will sometimes hear this spoken in the streets. Just to mix things up, the Valle d'Aosta also boasts a minority of German-speaking Swiss from the Valais.

QUAIL WITH ARTICHOKES

SERVES 4

In her book The Food of Rome and Lazio, *Oretta Zanini De Vita ascribes this dish to Tuscia, a historical region that now mostly coincides with the province of Viterbo but once included portions of Umbria and Tuscany as well. I've spent time around Viterbo and never encountered quail with artichokes, but the recipe intrigued me and the results were delicious.*

JUICE OF 2 LEMONS

8 MEDIUM ARTICHOKES

8 QUAIL, PREFERABLY WILD

8 LARGE, THIN SLICES PROSCIUTTO DI PARMA OR OTHER GOOD-QUALITY PROSCIUTTO

3 TABLESPOONS EXTRA-VIRGIN OLIVE OIL

1 CUP/240 MILLILITERS DRY RED WINE

2 GARLIC CLOVES, CRUSHED

¼ CUP/60 MILLILITERS CHICKEN BROTH, HOMEMADE (PAGE 372) OR COMMERCIAL

Mix together the lemon juice and 2 to 3 cups/480 to 720 milliliters water in a medium bowl.

Cut the stems off the artichokes. Follow this whole process with 1 artichoke at a time: Pull off the tough outer leaves by hand, then trim off more layers of leaves with a sharp knife until only the tenderest leaves, or heart, remains. Scoop out and discard the chokes, slice the hearts into four or six lengthwise wedges (depending on their size), and immediately put them in the acidulated water to stop them from turning black.

Wrap each quail in a slice of prosciutto. Heat the oil in a large frying pan with a cover over medium-high heat. Add the quail and fry, turning frequently, until lightly browned on all sides, 4 to 6 minutes. Deglaze the pan with the wine, scraping up the browned bits on the bottom.

Reduce the heat to low, add the artichokes, garlic, and broth, cover the pan, and braise the quail until just cooked through, 15 to 20 minutes. Serve immediately.

PARTRIDGE WITH CABBAGE

SERVES 4

This is a typical preparation of partridge in the Carnic Alps, in Friuli, north of Udine, near the Austrian and Slovenian borders. See page 382 for a source for wild partridge.

4 PARTRIDGES, 8 TO 10 OUNCES/250 TO 315 GRAMS EACH

SALT AND PEPPER

4 LARGE, THIN SLICES PROSCIUTTO DI SAN DANIELE OR OTHER GOOD-QUALITY PROSCIUTTO

½ CUP/125 GRAMS BUTTER

¼ POUND/125 GRAMS PANCETTA, CUT INTO ½-INCH/1.25-CENTIMETER CUBES

1 SMALL HEAD SAVOY CABBAGE, ABOUT ¾ POUND/375 GRAMS, CORED AND SHREDDED

1 ONION, THINLY SLICED

4 SAGE LEAVES, MINCED

8 JUNIPER BERRIES, CRUSHED

¼ CUP/60 MILLILITERS GRAPPA

½ CUP/120 MILLILITERS CHICKEN BROTH, HOMEMADE (PAGE 372) OR COMMERCIAL

Preheat the oven to 400°F/200°C/gas 6.

Season the partridges generously with salt and pepper, then wrap each bird in a slice of prosciutto. Put the partridges, breast side up, in a roasting pan/tray just large enough to hold them.

Roast the partridges until the prosciutto is lightly browned, 12 to 15 minutes. Remove the partridges from the oven and set them aside.

Meanwhile, melt the butter in a Dutch oven or other heavy pot over medium heat. Add the pancetta and cook, stirring frequently, until it has browned, 6 to 8 minutes. Add the cabbage, onion, sage, and juniper berries and cook, stirring frequently, until the cabbage has wilted, 10 to 12 minutes. Add the grappa and cook for about 5 minutes more, then stir in the broth. Reduce the heat to low, cover, and cook until sauce has thickened, about 45 minutes.

Add the partridges, breast side up, to the Dutch oven, re-cover, and cook until the partridges are done, 15 to 20 minutes. Partridges should be served slightly pink; to test for doneness, insert a fork between the breast and the thigh; the juices should run slightly pink.

To serve, divide the cabbage evenly between 4 warmed plates, and put 1 partridge on top of each serving.

STUFFED PHEASANT, FRIULI STYLE

SERVES 6 TO 8

I find domestically raised pheasant to be dry and flavorless most of the time, but the wild kind can be very good. See page 382 for a source for fresh wild pheasant in season, frozen the rest of the year.

2 THICK SLICES COUNTRY-STYLE BREAD, CRUSTS TRIMMED AND SOAKED IN 1 CUP/240 MILLILITERS WHOLE MILK

½ POUND/250 GRAMS GROUND/MINCED VEAL

4 CHICKEN LIVERS, OR 2 CHICKEN LIVERS AND 2 PHEASANT LIVERS, TRIMMED AND FINELY CHOPPED

¼ POUND/125 GRAMS FRESH PORCINI OR OTHER WILD MUSHROOMS, FINELY CHOPPED

6 TO 8 SAGE LEAVES, MINCED

6 TO 8 SPRIGS ITALIAN PARSLEY, MINCED

SALT AND PEPPER

1 EGG, LIGHTLY BEATEN

2 PHEASANTS, 1½ TO 2 POUNDS/750 GRAMS TO 1 KILOGRAM EACH

4 TABLESPOONS/60 GRAMS BUTTER

¼ CUP/60 MILLILITERS EXTRA-VIRGIN OLIVE OIL

1 CUP/240 MILLILITERS FRIULIAN MERLOT OR OTHER DRY RED WINE

¼ CUP/60 MILLILITERS GRAPPA

2 BAY LEAVES

Squeeze the milk out of the bread and place the bread in a medium bowl. Add the veal, livers, mushrooms, sage, and parsley and mix to combine. Season the mixture generously with salt and pepper, then mix in the egg.

Season the pheasants generously inside and out with salt and pepper. Divide the stuffing equally between the cavities of both birds, packing it in firmly. Put the butter and oil in a Dutch oven or other heavy ovenproof pot large enough to hold the birds side by side and place over medium-high heat. When the butter has melted, add the pheasants and cook, turning as needed, until browned on all sides, about 10 minutes. (If it is easier to turn them, brown 1 bird at a time. Be careful not to let the stuffing fall out.)

Meanwhile, preheat the oven to 350°F/175°C/gas 5.

Put the pheasants side by side, breast side up, in the Dutch oven. Pour the wine and then the grappa over them, then put the bay leaves into the liquid. Cover the pot, place in the oven, and cook, basting occasionally, for 1¾ hours.

Uncover the Dutch oven and cook, continuing to baste, until the birds are deep brown, about 15 minutes longer. Serve immediately.

PHEASANT WITH FIGS

SERVES 4

I had this dish years ago at a restaurant near Oristano, in Sardinian Muscat country. See page 382 for a source for fresh wild pheasant in season, frozen the rest of the year.

6 TABLESPOONS/90 GRAMS BUTTER

SALT AND PEPPER

1 PHEASANT, 1½ TO 2 POUNDS/750 GRAMS TO 1 KILOGRAM

10 FRESH FIGS, QUARTERED LENGTHWISE

JUICE OF 1 LEMON

1 CUP/240 MILLILITERS SARDINIAN OR OTHER SWEET MUSCAT

Preheat the oven to 350°F/175°C/gas 5.

Melt half the butter in a small saucepan over low heat, then season it generously with salt and pepper. Brush the seasoned butter all over the pheasant, inside and out.

Put the pheasant on a rack set in a roasting pan/tray and roast for 30 minutes.

Meanwhile, melt the remaining butter in a medium frying pan over medium heat. Add the figs and cook, stirring frequently, until they begin to soften, 6 to 8 minutes. Stir in the lemon juice and wine and season with salt and pepper. Cook for about 10 minutes more, then remove from the heat.

When the pheasant has finished roasting for 30 minutes, pour the figs and their butter over the bird. Continue roasting the pheasant, basting occasionally with the pan juices, until done, about 20 minutes longer. To test for doneness, insert a fork between the breast and the thigh; the juices should run clear. Serve immediately.

WILD BOAR STEAKS WITH JUNIPER-CURRANT SAUCE

SERVES 4

This recipe comes from the hinterlands around Bolzano in the Alto Adige. Unless you're a hunter, you won't have access to real wild boar in the United States, but the meat of free-range wild pigs (Sus scrofa) is available; see page 382 for a source.

4 TABLESPOONS/60 MILLILITERS EXTRA-VIRGIN OLIVE OIL

2 GARLIC CLOVES, MINCED

8 JUNIPER BERRIES

LEAVES FROM 1 SPRIG ROSEMARY

SALT AND PEPPER

4 WILD BOAR TENDERLOIN STRIPS, EACH ABOUT 6 OUNCES/175 GRAMS AND 1½ INCHES/ 3.75 CENTIMETERS THICK

¾ CUP/180 MILLILITERS ITALIAN MERLOT OR OTHER DRY RED WINE

¾ CUP/180 MILLILITERS VEAL BROTH (PAGE 373) OR COMMERCIAL BEEF BROTH

4 TEASPOONS RED CURRANT JELLY

2 TABLESPOONS COLD BUTTER, CUT INTO CUBES

BASIC POLENTA (PAGE 131), SOFT AND WARM, OR BUTTERED NOODLES (OPTIONAL)

Combine 2 tablespoons of the oil, the garlic, juniper berries, rosemary, and plenty of salt and pepper in a shallow dish large enough to hold the boar steaks in a single layer. Put the steaks into the marinade, turn to coat them on all sides, cover the dish with plastic wrap/cling film, and set aside for 2 to 3 hours at room temperature.

Remove the steaks from the marinade, discarding the marinade. Heat the remaining 2 tablespoons oil in a large frying pan over medium heat. Add the steaks and cook, turning once, just until tender, about 3 minutes per side. Transfer to a warmed plate, tent lightly with aluminum foil, and set aside.

Pour off the oil from the frying pan, then wipe it out with a paper towel. Add the wine and cook over medium heat until it is reduced by half, 1 to 2 minutes. Reduce the heat to medium-low, add the broth and the jelly, and stir well. Continue cooking for about 3 minutes, then whisk in the butter. Season the sauce with salt and pepper.

Return the steaks to the pan and cook for about 1 minute to heat through, then remove from the pan. Serve the steaks with the sauce on the side and accompanied by polenta, if you like.

SLOW-ROASTED WILD BOAR, SARDINIAN STYLE

SERVES 6

"Sardinian wild boar," Tobias Smollett noted back in the 1760s, *"although a little dry, certainly has a most excellent flavour."* This typically Sardinian method of cooking will help keep the meat moist. See page 382 for a source for wild pig.

½ CUP/120 MILLILITERS EXTRA-VIRGIN OLIVE OIL

JUICE OF 1 LEMON

1 ONION, THICKLY SLICED

2 GARLIC CLOVES, CRUSHED

6 JUNIPER BERRIES, CRUSHED

6 WHOLE CLOVES

1 BAY LEAF

2 WILD BOAR KNUCKLE ROASTS, 1½ POUNDS/ 750 GRAMS EACH, TIED

SALT AND PEPPER

2 TABLESPOONS LARD OR RENDERED BACON FAT

½ CUP/120 MILLILITERS SARDINIAN VERMENTINO OR OTHER DRY WHITE WINE

2 TABLESPOONS ROSEMARY LEAVES

Combine the oil, lemon juice, onion, garlic, juniper berries, cloves, and bay leaf in a medium bowl. Cover and refrigerate for 24 hours.

Transfer the marinade to a bowl or baking dish just large enough to hold the boar roasts side by side. Put the boar roasts into the marinade, turning them several times to coat them well, then cover and refrigerate for 24 hours, turning the meat about every 8 hours.

Preheat the oven to 300°F/150°C/gas 2.

Remove the boar from the marinade, discarding the marinade. Pat the meat dry with paper towels, then season generously all over with salt and pepper. Put the roasts into a roasting pan/ tray just large enough to hold them side by side without touching. Put the lard and the wine into the pan (not over the boar). Scatter the rosemary over the top of the meat.

Roast the meat, basting with the pan juices about every 30 minutes, until an instant-meat thermometer inserted into the center of a roast without touching bone registers 185°F/85°C, 1½ to 2 hours.

Snip the twine and let rest for 10 minutes before carving and serving.

AUSTRIAN ITALY

The streets of Merano are lined with gingerbread houses and alpine chalets. German is heard and seen as often as Italian. There is excellent wine made nearby, but much of the local citizenry seems to prefer lusty dark beer quaffed from oversize steins, and at least some of them sport lederhosen and feather-garnished Tyrolean hats. Well, fair enough, because though Merano is in Italy, it is also in the Tyrol—the South Tyrol, to be precise. The modern Italian region called Trentino–Alto Adige (and formerly known as Venezia Tridentina) has been part of Italy only since 1919; before that, at least since the late four-teenth century, it was part of the Austrian or Austro-Hungarian Empire.

Trentino–Alto Adige is divided into two prov-inces: Trento, to the south, is primarily Italian speak-ing today, despite its Austrian heritage. Its capital city is also called Trento, which I first became distantly aware of as a Catholic schoolboy (the Council of Trent, in the mid-sixteenth century, defined much of the Church doctrine I grew up with). The city of Bolzano-Bolzen is the capital of the more northerly portion of the region, Alto Adige—also known as the Südtirol—which borders Switzerland and Austria and which is also the province of Bolzano-Bolzen. (Both city and province officially bear both the Italian and German forms of the name.) Like Merano, a smaller city to the northwest, Bolzano has a distinctly Tyrolean feeling to it, and the food is hearty and Teutonic.

The region is famous for its game dishes and its sausages and other cured meats, most notably the superb smoked prosciutto known as speck. The most famous (notorious?) specialty of the area, though,

may well be the *piatto elefante*, or *Elefantenplatten*—the "elephant plate." One version of its story is that in 1551, the king of Portugal sent an elephant, appar-ently named Solomon, from Portuguese Goa in India as a gift to his nephew, the Archduke Maximilian II of Austria (later to become the Holy Roman Emperor). The beast and his keepers made it as far as Bressa-none (Brixen), northeast of Bolzano, on their way to the Brenner Pass and Vienna beyond, before get-ting snowed in. The elephant ended up spending two weeks there in late December and early January behind an inn called Herberge am Hohen Feld (Hostal in the High Field). When he left to continue his journey, the inn capitalized on the affair by renaming itself Am Hellephanten and introducing an "elephant plate" to its menu. This was considered a one-dish meal, even though it was served on two or three separate platters. The original was said to include at least six kinds of meat and a dozen varieties of vegetables. One account describes a version that involved a mountain of anti-pasto followed by steaks, pork chops, mutton chops, boiled ham, grilled liver, grilled kidneys, chunks of suckling pig, thick slices of speck, and several sorts of sausage, as well as rice, sauerkraut, four kinds of pota-toes, noodles, carrots, peas, asparagus, spinach, grilled tomatoes, zucchini/courgettes, white beans, cucum-bers, several cheeses, three kinds of cake, and both fresh and stewed fruit.

Am Hellephanten became the Hotel Elephant and exists to this day, still serving a version of the ele-phant plate on special request. Solomon the elephant, incidentally, reached Vienna in May of 1552, and died about eighteen months later in the royal menagerie.

TYROLEAN VENISON GOULASH

※

SERVES 4 TO 6

The paprika-flavored soup or stew we know as goulash (also spelled goulasch) is of course a version of Hungarian gulyàs, which spread throughout the Austro-Hungarian Empire from its country of origin and became a staple of the hearty cooking of what was once Austria's Südtirol and is now Italy's Trentino–Alto Adige region. The people of the Val Gardena, in the Dolomites northeast of Bolzano in Trentino, are particularly known for this dish, which they call golasc *in their regional language, Ladin (which is not a dialect of Italian but a Rhaeto-Romance tongue related to Friulian and the Romansh of Switzerland). The dish is usually made with beef, but is sometimes adapted to the wild game that abounds in the area. Venison works particularly well in goulash. See page 382 for a source for venison stew meat.*

4 TABLESPOONS/60 GRAMS LARD

3 ONIONS, SLICED

2 TABLESPOONS SWEET HUNGARIAN PAPRIKA

2 POUNDS/1 KILOGRAM VENISON STEW MEAT, CUT INTO 2-INCH/5-CENTIMETER CUBES

½ CUP/120 MILLILITERS RICH RED WINE

2 TABLESPOONS RED WINE VINEGAR

SALT AND PEPPER

2 BAY LEAVES

2 GARLIC CLOVES, CRUSHED

10 TO 12 JUNIPER BERRIES

10 TO 12 PEPPERCORNS

Melt the lard in a Dutch oven or other heavy pot over medium heat. Add the onions and cook, stirring occasionally, until they begin to soften, about 5 minutes. Stir in the paprika and cook, again stirring occasionally, until the onions are beginning to brown, about 5 minutes more.

Remove the onions from the Dutch oven with a slotted spoon and set them aside in a bowl. Raise the heat to medium-high, add the venison, and fry, turning it frequently, until it is lightly browned on all sides, 4 to 5 minutes. Return the onions and their juices to the Dutch oven, then deglaze the pot with the wine and vinegar, scraping up the browned bits on the bottom. Season with salt and pepper, and continue cooking until the liquid has almost evaporated, 3 to 4 minutes.

Reduce the heat to low and add the bay leaves, garlic, juniper berries, and peppercorns to the pot. Add just enough water to cover the ingredients, then cover the pot and cook until the venison is very tender, about 1½ hours.

Uncover the pot, raise the heat to medium-high, and let cook until the sauce has thickened, about 10 minutes more. Serve immediately.

OFFAL

NOTHING GOOD WASTED

One of the effects of the relative scarcity of meat is to force
people to utilize cuts which in more fortunate lands would be discarded.
—*Ada Boni*, The Talisman of Happiness

Er Monno è una trippetta, e ll'omo è un gatto / che jje tocca aspettà lla su' porzione.
[The world is a tripe, and man is a cat / who must wait for his portion.]
—*Giuseppe Gioachino Belli*, "Er Monno" (1833)

The (modern) Romans say it best: They call the assorted organs and extremities of a slaughtered animal the *quinto quarto*, or "fifth quarter." The expression simply means that the offal that is typically removed from a beast after it has been quartered amounts to approximately as much meat—if you want to call it that—as each of the four sections of more conventional flesh. Slaughterhouse workers were traditionally paid in offal—in the days before refrigeration, it was too perishable to last long in the markets anyway—and it was, for obvious reasons, a favored food of the poor if they happened to live close to an abbatoir. If offal was once the recourse of those who could afford nothing better, however, today the various aspects of the quinto quarto are considered delicacies in Lazio and virtually every other part of Italy.

Tripe is an institution in Tuscany, Emilia-Romagna, and Liguria—and not just the honeycomb tripe we're most familiar with, but tripe from all four of the cow's stomachs. Lamb, pork, and veal kidneys are eaten in many regions, as are sweetbreads, tongue, heart, and brains (goat's brains are eaten in Sicily). Whole calf's or pig's heads are split and roasted. Sandwiches of tripe and caciocavallo cheese, called *pani cà meusa* or *vastedda*, are more popular than Big Macs—so far—in Palermo and vicinity. The (ancient) Romans force-fed geese to fatten their livers, and in his sixteenth-century cookbook, Bartolomeo Scappi reports that Jewish farmers were doing the same thing. Chicken livers of ordinary size are well liked, and the livers not just of calves but of lambs and pigs are grilled or fried (fegato alla veneziana, the Venetian version of liver with onions, is probably the Italian offal dish most often seen outside Italy). The "liver of Piacenza," however, is not a culinary specialty: It is a bronze sculpture of a sheep's liver, covered in Etruscan script (which Sean O'Faolain once described as looking "as if a blind man were trying to write Greek with a blunt nail"), dating from around the third century BC. Now on display in a museum in Piacenza, in Emilia-Romagna, it was apparently used for an ancient form of divination.

It took me at least a small measure of courage to sample the old Roman specialty rigatoni alla pajata, in which the pasta is tossed in tomato sauce with pieces of the intestines of unweaned baby lamb or kid. The latter still have traces of milk in them, and it turns into a kind of creamy cheese that adds richness to the dish. I found it extraordinary, and now order it every time I see it on a menu. Next on my list: stigghiole, which are grilled intestines—Sicilian street food.

CALF'S LIVER, VALLE D'AOSTA STYLE

SERVES 6

In the trattorias and osterie of Saint-Vincent and the surrounding area, in the Valle d'Aosta, near the French border, this dish is made with pale, tender liver and often with surprisingly hearty red wine pressed from local Pinot Noir and Gamay grapes. See page 382 for a source for lardo (salt-cured pork fat).

2 GARLIC CLOVES, MINCED

5 TO 6 SPRIGS ITALIAN PARSLEY, MINCED

2 OUNCES/60 GRAMS LARDO OR UNSMOKED BACON, FINELY CHOPPED

2 POUNDS/1 KILOGRAM CALF'S LIVER, THINLY SLICED AND THEN CUT INTO STRIPS ABOUT ½ INCH/ 1.25 CENTIMETERS WIDE AND 2 TO 3 INCHES/5 TO 7.5 CENTIMETERS LONG

1 CUP/125 GRAMS FLOUR

4 TABLESPOONS/60 GRAMS BUTTER

2 ONIONS, FINELY CHOPPED

1 CUP/240 MILLILITERS PINOT NOIR OR OTHER DRY RED WINE

¼ TEASPOON FRESHLY GRATED NUTMEG

SALT AND PEPPER

Mix together thoroughly the garlic, parsley, and lardo in a small bowl. Mix together the liver strips and flour in a medium bowl, coating the liver evenly.

Melt the butter in a large frying pan over medium-high heat. Add the garlic mixture and cook, stirring frequently, until the garlic begins to color, 3 to 4 minutes. Add the onions, reduce the heat to medium, and cook, stirring frequently, until the onions soften, 6 to 8 minutes more.

Remove the liver strips from the bowl, shaking off the excess flour, and add to the pan. Cook, stirring frequently, until they begin to brown, 6 to 8 minutes. Add the wine and nutmeg and season with salt and pepper. Stir the ingredients together well, reduce the heat to low, and cook, stirring occasionally, until the liver is cooked through, about 10 minutes.

PORK LIVER WITH HONEY

SERVES 4

This is my version of a dish I had at a trattoria in the Sabine Hills of northern Lazio. Pork liver is delicious, and I can't imagine why it isn't more widely eaten in the United States. Your butcher should be able to special order it for you.

¼ CUP/60 MILLILITERS EXTRA-VIRGIN OLIVE OIL

1 POUND/500 GRAMS PORK LIVER, CUT INTO STRIPS ABOUT 2 INCHES/5 CENTIMETERS LONG AND ½ INCH/1.25 CENTIMETERS WIDE

1 GARLIC CLOVE, MINCED

4 SPRIGS ITALIAN PARSLEY, MINCED

½ CUP/120 MILLILITERS DRY WHITE WINE

JUICE OF 1 LEMON

2 TABLESPOONS WILDFLOWER HONEY

SALT AND PEPPER

Heat the oil in a large frying pan over medium-high heat. Add the liver and cook, turning frequently, until beginning to brown, 6 to 8 minutes.

Reduce the heat to low and add the garlic and parsley. Stir well and continue cooking until the garlic softens, 2 to 3 minutes. Stir in the wine and cook until the alcohol burns off, 2 to 3 minutes more. Stir in the lemon juice and honey, season with salt and pepper, and cook for 2 to 3 minutes more to glaze the liver.

GRILLED CHICKEN LIVERS WITH LEMON SAUCE

✳

SERVES 2 TO 4

I've converted more than one liver hater with this simple preparation, typical of Lazio.

- 1 POUND/500 GRAMS CHICKEN LIVERS, TRIMMED
- 2 TABLESPOONS EXTRA-VIRGIN OLIVE OIL
- SALT AND PEPPER
- 4 TABLESPOONS/60 GRAMS BUTTER
- JUICE OF 2 LEMONS
- 4 SPRIGS ITALIAN PARSLEY, MINCED

Soak four 6- to 8-inch/15- to 20-centimeter wooden skewers in water for 30 minutes.

Light the grill/barbecue and let the coals or wood get very hot (if using a gas grill, preheat to at least 600°F/315°C).

Divide the livers equally between the four skewers, then brush them with the oil and season them generously with salt and pepper.

Grill/barbecue the livers, turning once, until well browned and cooked through, 2 to 3 minutes per side.

Meanwhile, melt the butter in a small pan and mix in the lemon juice and parsley. When the livers are cooked, brush the lemon sauce over them thoroughly.

CHICKEN LIVERS WITH BUTTER AND SAGE

✳

SERVES 4

This is another simple, attractive presentation of chicken livers, typically Tuscan in style.

- 1 POUND/500 GRAMS CHICKEN LIVERS, TRIMMED AND HALVED
- SALT AND PEPPER
- ½ CUP/65 GRAMS FLOUR
- 3 TABLESPOONS BUTTER
- 1 SMALL ONION, VERY THINLY SLICED
- 4 TABLESPOONS/60 MILLILITERS EXTRA-VIRGIN OLIVE OIL
- 10 TO 12 SAGE LEAVES, COARSELY CHOPPED
- 1 TABLESPOON RED WINE VINEGAR
- 2 SPRIGS ITALIAN PARSLEY, MINCED
- 4 SLICES COUNTRY-STYLE BREAD, LIGHTLY TOASTED

Put the chicken livers into a medium bowl. Season them generously with salt and pepper, then sprinkle the flour over them and stir well so that all the livers are lightly coated. Set the bowl aside.

Melt about half the butter in a large nonstick frying pan over low heat. Add the onion, season it generously with salt and pepper, and cook, stirring frequently, until the onion is soft and beginning to brown, about 10 minutes.

With a slotted spoon, transfer the onion to a small bowl. Add half the oil to the pan and raise the heat to medium-high. Add half the livers and fry, turning as needed, until nicely browned on all sides, about 5 minutes in all. As the livers are ready, transfer them to paper towels/absorbent paper. Add the remaining oil to the same pan and repeat the process with the remaining livers.

Put the remaining butter into the same pan, leaving the heat on medium-high. Add the livers, onions, and sage and cook, stirring constantly, until livers are heated through, about 2 minutes. Add the vinegar and parsley, stir the livers, and cook for about 2 minutes more.

Put a slice of toast on each of 4 plates. Spoon the livers and their pan juices over over the toast.

SWEETBREADS ALLA CIOCIARA

SERVES 4

Ciociara is an historical name for a large but ill-defined region of central Italy, certainly including Lazio, as well as surrounding areas. (The name probably derives from the word ciocia, *a kind of sandal worn by shepherds in the Apennines, and thus ultimately from the Greek* sykchos, *meaning a variety of ancient shoe.) This recipe is based on one in Oretta Zanini De Vita's* The Food of Rome and Lazio.

2 TABLESPOONS WHITE WINE VINEGAR

1½ POUNDS/750 GRAMS SWEETBREADS

4 TABLESPOONS/60 MILLILITERS EXTRA-VIRGIN OLIVE OIL

¼ CUP/35 GRAMS FLOUR

1 CUP/240 MILLILITERS FRASCATI OR OTHER DRY WHITE WINE

¾ POUND/375 GRAMS WHITE MUSHROOMS, SLICED

½ POUND/250 GRAMS BOILED HAM, DICED

SALT AND PEPPER

Put the vinegar and 4 cups/1 liter water into a medium pot and bring to a boil over high heat. Reduce the heat to medium, add the sweetbreads, and blanch for 3 minutes. Drain the sweetbreads, peel them, cut out any veins or sinew, and cut them into four pieces of about equal size.

Heat the oil in a large frying pan over medium-high heat. Dredge the sweetbreads in the flour, shaking off the excess, then add to the pan. Fry, turning the pieces frequently, until golden brown, 6 to 8 minutes. Remove them from the pan with a slotted spoon and set aside on a plate.

Deglaze the pan with the wine, scraping up the browned bits on the bottom. Add the mushrooms and ham, season with salt and pepper, and continue cooking over medium-high heat, stirring frequently, until the mushrooms have given up their water and the sauce has thickened, about 5 minutes.

Reduce the heat to medium and return the sweetbreads to the frying pan. Stir well and cook until the sweetbreads are heated through, 2 to 3 minutes.

VEAL TONGUE WITH ANCHOVY SAUCE

SERVES 4 TO 6

This recipe is based on my recollection of a dish I ate years ago at a trattoria in Mestre, the urban mainland part of Venice.

SALT

2 ONIONS, 1 HALVED, 1 MINCED

1 VEAL OR SMALL BEEF TONGUE, 1½ TO 2 POUNDS/ 750 GRAMS TO 1 KILOGRAM

2 TABLESPOONS BUTTER

2 TABLESPOONS EXTRA-VIRGIN OLIVE OIL

2 TABLESPOONS CAPERS

12 ANCHOVY FILLETS, MASHED WITH A FORK

1 CUP/240 MILLILITERS DRY WHITE WINE

PEPPER

Bring a large pot of salted water to a boil over high heat. Add the halved onion and the tongue, reduce the heat to low, cover, and simmer until the tongue is tender, about 1½ hours. Transfer the tongue to a board and let it cool slightly. When it is cool enough to handle, slip off the outer skin (it will come off easily) and trim away any gristle.

When the tongue is almost finished cooking, melt the butter with the oil in a medium frying pan over medium heat. Add the minced onion and cook, stirring frequently, until it softens, 6 to 8 minutes. Add the capers and anchovies, stir well, and then add the wine. Raise the heat to high and bring the liquid to a boil, then reduce the heat to medium and simmer until the liquid has reduced by about half, 6 to 8 minutes. Season with salt and pepper.

Cut the tongue into slices about ½ inch/1.25 centimeters thick and arrange them on a serving platter. Drizzle the sauce over the tongue.

GRILLED VEAL HEART

✳

SERVES 4

Heart is probably the most accessible of organ meats. It may be daunting in appearance, but it is meaty and firm when cooked, and tastes very good. It is prepared in this manner in various corners of Lazio, Umbria, and Tuscany. Most butchers will special order veal heart for you.

½ CUP/120 MILLILITERS EXTRA-VIRGIN OLIVE OIL, PLUS MORE FOR DRIZZLING

JUICE OF 2 LEMONS

2 VEAL HEARTS, ABOUT ½ POUND/250 GRAMS EACH, TRIMMED OF SINEW AND HALVED CROSSWISE

SALT AND PEPPER

Combine the oil and lemon juice in a medium bowl or baking dish. Add the veal hearts, turn to coat, and marinate at room temperature for 2 hours, turning them several times.

Light a grill/barbecue and let the coals or wood get very hot (if using a gas grill, preheat to at least 600°F/315°C).

Remove the heart halves from the marinade and lightly blot off the excess oil with paper towels. Season them generously on both sides with salt and pepper, then grill/barbecue them, turning them once, until firm to the touch, 5 to 6 minutes total.

To serve, cut the halves into thin slices across the grain and arrange on a platter. Drizzle a little oil over the slices.

TRIPE, TREVISO STYLE

✳

SERVES 4 TO 6

There are scores of ways of preparing tripe in Italy, varying according to region and cook's preference—in white wine, in red wine, in meat sauce, with mushrooms, with pancetta, with cheese, and of course with tomatoes. This typical preparation from Treviso in the Veneto is a good example of the last of these. The traditionalists in the region consider this a "modern" recipe, however, dating only from the late 1700s or early 1800s, the era when the tomato first began to gain acceptance in northern Italian cooking. Before that, the Trevisano way with tripe was to cook it with herbs in beef broth, to produce a thick soup served over dried bread. In that form, it was considered a breakfast dish—not so strange when you consider that the Mexican tripe stew, menudo, is also consumed as a morning meal. In fact, in Italy, as in Mexico, tripe has long been consumed as an antidote to the effects of a hard night's drinking.

2 POUNDS/I KILOGRAM HONEYCOMB TRIPE

¼ CUP/60 MILLILITERS EXTRA-VIRGIN OLIVE OIL

2 ONIONS, FINELY CHOPPED

2 GARLIC CLOVES, MINCED

4 SPRIGS ITALIAN PARSLEY, MINCED

½ CUP/120 MILLILITERS DRY WHITE WINE

2 CUPS/480 MILLILITERS TOMATO SAUCE, HOMEMADE (PAGE 371) OR COMMERCIAL

SALT AND PEPPER

GRATED PARMIGIANO-REGGIANO FOR SERVING

Put the tripe in a medium pot with cold water to cover. Bring to a boil over high heat and cook for about 15 minutes. Drain the tripe and rinse it in cold water, then pat it dry with paper towels. Cut it into strips about 2 inches/5 centimeters long and ½ inch/ 1.25 centimeters wide.

Heat the oil in a large frying pan over medium heat. Add the onions and garlic and cook, stirring frequently, until the onions soften, 6 to 8 minutes. Add the tripe, parsley, and wine and stir well. Add the tomato sauce, season with salt and pepper, and stir well again.

Reduce the heat to low, cover, and simmer, stirring occasionally, until the tripe is tender, about 1½ hours. Serve with the cheese on the side.

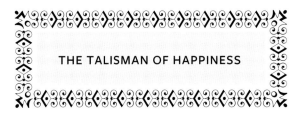

THE TALISMAN OF HAPPINESS

The first comprehensive Italian cookbook was Pellegrino Artusi's *La scienza in cucina e l'arte di mangiar bene* (*Science in the Kitchen and the Art of Eating Well*), published in 1891, but the first *modern* Italian cookbook was Ada Boni's *Il talismano della felicità* (*The Talisman of Happiness*). The very names of the two volumes tell you how different they were. Artusi published recipes he had collected, mostly from Tuscany and his native Emilia-Romagna, adding others sent in by readers in later editions. Boni was the Roman-born granddaughter of a famous chef named Adolfo Giaquinto, founder of the gastronomic periodical *Il Messaggero della Cucina*, and herself an editor for a "women's magazine" called *Preziosa*—in whose pages, starting in 1915, her own recipes, from all over Italy and beyond, began to appear. *Preziosa* published a collection of these in 1925, and a larger edition appeared under another imprint four years later.

Like Artusi's, Boni's volume is encyclopedic in scale—Artusi includes almost eight hundred recipes, later editions of Boni's book have almost two thousand—but her recipes are more, well, a later generation would have said "user-friendly." Because she knew food from the viewpoint of the kitchen, not just the dining table, she couched her formulas in a style that would almost pass muster today—"almost" only because, though she helpfully and articulately guided her readers through standard techniques and listed ingredients more precisely than was common in that era, she didn't always provide quantities. *Il talismano* nonetheless became the Italian *Joy of Cooking*, the go-to manual for home cooks, and a popular present for newlyweds, a distinction it holds to this day.

Boni's book was published in New York in English in 1950 as *The Talisman Italian Cookbook: Italy's Best-Selling Cookbook Adapted for American Kitchens*, translated and "augmented" by Matilde La Rosa, who edited out the obviously non-Italian recipes and added some Italian American specialties that she thought U.S. readers might expect. La Rosa's husband, the celebrated linguist Mario Pei, wrote the introduction. (He was quite a gourmet himself, and reportedly a more than capable cook; we once published his recipe for lasagna in *Saveur*.) It is probably safe to say that until Americans discovered Marcella Hazan in the early 1970s, Ada Boni taught them most of what they wanted to know about how to cook real Italian food.

LA PANARDA

Centuries ago, the story goes, a young mother in the wilds of Abruzzo left her baby alone at home to go out and forage food. When she returned, she found that a wolf had come through the door and was holding the baby in its jaws. Falling to her knees, she prayed for help to Saint Anthony of Abate, the patron saint of animals, and the wolf immediately let the infant fall to the ground. In gratitude, the woman vowed to feed the hungry in Saint Anthony's honor on his feast day, January 17, every year. Either that, I figure, or the people of the region's isolated mountain towns decided that by mid-January it was time for a party.

The celebration, which was well established by the 1600s, came to be called La Panarda—a word of uncertain etymology, perhaps connected with *pane*, "bread," or with the Greek suffix *pan-*, meaning "all." *All* would be appropriate, because La Panarda is nothing less than a gigantic feast, traditionally lasting all night—or, according to some, a day and a night. At least twenty courses must be served, and as many as sixty have been recorded. The large number of items may have become traditional because the first panarde were potluck affairs, with every household pitching in. The foods served are not prescribed, but might include all manner of cheese and salumi, veal or chicken broth, vegetable soups, boiled fava/broad beans dressed with olive oil, fried artichokes, boiled meats, lamb both roasted and stewed, deep-fried calf's brains, peas with prosciutto, *pizz'e foje* (cornmeal flatbread with assorted vegetables), and whole roasted fish, followed by fresh fruit, *ferratelle* (waffle cookies), and various cakes.

Though La Panarda began as a kind of religious observance, it evolved into a celebratory banquet, especially in the province of L'Aquila, that might be staged to honor the return of an emigrant, an election victory, a wedding or baptism, or any other signal occasion. The little village of Villavallelonga, southeast of Arrezano, maintains the tradition of hosting a panarda on January 17 to this day. The town of Villa Santo Stefano, in Lazio not far from the border with Abruzzo, has a panarda of its own, held every year on August 16, the feast of San Rocco, its patron saint. Far from being an all-night, multicourse feast, this panarda involves a ritual distribution of bread with chickpeas slow cooked overnight with olive oil, pepper, and rosemary.

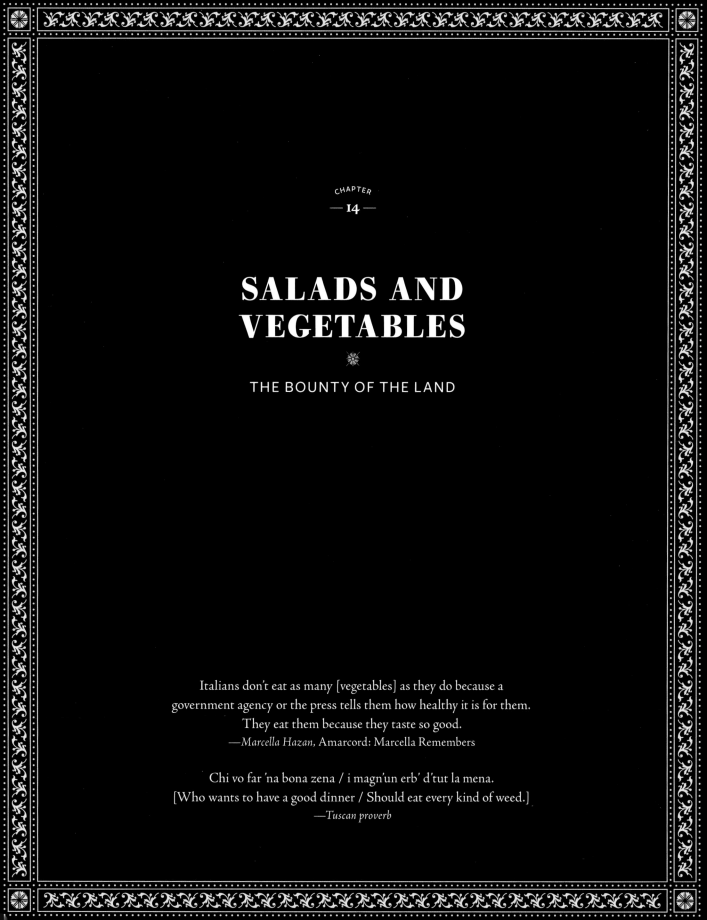

CHAPTER

— 14 —

SALADS AND VEGETABLES

✳

THE BOUNTY OF THE LAND

Italians don't eat as many [vegetables] as they do because a
government agency or the press tells them how healthy it is for them.
They eat them because they taste so good.
—*Marcella Hazan*, Amarcord: Marcella Remembers

Chi vo far 'na bona zena / i magn'un erb' d'tut la mena.
[Who wants to have a good dinner / Should eat every kind of weed.]
—*Tuscan proverb*

When I first started traveling regularly in Europe, spending weeks at a time in the countrysides of France and Italy, I noticed something interesting: though I ate heroic amounts of food and drank plenty of wine in both countries, I always felt healthier—less overstuffed—in the latter. What I eventually figured out was that, while I was shoveling in the protein and carbohydrates in both places, in Italy I was also eating a lot of vegetables, both raw and cooked. The vegetable I encountered most often in France was the potato. Occasionally, I would have a serving of asparagus, or a simple salad, but other than that, the greens and roots and such that did end up on my plate were mostly garnish. In Italy, without even meaning to, I was wolfing down immense servings of insalata mista (mixed salad), eating bean-filled soups, ordering bitter greens seared in olive oil with garlic, eating pasta stuffed with squash or Swiss chard or tossed with cauliflower or broccoli, and of course coloring almost every meal with tomatoes in some form or other.

Among the most important vegetables in Italy, both historically and today, are the legumes/pulses: chickpeas, lentils, fava/broad beans, and field peas, and the like, all with a long history in the country. Garden peas came a little later, and their American cousins, the shell beans of the Western Hemisphere, later still. It took the Italians a while to get used to tomatoes and potatoes, but once they did, these became essential to Italian cooking, the former in particular. Onions and especially garlic practically define the peninsula's cuisine—as do herbs (which, after all, are vegetables too, of a sort) like rosemary, basil, oregano, marjoram, thyme, borage, and bay leaves. Celery, esteemed by the Romans, is the secret ingredient in many pasta sauces and stews.

Greens of every kind are daily fare in Italy, from cultivated lettuces and chicory to the assorted wild ones that constitute Liguria's preboggion—and the weedlike rucola (known in America, for some reason, by one of its obscure dialect names, *arugula*, and in the United Kingdom as *rocket*). Curiously, not all early commentators thought that eating greens was a good thing. Sixteenth-century physician Constanzo Felici, from Piobbico in the Marche, wrote that "salad foods . . . are almost exclusive to greedy Italians, who have appropriated the food of those base animals that eat raw greens."

The first evidence of mushrooms being eaten *anywhere* comes from a Bronze Age site near Nola, in Campania. The Italians went on to become among the world's most fanatical collectors and consumers of fungi—prized varieties like funghi porcini (ceps, or *Boletus edulis*), morchelle (morels, or *Morchella esculenta*), and the justly revered ovoli (Caesar's amanita, or *Amanita caesaria*), but scores of other kinds, as well. One nineteenth-century source claimed that the inhabitants of Piteglio, near Pistoia in Tuscany, once collected three thousand pounds/fifteen hundred kilograms of wild mushrooms in a single day. Italians also consume, to this day, huge quantities of artichokes, cardoons, asparagus, fennel, dandelion greens, Swiss chard, spinach, carrots, leeks, broccoli, cauliflower, turnips—any savory plant that will grow in Italian soil. The citizens of Matera, in Basilicata, prepare one of the most exuberant and all-inclusive of all Italian vegetable dishes in what they call the *capriata*. A typical recipe might include white beans, chickpeas, fava/broad beans, lentils, peas, corn, potatoes, celery, onions, garlic, tomatoes, basil, parsley, and wheat berries. The word *capriata* means "food for goats."

THE GOLDEN APPLE

Probably no vegetable is more identified in the public imagination with Italy than the tomato. It was not always so. Everybody knows that tomatoes came from the New World, and thus couldn't have been part of Italian cuisine before Columbus, but what may surprise some people is that it wasn't until comparatively recently that most Italians really took to the *pomodoro*, or "golden apple," as they call it. (The first ones they saw were apparently yellow.)

Tomato plants did reach Italy fairly quickly after the Spanish first brought them to Europe from South America (where, incidentally, there is no evidence that tomatoes were considered edible): In 1544, in *De materia medica*, a book of commentaries by Greek physician Pedanius Dioscorides, a Siena-born naturalist named Pietro Andrea Mattioli or Matthiolus described the *mala aurea* ("apple of gold" in Latin) as being segmented, with the appearance of a flattened apple and green at the start, then "blood-red" or yellow when ripe. (Medieval trivia: Mattioli was also the first person to describe a case of cat allergy.) Antonio Latini, from the Marche, steward to Cardinal Antonio Barberini, published the first-known

Italian recipe for tomato sauce in 1692, in his influential cookbook and household manual *Lo scalco alla moderna* (*The Carver* [that is, the man in charge of the table], *Modern Style*), describing it as *alla spagnuola*, "in the Spanish style." He recommended it, though, not for pasta but as a sauce for boiled meats. Another tomato sauce recipe, also for meat, appeared in 1790, in the Neapolitan chef Francesco Leonardi's multivolume *L'Apicio moderno, ossia, L'arte di apprestare ogni sorta di vivande* (*The Modern Apicius, or the Art of Preparing Every Sort of Food*).

The first reference to tomato sauce with pasta—*viermicielli co le pommadoro*—appears in a cooking manual by Ippolito Cavalcanti, Duke of Buonvicino (a town in Calabria), published in Naples in 1839. But it would be another twenty years or so, after canned (or jarred) tomatoes from Campania reached the marketplace, that cooks all over the Italian peninsula began incorporating tomatoes—both preserved and fresh—into their dishes. In his famous cookbook, published in 1891, Artusi recalls a busybody priest in Romagna whom locals dubbed Don Pomodoro (Father Tomato), "since tomatoes are also ubiquitous."

MARINATED LETTUCE

SERVES 4

This unusual Calabrian salad is called mappina, *a dialect word for "dishrag," because the oil-cured lettuce is damp and limp.*

4 ROMAINE/COS LETTUCE HEARTS

2 GARLIC CLOVES, MINCED

¼ TEASPOON PEPERONCINI

½ CUP/120 MILLILITERS EXTRA-VIRGIN OLIVE OIL

SALT

Put the lettuce hearts into a rectangular glass or porcelain dish just large enough to hold them. Sprinkle them with the garlic and peperoncini, then drizzle the oil over them and season with salt.

Cut a piece of cardboard to fit snugly inside the dish, then wrap it in aluminum foil. Fit the cardboard on top of the lettuce, and weight it down with two or three large cans of tomatoes (or something else). Refrigerate for 2 days. Bring to room temperature before serving.

INSALATA MISTA

SERVES 4

Exuberance was the word that occurred to me the first time I saw a classic Italian insalata mista—"mixed salad"—being prepared tableside at a handsomely appointed small-town trattoria in Lazio many years ago. Our waiter wheeled a cart up to the table. On it were bowls of baby lettuce, arugula, radicchio, tomato wedges (the tomatoes firm and slightly green, the way Italians like them in salads), and shredded carrots. "Tutto?" he asked. (Everything?) We nodded. Into a big, wide wooden bowl went leaves of all the greens, six or eight tomato wedges, a scattering of carrots. Then oil, oil, oil; more vinegar than could possibly be right; and enough salt to give a cardiologist a heart attack at one hundred paces. Then the tossing—strenuous, almost operatic in its drama. Finally, the salads were set before us. Absolutely wonderful.

3 CUPS/150 GRAMS LOOSELY PACKED BABY LETTUCES

2 CUPS/100 GRAMS LOOSELY PACKED TENDER ARUGULA/ROCKET

1 SMALL HEAD RADICCHIO, SEPARATED INTO LEAVES

2 FIRM, RIPENING TOMATOES, CUT INTO 6 TO 8 WEDGES EACH

2 LARGE CARROTS, GRATED

¼ CUP/60 MILLILTERS EXTRA-VIRGIN OLIVE OIL

2 TO 3 TABLESPOONS RED WINE VINEGAR

SALT

Combine the lettuces, arugula, radicchio, tomatoes, and carrots in a large salad bowl. Drizzle the oil over the salad, then add the vinegar to taste. Salt generously and toss vigorously until all the greens are well coated. Add a little more oil if necessary before serving.

INSALATA CAPRESE

SERVES 4

I almost never order this famous, gloriously simple salad—named for the island of Capri, where it may or may not have been invented—in America, and I'm careful even in Italy. If it's made, as it all too often is, with cottony, flavorless tomatoes and rubbery, not-quite-fresh mozzarella, it is downright unpleasant. Made in prime tomato season, on the other hand, with tomatoes that are still firm (a little green doesn't hurt) but ripening and with fresh mozzarella—bufala if possible—that is no more than a day or so old (domestic or imported), it is one of the most delicious salads in the world.

4 FIRM, RIPENING TOMATOES, SLICED ABOUT ¼ INCH/6 MILLIMETERS THICK

¼ POUND/125 GRAMS FRESH MOZZARELLA, PREFERABLY BUFALA, SLICED ABOUT ¼ INCH/6 MILLIMETERS THICK

8 TO 10 BASIL LEAVES, TORN INTO LARGE PIECES

¼ CUP/60 MILLILITERS EXTRA-VIRGIN OLIVE OIL

SALT

Arrange the tomato slices on a platter, and arrange the mozzarella slices over them. Scatter the basil leaves over the top of the salad. Drizzle with the oil and season generously with salt before serving.

TUNA AND WHITE BEAN SALAD

SERVES 4

This simple salad can be made with any top-quality olive oil–packed Italian or Spanish tuna, but when I make it for company, I often splurge on ventresca, or tuna belly, the richest and most delicious of canned tunas and also by far the most expensive (I've seen it for as much as thirty-two dollars/twenty pounds for a 10.8-ounce/305-gram can). Like other good canned tuna, it comes from both Italy and Spain, and the term ventresca is common to both countries.

TWO 6-OUNCE/175-GRAM CANS OR JARS VENTRESCA OR OTHER TOP-QUALITY OLIVE-OIL–PACKED ITALIAN OR SPANISH TUNA

4 CUPS/400 GRAMS DRAINED COOKED WHITE BEANS (SEE PAGE 308)

I SMALL RED ONION, VERY THINLY SLICED

LEAVES FROM 2 TO 3 SPRIGS ITALIAN PARSLEY

SALT AND PEPPER

EXTRA-VIRGIN OLIVE OIL, IF NEEDED

Put the tuna and its packing oil into a salad bowl. Break up the tuna with a fork.

Add the white beans, onion, and parsley, and season with salt and pepper. Gently toss the salad, adding a bit of extra-virgin olive oil if the packing oil isn't sufficient to moisten the salad. Serve immediately.

FENNEL, ORANGE, AND ONION SALAD

SERVES 4

This is a popular wintertime salad in Sicily. Blood oranges make for a particularly attractive presentation. If possible, use a mandoline for slicing the fennel and onion.

3 OR 4 MEDIUM-SIZE ORANGES OR BLOOD ORANGES, PEELED, WITH PITH REMOVED, AND CUT CROSSWISE INTO SLICES ¼ INCH/6 MILLIMETER THICK

I SMALL BULB FENNEL, SLICED PAPER-THIN

I SMALL RED ONION, SLICED PAPER-THIN AND SEPARATED INTO RINGS

COARSE SALT AND COARSE PEPPER

3 TABLESPOONS EXTRA-VIRGIN OLIVE OIL

Arrange the orange slices on a platter. Arrange the fennel slices on top of the oranges, then scatter the onion rings over the fennel and oranges. Season generously with salt and pepper, and drizzle the oil over the salad before serving.

SAVING YOUR BREAD

The word *panzanella* comes from the Italian words *pane*, or "bread," and *zanella*, "soup bowl." Or is that *zana*, "valley" or "hollow"? Or, maybe the word derives from *pantanella*, meaning "little swamp"; or *panza*, meaning "belly." I've read all those theories, which leads me to believe that nobody has any idea *where* it comes from. (For the record, I can't find *zanella*, *zana*, *pantanella*, or *panza* in my quite-good Italian dictionary; the word for "belly" in Italian is *pancia*.) Well, never mind. The culinary origins of this quintessential Tuscan summer salad are clearer: Tuscans traditionally bake their bread without salt—this practice is said to descend from popular resistance to a salt tax imposed by the Medicis in medieval times—and thus it dries out quickly. There are ingenious uses for day-old (or older) bread all over Italy, but the Tuscans took to dressing chunks of it with two substances they had in abundance: olive oil and wine vinegar. Later, in the nineteenth century, when tomatoes became popular in Italy, they were added to the mix—and they have since become essential. Other ingredients—onions, bell peppers/ capsicums, olives, anchovies, capers, and on—are not only allowed but encouraged. The same kind of salad, incidentally, is eaten elsewhere in central Italy, especially in Umbria and Lazio. In these places, it is usually called *panmolle*. No mystery there: the name simply means "moistened bread."

PANZANELLA

SERVES 6

While Italians tend to prefer firm, just-ripening tomatoes in their salads, this summertime Tuscan standard is an exception: use the ripest, juiciest tomatoes you can find. One other note: do not be tempted to make this salad with balsamic vinegar, as some Italian restaurants in the United States now do. It changes its character dramatically; use good-quality Italian red wine vinegar instead. This is a basic panzanella recipe. If you like, toss in some capers, anchovies, olives, thin-sliced fennel or celery, or other appropriate ingredients.

2 POUNDS/1 KILOGRAM VERY RIPE TOMATOES, PEELED, SEEDED, AND HALVED, THEN PLACED IN A BOWL TO CONSERVE THE JUICES

2 GARLIC CLOVES, MINCED

¼ CUP/60 MILLILITERS RED WINE VINEGAR, PREFERABLY ITALIAN

½ SMALL RED ONION, VERY THINLY SLICED

2 RED BELL PEPPERS/CAPSICUMS, CHARRED AND PEELED (PAGE 376), THEN CUT INTO NARROW STRIPS (OPTIONAL)

LEAVES FROM 1 SMALL BUNCH BASIL

1¼ CUPS/300 MILLILITERS EXTRA-VIRGIN OLIVE OIL

ONE 1-POUND/500-GRAM LOAF CIABATTA, 2 OR 3 DAYS OLD, CUT ROUGHLY INTO SLICES ABOUT 1 INCH/2.5 CENTIMETERS THICK

SALT

Combine the tomatoes, garlic, vinegar, onion, bell peppers (if using), basil, and 1 cup/240 milliliters of the oil in a large salad bowl and toss together well.

Tear the bread slices into large, irregular pieces, then add to the bowl and toss well, making sure that all the bread is soaked in liquid. If necessary, add a little more olive oil.

Season the salad generously with salt, then drizzle the remaining ¼ cup/60 milliliters oil over the top before serving.

CIANFOTTA

SERVES 4

Cianfotta, also known as ciambotta, might be described as the southern Italian ratatouille—except that, unlike its Provençal counterpart (or the closely related samfaina or chanfaina of Catalan Spain), it almost always contains potatoes.

¼ CUP/60 MILLILITERS EXTRA-VIRGIN OLIVE OIL

1 ONION, HALVED LENGTHWISE AND SLICED

4 GARLIC CLOVES, FINELY CHOPPED

2 STALKS CELERY, SLICED CROSSWISE INTO ½-INCH/1.25-CENTIMETER PIECES

2 RED BELL PEPPERS/CAPSICUMS, CORED, HALVED LENGTHWISE, AND SLICED THINLY CROSSWISE

4 TO 6 SMALL POTATOES, HALVED LENGTHWISE AND SLICED

4 RIPE TOMATOES, SEEDED AND GRATED (SEE RAW TOMATO COULIS, PAGE 371)

1 EGGPLANT/AUBERGINE, CUT INTO BATONS ABOUT 2 INCHES/5 CENTIMETERS LONG AND ½ INCH/ 1.25 CENTIMETERS WIDE

6 TO 8 BASIL LEAVES, ROUGHLY TORN

SALT

GRATED PECORINO SARDO FOR SERVING

Heat the olive oil in a Dutch oven or other heavy pot over medium heat. Add the onion, garlic, and celery and cook, stirring frequently, until the vegetables soften, 6 to 8 minutes. Add the bell peppers, potatoes, tomatoes, eggplant, and basil and season with salt.

Cover the pot, reduce the heat to low, and cook, stirring occasionally, until all the vegetables are very soft, about 30 minutes. Serve with the cheese on the side.

PLUM GOOD

The most famous—and best—canned tomatoes in Italy are a variety of oversize plum tomatoes named for and grown around the town of San Marzano sul Sarno, in the Agro Nocerino region of Campania, just east of Naples. Locals like to say that the variety, or its direct ancestor, came to San Marzano in the late eighteenth century, as a gift from the Viceroyalty of Peru to the Kingdom of Naples. That's doubtful for all kinds of reasons, and San Marzanos weren't identified as a specific cultivar until roughly a century after that. By the early twentieth century, though, they had become an important product for the Italian canning industry, which had been founded by Francesco Cirio in 1856—far from Campania, in Turin. Cirio later built facilities in the region, however, and scientists from the company's research center were influential in identifying the best San Marzano clones in the 1990s, with a resulting increase in quality.

San Marzanos grow in volcanic soil (Mount Vesuvius is nearby) and ripen—quickly—in full meridional sun. They are ideal for canning for two reasons: they have only two shallow seed pockets (conventional round tomatoes have between five and seven) and thus fewer seeds, easier to remove; and they have skin that's strong enough to resist cracking on the vine but is loosely attached to their flesh, making them a cinch to peel, whether mechanically or by hand. Their suitability for canning aside, they taste very good, bright and tomatoey, with low levels of both sugar and acidity. They are perfect for tomato sauce, and add real dimension to any cooked dish calling for tomatoes. (So far, to the best of my knowledge, nobody has come up with a canned tomato—San Marzano or otherwise—that has the right texture for salads.)

Be careful, though: "San Marzano" applies both to a variety of tomato and a geographically specific region. There are Roma tomatoes and assorted hybrids grown in San Marzano—perfectly fine, but not as delicious as San Marzanos—and San Marzano tomatoes grown as far from Campania as Australia and California. What you want are San Marzanos *from* San Marzano. Some brands widely exported, besides Cirio, include Cento, La Bella San Marzano, La Valle, Strianese, Titina's, and Carmelina. Some, but not all, of these qualify for a European Union "denomination of protected origin" designation (DOP in Italian), and the cans bear stamps certifying this fact, as well as membership in the Consorzio San Marzano. In general, these are the best ones to buy—though non-DOP San Marzanos can be very good, too.

PEAS, UMBRIAN STYLE

SERVES 4

The green peas grown in and around Bettona, a village just south-east of Perugia in central Umbria, are famous in the region for their sweetness and intensity of flavor. This is how the locals cook them.

SALT

2 CUPS/140 GRAMS SHELLED GREEN PEAS (ABOUT 2 POUNDS/1 KILOGRAM IN THE POD)

4 TABLESPOONS/60 GRAMS BUTTER

2 OUNCES/60 GRAMS PROSCIUTTO OR PANCETTA (NOT SLICED), FINELY DICED

1 SMALL WHITE ONION, VERY THINLY SLICED

1 CUP/240 MILLILITERS VEAL BROTH (PAGE 373) OR COMMERCIAL BEEF BROTH

PEPPER

Bring a medium pot of salted water to a boil, add the peas, and blanch for about 10 seconds. Drain and refresh with cold water.

Melt the butter in a medium frying pan over medium heat. Add the prosciutto, onion, and peas and cook, stirring frequently, until the onion begins to soften, 5 to 6 minutes. Add about half the broth and continue cooking, stirring frequently, until it has evaporated. Add the remaining broth and repeat the process.

Season generously with salt and pepper before serving.

BLACK-EYED PEAS, TUSCAN STYLE

SERVES 6 TO 8

This is the simplest possible recipe. Dress it up with a few shreds of prosciutto, if you like.

2 CUPS/500 GRAMS DRIED BLACK-EYED PEAS, SOAKED OVERNIGHT IN WATER TO COVER

¼ CUP/60 MILLILITERS EXTRA-VIRGIN OLIVE OIL

SALT

Drain the peas and put them into a large pot with 3 quarts/ 3 liters cold water. Cover the pot and bring just to a simmer over medium heat (do not boil). Continue cooking for about 1 hour. Reduce the heat to low and continue cooking until the peas are tender but just before the skins begin to split, 30 to 45 minutes, depending on the age of the peas.

Drain the peas, transfer them to a bowl, and drizzle in the oil, stirring the peas to coat them well. Season generously with salt before serving.

LENTILS WITH PANCETTA

SERVES 4

This simple preparation is the classic accompaniment (along with pureed potatoes) to cotechino, the coarse-textured pork sausage that is a specialty of the gastronomic capital of Modena, in Emilia-Romagna, or to the same area's celebrated zampone, a cotechino variation stuffed into a pig's trotter. See page 382 for sources for Italian lentils (though these aren't essential).

1⅔ CUPS/325 GRAMS LENTILS, PREFERABLY ITALIAN, SOAKED IN WATER TO COVER OVERNIGHT

1 ONION, MINCED

2 OUNCES/60 GRAMS PANCETTA (NOT SLICED), FINELY CHOPPED

6 TO 8 SAGE LEAVES

SALT

Drain the lentils, then combine them in a pot with the onion, pancetta, and sage. Add cold water just to cover, bring to a boil over high heat, then reduce heat to low and simmer, uncovered, until the water has evaporated and the lentils are tender, about 1 hour. Season with salt before serving.

BLACK-EYED PISELLI

Until I first encountered them in Catalonia about twenty years ago, I had naively thought that black-eyed peas were eaten today mostly in the Caribbean and the American South. In fact, this species of cowpea (*Vigna unguiculata* subsp. *unguiculata*) was apparently first cultivated in Africa and later widely planted all over Asia and the Middle East. (The tradition of eating black-eyed peas for good luck at the New Year goes back to ancient Babylonia.) It didn't reach the southern United States until the seventeenth century, by which time it had already been known in Europe—Italy most definitely included—for at least a hundred years. According to legume lore, black-eyed plants or seeds were given to Pope Clement VII in the 1520s by Charles V, the Holy Roman Emperor, and the prelate, who was active in Florentine politics, in turn took them to Tuscany, where they are still popular, especially in the Maremma. They are not really called *piselli*, "peas," incidentally; the Italian term for them is *fagioli con l'occhio*, "beans with the eye."

CHICKPEAS WITH FRIED BREAD

SERVES 4

I sometimes serve this definitively rustic dish—which would have been dinner for poorer farm families in the Abruzzo in earlier times— as part of a large Italian meal, in place of a pasta course.

2¼ CUPS/250 GRAMS DRIED CHICKPEAS, SOAKED OVERNIGHT IN WATER TO COVER

½ CUP/120 MILLILITERS EXTRA-VIRGIN OLIVE OIL

2 SPRIGS ROSEMARY

2 GARLIC CLOVES, CRUSHED

4 THICK SLICES COUNTRY-STYLE BREAD

1 ONION, FINELY CHOPPED

SALT AND PEPPER

Drain the chickpeas and put them in a pot with 8 cups/2 liters cold water. Cover the pot and bring just to a simmer over medium heat (do not boil). Continue cooking for about 1 hour. Reduce the heat to low and continue cooking until chickpeas are tender but just before the skins begin to split, 45 minutes to 1 hour, depending on the age of the chickpeas.

Meanwhile, heat the oil in a medium frying pan over low heat and add the rosemary and garlic. Let cook slowly for 15 minutes, then remove and discard the rosemary and garlic.

Pour half the flavored oil into a large frying pan. Raise the heat in the first frying pan to medium-high. Working in two batches if necessary, fry the bread, turning once, until it turns golden brown, 2 to 3 minutes per side. Drain the fried bread on paper towels, then put 1 piece on each of 4 warmed plates.

While the bread is frying, heat the oil in the large frying pan over medium heat. Add the onion and cook, stirring frequently, until it begins to soften, 5 to 6 minutes. Drain the chickpeas and add them to the pan, stirring well to coat them with the oil. Season generously with salt and pepper.

Spoon the chickpeas over the fried bread, dividing it equally between the plates to serve.

WHITE BEANS, TUSCAN STYLE

SERVES 6 TO 8

Cannellini beans are the ones most often found in Tuscany today. This recipe is classically cooked in a fiasco, an old-style round-bottomed Chianti bottle, nestled in the embers of the fire. This is a more conventional method of preparing them.

2 CUPS/500 GRAMS DRIED CANNELLINI BEANS, SOAKED OVERNIGHT IN WATER TO COVER

⅓ CUP/80 MILLILITERS EXTRA-VIRGIN OLIVE OIL

6 SAGE LEAVES

SALT AND PEPPER

Put the beans into a flameproof earthenware dish or metal pot with 3 quarts/3 liters cold water, about half the oil, and the sage leaves. Cover the pot and bring just to a simmer over medium heat (do not boil). Continue cooking for about 1 hour. Reduce the heat to low and continue cooking until the beans are tender but just before the skins begin to split, 45 minutes to 1½ hours, depending on the age of the beans.

Drain the beans and season generously with salt and pepper. Drizzle the remaining oil over them before serving.

CATO ON CABBAGE

De agri cultura (*On Farming*) is both the oldest surviving work of prose in the Latin language and the only piece of writing by Marcus Porcius Cato (234–149 BC), the Roman statesman commonly known as Cato the Elder, that we have in its entirety. It is a practical manual, containing instructions for establishing and equipping a farm, feeding cattle, planting and harvesting olives, and managing slaves, among other things. There are also sections on contractual arrangements and religious rites concerning farming, some recipes (see page 155), and some passages on folk medicine—the most famous of which involves cabbage.

"Cabbage surpasses all other vegetables," writes Cato. "It may be eaten cooked or raw; to eat it raw, dip it into vinegar. It encourages digestion wonderfully and is an excellent laxative. . . . If your desire is to drink seriously at a banquet and to enjoy the meal, eat as much raw cabbage as you would like, seasoned with vinegar, before the meal and also after the meal eat half a dozen leaves; this will give you the feeling that you have not dined, and you will be able to drink all you want."

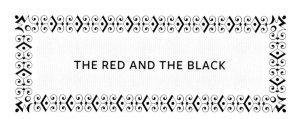

THE RED AND THE BLACK

These days, probably hundreds of varieties of Italian olive oil are sold in shops, and fifty kinds of balsamic vinegar, and thirty kinds of (pardon the expression) truffle oil, but there are still many, many delicious and regionally important food products in Italy that remain all but unknown beyond its borders. I encountered two salient examples not long ago in Basilicata: peperoni di Senise, which are sweet peppers from the town of Senise in the southern portion of the region, in the foothills of the Pollino Mountains; and olive di Ferrandina, from the town of that name in eastern Basilicata. Peperoni di Senise are mild chiles that are dried in the sun to a brick red and an attractive sweetness. These are sold in that form, or are further processed into peperoni cruschi, for which the dried

peppers are slowly fried in olive oil until they get very crisp, almost crackly. The latter are eaten as a snack or crumbled (or ground into a powder) as a seasoning for pasta—very good.

Ferrandina, about thirty-five miles/sixty kilometers northeast of Senise, grows a variety of smallish black olives called Majatica (the name comes from *majo*, local dialect for *maggio*, the month of May, which is when the trees flower). These are partially dried, then cured in brine flavored with oregano. Finally, they are put into ovens—preferably wood burning—and slowly roasted. The resulting olives aren't particularly complex in flavor, but they are dense and concentrated, like olives reduced to their essence.

BEAN EATERS

The ancient Romans were great fans of fava/broad beans, chickpeas, black-eyed peas, and lentils, but of course they didn't have what we think of as real beans, exemplars of the genus and species *Phaseolus vulgaris*, like green beans and red or white shell beans. These didn't reach Italy from the New World until the sixteenth century, when they found their way there thanks to the Spanish. The Italians took to these beans quickly, almost certainly because of their familiarity with their not dissimilar Old World relatives like favas and chickpeas, and by the seventeenth century, they had become an important part of the diet all over the country.

For whatever reasons, the Tuscans became particularly enamored with them. They got an early start—there are records of beans being grown in the region as early as 1528—and beans became such an important means of sustenance that they were sometimes called *la carne dei poveri*, "the poor man's meat." Tuscans still eat so many beans today that they are called slangily *mangiafagioli*, "bean eaters."

BORLOTTI BEANS WITH PORK CRACKLINGS

SERVES 6 TO 8

I found this recipe in the notes I had made on a trip through Lazio, Umbria, and Tuscany in 1985. I have no idea where I got it, except that it must have been at some modest trattoria in one of those regions. Coincidentally, the recipe as I wrote it uses a bean-cooking method we often used at Saveur, with two boils and less water than usual.

2 CUPS/500 GRAMS DRIED BORLOTTI (CRANBERRY) BEANS, SOAKED OVERNIGHT IN WATER TO COVER

1 ONION, HALVED

3 GARLIC CLOVES, LIGHTLY CRUSHED

¾ CUP/180 MILLILITERS EXTRA-VIRGIN OLIVE OIL

½ POUND/250 GRAMS SALT PORK, CUT INTO SLICES ⅛ INCH/3 MILLIMETERS THICK

1 TABLESPOON THYME LEAVES

SALT AND PEPPER

Drain the beans and put them into a large pot with water to cover. Cover the pot and bring the water to a boil over high heat, then remove from the heat and drain the beans. Return the beans to the pot and add water to cover again.

Add the onion, garlic, and ½ cup/120 milliliters of the oil to the pot. Cover the pot and bring the water to a boil over high heat. Reduce the heat to low and cook, tightly covered, until the beans are tender but just before the skins begin to split, 45 minutes to 1½ hours, depending on the age of the beans.

Meanwhile, preheat the oven to 500°F/260°C/gas 10. Arrange the salt pork slices in a single layer in a shallow baking pan/tray and roast for about 5 minutes. Reduce the oven temperature to 350°F/175°C/gas 5 and continue to roast until the pork fat is crisp and brown, about 25 minutes more. Transfer the cracklings to paper towels to drain, and reserve the rendered fat for cooking other dishes.

Remove the bean pot from the heat, uncover it, and allow the beans to cool in their liquid. Drain the beans, then put them into a large bowl. Stir in the thyme and the remaining oil. Crumble or chop the pork cracklings and stir them into the beans, then season with salt and pepper. Serve at room temperature.

PIEDMONTESE BAKED BEANS

SERVES 4 TO 6

The food-related tradition for which the Piedmontese town of Ivrea, north of Turin, used to be best known was the Battle of the Oranges, waged during Carnival every year. Since 1975, it has competition from another Carnival event—the Fagiolata, a celebration of local borlotti beans and a dish called fagiolata—*complete with a parade and a blessing of the beans and those who cook them. This is an adaptation of Ivrea's official fagiolata recipe.*

2 HAM HOCKS

2 CUPS/500 GRAMS DRIED BORLOTTI (CRANBERRY) BEANS, SOAKED OVERNIGHT IN WATER TO COVER

4 TABLESPOONS/60 GRAMS BUTTER OR LARD

½ POUND/250 GRAMS MILD ITALIAN SAUSAGES, CASINGS REMOVED AND CHOPPED

1 ONION, FINELY CHOPPED

1 STALK CELERY, FINELY CHOPPED

2 GARLIC CLOVES, MINCED

4 WHOLE CLOVES

3 SPRIGS ROSEMARY

1 PINCH FRESHLY GRATED NUTMEG

SALT AND PEPPER

Put the ham hocks into a medium pot with cold water to cover and bring to a boil over high heat. Reduce the heat to low, cover, and simmer for 30 minutes.

Meanwhile, drain the beans and put them into a large pot with water to cover. Cover the pot and bring the water to a boil over high heat. Reduce the heat to low and cook, tightly covered, until the beans are tender but just before the skins begin to split, 45 minutes to 1½ hours, depending on the age of the beans.

Remove the ham hocks from their pot and let them cool until they can be handled, then pull or cut off the rind and pick the meat off the bones. Chop the meat finely. Melt the butter in a Dutch oven or other heavy pot over medium heat. Add the chopped ham hock, sausages, onion, celery, garlic, cloves, rosemary, and nutmeg and cook, stirring frequently, until onion is very soft and begins to caramelize and the sausage is browned, 12 to 15 minutes. Season generously with salt and pepper.

Drain the beans and add them to the Dutch oven. Stir well and continue cooking for about 5 minutes to blend the flavors. Serve immediately.

SCAFATA
(SAUTÉED SPRING VEGETABLES)

SERVES 4

I'm not sure that the Umbrian farmhouse where I first ate this dish was officially an agriturismo (see page 228). In fact, it was so long ago that I'm not even sure the agriturismo program was running back then. If the place had a name, I don't remember it—but I can picture a long, well-worn wooden table outside, in front of the house, and a seemingly nonstop progression of dishes, of which this spring vegetable dish—related to the resolutely seasonal Roman specialty called vignarola—was a star. Scafata is the feminine form of scafato, meaning "cunning" or "savvy," and it was surely a cunning, savvy farmwife who first thought of combining these ingredients.

JUICE OF 1 LEMON

4 BABY ARTICHOKES

1 CUP/150 GRAMS SHELLED FRESH FAVA/BROAD
BEANS (ABOUT 1 POUND/500 GRAMS IN THE POD)

SALT

1 CUP/150 GRAMS SHELLED GREEN PEAS (ABOUT
1 POUND/500 GRAMS IN THE POD)

6 TABLESPOONS/90 MILLILITERS EXTRA-VIRGIN
OLIVE OIL

6 GREEN/SPRING ONIONS, FINELY CHOPPED

PEPPER

½ CUP/120 MILLILITERS ORVIETO OR OTHER
DRY WHITE WINE

2 OUNCES/60 GRAMS PECORINO ROMANO,
THINLY SLICED

Fill a bowl three-quarters full of water and add the lemon juice. Cut the stems off the artichokes. Follow this whole process with one artichoke at a time: Pull off the tough outer leaves by hand, then trim off more layers of leaves with a sharp knife until only the tenderest leaves, or heart, remain. Halve the artichoke lengthwise, then cut or scrape out and discard the choke and immediately put the halves in the acidulated water to stop them from turning black. Set aside.

Bring a medium pot of unsalted water to a boil over high heat, add the shelled favas, and blanch for about 30 seconds. Reduce the heat to a simmer and, with a slotted spoon, transfer the favas to a colander. Rinse the favas with cold water, then peel them by squeezing them gently from one end so they slip out of their skins. Set them aside.

Salt the water in the pot, raise the heat to high, and bring to a boil again. Drain the artichokes, add to the boiling water, and cook for 3 to 4 minutes, then add the peas. Cook for about 5 minutes longer, then drain the vegetables in the colander and rinse them with cold water. Set them aside.

Heat the oil in a large frying pan over medium heat. Add about two-thirds of the green onions and cook, stirring frequently, for 3 to 4 minutes. Add the fava beans, peas, and artichokes, season generously with salt and pepper, then add the wine. Raise the heat to medium-high and cook, stirring frequently, until the wine is absorbed, 2 to 3 minutes.

Transfer the vegetables to a warmed bowl, sprinkle with remaining green onions, and lay the slices of cheese on top to melt before serving.

Note: This dish is sometimes served as a soup. Follow the instructions above, omitting the cheese. After the vegetables are cooked, add 2 to 3 cups/480 to 720 milliliters chicken broth, homemade (page 372) or commercial, bring to a boil over high heat, reduce heat to low, and simmer for about 5 minutes. Serve over slices of day-old or lightly toasted country-style bread.

FAVA BEAN PESTO

MAKES ABOUT 1 CUP/240 MILLILITERS

This unusual condiment is a specialty of Sanremo, on the western Riviera in Liguria, where it is called salsa marò. *Unlike pesto, it is rarely used on pasta, but instead is served as a condiment for roasted lamb or goat, or simply spread on toasted country-style bread.*

1 CUP/150 GRAMS FRESH FAVA/BROAD BEANS
(ABOUT 1 POUND/500 GRAMS IN THE POD)

SALT

1 GARLIC CLOVE, MINCED

6 MINT LEAVES

2 ANCHOVY FILLETS

3 TABLESPOONS GRATED PARMIGIANO-REGGIANO

2 TO 3 TABLESPOONS EXTRA-VIRGIN OLIVE OIL

Bring a medium pot of unsalted water to a boil over high heat, add the shelled favas, and blanch for about 30 seconds. Drain them and rinse under cold running water, then peel them by squeezing them gently from one end so they slip out of their skins.

Scatter a pinch or two of salt into a good-size mortar, add the garlic and mint, and crush into a paste with a pestle. Work in the anchovy fillets, then add the favas a few at a time, crushing them into the paste.

Work in the cheese a little at a time, then drizzle in enough oil, working it into the fava mixture, to form a coarse paste.

Use immediately or store, covered, in the refrigerator for no more than 48 hours.

PUREED FAVAS WITH CHICORY

SERVES 4

This is perhaps the most typical of all Puglian vegetable dishes, made in every traditional household and served by most restaurants. Locals will proudly tell you that they eat it at least once a week, and sometimes more. In some versions, the pureed favas are very moist, almost like a thick soup. Though I've put this recipe in the vegetables chapter, in fact, it is usually consumed in place of soup or pasta, not as a side dish. Some recipes add a potato or two to the puree, but I like the more intense pure-fava flavor. Wild chicory is the preferred green, though anything leafy and a little bitter may be substituted.

1½ CUPS/375 GRAMS DRIED FAVA/BROAD BEANS, SOAKED OVERNIGHT IN WATER TO COVER

2 TABLESPOONS EXTRA-VIRGIN OLIVE OIL, PLUS MORE FOR DRIZZLING

SALT

SAUTÉED BITTER GREENS WITH GARLIC AND PEPERONCINI (PAGE 320)

Drain the favas and put them into a medium pot. Add just enough water to cover them and bring to a boil over high heat. Reduce the heat to low and simmer uncovered, skimming off any foam that appears on the surface and replenishing the water to cover barely as necessary, until the favas have completely broken apart, about 2 hours. Stir every 10 to 15 minutes.

When the favas are very soft and only a little water is left in the pot, add the oil, season with salt, and mash the beans with a fork into a coarse puree.

To serve, divide the puree equally between 4 plates, then divide the just-cooked greens between the same plates, placing them alongside the puree. Drizzle the puree with a little more olive oil.

CARDOONS WITH BAGNA CAUDA

SERVES 6 TO 8

The town of Chieri, just southeast of Turin, has an illustrious past: founded by the Romans about two thousand years ago, it was mentioned by Pliny the Elder as an important fortified settlement; in the thirteenth century, it was the capital of a small republic considered as prosperous as those of Asti or Pisa; in the late 1800s, it was a principality owing allegiance to the Duke of Aosta. To Italian gourmets today, however, Chieri is most famous for a vegetable: from the farms and in the market gardens around the town come what are arguably Italy's best and most famous cardoons. There are two main types, gobbi *(hunchbacks) and* spadoni *(swords). These terms have to do with the way the vegetables grow. Gobbi are called that because when the stalks begin to rise, they are bent back down into the earth, so that they grow blanched and less bitter. Spadoni, which are much less work to raise, grow straight up. Around Turin, cardoons are often eaten, either by themselves or with raw carrots, celery, fennel, and other vegetables with a bagna cauda, or "hot bath," of butter and olive oil flavored with garlic and anchovies.*

3 POUNDS/1.5 KILOGRAMS CARDOONS, SEPARATED INTO STALKS

SALT

JUICE OF 3 LEMONS

½ CUP/125 GRAMS BUTTER

10 GARLIC CLOVES, THINLY SLICED LENGTHWISE

20 TO 25 ANCHOVY FILLETS, COARSELY CHOPPED

2 CUPS/480 MILLILITERS EXTRA-VIRGIN OLIVE OIL

PEPPER

Carefully trim the thorns and leaves off the cardoon stalks with a sharp knife or shears, then, using a vegetable peeler, remove the tough strings from the backs of the stalks.

Cut the stalks into pieces about 3 inches/7.5 centimeters long and put them into a large pot of salted water. Stir in the lemon juice, then cover the pot and bring the water to a boil over high heat. Reduce the heat to low and simmer until the cardoons are tender but still firm, about 30 minutes.

Drain the cardoons, then rinse in cold water and pat dry with paper towels. Set aside.

Melt the butter in a small saucepan over low heat. Stir in the garlic and anchovies and simmer for about 5 minutes, then stir in the oil. Simmer for about 15 minutes longer, then season generously with salt and pepper.

To serve, arrange the cardoons on a plate to be dipped into the bagna cauda. Put the bagna cauda in a thick bowl, returning it to the saucepan after a few minutes to keep it warm if necessary (or serve in a small chafing dish).

FRIED CARDOONS

SERVES 6 TO 8

This is another popular way to eat cardoons in Italy.

3 POUNDS/1.5 KILOGRAMS CARDOONS

3 EGGS

1½ CUPS/185 GRAMS FLOUR

2 CUPS/480 MILLILITERS EXTRA-VIRGIN OLIVE OIL OR CANOLA OIL

SALT

¼ CUP/25 GRAMS GRATED PARMIGIANO-REGGIANO

Prepare and cook the cardoons as directed for Cardoons with Bagna Cauda (at left), through draining the cooked pieces and patting them dry.

Lightly beat the eggs in a medium bowl, and put the flour in another medium bowl. Add the cardoon pieces to the flour and toss well to coat evenly. Remove from the flour and shake off the excess.

Heat the oil in a large frying pan over medium-high heat until it begins to pop. Working in batches, dip the flour-coated cardoon pieces into the eggs, allowing the excess egg to drip back into the bowl, add to the hot oil. Fry until golden, 5 to 6 minutes. As the pieces are done, drain them on paper towels.

Season the hot cardoon pieces generously with salt and toss with the cheese before serving.

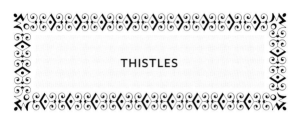

THISTLES

The cardoon—*cardo* in Italian—is a relatively obscure vegetable these days, but it was once greatly favored around the Mediterranean, to which it is probably native, and is still popular in many parts of Italy, including Sicily, the Abruzzo, Piedmont, and Liguria. A kind of thistle, related to the artichoke—which may have been developed from it by Moorish horticulturists—the cardoon (*Cynara cardunculus*) was known to the Greeks and Romans (it was one of the most popular garden plants in Rome), and was an important crop in medieval Spain and North Africa. It is best grown in the winter months in temperate climates—it needs cool weather to develop properly, but doesn't much like frost—and is a traditional Christmastime dish, especially around Nice and in Piedmont and Liguria. It is also enjoyed farther south, though. A young man in Basilicata once told me that when he was a kid, he and his friends would forage for snacks in the countryside, including cardoons, which they would trim and peel and eat raw on the spot. (Licorice root and acacia flowers were also part of their diet.)

The cardoon has a flavor somewhere between those of artichokes and celery, often with a pronounced but not unpleasant bitterness. It is full of vitamins A and C and assorted minerals, including potassium and iron, and has a reputation as a restorative. In appearance, the cardoon suggests overgrown, excessively fibrous celery. Indeed, it is not an easy vegetable to deal with: it must be trimmed of its thorns (carefully), then peeled of its thick strings. Farmers sometimes save the strings along with the plant's attractive purple blossoms as both contain an enzyme that can coagulate milk into cheese, the same way rennet does. It is said that this only works with sheep's or goat's milk, though, as the enzyme infects cow's milk with some of the cardoon's native bitterness.

Some sources maintain that artichokes were known to the Greeks and Romans, and were cultivated by the Greeks in Sicily, but they are probably talking about the cardoon. The history of the artichoke as we know it today is a bit mysterious. There are reports of its cultivation around Naples as early as the ninth century, but most sources maintain that it first appeared—there—only in the early 1400s. It traveled from Naples soon thereafter to Florence and Venice, and then on to France and beyond. The word *artichoke* and its Italian equivalent, *carciofi*, derive—like most European words for the thing—from the vegetable's Arabic name, *al-khursufa*.

Artichokes are known and enjoyed in almost every part of Italy today, but among its most ardent fans are the Venetians. The market-garden island of Sant'Erasmo in the Venetian lagoon is famous for producing a springtime treat called *castraure*, "castrated ones," which are the first buds of the artichoke, cut out of the heart of the plant. "You know," Arrigo Cipriani of Harry's Bar once told me, "that the Venetians do this because they simply can't wait for the artichoke to mature." Castraure, of course, are expensive. My Buranese friend Bepi D'Este told me that, in 2010, he was offered these little gems at 1.50 euros (then worth about $1.80 or £1.25) apiece. "Okay," he said to the would-be seller, "I'll take twenty-two of them." The seller asked, why the specific number? "Because at that price, I will give them to my wife," he said, "and she will wear one hanging from each ear, six around her wrist as a bracelet, and the rest as a necklace around her neck."

SAUTÉED BITTER GREENS WITH GARLIC AND PEPERONCINI

SERVES 4

I've eaten variations on this basic Italian vegetable dish all over the country, from the outskirts of Rome to the hills of Puglia. One of my favorite versions, served alongside wonderful chargrilled pork liver, was made with wild chicory, at Degli Angeli near Magliano Sabina, east of Viterbo. It is good as a side dish or as a topping for Bruschetta (page 37).

¼ CUP/60 MILLILITERS EXTRA-VIRGIN OLIVE OIL

2 GARLIC CLOVES, MINCED

¼ TEASPOON PEPERONCINI, OR MORE TO TASTE

2 LARGE BUNCHES CHICORY, DANDELION OR MUSTARD GREENS, OR REGULAR, BLACK, OR RUSSIAN KALE, COARSELY CHOPPED

SALT

Heat the oil in a very large frying pan over medium heat. Add the garlic and peperoncini and cook, stirring frequently, until the garlic begins to brown (don't let it burn), 4 to 5 minutes.

Rinse the greens in a colander, even if they are already clean, and shake off the excess water. Add them to the pan carefully (the oil will spatter slightly when the water from the greens hits it), heaping them up, then pushing them down into the pan with a wooden spoon. Gently stir the greens as they start to cook and lose their volume, turning them over so that the raw greens reach the bottom of the pan. When the greens have darkened and cooked down to about one-fourth of their former volume (do not cook them down too far), season them with salt and serve.

WHITE ASPARAGUS WITH BOZNER SAUCE

SERVES 4

White asparagus is the object of cultish adoration each spring in Germany and Austria, and, by extension, in the formerly Austrian Südtirol—the Italian province now known as Alto Adige. The provincial capital is Bolzano, Bozen in German; bozner means "of Bozen." White asparagus with this sauce is traditionally eaten at Easter Sunday lunch in and around Bolzano.

2 POUNDS/1 KILOGRAM WHITE ASPARAGUS

SALT

4 HARD-BOILED EGGS, CRUMBLED

2 TABLESPOONS WHITE WINE VINEGAR

1 TABLESPOON SOUR CREAM

1 TABLESPOON MAYONNAISE

1 TEASPOON DIJON MUSTARD

1 SMALL ONION, MINCED

1 TABLESPOON CHOPPED GHERKINS

6 CHIVES, MINCED

4 SPRIGS ITALIAN PARSLEY, MINCED

Trim the tough bottom ends off the asparagus, then use a sharp vegetable peeler or small knife to peel the bottom three-fourths of each stalk. (If using a vegetable peeler, lay the asparagus on a cutting board to work so the stalks won't break.)

Lay the asparagus in a lidded pan large enough to hold them in a single layer, then fill the pan about three-fourths full of water. Sprinkle in 2 teaspoons salt. Cover the pan and bring the water to a boil over medium heat. Reduce the heat to low and simmer until the spears are cooked through but still slightly firm, 5 to 7 minutes. (White asparagus takes longer to cook than green.)

Meanwhile, put the eggs, vinegar, sour cream, mayonnaise, mustard, onion, and gherkins into a medium bowl and whisk the ingredients vigorously until well combined. Gently stir in the chives and parsley and season with salt.

Lift the asparagus out of its cooking water with tongs and blot it dry with paper towels. Divide it evenly among 4 plates and spoon the sauce over the peeled portions to serve.

FENNEL WITH BUTTER AND PARMIGIANO

SERVES 4

The use of fennel as a medicinal plant dates back thousands of years, to ancient Egypt if not earlier, and the Romans believed that it cured everything from poor eyesight to flatulence. Today it is much appreciated around Italy, and seems particularly popular in Tuscany, where it is sometimes prepared in the following manner.

2 BULBS FENNEL, HALVED LENGTHWISE

2 TABLESPOONS BUTTER, SOFTENED

2 GARLIC CLOVES, MINCED

SALT

1½ CUPS/360 MILLILITERS CHICKEN BROTH, HOMEMADE (PAGE 372) OR COMMERCIAL, HEATED

2 TABLESPOONS HEAVY/DOUBLE CREAM

⅓ CUP/35 GRAMS GRATED PARMIGIANO-REGGIANO

COARSE PEPPER

Preheat the oven to 350°F/175°C/gas 5.

Put the fennel bulbs, cut side up, in a baking pan/tray just large enough to hold them in a single layer. Spread the butter over the fennel, dividing it equally, then scatter the garlic over the top. Season with salt. Pour the broth into the baking pan around the fennel (don't pour it over the top).

Bake the fennel until very soft, about 1½ hours. Remove from the oven, and preheat the broiler/grill.

Spoon any pan juices over the fennel, then drizzle the cream over the fennel and sprinkle with the cheese. Broil/grill until the top is golden brown, about 2 minutes. Sprinkle with pepper before serving.

BROCCOLI RABE WITH OLIVE OIL AND SEA SALT

SERVES 4

Broccoli rabe is one of those vegetables with lots of names, in this case including broccoli rape, rapini, broccoli di rape, cima (or cime) di rapa, and broccoletti (not to be confused with the slender stalks of broccoli that also go by that name). Broccoli rabe is more closely related to turnips than to broccoli, and despite the fact that it has small florets that resemble those of broccoli, its serrated leaves taste a lot like turnip greens. It is a bitter vegetable overall, and something of an acquired taste, but is extremely popular in southern Italy. This recipe is from the region of Bari, in Puglia.

1½ POUNDS/750 GRAMS BROCCOLI RABE, TOUGH ENDS TRIMMED THEN STEMS SPLIT LENGTHWISE BUT LEFT ATTACHED

6 TABLESPOONS/90 MILLILITERS EXTRA-VIRGIN OLIVE OIL

2 GARLIC CLOVES, CRUSHED

¼ TEASPOON PEPERONCINI (OPTIONAL)

COARSE SEA SALT

Bring a medium pot of water to a boil over high heat. Add the broccoli rabe and cook for about 5 minutes.

Meanwhile, heat 4 tablespoons/60 milliliters of the oil in a large frying pan over medium heat. Add the garlic cloves and peperoncini (if using) and cook, stirring, for about 2 minutes. Add the broccoli rabe, lifting it straight from the pot into the frying pan with tongs or a slotted spoon without draining it.

Raise the heat to high and cook, stirring constantly, until the broccoli rabe just begins to brown and the water has evaporated, 4 to 5 minutes. Season generously with salt and drizzle the remaining 2 tablespoons oil on top. Serve hot or at room temperature.

TOO MUCH GARLIC

In her book The Cook's Decameron: A Study in Taste Containing Over Two Hundred Recipes for Italian Dishes, *originally published in London in 1901, one Mrs. W. G. Waters notes that "the culinary experiences of Englishmen in Italy have led to the perpetuation of the legend that the traveller can indeed find decent food in the large towns . . . but that, if he should deviate from the beaten track, unutterable horrors, swimming in oil and reeking with garlic, would be his portion. Oil and garlic are in popular English belief the inseparable accidents of Italian cookery, which is supposed to gather its solitary claim to individuality from the never-failing presence of these admirable, but easily abused, gifts of Nature."*

Sixty years later, in Bemelmans' Italian Holiday, *Ludwig Bemelmans addresses the question of garlic quite differently: he is in the dining car of a train bound from Paris into Italy, and, with an Italian he has just met, a wealthy nobleman he calls Don Basilio, he has just eaten a pleasing dish of spaghetti tossed with nothing more than butter, garlic, and parsley. The pasta causes Don Basilio to reflect:*

Some people condemn the Italian kitchen . . . and also the French. They say that they can't eat the food on account of the garlic. Now there is no good cooking except with garlic—but in the hands of a bad cook it's poisonous. It must be used with extreme care. . . . For example, in Aix-en-Provence—a city where they overdo garlic—once I was served truffles wrapped in bacon, a very good dish. The truffles profit by the flavor of the bacon, the bacon is enhanced by the truffles, and I like it. But at that luncheon I bit into a truffle and inside was a whole clove of garlic. Both the truffle and bacon were ruined. And the garlic, which, incidentally, was also in the chicken we were served and on the toast that came with the cheese and in the salad—it was so predominant that the whole meal was ruined. Now take this spaghetti—simple, ultrasimple—but with a bouquet like the finest wine.

OPPOSITE, BOTTOM: *A vegetable seller in Naples, date unknown.*

CAULIFLOWER WITH SPICY ANCHOVY SAUCE

SERVES 4

I have a vivid memory of rounding a corner one morning in Palermo and coming upon a small street market, at which one table was absolutely buried in cauliflower—cauliflower so large and unruly that it seemed almost threatening. The heads—not the usual slightly dirty looking, off-white but luminous yellow-green— were the size of soccer balls. The stems were 2 or 3 inches thick, like branches from a tree, and the leaves were so lush and expansive that they looked like small tropical shrubs. You would have to be pretty fearless in the kitchen, I remember thinking, to face down one of those. In other words, you would have to be a Sicilian housewife. I've had delicious cauliflower all over Sicily, always cooked with something strong in flavor—black olives, anchovies, chiles. This is an amalgam of several of my favorite versions.

JUICE OF I LEMON

SALT

I MEDIUM TO LARGE HEAD CAULIFLOWER ABOUT 2 POUNDS/I KILOGRAM, CORED AND SEPARATED INTO FLORETS

8 ANCHOVY FILLETS, CHOPPED

2 GARLIC CLOVES, MINCED

¼ TO ½ TEASPOON PEPERONCINI

3 TABLESPOONS EXTRA-VIRGIN OLIVE OIL

Add the lemon juice to a large pot of salted water, then bring to a boil over high heat. Add the cauliflower florets and cook until soft, 8 to 10 minutes.

Meanwhile, crush together the anchovies, garlic, and peperoncini with a mortar and pestle to form a coarse paste. Work 1 tablespoon of the oil into the mixture.

Heat the remaining olive oil in a large frying pan over medium-high heat. Drain the cauliflower, then add to the pan and cook, stirring constantly, until the cauliflower begins to brown slightly, 3 to 4 minutes. Remove the pan from the heat and stir in the anchovy sauce before serving.

SWEET-AND-SOUR EGGPLANT

SERVES 4

Eggplant has been one of the defining vegetables of Sicilian cuisine since the fourteenth century, if not earlier, and is popular today all over southern Italy—where sweet-and-sour flavors are common.

2 EGGPLANTS/AUBERGINES, ABOUT I½ POUNDS/ 750 GRAMS TOTAL, SEEDED AND COARSELY CHOPPED

2 TABLESPOONS FLOUR

I CUP/240 MILLILITERS MILD EXTRA-VIRGIN OLIVE OIL, OR MORE IF NEEDED

I RED ONION, MINCED

2 TABLESPOONS RED WINE VINEGAR

2 TEASPOONS SUGAR

I TABLESPOON PINE NUTS, LIGHTLY TOASTED IN A SMALL, DRY FRYING PAN

SALT

Put the eggplant into a large bowl, sprinkle in the flour, and toss to coat the pieces lightly and evenly.

Heat the oil in a large frying pan over medium-high heat. Working in batches, add the eggplant and fry, stirring constantly, until cooked through and golden brown on all sides, 5 to 6 minutes. As the eggplant is done, drain it on paper towels.

Cook the onion in the same pan over medium-high heat, adding a bit more oil if necessary, until it softens, 3 to 4 minutes. Deglaze the pan with the vinegar, scraping up the browned bits on the bottom, then quickly stir in the sugar until it dissolves.

Combine the eggplant with the onions and sweetened vinegar in a large bowl. Stir in the pine nuts and season with salt. Cover and let marinate for about 1 hour at room temperature.

Serve at room temperature, or reheat in a dry medium frying pan over low heat, stirring frequently, for 3 to 4 minutes.

STUFFED EGGPLANT

SERVES 4

Stuffed vegetables are known all over Italy, but seem to be especially popular in Liguria and the far south—and the south, of course, is eggplant country. Stuffed eggplant is so basic to Calabrian cooking, for example, that the town of Castrovillari holds an annual Stuffed Eggplant Festival in August. This is a typical way of preparing the dish.

2 EGGPLANTS/AUBERGINES, I TO I½ POUNDS/500 TO 750 GRAMS TOTAL, HALVED LENGTHWISE

5 TABLESPOONS/75 MILLILITERS EXTRA-VIRGIN OLIVE OIL

2 GARLIC CLOVES, MINCED

I TABLESPOON CAPERS

8 ANCHOVY FILLETS, FINELY CHOPPED

4 OR 5 SPRIGS ITALIAN PARSLEY, MINCED

I TEASPOON FRESH OR DRIED OREGANO

½ CUP/30 GRAMS TOASTED BREAD CRUMBS, HOMEMADE (PAGE 378) OR COMMERCIAL

½ CUP/50 GRAMS GRATED RICOTTA SALATA

SALT AND PEPPER

Scoop about two-thirds of the flesh out of each eggplant half with a spoon or melon baller, being careful not to puncture the walls of the eggplant. Finely chop the extracted flesh.

Rub all surfaces of the eggplant halves lightly with about 2 tablespoons of the oil, then arrange them, side by side and hollow side up, in a baking dish or on a baking sheet/tray large enough to hold them in a single layer.

Preheat the oven to 325°F/160°C/gas 3.

Heat the remaining 3 tablespoons oil in a large frying pan over medium heat. Add the chopped eggplant, garlic, capers, anchovies, parsley, and oregano and cook, stirring frequently, until the eggplant has softened, 6 to 8 minutes. Stir in the bread crumbs and cheese and season generously with salt and pepper.

Fill the eggplant cavities with the eggplant mixture, pressing it down and mounding it gently on top. Bake until the eggplant shells are very soft and the top of the stuffing is browned, about 1 hour. Serve hot or at room temperature.

EGGPLANT ALLA PARMIGIANA

SERVES 4

The name of this familiar Italian specialty is misleading. The term alla parmigiana *means "in the style of Parma" (or "of a woman of Parma"), but the dish has nothing to do with the cooking of that famous city in Emilia-Romagna. It is a southern Italian dish, claimed by both Sicily and Naples—probably the two parts of Italy where eggplant is eaten most. The familiar explanation for the name is that the dish usually includes, in addition to the mozzarella that is its second most-important ingredient, a sprinkling of parmigiano-reggiano. If that were the case, though, it would be "al [or col] parmigiano." A more likely explanation seems to be that "parmigiana" is a corruption of a Sicilian dialect word for the pattern of wooden slats that overlap in window shutters (like the slices of eggplant in this dish)—*palmigiana *(according to Mary Taylor Simeti) or* parmiciana *(according to Anna Pomar). Italian American versions of this dish often fry the eggplant slices first in an egg batter or bread crumbs, but that is rare in Italy.*

I½ CUPS/360 MILLILITERS EXTRA-VIRGIN OLIVE OIL

3 GARLIC CLOVES, MINCED

2 CUPS/480 MILLILITERS TOMATO SAUCE (PAGE 371) OR ONE 28-OUNCE/875-GRAM CAN WHOLE SAN MARZANO TOMATOES, DRAINED AND FINELY CHOPPED

SALT AND PEPPER

15 TO 20 BASIL LEAVES, 6 JULIENNED, THE REST WHOLE

2 LARGE EGGPLANTS/AUBERGINES, ABOUT 3 POUNDS/1.5 KILOGRAMS TOTAL, CUT CROSSWISE INTO SLICES ½ INCH/1.25 CENTIMETERS THICK

½ POUND/250 GRAMS FRESH MOZZARELLA, THINLY SLICED

½ CUP/50 GRAMS GRATED PARMIGIANO-REGGIANO

Heat 3 tablespoons of the oil in a medium saucepan over medium heat. Add the garlic and cook, stirring frequently, until it begins to color, 1 to 2 minutes. If using the tomato sauce, stir it into the garlic and oil and cook for 2 to 3 minutes. Stir in the julienned basil and cook for 5 minutes more, then set aside. If using the canned tomatoes, add them to the garlic and oil, season with salt and pepper, reduce the heat to medium-low, and simmer, stirring frequently, until thickened to a sauce, about 30 minutes. Stir in the julienned basil the last 5 minutes of cooking. Set the sauce aside.

Preheat the oven to 375°F/190°C/gas 5.

Heat the remaining oil in a large frying pan over medium-high heat. Working in batches, add the eggplant slices and fry, turning them once, until soft and golden brown, 2 to 3 minutes per side. As the eggplant is done, drain it on paper towels.

Spread a layer of the tomato sauce over the bottom of a 9-by-13-inch/23-by-33-centimeter baking dish. Cover the sauce with a layer of eggplant slices, overlapping them slightly. Arrange slices of the mozzarella over the eggplant, then spread another layer of tomato sauce on top of the cheese. Repeat the process to use all the tomato sauce, eggplant, and mozzarella, ending with a layer of sauce. Scatter the whole basil leaves over the sauce, then sprinkle the parmigiano over the top.

Bake until the sauce is bubbling and the cheese is golden brown, 25 to 30 minutes. Serve immediately.

BAKED WINTER SQUASH

❋

SERVES 6 TO 8

A Sicilian proverb maintains that, Cònzala comu voi sempri è cucuzza *(However you season it, it's still squash). Well, yes, and good squash, too, if seasoned like this.*

I KABOCHA OR OTHER LARGE WINTER SQUASH, 3 TO 4 POUNDS/1.5 TO 2 KILOGRAMS

2 TABLESPOONS EXTRA-VIRGIN OLIVE OIL

SALT AND PEPPER

2 CUPS/120 GRAMS TOASTED BREAD CRUMBS, HOMEMADE (PAGE 378) OR COMMERCIAL

4 TABLESPOONS/60 GRAMS BUTTER, MELTED

¼ TEASPOON THYME LEAVES

¼ TEASPOON MARJORAM OR OREGANO LEAVES

½ CUP/50 GRAMS GRATED PARMIGIANO-REGGIANO

Preheat the oven to 400°F/200°C/gas 6.

Halve the squash lengthwise and scoop out and discard the seeds. Rub the oil over the cut surfaces, then season them generously with salt and pepper. Put the squash halves, cut side up, on a baking sheet/tray, tent them loosely with aluminum foil, and bake until soft, about 1 hour.

Meanwhile, in a medium bowl, mix together the bread crumbs, butter, thyme, marjoram, and cheese and season with salt and pepper.

When the squash is ready, remove from the oven, remove the foil, and fill the cavities with the bread crumb mixture, dividing it evenly. Return to the oven uncovered and bake until the filling is well browned, about 15 minutes. Serve immediately.

THE MAD APPLE

You will often read that the Italian word for eggplant/aubergine, *melanzane*, derives from *mela insana*, meaning "mad apple." Not so, says my longtime friend and colleague Charles Perry, who is an expert on the food and languages of the Middle East and my etymological maven. "The word comes from the same root as *aubergine*," he says, "and that is the Arabic word *badhinjan*. It evidently entered standard Italian as something like *melingiana*, but this was altered to *melanzana*, from *mela insana*, under the influence of folk etymology. Why mad apple? Eggplant was domesticated in Southeast Asia. When it entered India, it came under a name that appears variously as *varttaka*, *vangana*, *vatigama*, and *vatingana*. Eventually Sanskrit settled on the last of these, which looks as if it means 'something of the wind class.' In India, wind is associated with madness the way the moon is associated with madness in Europe. So when the eggplant spread to Iran and then the Arab countries, it came saddled with an association of madness. Medieval Arab doctors gravely scolded people for eating eggplant because of this danger, but after a period when the Arabs considered the eggplant to be repulsively bitter, the public chose to ignore their doctors. Tenth-century Aleppo poet Kushajam wrote, 'The doctor blames me for loving eggplant, but I will not give it up. / Its flavor is like the saliva generously exchanged by lovers in kissing.' Still, when eggplant entered Europe, it was encumbered by prejudice because medieval European scholars had eagerly studied those Arab medical writers."

A SCOTSMAN
DISCOVERS EGGPLANT

In a letter written in 1764 from Nice—which was then as much Italian as it was French—Scottish poet and novelist Tobias Smollett first encountered the vegetable (fruit, actually) we know as eggplant or aubergine, and described it thus: "Badenjean, which the Spanish call berengena . . . is much eaten in Spain and the Levant, as well as by the Moors in Barbary. It is about the size and shape of a hen's egg, inclosed in a cup like an acorn; when ripe, of a faint purple colour. It grows on a stalk about a foot high, with long spines or prickles. The people here have different ways of slicing and dressing it, by broiling, boiling, and stewing, with other ingredients: but it is at best an insipid dish." He adds in a footnote that "this fruit is called Melanzana in Italy and is much esteemed by the Jews in Livorno. Perhaps Melanzana is a corruption of malamsana."

WINTER SQUASH PUDDING

SERVES 6 TO 8

I had this unusual savory pudding at the delightful Ristorantino di Colomba in Ferrara one chilly February evening, served as a side dish to the hearty sausage called salama. *Ferrara has had a Jewish community since 1275, when the prominent Este family offered a safe haven for Jews within the city walls. The community grew in the sixteenth century as a haven for those fleeing the Spanish Inquisition. Sweet winter squash is a favorite vegetable in the area's Jewish cuisine, and this pudding is a Ferrara specialty, often served (without the sausage) at Yom Kippur.*

SALT

I TO 2 BUTTERNUT OR OTHER WINTER SQUASHES, ABOUT 3 POUNDS/1.5 KILOGRAMS TOTAL, PEELED, SEEDED, AND CUT INTO 2-INCH/5-CENTIMETER CUBES

I CUP/240 MILLILITERS CLARIFIED BUTTER (PAGE 376), PLUS MORE FOR GREASING

I CUP/125 GRAMS FLOUR

2 CUPS/480 MILLILITERS WHOLE MILK

2 EGG YOLKS

3 TABLESPOONS GRATED PARMIGIANO-REGGIANO

Bring a large pot of salted water to a boil over high heat. Add the squash, reduce the heat to medium, and cook until the squash is very soft, 20 to 30 minutes.

Meanwhile, heat the butter in a medium saucepan over the lowest possible heat, then whisk in the flour. Raise the heat to medium-low and continue stirring until the mixture turns light golden brown, 5 to 6 minutes. At the same time, in another medium saucepan, heat the milk over medium heat to just below boiling. Immediately pour the milk into the flour mixture in a slow, steady stream, whisking constantly. Raise the heat to medium-high and bring to a boil. Then reduce the heat to medium, stir in the egg yolks and parmigiano, and continue stirring until nicely thickened, about 10 minutes. Remove from the heat.

Preheat the oven to 350°F/175°C/gas 5. Lightly butter a 2-quart/2-liter soufflé dish or pudding bowl.

Drain the squash and put it into a large bowl. Mash it with a fork or potato masher, then pour in the white sauce, stirring constantly with a wooden spoon or whisk until the mixture is smooth.

Pour the squash mixture into the prepared dish. Put the dish into a deep ovenproof pot, then fill the pot with water to reach halfway up the sides of the dish. Bake until the pudding is set and lightly browned on top, 50 to 55 minutes. Serve immediately.

CALABRIAN MUSHROOM STEW

SERVES 6

The Italian expression Fare le nozze con i funghi—*literally, "To put on a wedding with mushrooms"—means to overreach, to stage a great celebration with nothing more than what can be gathered in the fields. ("To put on a wedding with dried figs" is a related saying.) In the poorer parts of Italy, like Calabria, it is common to make pasta sauces and stews with the field's produce, generally an assortment of mushroom varieties. This is a typical Calabrese way of fixing them, based on a recipe from Clifford Wright's masterful* A Mediterranean Feast. *It also makes a good pasta sauce.*

I CUP/240 MILLILITERS EXTRA-VIRGIN OLIVE OIL

4 GARLIC CLOVES, CHOPPED

I TABLESPOON OREGANO LEAVES

4 POUNDS/2 KILOGRAMS ASSORTED WILD MUSHROOMS (AT LEAST 4 KINDS), LARGER ONES HALVED OR QUARTERED, SMALLER ONES LEFT WHOLE

SALT AND PEPPER

4 TO 6 RIPE TOMATOES, SEEDED AND GRATED (SEE RAW TOMATO COULIS, PAGE 371)

I TEASPOON PEPERONCINI

½ CUP/8 GRAMS LOOSELY PACKED MINT LEAVES, CHOPPED

TOASTED COUNTRY-STYLE BREAD SLICES FOR SERVING

Heat the oil in a Dutch oven or other heavy pot over medium heat. Add the garlic and oregano and cook, stirring constantly, for 2 to 3 minutes. Add the mushrooms, reduce the heat to medium-low, and toss the mushrooms to coat them well with the oil. Season generously with salt and pepper.

Add the tomatoes, peperoncini, and mint and cook uncovered, stirring frequently, until most of the moisture has evaporated, about 30 minutes. Serve over the toasted bread slices.

POTATOES PUREED WITH OLIVE OIL

SERVES 4 TO 6

Use mild, golden-hued extra-virgin olive oil for this dish, which is especially popular as an accompaniment to various kinds of sausages.

2 POUNDS/1 KILOGRAM RUSSET OR OTHER FLOURY POTATOES, PEELED AND QUARTERED

SALT

⅔ CUP/160 MILLILITERS EXTRA-VIRGIN OLIVE OIL

PEPPER

Put the potatoes into a large pot with salted cold water to cover. Bring to a boil over medium-high heat, reduce the heat to low, and simmer until easily pierced with a fork, 20 to 30 minutes.

Drain the potatoes, reserving about ¼ cup/60 milliliters of the cooking water. Press the potatoes through a ricer back into the pot, then stir in the oil and the reserved cooking water. Season generously with salt and pepper before serving.

ROASTED POTATOES WITH FRESH HERBS

SERVES 4

Roasted potatoes are an almost obligatory accompaniment to roasted meat—lamb, pork, kid—in Italy.

2 POUNDS/1 KILOGRAM RUSSET OR OTHER FLOURY POTATOES, UNPEELED, QUARTERED LENGTHWISE AND CUT INTO PIECES ABOUT 2 INCHES/5 CENTIMETERS LONG

½ CUP/120 MILLILITERS EXTRA-VIRGIN OLIVE OIL

SALT AND PEPPER

2 TEASPOONS THYME LEAVES

2 TEASPOONS MARJORAM OR OREGANO LEAVES

1 TEASPOON ROSEMARY LEAVES

Preheat the oven to 450°F/230°C/gas 8.

Put the potatoes into a large bowl, then pour in the oil and season generously with salt and pepper. Mix the ingredients together very well so the potatoes are completely coated in oil.

Put the potatoes into a large baking dish, arranging them in a single layer (use two dishes if they don't fit). Roast for 30 minutes. Remove the baking dish(es) from the oven, add the thyme, marjoram, and rosemary, and then stir and turn the potatoes over so they will brown evenly.

Return the dish to the oven and roast until the potatoes are golden brown and tender, about 20 minutes more. Serve immediately.

POTATOES, TRIORA STYLE

SERVES 4

Triora is a fortified village in the Valle Argentina, in the mountains of backcountry Liguria, famous historically as the site of the last witch trials in Italy, held in the late sixteenth century (an annual festival commemorates this dubious honor today). The cooking of the region is plain but savory, and it is one of the few parts of Liguria where dairy products are abundant.

2 POUNDS/1 KILOGRAM WAXY POTATOES, PEELED AND THINLY SLICED

3 TABLESPOONS FLOUR

1½ CUPS/360 MILLILITERS WHOLE MILK

2½ CUPS/250 GRAMS GRATED PARMIGIANO-REGGIANO

½ POUND/250 GRAMS FRESH MOZZARELLA, CUT INTO ½-INCH/1.25-CENTIMETERS CUBES

1 SMALL ONION, MINCED

2 TABLESPOONS EXTRA-VIRGIN OLIVE OIL, PLUS MORE FOR GREASING

SALT

2 TABLESPOONS COLD BUTTER, THINLY SLICED

Preheat the oven to 325°F/160°C/gas 3.

Put the potatoes into a large bowl, then add the flour, milk, about three-fourths of the parmigiano, the mozzarella, onion, and oil and season with salt. Mix the ingredients together gently with your hands, trying not to break up the potato slices.

Lightly oil a baking dish large enough to hold the potato mixture at a thickness of about 1 inch/2.5 centimeters. Add the potato mixture to the prepared dish. Distribute the butter slices evenly over the top, then sprinkle evenly with the remaining parmigiano.

Bake until the potatoes are tender and the top is golden brown, about 1 hour. Serve immediately.

POTATOES WITH PORCINI

SERVES 4

Because Italy's famous porcini are greatly treasured all over the country but have a limited season, they tend to be expensive. The notoriously frugal (and, to be fair, long poverty-wracked) Ligurians figured out a way to make the mushrooms go further by intentionally muddling them up with potatoes, so that the latter take on the former's flavor and it is not always possible to tell where the porcini stop and the potatoes begin. I first learned of this thrift-minded recipe, ironically, from Luigi Miroli, proprietor of the now-vanished Ristorante da Puny in the very un-thrift-minded village of Portofino.

I POUND/500 GRAMS FRESH PORCINI MUSHROOMS

I SMALL BUNCH ITALIAN PARSLEY, MINCED

2 GARLIC CLOVES, MINCED

3 TABLESPOONS EXTRA-VIRGIN OLIVE OIL

I POUND/500 GRAMS WAXY POTATOES, PEELED AND VERY THINLY SLICED

SALT

Preheat the oven to 350°F/175°C/gas 5.

Carefully remove the stems from the mushrooms and set the caps aside. Mince the stems and mix them with the parsley and garlic.

Using the oil, generously grease the sides and bottom of a wide, shallow baking dish with a tight-fitting cover. Arrange the potatoes in overlapping layers on the bottom of the dish, salting each layer. Sprinkle half the parsley mixture over the potatoes, then arrange the mushroom caps, cap side up, in a single layer over the potatoes. Sprinkle the remaining parsley mixture over the mushrooms.

Seal the the baking dish tightly with aluminum foil, then top the dish with its cover. Bake until the potatoes and mushrooms are tender, about 1 hour. Serve immediately.

PATATE INCAGRUMÀ

SERVES 4 TO 6

These potatoes are a specialty of the island of Burano, in the Venetian lagoon, where they are typically eaten in autumn with wild game birds, in place of the usual polenta. In the island's dialect, Incagrumà means "made with no care," "made in a hurry."

2 POUNDS/I KILOGRAM RUSSET OR OTHER FLOURY POTATOES, PEELED AND QUARTERED

SALT

½ CUP/120 MILLILITERS CLARIFIED BUTTER (PAGE 376)

I ONION, MINCED

LEAVES FROM I SPRIG ROSEMARY

2 TABLESPOONS TOMATO PASTE, HOMEMADE (PAGE 371) OR COMMERCIAL

Put the potatoes into a large pot with cold salted water to cover. Bring to a boil over medium-high heat, reduce the heat to low, and simmer until easily pierced with a fork, 20 to 30 minutes.

Meanwhile, melt the butter in a medium pot over medium heat. Add the onion and rosemary, reduce the heat to low, and cook, stirring frequently, until the onion is very soft and beginning to caramelize, about 20 minutes.

Drain the potatoes and add them to the pot with the onion. Mash them coarsely with a potato masher, then stir in the tomato paste and season with salt. Continue mashing and stirring until the tomato paste is completely amalgamated into the potatoes.

DESSERTS AND CONFECTIONS

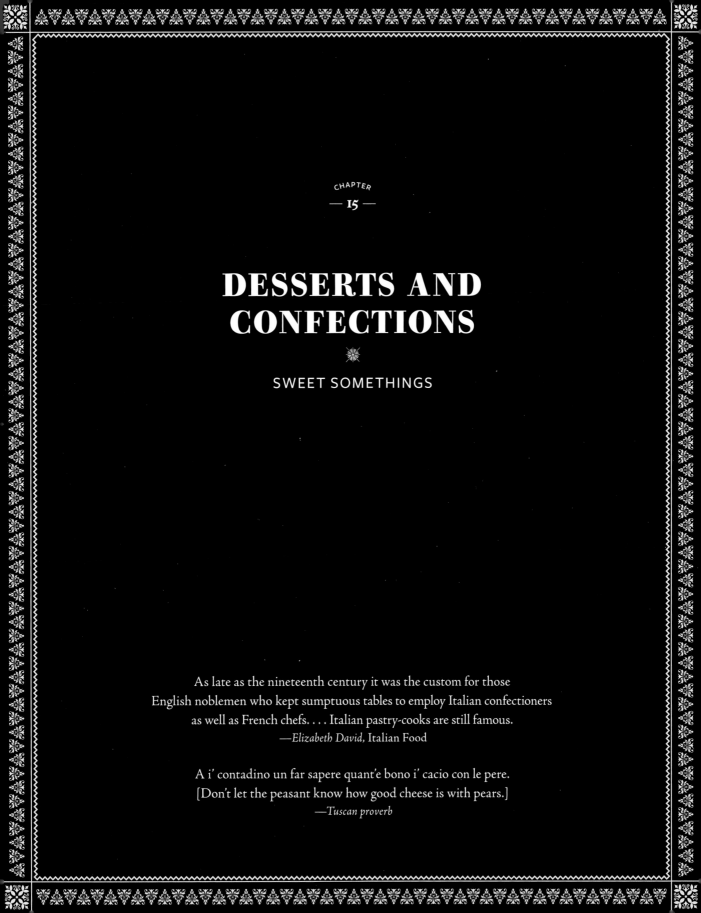

SWEET SOMETHINGS

As late as the nineteenth century it was the custom for those
English noblemen who kept sumptuous tables to employ Italian confectioners
as well as French chefs. . . . Italian pastry-cooks are still famous.
—*Elizabeth David*, Italian Food

A i' contadino un far sapere quant'e bono i' cacio con le pere.
[Don't let the peasant know how good cheese is with pears.]
—*Tuscan proverb*

Sugar was probably first refined in India in the early years of the first millennium AD, and was eventually brought to southern Italy by the Moors. Sugarcane was being grown in the eastern Mediterranean by the tenth century, but it wasn't until Crusaders returning from the Holy Land brought sugar to Venice in the twelfth century that the Italians first paid close attention to it—and that the Venetians saw in it a source of profit. By the fourteenth century,

before most of their neighbors, Italians were incorporating sugar as a matter of course into their pastries and desserts, finding that it produced more delicate sweetmeats than honey. (They even used it in savory dishes; the sixteenth-century physician Constanzo Felici quotes the adage, "Sugar never spoils a soup.") It's little wonder, then, that the Italians soon earned an international reputation for such things.

That reputation aside, I have rarely concluded a meal in Italy with dessert. That's partly because I will typically have consumed three courses by the end of the repast—antipasto, pasta, and main dish—and usually don't feel the need for anything else. But it's also partly because, at least when I'm eating in somebody's home, dessert as such is rarely offered. A little cheese (frequently just some shards of good parmigiano-reggiano, which is fine with me), maybe some fruit, occasionally some small cookies to go with a thimble of sweet wine . . . that's how Italians are likely to finish up—and that always seems like more than enough. In trattorias and restaurants, of course, there will be a choice of sweet conclusions: gelato, probably; an open-face or lattice-top tart, or crostata, filled with preserves, fresh fruit, ricotta, or nuts; possibly something like Montebianco (Mont Blanc), an over-the-top arrangement of chestnut puree and whipped cream on a base of meringue; or zuppa inglese, "English soup," an Italian version of trifle. (After having a particularly good example of this last dessert at a trattoria on the island

of Ischia, off the coast of Naples, Sean O'Faolain noted, "If one orders Zuppa Inglese in an ordinary ristorante one may be unlucky enough to get something no better than the mess of leftovers sunk in custard which one girls' school I know has well named 'Resurrection Puddin'.' Not all Italians can cook.")

Indeed, Italy boasts a vast repertoire of desserts, including whole classes of specialties based on egg yolks (mostly convent sweets in origin; monks used egg whites to fine their wine, leaving an excess of yolks, which nuns put to good use); almonds (a legacy of the Moors, including marzipan in countless forms); and cream (thanks to the influence of the French in Sicily, Piedmont, Lombardy, and Emilia-Romagna and the Austrians in Friuli and the Veneto). But the sweet indulgences for which Italy is famous—including the aforementioned gelato—are more likely to be encountered in pastry shops and caffès than in serious eating places, and are frequently eaten outside of regular mealtimes. Patience Gray, for instance, describes the scene at the Caffè Alvino in Lecce, in Puglia, at ten o'clock one morning: "The more well-to-do inhabitants were already . . . gorging themselves on magnificent cakes: conch shells of crumbling cinnamon-flavoured *pâte feuilletée* with a ricotta filling and pralinated almonds; éclairs light as air, containing a dense chestnut syrup, the exterior reinforced with a delicate carapace of curled bitter chocolate." If that's breakfast, who needs dessert at lunch?

FICHI MANDORLATI

✳

SERVES 4 TO 6

Waverley Root wrote that around Bari, a region famous for its figs, the confection called fichi mandorlati—*which means something like "almonded figs"—consists of figs that "have been not quite cooked, but heated, and flavored with almonds, fennel seeds, and bay leaves." (I've never seen bay leaves included myself.) He added that "unlike other dried figs, they somehow remain moist and juicy." Sometimes jocularly called* fichi sposati, *"married figs," these are traditionally made with fruit that has been partially dried in the sun. They go very nicely with a good Italian sweet Muscat.*

24 TO 30 FRESH FIGS, HALVED LENGTHWISE

24 TO 30 WHOLE BLANCHED ALMONDS

I TEASPOON FENNEL SEEDS

Preheat the oven to 200°F/95°C.

Arrange the figs, cut side up, on a baking sheet/tray large enough to hold them in a single layer. Bake until very soft, about 1 hour.

Meanwhile, heat a dry medium frying pan over medium-high heat. Add the almonds and toast them, shaking the pan constantly, until they brown slightly. Transfer them to paper towels, then add the fennel seeds to the same pan and toast until they release their aroma, about 30 seconds. Transfer them to paper towels, too.

Set an almond on the cut side of half of the fig halves, sprinkle the almond-topped halves with the fennel seeds, dividing them evenly, and top with the remaining halves, cut side down. Return the figs to the oven and continue baking for 20 minutes more. Let cool before serving.

FIGS WITH GORGONZOLA

✳

SERVES 6

It is well-known that blue cheese and pears have a natural affinity, but creamy, salty gorgonzola—the great Italian blue produced in Piedmont and Lombardy—also works wonderfully with the earthy sweetness of fresh figs. For this simple dessert, use gorgonzola with enough age that it can be crumbled. Young gorgonzola is too moist.

½ CUP/120 MILLILITERS EXTRA-VIRGIN OLIVE OIL

JUICE OF I LEMON

3 TO 4 OUNCES/90 TO 125 GRAMS FIRM GORGONZOLA, CRUMBLED

SALT AND PEPPER

18 FRESH FIGS, HALVED LENGTHWISE

Mix together the oil, lemon juice, and gorgonzola in a small bowl to form a thick sauce, then season with salt and pepper.

Divide the fig halves, cut side up, equally between 6 plates, then spoon the gorgonzola dressing over them. Serve immediately.

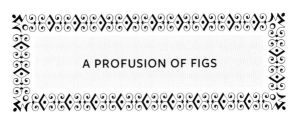

A PROFUSION OF FIGS

Passing through Basilicata on his way from Puglia to Calabria about a century ago, the English writer Norman Douglas paused in Venosa, in the province of Potenza, where he learned—among other things—a lot about figs from an unexpected source. He recounted the lesson in Old Calabria *(1915).*

A small boy . . . informed me that the fig-tree was *innamorato delle pietre e cisterne*–enamoured of stones and cisterns; meaning, that its roots are searchingly destructive to masonry and display a fabulous intuition for the proximity of water. He also told me, what was news to me, that there are more than two or three varieties of figs. Will you have his list of them? Here it is:

There is the *fico arnese*, the smallest of all, and the *fico santillo*, both of which are best when dried; the *fico vollombola*, which is never dried, because it only makes the spring fruit; the *fico molegnano*, which ripens as late as the end of October and must be eaten fresh; the *fico coretorto* ("wry-heart"—from its shape), which has the most leathery skin of all and is often destroyed by grubs after rain; the *fico troiano*; the *fico arzano*; and the *fico vescovo*, which appears when all the others are over, and is eaten in February (this may be the kind referred to in Stamer's "Dolce Napoli" as deriving from Sorrento, where the first tree of its kind was discovered growing out of the garden wall of the bishop's palace, whence the name). All these are *neri*—black. Now for the white kinds. The *fico paradiso* has a tender skin, but is easily spoilt by rain and requires a ridiculous amount of sun to dry it; the *fico vottato* is also better fresh; the *fico pezzottolo* is often attacked by grubs, but grows to a large size every two or three years; the *fico pascarello* is good up till Christmas; the *fico natalino*; lastly, the *fico*—whose name I will not record, though it would be an admirable illustration of that same anthropomorphic turn of mind. The *santillo* and *arnese*, he added, are the varieties which are cut into two and laid lengthwise upon each other and so dried (Query: Is not this the "duplex ficus" of Horace?). "Of course there are other kinds," he said, "but I don't remember them just now."

APRICOTS WITH HONEY AND PISTACHIOS

SERVES 4 AS FRUIT DESSERT OR 6 AS A TOPPING FOR CAKE

Italy produces more apricots than any other country in Europe (the majority are grown in Emilia-Romagna), and honey has been an important food from the Alps to Sicily for thousands of years. In recent years, disease and environmental poisons have been killing off Italian bees, and the honey industry is threatened. Good Italian honey, in both sweet and bitter varieties, is still exported in small quantities, and well worth looking for. I first had this simple dessert in a caffè in Sardinia.

2 CUPS/480 MILLILITERS CLOVER OR ACACIA HONEY, PREFERABLY ITALIAN

JUICE OF 2 LEMONS

24 RIPE APRICOTS, HALVED AND PITTED

⅓ CUP/80 GRAMS PISTACHIO NUTS

HEAVY/DOUBLE CREAM OR POUND CAKE FOR SERVING (OPTIONAL)

Combine the honey, lemon juice, and ½ cup/120 milliliters water in a medium saucepan. Bring to a boil over medium heat, then reduce the heat to medium-low. Add 12 of the apricot halves and poach until soft, 5 to 6 minutes. Remove the apricots with a slotted spoon and put them into a glass or ceramic bowl large enough to hold all the apricots. Poach the remaining apricot halves the same way and add them to the bowl.

Stir the pistachios into the apricots, then cover the bowl with plastic wrap/cling film and refrigerate for 2 to 3 days.

Bring to room temperature before serving. Serve in individual bowls plain, garnished with a little heavy cream, or spooned over pound cake.

APFELKUCHEL
TRENTINO APPLE FRITTERS

SERVES 4

The Val di Non, northwest of Trento, southwest of Bolzano, is famous for its apples, and the fruit figures prominently in the local cuisine, in preparations both sweet and savory (and as juice, hard cider, and a potentially dangerous distillate). This is one of the simplest preparations, called fanziuetes da meiles *in the local dialect.*

1¼ CUPS/160 GRAMS FLOUR

2 EGGS, LIGHTLY BEATEN

½ CUP/120 MILLILITERS WHOLE MILK

¼ TEASPOON SALT

4 CUPS/1 LITER CANOLA OIL

4 SWEET EATING APPLES, PEELED, CORED, AND CUT INTO SLICES ¼ INCH/6 MILLIMETERS THICK

SUGAR FOR DUSTING

Put the flour into a medium bowl, then whisk in the eggs and milk to make a thick batter. Stir in the salt.

Heat the oil in a deep frying pan or wide pot to 375°F/190°C. Working in batches, dip the apple slices in the batter, allowing the excess to drip back into the bowl, and add to the hot oil. Fry them, turning as needed to cook evenly, until golden brown, 3 to 4 minutes. As they are done, drain them on paper towels.

Dust the fritters with sugar and serve warm.

The most famous varieties of fruit in Italy, and quite possibly the most widely grown, are the grape and the olive (which, yes, is technically a fruit), both of them arguably better known for the wondrous liquid substances they yield than for themselves. These are only the beginning, however. The soil and climate of the Italian peninsula—or, I should say, the vast range of soils and climates—create ideal growing conditions for virtually every kind of nontropical fruit imaginable. As early as the first century BC, the Roman poet Horace wrote that Italy had become one immense fruit orchard, and proposed that the perfect meal would end with apples. (The Romans are generally credited with having disseminated the apple tree throughout the western Mediterranean, taking the fruit as far as France and England.) The apples of Trentino–Alto Adige are particularly good in my experience, even though the majority of them are

Golden Delicious, an easy-to-grow variety that has taken over most European apple orchards from less fecund local cultivars. (The Laimburg agricultural station in Ora, in the Alto Adige, is preserving heirloom varieties.)

Certain other parts of Italy have become famous for crops of their own. When I first started spending time in Rome, I remember my local friends telling me that they couldn't wait until springtime to go out to the hills of the Castelli Romani to eat the famous strawberries of Nemi. (They are indeed very good.) I've heard similar enthusiasm about the apricots grown around Mount Vesuvius, near Naples, and the pears and peaches of the Marche. The cantaloupe of Cantalupo in Sabina, in Lazio—said to be the fruit's birthplace and certainly its namesake—is renowned, as are the cherries of Vignola in Emilia-Romagna. The region of Bari in Puglia has famous cherries, too,

known as *ciliegie ferrovia*, or "railroad cherries" (the first tree is said to have been grown from a pit found near the railroad tracks outside the town of Sammichele di Bari). Among the more exotic fruits enjoyed in Italy are those known as *fichi d'India*, "Indian figs" (that is, cactus pears or prickly pears), which are eaten from Puglia and Basilicata south, and *nespola*, or "medlar," a tart, distant relative of the apple.

The first citrus grown on the Italian peninsula was probably the citron, which made its appearance around AD 300. The fourth-century agricultural specialist known as Palladius devotes a whole chapter of his masterwork, *Opus agriculturae*, to the citron tree. (The Romans used lemons, but they imported them from Greece or North Africa and apparently never attempted to cultivate the fruit.) The Moors first propagated oranges and lemons and other citrus on a large scale in Sicily. In his book *Oranges*, John McPhee describes a banquet given in 1529 by the Archbishop of Milan, which employed that orange globe in all sixteen courses; dishes included caviar with fried oranges flavored with cinnamon and sugar, oysters with oranges and pepper, and fried sparrows with oranges. Sicily remains Italy's most important citrus country—its blood oranges are nonpareil—but there's a lot of the fruit in Calabria, Liguria, and other regions, too. Surprisingly, there has also been extensive lemon and orange cultivation in Lombardy, in a warm microclimate on the western side of Lake Garda, since the fifteenth century. (D. H. Lawrence, visiting the region's famous lemon houses [see page 142], describes "dozens of oranges hanging like hot coals in the twilight.") I was not surprised to learn that the Italian word *frutta*, like our word *fruit*, derives ultimately from the Latin verb *fruor*, meaning "to take delight in."

LEMON MARMELLATA

MAKES SIX TO EIGHT 1-PINT/500-MILLILITER JARS

This Italian version of marmalade may be used as a filling for a crostata (see page 360) and other baked goods, but I also like it as a chutney-like condiment for grilled chicken or roasted pork. Always wash lemons well before using.

2 POUNDS RIPE LEMONS, PREFERABLY ORGANIC, QUARTERED LENGTHWISE

8 CUPS/1.75 KILOGRAMS SUGAR

2 TABLESPOONS LIMONCELLO, HOMEMADE (RECIPE FOLLOWS) OR COMMERCIAL

Squeeze the juice from the lemons into a large glass or ceramic bowl. With a sharp spoon or grapefruit knife, scrape out and discard the flesh, seeds, and pith from the peels.

Slice the lemon peels into narrow strips no more than 2 inches/ 5 centimeters long, and add to the bowl holding the juice. Add 4 cups/1 liter cold water to the bowl and stir gently. Cover and refrigerate overnight.

Put the lemon peels and liquid into a large nonreactive pot and bring to a boil over high heat. Reduce the heat to a simmer and cook, uncovered, until the peel strips are very soft and the liquid is reduced by about half, 2 to 2½ hours.

Put a couple of small saucers into the freezer to chill. Then stir the sugar into the lemon peel mixture a little at a time, making sure it dissolves thoroughly. Raise the heat to medium-high and boil gently until the temperature registers 220°F/105°C on a candy thermometer, 15 to 20 minutes. Reduce the heat to medium and test to see if the marmalade has set by spooning a small amount onto a chilled saucer. Allow the marmalade to cool slightly, then tilt the saucer to one side. If the marmalade remains in place, it's ready. If not, cook a little longer and test again.

Remove the pot from the heat and allow the marmalade to cool for 10 to 15 minutes, then stir in the limoncello.

Ladle the marmalade into six to eight sterilized 1-pint/500-milliliter canning jars, filling them to within ½ inch/1.25 centimeters of the rim. Wipe the rims clean, and then seal with sterilized lids and rings. Transfer the filled jars to a canning rack, submerge them in a pot of gently boiling water (make sure the jars are covered by at least 1 inch/2.5 centimeters of water), and boil for 5 minutes. Carefully lift the jars from the water with jar tongs, and place on a kitchen towel to cool undisturbed for 24 hours.

Check the seal of each jar by pressing down firmly in the center of the lid; if it doesn't move up or down, it is properly sealed. Improperly sealed jars will keep in the refrigerator for no more than 3 days. Properly sealed ones may be stored for up to 1 year in a cool, dark place.

HOMEMADE LIMONCELLO

MAKES ABOUT 2 QUARTS/2 LITERS

Limoncello is an intensely lemon-flavored—and often brightly lemon-hued—liqueur found, in one version or another, everywhere in Italy that citrus grows. This recipe comes from the fabled Sorrento Peninsula, which faces the Isle of Capri off the coast of Campania. Citrus fruits tend to carry heavy residue from pesticides and other agricultural applications, so wash your lemons very well in warm water—even if they are organic.

25 RIPE LEMONS, PREFERABLY ORGANIC

4 CUPS/1 LITER EVERCLEAR OR OTHER NEUTRAL GRAIN ALCOHOL, OR MORE IF NEEDED

3½ CUPS/700 GRAMS SUGAR

With a very sharp paring knife or vegetable peeler, remove the zest from the lemons in wide strips. (Squeeze lemons for lemonade, or freeze the juice for future use.) Combine the zest and the Everclear in a large glass jar with a tight-fitting lid, making sure all the zest is submerged. Add a little more Everclear if necessary. Cover tightly and place in a cupboard or other cool, dark place for 48 hours.

Combine the sugar with 4 cups/1 liter cold water in a large nonreactive pot and bring to a boil over medium-high heat, stirring occasionally to dissolve the sugar. Remove from the heat and let the syrup cool in the pot to room temperature. Set a fine-mesh sieve over the pot, and strain the lemon alcohol into the pot, discarding the zest. Stir well and return the liquid to the jar.

Allow to settle for 24 hours before serving. Store, tightly covered, in a cool, dark place for up to 3 months.

FRUITLESS SICILY

Lawrence Durrell wrote eloquently about the Mediterranean, in poetry, fiction, and nonfiction alike (he is most famous for The Alexandria Quartet*). He seemed particularly drawn to large islands, and penned evocative accounts of travel in Corfu, Cyprus, and Sicily, among other places. In his book* Sicilian Carousel, *published in 1977, he noted that Sicily was not always what it later became:*

So much of what surrounds us today came to the island very late in its history, sometimes as late as the sixteenth century. The long straggly hedges of prickly pear came from the Americas, as did the agave and the tomato. The Arabs imported lemon, orange, mulberry and sumach. The land is bounteous, and it varies in exposure and elevation to a considerable degree. . . . Everything "takes" and there is a suitable corner where soil and temperature combine to welcome almost everything. . . . Here for example one can see stands of banana, grape-fruit and sugar-cane in the hot lowlands. . . . But how hard it is to imagine this "granary of Rome" without lemons, oranges or grapes, without the cactus and the sentinel aloe.

LIMONCELLO SORBETTO

✳

MAKES 1 QUART/1 LITER

This is a very refreshing, slushy sorbet—almost a granita. For an even simpler alternative, splash limoncello over store-bought lemon sorbet.

½ CUP/120 MILLILITERS LIMONCELLO, HOMEMADE (PAGE 344) OR COMMERCIAL

1 CUP/200 GRAMS SUGAR

½ CUP/120 MILLILITERS FRESH LEMON JUICE

Combine the limoncello, sugar, and 2 cups/480 milliliters water in a medium saucepan and bring to a boil over medium-high heat, stirring constantly. When the sugar has dissolved, remove the pan from the heat.

Let the syrup cool to room temperature, then stir in the lemon juice. Transfer the syrup to a bowl, cover, and refrigerate for at least 3 hours to chill thoroughly.

Pour into an ice cream maker and freeze according to the manufacturer's instructions. The sorbet will keep in the freezer, in a tightly sealed container, for at least 1 month, but it is best made to order and eaten fresh.

PEAR SORBETTO

MAKES 1 QUART/1 LITER

I first had this grappa-spiked sorbet one autumn at Le Tre Vaselle, the comfortable hotel-restaurant owned by the Lungarotti winery in Torgiano, in the heart of Umbria.

1 CUP/200 GRAMS SUGAR

4 LARGE, VERY RIPE ANJOU PEARS, PEELED, CORED, AND FINELY CHOPPED

2 TABLESPOONS GRAPPA

Combine the sugar and 2 cups/480 milliliters water in a medium saucepan and bring to a boil over medium-high heat, stirring constantly. When the sugar has dissolved, remove the pan from the heat and let the syrup cool to room temperature.

Meanwhile, put the pears into a metal or other unbreakable bowl and gently mash them with a potato masher until they form a coarse puree. When the syrup has cooled, mix in the pears and grappa. Transfer the pear mixture to a bowl, cover, and refrigerate for at least 3 hours to chill thoroughly.

Pour into an ice cream maker and freeze according to the manufacturer's instructions. The sorbet will keep in the freezer, in a tightly sealed container, for at least 1 month, but it is best made to order and eaten fresh.

POMEGRANATE SORBETTO

MAKES 1 QUART/1 LITER

Pomegranates are Persian in origin, and came to Italy, by way of North Africa, in Roman times. The Romans not only ate them, but also used their juice to tan leather. I figured out how to make this simple sorbetto many years ago, after sampling something very much like it at a caffè on the Via Vittorio Veneto in Bordighera, on the Ligurian coast.

12 TO 14 VERY RIPE POMEGRANATES OR 3 CUPS/
720 MILLILITERS PURE POMEGRANATE JUICE

¾ CUP/150 GRAMS SUGAR

If extracting your own juice, roll the pomegranates one at a time on the kitchen counter, pressing down firmly and rolling them to crush the interiors evenly. When all the pomegranates have been treated this way, hold a pomegranate over a medium bowl, puncture it with a sharp knife, and squeeze it firmly to extract all the juice. Repeat with the remaining pomegranates. Strain the juice and discard any seeds that have emerged, or save them for another use.

Combine 3 cups/720 milliliters pomegranate juice and 1 cup/ 240 milliliters cold water in a large saucepan over low heat. Stir in the sugar, raise the heat to medium-low, and bring just to a boil, stirring constantly. When the sugar has dissolved, remove the pan from the heat. Let cool to room temperature, then transfer to a bowl, cover, and refrigerate for at least 3 hours to chill thoroughly.

Pour into an ice cream maker and freeze according to the manufacturer's instructions. The sorbet will keep in the freezer, in a tightly sealed container, for at least 1 month, but it is best made to order and eaten fresh.

ESPRESSO GRANITA

SERVES 4 TO 6

Coffee and ice cream became popular in Italy at roughly the same time, in the mid- to late seventeenth century, but espresso—whose concentration makes it ideal for granita—wasn't invented until the early 1900s. So this concoction, though ancient in conception, is probably a fairly recent invention.

⅔ CUP/130 GRAMS SUGAR

2¼ CUPS/540 MILLILITERS STRONG, FRESHLY BREWED ESPRESSO

Add the sugar to the espresso in a medium bowl, stirring well so that it thoroughly dissolves.

Pour the sweetened espresso into a shallow cold-proof glass or plastic container and put it into the freezer. Stir the mixture with a fork every 30 minutes, stirring the frozen portion from around the edges of the container into the center, until the mixture has become a uniformly frozen slush, about 4 hours. Serve immediately.

ICE CREAM SANDWICH

Who invented ice cream? It depends on how you define it. There are all kinds of romantic tales, some of them possibly true, about the shahs of Persia, the caliphs of Baghdad, the emperors of China and Mogul India, and the noble epicures of Greece and Rome importing snow from various mountain ranges to mix with fruit and honey or, later, sugar. (The first sorbets were liquid, like slushies; the term itself comes from the Arabic *shariba*, "he drank"—the same word that gives us the term *syrup*.) Frozen desserts made with milk or cream, often flavored with rose water, were known in the Arab world as early as the tenth century, and the Arabs almost certainly took the art of making sorbet (and ice cream?) to Sicily and other parts of southern Italy around that time. Ice cream in more or less the modern sense was known by the seventeenth century (some sources give its birth year as 1650), and by the late 1600s, ice cream vendors had become a familiar sight on Italian streets. Sicily claims to have invented gelato as we know it, though the Neapolitans and the Florentines sometimes do, too. (Vittorio Amedeo II famously dismissed the eighteenth-century Sicilian legislature as "an ice cream and sorbet parliament.")

In any case, it was a Sicilian named Procopio Cutò, later known as Procopio dei Coltelli, who first developed a machine in the 1670s that could produce large quantities of ice cream. In 1686, he opened a café featuring the confection in Paris, thus introducing it to France. (Café Procope was considered the first literary coffeehouse, and is still open, today the city's oldest café.) Just as *prosciutto* is the Italian word for not only the cured ham we call by that name but for ham in general, *gelato* in Italy means ice cream, period—not a specific style of same. (An Italian would call what Edy's or Häagen-Dazs makes gelato.) That said, ice cream—gelato—in Italy in general tends to be lower in both butterfat and sugar than its American or British equivalent, and has a distinctive texture, creamy but sometimes faintly grainy.

Sicily is today the home of Italy's most famous gelato—but Naples is famous for its spumone, studded with dried fruit and nuts, and the town of Pizzo, on Calabria's Tyrrhenian coast, has developed a reputation as an ice cream capital. Only the Sicilians, however, have had the genius to eat gelato, especially in the morning, in sandwich form: two or three scoops of assorted flavors (chocolate and pistachio go together brilliantly) in a plump brioche roll. Now, that's breakfast.

OPPOSITE: *An ice cream and lemonade vendor in Naples, 1885.*

PISTACHIO GELATO

❈

MAKES ABOUT 1 QUART/1 LITER

Sicilian gelato is very particular indeed: it is a rich ice cream made without eggs or cream, related more to blancmange—which is a kind of pudding thickened with gelatin or cornstarch and often made with almond milk, popular in medieval times—than to the custardlike preparation that serves as the base for some other rich ice creams. So-called pistachio flour is just finely ground pistachios (see page 382 for a source).

1 CUP/200 GRAMS SUGAR

3 TABLESPOONS CORNSTARCH/CORNFLOUR

4 CUPS/1 LITER WHOLE MILK

1 CUP/100 GRAMS PISTACHIO FLOUR

Stir the sugar and cornstarch into 1 cup/240 milliliters of the milk in a small bowl, then set aside. Put the pistachio flour into a medium heatproof bowl.

Heat the remaining milk in a medium saucepan over medium heat until it reaches a simmer (do not boil). Remove from the heat and stir in the sweetened milk. Return the pan to the heat and cook, stirring constantly, until the mixture thickens slightly, about 10 minutes.

Slowly pour the hot milk mixture into the pistachio flour, whisking gently but constantly. Allow the mixture to cool to room temperature, then cover and refrigerate overnight.

Strain the mixture through a fine-mesh sieve into another medium bowl, pressing down on the pistachio solids with the back of a wooden spoon, then discard the contents of the sieve.

Pour into an ice cream maker and freeze according to the manufacturer's instructions.

CHOCOLATE GELATO

❈

MAKES ABOUT 1 QUART/1 LITER

Chocolate was introduced to Sicily by the Spanish in the mid-1600s. The city of Modica, near Ragusa in southeastern Sicily, became the island's chocolate capital, and to this day chocolate is used there not only in desserts, but also in savory dishes, including two different pastries: 'mpanatigghi, filled with sweetened, chocolate-flavored ground beef, and liccumie, with a filling of eggplant preserves accented with chocolate. Of course, chocolate desserts are more common—ice cream most definitely among them. This is a basic Sicilian-style gelato.

3 CUPS/720 MILLILITERS WHOLE MILK

¾ CUP/150 GRAMS SUGAR

2 TABLESPOONS CORNSTARCH/CORNFLOUR

¾ CUP/75 GRAMS UNSWEETENED COCOA POWDER

Whisk together 1 cup/240 milliliters of the milk, the sugar, cornstarch, and cocoa powder in a medium bowl.

Put the remaining milk into a medium saucepan and bring just to a simmer over low heat. Add the cocoa mixture and whisk gently until the sugar and cocoa powder have thoroughly dissolved. Remove from the heat, let cool to room temperature, then cover and refrigerate for 12 hours.

Whisk the mixture gently, then pour into an ice cream maker and freeze according to the manufacturer's instructions.

LIGURIAN COOKIES

✳

MAKES 20 TO 25 COOKIES

The word canestrello *has two meanings in Italian: it is one of the words for scallop, as in the shellfish (also called* capesante *or* pettina*); and it is a kind of cookie, usually round, eaten in Piedmont and Liguria. I encountered this variation of the latter—not round—years ago in a little pastry shop in Crocefieschi, a hill town north of Genoa near the Liguria-Piedmont line. I sometimes make "dessert," after a substantial Italian dinner, out of a few of these cookies and a glass of Moscato d'Asti or other good dessert wine.*

I CUP/250 GRAMS BUTTER, SOFTENED, PLUS MORE FOR GREASING

3 CUPS/375 GRAMS FLOUR, PLUS MORE FOR DUSTING

⅔ CUP/130 GRAMS SUGAR

GRATED ZEST OF I LEMON

2 EGG YOLKS

I EGG WHITE, LIGHTLY BEATEN

Preheat the oven to 375°F/190°C/5. Lightly butter a baking sheet/tray.

Combine the flour, sugar, and lemon zest in a large bowl. Make a well in the center and add the egg yolks and butter. Work the ingredients together with your hands until a smooth dough forms.

Transfer the dough to a floured work surface. Flour a rolling pin, then roll the dough out about ¼ inch/6 millimeters thick. With a small, sharp knife, cut the dough into strips, circles, and stars. Place the cutouts on the prepared baking sheet, spacing them about 1 inch/2.5 centimeters apart. Gather up the dough scraps, press them together, reroll, and cut out more shapes. Add them to the baking sheet and brush the tops with the egg white.

Bake the cookies until golden brown, about 15 minutes. Let cool in the pan on a rack, then store in an airtight container at room temperature.

PIANEZZA CORNMEAL COOKIES

MAKES ABOUT 30 COOKIES

These cookies, called pasta di meliga *in their native Piedmont, are a specialty of Pianezza, just northwest of Turin, but are found all over the region.*

2 CUPS/250 GRAMS FLOUR, PLUS MORE FOR DUSTING

¾ CUP/120 GRAMS FINE-GRIND YELLOW CORNMEAL

I CUP/200 GRAMS SUGAR

½ TEASPOON SALT

GRATED ZEST OF ½ LEMON

I½ CUPS/375 GRAMS BUTTER, SOFTENED

2 EGG YOLKS

Combine the flour, cornmeal, sugar, salt, and lemon zest in a large bowl. Add the butter and egg yolks, then work the mixture with your fingers until a soft dough forms.

Transfer the dough to a floured work surface and knead a few times until smooth. Cover the dough with a clean kitchen towel and let it rest for 1 hour.

Preheat the oven to 300°F/150°C/gas 2. Line two baking sheets/trays with parchment/baking paper.

Transfer the dough to a pastry/piping bag fitted with a ⅜-inch/1-centimeter star-shaped pastry tip. Pipe the dough into 2-inch/5-centimeter spirals on the prepared baking sheets, spacing them about 2 inches/5 centimeters apart.

Bake the cookies until the edges begin to brown, 20 to 25 minutes. Transfer to racks to cool, then store in an airtight container at room temperature.

CUCCÌA

(SWEET WHEAT BERRY PORRIDGE)

❋

SERVES 10 TO 12

Wheat berries, which are husked whole kernels (bran included), were eaten long before anybody figured out how to turn them into flour and then into bread and pasta, and they are still eaten in Liguria, Lazio, Basilicata, and other regions. This unusual dessert, a kind of sweetened gruel, is Sicilian and is associated with Santa Lucia, the patron saint of Syracuse. Her feast day is December 13, and tradition holds that no bread or pasta should be eaten on that day—that wheat should be consumed only in this form. The name cuccìa is believed to derive either from a Greek term, xuxeon, which is a mixture of sweetened flour, or from the Arabic kiskiya, a type of grain. (Without the diacritical mark, cuccia is Italian for "kennel" or "dog's bed.") There are many recipes for the porridge, flavored with such ingredients as dried pumpkin, honey, or sweet wine.

- 3 CUPS/500 GRAMS WHEAT BERRIES, SOAKED FOR 48 HOURS IN WATER TO COVER
- 2 POUNDS/1 KILOGRAM FRESH RICOTTA
- 2 CUPS/400 GRAMS SUGAR
- 1 CUP/175 GRAMS SEMISWEET/PLAIN CHOCOLATE BITS
- 1 TABLESPOON SALT
- 1 TEASPOON GROUND CINNAMON
- ½ CUP/50 GRAMS FINELY CHOPPED CANDIED ORANGE OR LEMON PEEL

Drain the wheat berries and put them into a large pot with cold water to cover. Bring to a boil over high heat, reduce the heat to low, cover the pot, and simmer for 6 hours. Remove the pot from the heat and set it aside for at least 8 hours but no longer that 12 hours.

Drain the wheat berries thoroughly and transfer them to a large bowl. In another bowl, whisk together the ricotta, sugar, chocolate, salt, cinnamon, and orange peel until well combined. Stir the mixture into the wheat berries. Serve immediately.

RICOTTA WITH HONEY

❋

SERVES 4

Fresh cheese is eaten with honey all over the Mediterranean. When presenting this interesting variation on the theme, the ebullient Federico Valicenti, of Luna Rossa restaurant in Terranova di Pollino, in southern Basilicata, quotes the ambiguous Biblical verse Isaiah 7:15, which goes something like: "He shall eat cheese and honey until [when?] he knows how to reject evil and choose good." Chestnut honey has an appealing bitterness to offset the sweetness; see page 382 for a source.

- 2 TABLESPOONS EXTRA-VIRGIN OLIVE OIL
- 1½ CUPS/375 GRAMS FRESH RICOTTA
- 2 TABLESPOONS SESAME SEEDS, TOASTED
- 1 TEASPOON GROUND CINNAMON
- 2 TABLESPOONS SLIVERED BLANCHED ALMONDS
- 2 TABLESPOONS CHESTNUT HONEY

Heat the oil in a medium nonstick frying pan over medium-high heat. Add the ricotta and quickly stir in the sesame seeds and cinnamon with a rubber spatula. Cook for about 2 minutes, turning the ricotta over several times so that it browns slightly.

Set a 6- to 8-inch/15- to 20-centimeter pastry ring on a serving platter, then scatter the platter inside the ring evenly with the almonds. Pour in the ricotta, then gently lift off the ring. Drizzle the honey over the top. Serve warm.

CURIOUS CHEESES

Years ago, I read an article about the cheese section at Peck, the famous food shop and restaurant in Milan. Surveying the wide selection of top-quality formaggi, the writer asked the cheesemonger why there were so few French cheeses. "The best French cheese," the man reportedly sniffed, "is Normandy butter." This was rank culinary chauvinism, of course, but an Italian cheese lover, considering all that is available from Italy itself, might well ask why his attentions should stray across the border. There are at least four hundred different kinds of cheese in Italy—more, if you count variations in flavorings and in age—including some of the world's greatest. Parmigiano-reggiano (see page 92), mozzarella di bufala (see page 35), gorgonzola, taleggio, fontina, the various types of pecorino—these are true gastronomic treasures.

There is a lot more to Italian cheese than just the big names, however. Here are eight more obscure Italian cheeses worth looking for (and more easily found in their regions of origin, than abroad): Pannerone is an unsalted cow's milk cheese from Lodi in Lombardy; though it is sometimes referred to as "white gorgonzola" (it has approximately the same size and shape), it is a mild cheese—its name comes from the word *panera*, Milanese dialect for "cream"—but with a faintly bitter aftertaste. Another Lombardian cheese from more or less the same area is salva cremasco, named for the town of Crema; also from cow's milk, it reminds me a little of Caerphilly or Wensleydale, with a slightly flaky texture and a smack of damp leaves in the finish. Still another interesting cheese from Lombardy is a trademarked offering called Rossini, a pungent, engaging blue-veined cheese cured in the must of the dried Muscat grapes used to make the extraordinary dessert wine of the island of Pantelleria, off the coast of Sicily. Piacentinu is not, as its name might suggest, from Piacenza in Emilia-Romagna, but from around Enna in Sicily; it's a love-it-or-hate-it

sheep's milk cheese, strong and sort of funky, spiked with peppercorns and also infused with saffron. The name *cacio di fossa* means "cheese from the pit," and this unusual sheep's milk cheese from Sogliano al Rubicone in Emilia-Romagna is actually wrapped in burlap and packed into small hermetically sealed pits in the ground, where it ages for about three months, apparently refermenting in the process. The cheese is sharp and complex, with a faint suggestion of mold. Testun is a dense tomme-style cheese, made from cow's and/or sheep's milk (and occasionally the milk of goats) in the province of Cuneo in Piedmont. (Its name means "hard-headed" in the local dialect.) It has a grassy flavor, with a touch of caramel. A cheese I would like to try but haven't been able to find, even in its home region, is the mozzarella nell'asfodelo of Basilicata, fresh cow's milk cheese wrapped in the strong-smelling, bitter leaves of asphodel (*Asphodelus ramosus*).

And then there's a cheese that I've never tasted but am happy to continue avoiding: the infamous casa marzu, or "rotten cheese," of Sardinia (a similar one is made in Abruzzo, where it is called *cacio marcetto*, which means the same thing)—otherwise known as maggot cheese. This is a sheep's milk cheese that has been overaged outside, with the larvae of cheese flies (*Piophila casei*) introduced into it. These tiny creatures eat through the cheese, softening it and reportedly giving it a unique texture and flavor. Some connoisseurs eat the cheese with the maggots still living in it (because the maggots can jump six inches/fifteen centimeters or more, people sometimes wear glasses while they slather the casu marzu onto their flatbread), but others wait until they have departed. Ingesting the flies is dangerous, in any case, and for some years the cheese was banned by European Union health regulations. You will be happy to hear that it has since been given an exemption as a traditional food, and is now readily available again. Me, I'll have the parmigiano.

RICOTTA FRITTERS

✳

MAKES 30 TO 35 FRITTERS

These unexpectedly light-textured Sicilian confections go well with a glass of good Marsala.

3 EGGS

2 TABLESPOONS GRANULATED SUGAR

2 CUPS/500 GRAMS FRESH RICOTTA

1 CUP/125 GRAMS FLOUR

4 TEASPOONS BAKING POWDER

¼ CUP/60 MILLILITERS LIMONCELLO, HOMEMADE (PAGE 344) OR COMMERCIAL

2 TEASPOONS FINELY CHOPPED LEMON ZEST

1 PINCH SALT

4 CUPS/1 LITER CANOLA OIL

2 TO 3 TABLESPOONS POWDERED/ICING SUGAR

Lightly beat the eggs in a large bowl, then stir in the granulated sugar, ricotta, flour, baking powder, limoncello, lemon zest, and salt. Cover the bowl and refrigerate the dough until firm, 1 to 2 hours.

Heat the oil in a deep fryer or a deep saucepan fitted with a frying basket to 375°F/190°C. Working in batches, carefully drop rounded teaspoons of the dough into the oil and fry until golden brown, 4 to 5 minutes. As they are done, drain on paper towels.

Dust the fritters with the powdered sugar and serve warm.

CROSTATA DI RICOTTA

✳

SERVES 6 TO 8

This tart is a popular confection in Rome and the surrounding countryside. The recipe is said to date back hundreds of years.

2½ CUPS/320 GRAMS FLOUR, PLUS MORE FOR DUSTING

1 CUP/200 GRAMS SUGAR

1 TEASPOON BAKING POWDER

½ CUP/125 GRAMS PLUS 1 TABLESPOON BUTTER, SOFTENED, PLUS MORE FOR GREASING

1 EGG, LIGHTLY BEATEN

6 EGG YOLKS, 2 LIGHTLY BEATEN

2 POUNDS/1 KILOGRAM FRESH RICOTTA

1 TEASPOON SALT

GRATED ZEST OF ½ LEMON

2 TABLESPOONS GOLDEN RAISINS/SULTANAS

2 TABLESPOONS PINE NUTS

Sift together the flour, ½ cup/100 grams of the sugar, and baking powder into a large bowl. Make a well in the mixture and add the butter, the beaten egg, and the beaten egg yolks. Using two dinner knives, work the ingredients together until the mixture resembles coarse meal.

Turn the dough out onto a floured work surface. Coat your hands with flour, then knead the dough until it is smooth and elastic, 2 to 3 minutes. Form the dough into a ball and flatten slightly into a disk. Wrap the disk in plastic wrap/cling film and refrigerate for at least 1 hour or up to 8 hours.

Preheat the oven to 350°F/175°C/gas 5. Line a baking sheet/tray with parchment/baking paper and lightly butter the paper.

Remove the dough from the refrigerator and allow it to come to room temperature. Roll it out on a floured work surface into a round about 12 inches/30 centimeters in diameter and about ¼ inch/6 millimeters thick. Center the ring portion of a 10-inch/25-centimeter springform pan over the dough, then press it down so that it cuts an even-sided round. Lift the ring up and carefully transfer the pastry round to the prepared baking sheet.

Gather up the pieces of dough left outside the ring, form them into a ball, flatten into a disk, and roll out into a round 9 inches/23 centimeters in diameter and about ¼ inch/6 millimeters thick. Cut the round into uniform strips about ¼ inch/6 millimeters wide.

Combine the ricotta, the whole egg yolks, the remaining sugar, and the salt and whisk vigorously until well combined. Stir in the lemon zest, raisins, and pine nuts.

Spoon the ricotta mixture onto the pastry round, flattening it gently with a rubber spatula and leaving about 2 inches/5 centimeters around the rim of the pastry uncovered. Roll up the uncovered edge of the pastry to meet the filling, creating a rim. Arrange the pastry strips on top of the filling in a lattice pattern.

Bake the crostata until the crust is golden brown, 30 to 35 minutes. Let cool completely on a rack before serving.

CROSTATA DI MARMELLATA

SERVES 6 TO 8

Tarts filled with fruit were eaten in ancient Rome, when pastry chefs, known as crustularii, *made them with honey-sweetened dough. The first recipe for crostata as we know it today dates from the sixteenth century. Today, crostate are made in many parts of Italy, but I particularly associate them with Tuscany, where they are a staple dessert in private homes and at agriturismi, and a common sight in pastry-shop windows.*

2½ CUPS/320 GRAMS FLOUR, PLUS MORE FOR
DUSTING

½ CUP/100 GRAMS SUGAR

1 TEASPOON BAKING POWDER

½ CUP/125 GRAMS PLUS 1 TABLESPOON BUTTER,
SOFTENED, PLUS MORE FOR GREASING

1 EGG, LIGHTLY BEATEN

2 EGG YOLKS, LIGHTLY BEATEN

1 CUP/350 GRAMS LEMON MARMELLATA (PAGE 344)
OR OTHER FRUIT PRESERVES, PREFERABLY
HOMEMADE

Sift together the flour, sugar, and baking powder into a large bowl. Make a well in the mixture and add the butter, the egg, and the egg yolks. Using two dinner knives, work the ingredients together until the mixture resembles coarse meal.

Turn the dough out onto a floured work surface. Coat your hands with flour, then knead the dough until it is smooth and elastic, 2 to 3 minutes. Form the dough into a ball and flatten slightly into a disk. Wrap the disk in plastic wrap/cling film and refrigerate for at least 1 hour or up to 8 hours.

Preheat the oven to 350°F/175°C/gas 5. Line a baking sheet/tray with parchment/baking paper and lightly butter the paper.

Remove the dough from the refrigerator and allow it to come to room temperature. Roll it out on a floured work surface into a round about 12 inches/30 centimeters in diameter and about ¼ inch/6 millimeters thick. Center the ring portion of a 10-inch/25-centimeter springform pan over the dough, then press it down so that it cuts an even-sided round. Lift the ring up, then carefully transfer the pastry round to the prepared baking sheet.

Gather up the pieces of dough left outside the ring, form them into a ball, flatten into a disk, and roll out into a round 9 inches/23 centimeters in diameter and about ¼ inch/6 millimeters thick. Cut the round into uniform strips about ¼ inch/6 millimeters wide.

Spread the marmelatta evenly on top of the pastry round, leaving about 2 inches/5 centimeters around the rim of the pastry uncovered. Roll up the uncovered edge of the pastry to meet the marmelatta. Arrange the pastry strips on top of the marmelatta in a lattice pattern.

Bake the crostata until the crust is golden brown, 30 to 35 minutes. Let cool completely on a rack before serving.

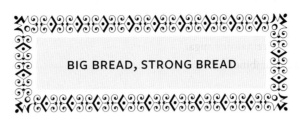

BIG BREAD, STRONG BREAD

The annual autumn appearance of panettone in Italy—the handmade version proudly displayed at fine pastry shops all over the country, the commercial stuff stacked high in gaudy boxes almost everywhere food is sold, from grocery stores to caffès to gas-station shops—is a sign that the holidays are coming. This sweet bread—in fact a sort of fruitcake, though far lighter and taller than fruitcake of the Anglo-Saxon variety—is traditionally consumed throughout the season, from November through February 2, Candlemas Day, usually with coffee or a small glass of sweet wine.

Waverley Root mentions a silly folk etymology that attributes the bread's name to the phrase *pan de Tonio*, "Tonio's bread," a supposed reference to a fifteenth-century baker said to have invented it. Another etymology relates it to the Milanese phrase *pan de ton*, "bread of distinction" (think "tony"). In fact, while panettone may claim Milanese parentage, its name is simply an augmentative form of *pane*; it just means "big bread." The antecedents of modern-day panettone can be traced at least back to medieval times, but the bread as we know it today—large dome-shaped loaves (their form is said to have been inspired by the domes of Lombardian churches) made from a butter-and-egg-enriched sourdough sponge and flavored with various combinations of dried and/or candied fruits and sometimes chocolate—is a more recent invention, probably from the nineteenth century.

Motta and Alemagna, the two big commercial brands whose panettones are ubiquitous in Italy and in many other parts of the world during the holiday season, both date from early-twentieth-century Milan. (They are under the same ownership today.)

Contemporary producers of panettone sometimes work variations on the conventional recipe. The firm of Loison, based in Vicenza, in the Veneto, has been particularly imaginative, selling whole-wheat/wholemeal panettone with rolled oats and versions made with white figs from Calabria, sour Amarene cherries, and chinotto (*Citrus aurantium* var. *myrtifolia*), a small, bitter citrus fruit better known as an essential flavoring in Campari and many brands of amaro (Italian bitters). Verona is known for pandoro, "golden bread," a panettone relative so-called because a high percentage of butter and eggs give its dough a distinctly yellowish color. Pandoro has an eight-pointed star-shaped top and is made without fruit, but is generously dusted with vanilla sugar. Sometimes the bottom is hollowed out and filled with whipped cream or gelato. The Veronese often claim Roman origins for the bread, on the grounds that Pliny the Elder described a bread made with eggs, butter, and oil.

"I once talked to a Florentine," Irish writer Sean O'Faolain reported back in the 1950s, "to whom, as far as I could discover, Siena meant nothing except the place from which one got, at Christmas time, a special kind of cake called panforte." Panforte—"strong bread"—is indeed a specialty of that Tuscan city. Unlike panettone, it is dark, flat, and dense, more like what we would call fruitcake. In its original form, it was known as panpepato, "peppered bread," because it was strongly dosed with the spice; panpepato is mentioned in records from the Montecellesi monastery in 1205. Panforte is made elsewhere than Siena today, but is so identified with the city that some bakers believe it must contain seventeen different ingredients, corresponding to the number of its neighborhoods.

OLIVE OIL CAKE

SERVES 8 TO 10

Anywhere in Italy that olive oil is produced, which is almost everywhere, some version of this dense white cake is made, using olive oil as shortening. This is an adaptation of a recipe from the Veneto.

¾ CUP/180 MILLILITERS EXTRA-VIRGIN OLIVE OIL, PLUS MORE FOR GREASING

3 CUPS/375 GRAMS FLOUR, PLUS MORE FOR DUSTING

4 EGGS

1 CUP/200 GRAMS SUGAR

1 TABLESPOON GRATED ORANGE ZEST

1 TEASPOON GRATED LEMON ZEST

⅓ CUP/80 MILLILITERS WHOLE MILK

⅓ CUP/80 MILLILITERS HEAVY/DOUBLE CREAM

2 TABLESPOONS BAKING POWDER

Preheat the oven to 325°F/160°C/gas 3. Lightly oil a 10- to 12-inch/25- to 30-centimeter Bundt pan or angel-food cake pan, then dust with flour, shaking off the excess by turning the pan upside down and gently banging it several times on a countertop.

Combine the eggs and sugar in the bowl of a stand mixer fitted with the paddle attachment and beat on medium-high speed until pale yellow, about 1 minute. Add the flour, orange and lemon zest, oil, milk, and cream and mix on low speed until well combined. Add the baking powder and mix in thoroughly.

Spoon the batter into the prepared pan, smoothing the top with the back of a wooden spoon. Bake the cake until the top is golden brown and a wooden skewer inserted into the center comes out clean, 35 to 45 minutes. Let the cake cool completely in the pan on a rack before unmolding and serving.

SBRISOLANA

(ALMOND CAKE, MANTUA STYLE)

SERVES 8

This rough-textured shortbread-like almond cake is a specialty of the historic city of Mantua, in Lombardy, where is it often eaten alongside a glass of sweet wine. It takes its Italian name from the verb sbriciolare, "to crumble." You'll see why when you eat it.

¾ CUP PLUS 2 TABLESPOONS/200 GRAMS BUTTER, SOFTENED, PLUS MORE FOR GREASING

1½ CUPS/240 GRAMS FINE-GRIND YELLOW CORNMEAL

1½ CUPS/185 GRAMS FLOUR

1 CUP/100 GRAMS GROUND ALMONDS

1¼ CUPS/250 GRAMS SUGAR

1 TEASPOON SALT

2 EGG YOLKS, LIGHTLY BEATEN

GRATED ZEST OF 1 LEMON

1½ CUPS/325 GRAMS COARSELY CHOPPED ALMONDS

Preheat the oven to 350°F/175°C/gas 5. Lightly butter a 10- to 12-inch/25- to 30-centimeter cake pan/tin.

Sift together the cornmeal, flour, ground almonds, sugar, and salt into a large bowl. Make a well in the center and add the butter, egg yolks, and lemon zest. Quickly work the ingredients together with your hands until a crumbly dough forms. Mix in the chopped almonds.

Sprinkle the dough evenly into the prepared pan. Do not pack down the dough. Bake the cake until golden brown and a wooden skewer inserted into the center comes out clean, 40 to 45 minutes. Let the cake cool completely in the pan on a rack before unmolding and serving.

PRESNITZ

TRIESTINO WALNUT CAKE

SERVES 16 TO 20

One fanciful account of the origins of this horseshoe-shaped pastry, popular in and around Trieste, holds that it was invented in 1832 by a local baker to celebrate the visit to the city of princess Elisabeth of Bavaria. He dubbed it (in German; remember that Trieste was the Mediterranean seaport for the Austro-Hungarian Empire) Preis Prinzessin, "prize princess," of which its name is a corruption. Unfortunately for this tale, Elisabeth wasn't born until 1837. (Folk etymology is such fun.) Another source says that it was first devised at the monastery of Castagnevizza, today called Kostanjevica and just across the border from Gorizia, in Slovenia. Several princesses are associated with Kostanjevica, too, as many exiled members of France's House of Bourbon lived in Gorizia and are buried in the monastery's crypt. Presnitz, incidentally, is said to have been one of James Joyce's favorite pastries when he lived in Trieste.

I CUP/200 GRAMS SUGAR

2 TABLESPOONS BUTTER, SOFTENED

I TEASPOON HONEY

1½ CUPS/150 GRAMS RAISINS, I CUP/100 GRAMS FINELY CHOPPED, THE REST WHOLE

6 CUPS/600 GRAMS WALNUTS, FINELY CHOPPED

2 CUPS/150 GRAMS CRUMBLED SPONGE CAKE

¾ CUP/125 GRAMS CANDIED ORANGE PEEL, CHOPPED

6 EGGS

ONE I-POUND/500-GRAM SHEET FROZEN PUFF PASTRY, THAWED ACCORDING TO PACKAGE DIRECTIONS

FLOUR FOR DUSTING

Preheat the oven to 375°F/190°C/gas 5. Line two baking sheets/trays with parchment/baking paper.

Put the sugar, butter, and honey into the bowl of a stand mixer fitted with the paddle attachment and beat on medium-high speed until the mixture is light and fluffy, about 1 minute. Add the whole and chopped raisins, walnuts, sponge cake, and orange peel and beat on medium speed until well combined, about 1 minute. Add 5 of the eggs, one at a time, beating thoroughly after each addition. When 5 eggs have been added, increase the speed to high and beat until the mixture has the consistency of a thick, rough paste, 2 to 3 minutes. Set the filling aside.

Cut the puff pastry sheet in half lengthwise. Roll out each half on a lightly floured work surface into a rectangle about 8 by 18 inches/20 by 45 centimeters. Place one sheet on each of the prepared baking sheets. With the long side of one rectangle facing you, spread half the filling on the third of the sheet nearest you, leaving a 1-inch/2.5-centimeter border uncovered at each end. Carefully roll the pastry around the filling like a jelly roll, then pinch the ends to seal them. Turn the pastry seam side down, then curve the ends toward each other to make a horseshoe shape. Repeat with the second pastry sheet and the remaining filling.

Beat the remaining egg with 1 teaspoon water in a small bowl, and brush the pastries with the egg wash. Bake the pastries until golden brown, 30 to 40 minutes. Let the pastries cool completely on the pans on a rack before serving.

GUBANE

FRIULANO NUT CAKE

SERVES 10 TO 12

This traditional fruitcake is eaten all over Friuli. The recipe is based on one from the Agriturismo de Carvalho in Manzano, a farming town between the Friulian capital of Udine and the Slovenian border.

¾ CUP/180 MILLILITERS WHOLE MILK, WARMED

ONE ¼-OUNCE/7-GRAM PACKET ACTIVE DRY YEAST

¾ CUP/150 GRAMS SUGAR

4 EGG YOLKS

½ CUP/120 GRAMS BUTTER, 4 TABLESPOONS/60 GRAMS SOFTENED AND 4 TABLESPOONS/60 GRAMS MELTED

3 CUPS/375 GRAMS FLOUR, PLUS MORE FOR DUSTING

GRATED ZEST OF 1 LEMON

2 PINCHES SALT

½ CUP/120 MILLILITERS DARK RUM

CANOLA OIL FOR GREASING

¾ CUP/75 GRAMS RAISINS

6 PRUNES, PITTED AND CHOPPED

6 DRIED FIGS, CHOPPED

¾ CUP/110 GRAMS PINE NUTS, FINELY CHOPPED

¾ CUP/75 GRAMS WALNUTS, FINELY CHOPPED

½ CUP/110 GRAMS HAZELNUTS, FINELY CHOPPED

½ CUP/110 GRAMS ALMONDS, FINELY CHOPPED

3 TABLESPOONS GRATED SEMISWEET/PLAIN CHOCOLATE

1 TABLESPOON CANDIED ORANGE PEEL

¼ CUP/20 GRAMS CRUSHED AMARETTI

1 TEASPOON VANILLA EXTRACT

2 EGGS, LIGHTLY BEATEN

Pour ¼ cup/60 milliliters of the warm milk in a small bowl, dissolve the yeast and 1 tablespoon of the sugar in the milk, and let stand until foamy, about 5 minutes.

Combine the egg yolks, softened butter, and ½ cup/100 grams of the sugar in the bowl of a stand mixer fitted with the paddle attachment and beat on medium speed until well mixed. Continuing to beat, gradually add the flour, then add the lemon zest, 1 pinch of the salt, 2 tablespoons of the rum, and the yeast mixture. Gradually mix in the remaining ½ cup/120 milliliters milk, beating until the dough is smooth.

Turn the dough out onto a lightly floured work surface and knead until smooth, 5 to 7 minutes. Lightly oil a medium bowl. Shape the dough into a ball and transfer to the bowl. Cover the bowl with a kitchen towel and set the bowl aside in a warm spot until the dough doubles in size, 1 to 2 hours.

Meanwhile, combine the raisins, prunes, figs, pine nuts, walnuts, hazelnuts, almonds, chocolate, candied orange peel, amaretti, 2 tablespoons of the remaining sugar, the melted butter, the vanilla, and the remaining pinch of salt in a large bowl. Stir until well combined.

Turn the dough out onto a lightly floured work surface and roll out into a rectangle about 12 by 16 inches/30 by 40 centimeters. Brush some of the beaten egg around the edges, then spread the filling evenly in the center of the rectangle, flattening it out with a spatula but avoiding the egg-washed edges.

With a long side of the rectangle facing you, gently roll the dough up like a jelly roll and lightly press the seam to seal it. Curl the roll into a spiral with the edges touching. Lightly oil a baking sheet/tray, then put the spiral on the sheet, cover it with a kitchen towel, and set it aside for 30 minutes.

Meanwhile, preheat the oven to 375°F/190°C/gas 5.

Brush the top of the spiral lightly with beaten egg, then sprinkle it with the remaining sugar. Bake until well browned, 45 to 55 minutes. Let cool completely on the pan on a rack before serving.

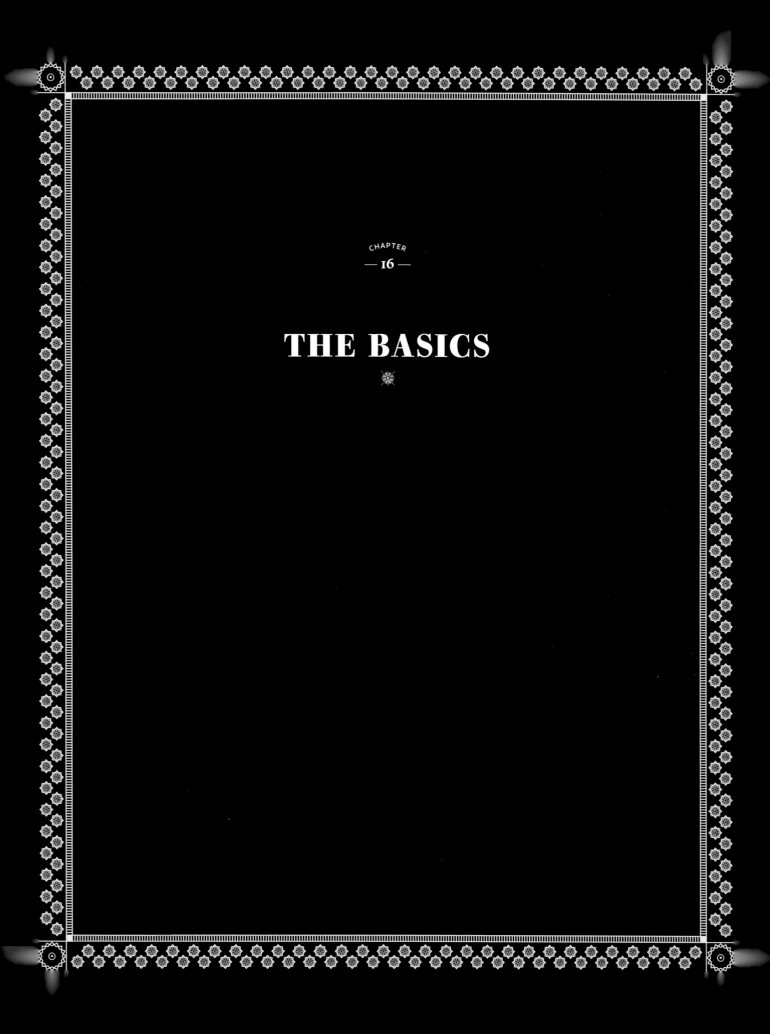

CHAPTER

— 16 —

THE BASICS

FRESH PASTA NO. 1 (WITHOUT EGGS)

MAKES ABOUT 1 POUND/500 GRAMS

Making your own fresh pasta is like making bread: it is a simple process that is almost impossible to get right the first time. But don't be discouraged: The more you make pasta, the better it will be.

I CUP/125 GRAMS ALL-PURPOSE FLOUR, PLUS MORE FOR DUSTING

I CUP/125 GRAMS SEMOLINA PASTA FLOUR

Sift the flours together into a mound on a large, lightly floured work surface, and make a well in the center. Pour ⅔ cup/160 milliliters warm water into the well.

Working from the inside rim of the well outward, slowly and gently incorporate the water into the flour with a fork. When the dough starts to stiffen, lightly flour your hands and knead it for about 1 minute, then form it into a ball.

Adding more flour to the work surface and to your hands if necessary, knead the ball with the heels of your hands until it is very smooth, 5 to 7 minutes.

Wrap the dough in plastic wrap/cling film and set aside to rest for 30 minutes to 1 hour.

Set the rollers of a hand-cranked pasta machine at the widest setting. Cut the dough into four equal pieces. Working with one piece at a time (keep the other pieces wrapped), flatten the dough with your hands so that it will feed into the machine, then pass it through the rollers. Fold the pasta sheet into thirds, as if you are folding a letter, then pass the narrow end through the rollers again. Repeat this process two more times. At this point, the dough should be silky smooth. Repeat with the remaining three pieces, keeping the pieces you are not working with wrapped to prevent them from drying out.

Decrease the setting on the machine by one notch and pass one piece of the dough through the rollers. Then pass the dough through each narrower setting until you have reached the second to the last setting and you have a long, thin sheet. (If the sheet begins to stick to the rollers, dust it lightly with flour.)

Cover the pasta sheets with a damp kitchen towel until you are ready to cut them into the desired form. If your pasta machine doesn't have blades to cut the pasta sheets into the size you want (many machines can be equipped with an attachment to handle different sizes), do it yourself: lay the sheet on a generously floured work surface and draw the tip of a small, very sharp paring knife along its length at the desired width (some cooks find the irregular "freehand" look of hand-cut pasta desirable). If cutting pasta into long, narrow forms, hang the noodles over a clean curtain rod or towel rack for 1 to 3 hours to dry slightly before using.

FRESH PASTA NO. 2
(WITH EGGS)

✳

MAKES ABOUT 1 POUND/500 GRAMS

If you don't make pasta regularly, you will find this recipe easier
than the version that uses water.

2 CUPS/250 GRAMS FLOUR, PLUS MORE FOR DUSTING

3 EGGS

Sift the flour into a mound on a large, lightly floured work surface, and make a well in the center. Break the eggs into the well.

Working from the inside rim of the well outward, slowly and
gently incorporate the eggs into the flour with a fork. When the
dough starts to stiffen, lightly flour your hands and knead it for
about 1 minute, then form it into a ball.

Adding more flour to the board and to your hands if necessary,
knead the ball with the heels of your hands until it is very
smooth, 5 to 7 minutes. Wrap the dough in plastic wrap/cling
film and set aside to rest for 30 minutes to 1 hour.

Set the rollers of a hand-cranked pasta machine at the widest
setting. Cut the dough into four equal pieces. Working with
one piece at a time (keep the other pieces wrapped), flatten the
dough with your hands so that it will feed into the machine,
then pass it through the rollers. Fold the pasta sheet into thirds,
as if you are folding a letter, then pass the narrow end through
the rollers. Repeat this process two more times. At this point, the
dough should be silky smooth. Repeat with the remaining three
pieces, keeping the pieces you are not working with wrapped to
prevent them from drying out.

Decrease the setting on the machine by one notch and pass one
piece of the dough through the rollers. Then pass the dough
through each narrower setting until you have reached the second
to the last setting and you have a long, thin sheet. (If the sheet
begins to stick to the rollers, dust it lightly with flour.)

Cover the pasta sheets with a damp kitchen towel until you
are ready to cut them into the desired form. For tagliolini,
taglierini, tagliatelle, linguine, fettuccine, pappardelle, and the
like, follow the instructions with your pasta machine. If your
pasta machine doesn't have blades to cut the dough into the
sizes you want, do it yourself: lay one pasta sheet at a time on
a generously floured board, roll it up like a jelly roll, and cut
through it with a sharp knife at regular intervals according to
the desired width (some cooks find the irregular "freehand"
look of hand-cut pasta desirable). If cutting pasta into long,
thin forms, hang the noodles over a clean curtain rod or towel
rack for about 1 hour to dry slightly before using.

BASIC TOMATO SAUCE

MAKES ABOUT 3 CUPS/720 MILLILITERS,
ENOUGH TO SAUCE 1 POUND/500 GRAMS PASTA

**4 TO 6 VERY RIPE TOMATOES, PEELED, SEEDED,
AND CHOPPED, OR ONE 28-OUNCE/875-GRAM CAN
WHOLE SAN MARZANO TOMATOES, DRAINED,
SEEDED, AND CHOPPED**

**4 TABLESPOONS/60 MILLILITERS EXTRA-VIRGIN
OLIVE OIL**

I TEASPOON OREGANO LEAVES

6 TO 8 LARGE BASIL LEAVES, JULIENNED

I SMALL ONION, MINCED

2 GARLIC CLOVES, MINCED

**2 TABLESPOONS TOMATO PASTE, HOMEMADE
(AT RIGHT) OR COMMERCIAL (OPTIONAL)**

SALT AND PEPPER

Put the tomatoes into a medium saucepan, add 2 tablespoons of
the oil, the oregano, and basil, and bring to a boil over medium-
high heat. Reduce the heat to low, cover, and simmer for about
30 minutes, stirring occasionally.

Meanwhile, heat the remaining oil in another medium saucepan over medium-low heat, add the onion and garlic, and cook,
stirring frequently, until the onion softens, 6 to 8 minutes.

Put the tomatoes through a food mill or small-holed colander
to remove any errant seeds and skin, then add to the onion mixture. Stir in the tomato paste (if using), season with salt and
pepper, then reduce the heat to low and cook uncovered, stirring occasionally, until it thickens and has turned brick red,
about 20 minutes more.

Use immediately or store, covered, in the refrigerator for no
more than 48 hours.

TOMATO PASTE

MAKES ABOUT 1 CUP/240 MILLILITERS

In Sicily, tomato paste, called strattu ri pumaroru, *literally
"extract of tomato," in dialect, is traditionally made by drying
tomato sauce in flat wooden boxes in the sun, protected from insects
by fine wire mesh. The best is said to come from the Hyblaean
Mountains near Syracuse.*

EXTRA-VIRGIN OLIVE OIL FOR GREASING

BASIC TOMATO SAUCE (AT LEFT)

Preheat the oven to 225°F/110°C/gas ¼. Very lightly oil a large,
shallow baking dish.

Press the tomato sauce through a fine-mesh sieve (to remove all
solid matter) into the prepared baking dish. Spread it out evenly.
It should be no more than about ¾ inch/2 centimeters deep.

Bake the sauce, stirring it about every 30 minutes, until it is
dark red and concentrated, 2 to 2½ hours. Store refrigerated,
in a tightly sealed container, for up to 2 weeks.

RAW TOMATO COULIS

MAKES ABOUT 2 CUPS/480 MILLILITERS

Use tomatoes prepared this way in sauces, soups, and stews.

3 OR 4 LARGE RIPE TOMATOES

Halve the tomatoes crosswise and flick out the seeds with your
finger. Stand a four-sided (box) grater in a shallow bowl. Cup a
tomato half in your hand and gently but firmly grate it on the
large holes of the grater, so that the skin splays out and flattens.
Repeat the process with the remaining tomato halves. Discard
the skins. Use immediately.

SEAFOOD BROTH

✳

MAKES 2 TO 3 QUARTS/2 TO 3 LITERS

3 POUNDS/1.5 KILOGRAMS ASSORTED SALTWATER
FISH FRAMES OR HEADS AND TAILS (ASK YOUR
FISHMONGER TO REMOVE THE GILLS)

6 TO 8 MEDIUM SHELL-ON SHRIMP/PRAWNS

1 JUMBO CRAB LEG, CRACKED

1 LARGE ONION, COARSELY CHOPPED

2 CARROTS, COARSELY CHOPPED

1 STALK CELERY, COARSELY CHOPPED

1 LEEK, WHITE PART ONLY, COARSELY CHOPPED

2 OR 3 FENNEL FRONDS

Put the fish parts, shrimp, crab, onion, carrots, celery, leek, and fennel fronds into a large pot and add cold water to cover. Cover the pot and bring to a boil over high heat. Uncover, reduce the heat to low, and simmer, skimming any foam that forms on the surface as needed, for 1 hour.

Strain the broth through a fine sieve, discarding the solids. Rinse out the pot, then return the broth to it and simmer for about 30 minutes longer.

Remove from the heat and use immediately, or let cool to room temperature, transfer to conveniently sized airtight containers, and refrigerate for up to 3 days or freeze for up to 2 months.

CHICKEN BROTH

✳

MAKES 2 TO 3 QUARTS/2 TO 3 LITERS

1 CHICKEN, 3 POUNDS/1.5 KILOGRAMS

1 LARGE ONION, COARSELY CHOPPED

2 CARROTS, COARSELY CHOPPED

1 STALK CELERY, COARSELY CHOPPED

1 LEEK, WHITE PART ONLY, COARSELY CHOPPED

1 BAY LEAF

Put the chicken, onion, carrots, celery, leek, and bay leaf into a large pot and add cold water to cover completely. Cover the pot and bring to a boil over high heat. Uncover, reduce the heat to low, and simmer, skimming any foam that forms on the surface as needed, for 2½ hours.

Lift out and set the chicken aside. Strain the broth through a fine-mesh sieve, discarding the solids. When the chicken is cool enough to handle, pick off the meat and reserve for another use. Rinse out the pot, then return the broth to it and simmer for about 30 minutes longer.

Remove from the heat, let cool to room temperature, cover, and refrigerate until chilled, then remove the fat that has solidified on the surface. Use immediately, or transfer to conveniently sized airtight containers and refrigerate for up to 5 days or freeze for up to 2 months.

VEAL BROTH

✳

MAKES 2 TO 3 QUARTS/2 TO 3 LITERS

3 POUNDS/1.5 KILOGRAMS VEAL BONES WITH BITS
OF MEAT ATTACHED

I LARGE ONION, COARSELY CHOPPED

2 CARROTS, COARSELY CHOPPED

I POUND/500 GRAMS VEAL STEW MEAT

I STALK CELERY, COARSELY CHOPPED

2 OR 3 LARGE SPRIGS ITALIAN PARSLEY

2 OR 3 LARGE SPRIGS THYME

2 BAY LEAVES

2 WHOLE CLOVES

3 GARLIC CLOVES, UNPEELED

2 TABLESPOONS TOMATO PASTE, HOMEMADE
(PAGE 371) OR COMMERCIAL

Preheat the oven to 450°/230°C/gas 8.

Spread the bones out in a roasting pan/tray and roast for
30 minutes. Add the onion and carrots to the pan and continue
roasting for 20 minutes more.

Transfer the roasted bones, onion, and carrots to a large pot
and add the stew meat, celery, parsley, thyme, bay leaves,
cloves, garlic, and tomato paste. Place the roasting pan on the
stove top over high heat, add about 1 cup/240 milliliters water
and deglaze the pan, scraping up the browned bits from the
bottom. Add the contents of the roasting pan to the pot, and
then add 6 quarts/6 liters water to the pot, or as much as you
need to cover the ingredients completely. Cover the pot and
bring to a boil over high heat. Uncover, reduce the heat to low,
and simmer, skimming any foam that forms on the surface as
needed, until the liquid has reduced by half, 3 to 4 hours.

Strain the broth through a fine-mesh sieve, discarding the
solids. (Or, you can reserve the veal for another use, if you like.)
Rinse out the pot, then return the broth to it and simmer over
low heat for about 30 minutes longer.

Remove from the heat, let cool to room temperature, cover, and
refrigerate until chilled, then remove the fat that has solidified
on the surface. Use immediately, or transfer to conveniently
sized airtight containers and refrigerate for up to 5 days or
freeze for up to 2 months.

LAMB BROTH

✳

MAKES 2 TO 3 QUARTS/2 TO 3 LITERS

4 POUNDS/2 KILOGRAMS MEATY LAMB BONES

I LARGE ONION, COARSELY CHOPPED

2 CARROTS, COARSELY CHOPPED

I STALK CELERY, COARSELY CHOPPED

2 TABLESPOONS EXTRA-VIRGIN OLIVE OIL

Put the bones, onion, carrots, celery, and oil into a large pot.
Add 6 quarts/6 liters water, or as much as you need to cover the
ingredients completely. Cover the pot and bring to a boil over
high heat. Uncover the pot, reduce the heat to low, and simmer,
skimming any foam that forms on the surface as needed, until
the liquid has reduced by half, 3 to 4 hours.

Strain the broth through a fine-mesh sieve, discarding the solids.
Rinse out the pot, then return the broth to it and simmer over
low heat for about 30 minutes longer.

Remove from the heat, let cool to room temperature, cover, and
refrigerate until chilled, then remove the fat that has solidified
on the surface. Use immediately, or transfer to conveniently sized
airtight containers and refrigerate for up to 5 days or freeze for
up to 2 months.

SALSA BESCIAMELLA

✻

MAKES ABOUT 5 CUPS/1.25 LITERS

The Italians also call this basic white sauce balsamella, *and sometimes claim that it was named for, if not invented by, the eighteenth-century Sicilian adventurer and occultist Alessandro Cagliostro, né Giuseppe Balsamo. Non-Italians realize, of course, that this is sauce béchamel, apparently named for Louis de Béchameil (sic), a courtier to Louis XIV, who died forty years before Balsamo was born.*

¾ CUP/180 MILLILITERS CLARIFIED BUTTER
(PAGE 376)

¾ CUP/90 GRAMS FLOUR

4 CUPS/1 LITER WHOLE MILK

¼ TEASPOON FRESHLY GRATED NUTMEG

SALT

Heat the butter over the lowest possible heat in a medium saucepan, then whisk in the flour. Raise the heat to medium-low and continue stirring until the butter-flour mixture turns light golden brown, 5 to 6 minutes. At the same time, in another medium saucepan, heat the milk to just below the boiling point over medium heat.

As soon as the butter-flour mixture is ready, pour in the milk in a slow, steady stream, whisking constantly. Raise the heat to medium-high and bring the mixture just to a boil, then reduce the heat to medium and continue stirring for about 10 minutes. The sauce should be medium thick and very smooth.

Remove from the heat and season with the nutmeg and with salt. Use immediately, or transfer to a tightly sealed container and refrigerate for up to 3 days or freeze for up to 3 months. Reheat the sauce in a bain-marie.

PESTO GENOVESE

✻

MAKES ABOUT 1 CUP/240 MILLILITERS,
ENOUGH TO SAUCE 1 POUND/500 GRAMS PASTA

This recipe produces a coarse pesto, of the kind you might be served in a farmhouse in the Ligurian countryside. For the smooth, homogenized restaurant variety, make and dilute the pesto as directed, then (without mentioning this step to your Genoese friends), puree it briefly in a blender or food processor. For pesto-making tips, see Pesto Presto *(page 106).*

1 GARLIC CLOVE, ANY GREEN CORE DISCARDED,
MINCED

3 TABLESPOONS PINE NUTS

COARSE SEA SALT

2 CUPS/30 GRAMS TIGHTLY PACKED YOUNG BASIL
LEAVES

¼ CUP/25 GRAMS EACH GRATED PARMIGIANO-
REGGIANO AND PECORINO SARDO OR ½ CUP/
50 GRAMS PARMIGIANO-REGGIANO (OMIT THE
CHEESE IF MAKING PESTO FOR MINESTRONE)

½ CUP/120 MILLILITERS EXTRA-VIRGIN OLIVE OIL,
PREFERABLY LIGURIAN

Place the garlic and pine nuts and a pinch of salt in a large mortar, then crush with a pestle, using smooth, regular motions, to make a paste.

Add the basil to the mortar a little at a time. Crush to a coarse paste, grinding the leaves against the side of the mortar with the pestle. Add a pinch more salt and continue crushing, then gradually stir and crush in the cheese.

Drizzle in the oil and continue working until the mixture becomes smoother and no large pieces of basil are visible.

Store in a tightly sealed container in the refrigerator for up to 1 week; do not freeze.

If serving on pasta, dilute the pesto with 1 to 2 tablespoons of the pasta cooking water before tossing it with the pasta.

CLARIFIED BUTTER

MAKES ABOUT 1¾ CUPS/420 MILLILITERS

1 POUND/500 GRAMS BUTTER

Melt the butter in a small saucepan over low heat. Remove from the heat and spoon off and discard any white solids that have risen to the top. Carefully pour off the clear yellow liquid into a heatproof glass jar or bowl, stopping before you reach the cloudy milk solids and liquid at the bottom of the pan. Discard the cloudy liquid, or add to cream sauces.

Use immediately, or transfer to a tightly sealed container and refrigerate for up to 1 month or freeze for up to 6 months.

CHARRED, PEELED BELL PEPPERS

Char red, yellow, or green bell peppers on a hot gas-, briquette-, or wood-fired grill/barbecue, turning frequently, until blistered and blackened on all sides. Alternatively, char one pepper at a time by placing it on a long fork and blackening it over the flames of a gas burner on the stove top turned on high.

Put the charred peppers into a brown-paper grocery bag, close the bag by rolling the top over, and let them steam for about 5 minutes.

To peel each pepper, halve it lengthwise; cut out the stem, seeds, and ribs; and then flatten it, interior side down, on a cutting board. Pull the charred peel off with your fingers, using a sharp knife to scrape or to cut off patches that don't readily come off. Leave little bits of black on for flavor.

Use the peppers immediately in salads and other dishes, or store them in a plastic container, refrigerated, for up to 1 week.

TOASTED BREAD CRUMBS

※

MAKES ABOUT 1½ CUPS/90 GRAMS

In the poorer reaches of southern Italy, toasted bread crumbs are often used in place of (more expensive) grated cheese on pasta. I've had orecchiette in Puglia so densely covered with them that the pasta itself disappears.

ONE 6-INCH/15-CENTIMETER LENGTH COUNTRY-STYLE BREAD (ABOUT 6 OUNCES/175 GRAMS), LEFT UNCOVERED TO DRY FOR 3 TO 4 DAYS

3 TABLESPOONS EXTRA-VIRGIN OLIVE OIL

Stand a four-sided (box) grater in a wide bowl with high sides, then grate the bread on the large holes of the grater.

Heat the oil in a large frying pan over medium heat (don't let it get too hot). Add the bread crumbs and stir them thoroughly with a wooden spoon to coat them with the oil. Then continue to stir constantly until the crumbs are toasted and golden brown, about 5 minutes.

Let cool completely before using. Store in an airtight container at room temperature for up to 1 year.

PREPARING SALT COD FOR COOKING

※

The best salt cod—which is simply Atlantic cod (Gadus morhua) cured in salt and partially dried—comes from Norway and Iceland. Canadian salt cod is common in the United States and varies greatly in quality. In general, it is best to buy thick, unwrapped filleted slabs (loins) of salt cod from a fishmonger, rather than the thin, sometimes shredded variety that comes in small wooden boxes.

To prepare salt cod for cooking, put it into a glass or ceramic bowl or baking dish large enough to hold it comfortably and cover it with water. Cover the bowl and refrigerate for about 48 hours, changing the water twice a day. To prepare the cod for the recipes in this book (see pages 172 and 185), bring a large pot of water to a boil over high heat. Remove the cod from its soaking water, add it to the boiling water, reduce the heat to low, and cook gently for about 20 minutes. Remove it from the water, allow it to cool to room temperature, then remove any skin or bones with your fingers, leaving the salt cod in large pieces.

BOOKS CONSULTED

Books that have been particularly useful are marked with an asterisk.

Albala, Ken. *Eating Right in the Renaissance.* Berkeley and Los Angeles: University of California Press, 2002.

Andrews, Colman. *Flavors of the Riviera: Discovering Real Mediterranean Cooking.* New York: Bantam Books, 1996.

(*) Artusi, Pellegrino. *Science in the Kitchen and the Art of Eating Well.* Translated by Murtha Baca and Stephen Sartarelli. Toronto: University of Toronto Press, 2003.

Bastianich, Lidia, and Jay Jacobs. *La Cucina di Lidia.* New York: Doubleday, 1990.

Bayle, Pierre. *A Historical and Critical Dictionary: Selected and Abridged from the Great Work of Peter Bayle (1732).* Vol. 1. No translator given. Whitefish, Montana: Kessinger, 2009.

Bemelmans, Ludwig. *Bemelmans' Italian Holiday.* Boston: Houghton Mifflin / Cambridge, MA: Riverside Press, 1961.

Boni, Ada. *The Talisman Italian Cookbook: Italy's Best-Selling Cookbook Adapted for American Kitchens.* Translated and augmented by Matilde La Rosa. New York: Crown, 1978.

Caffarella, Giovanni. *Il mondo di Lucania: Un viaggio.* lulu.com, n.d.

Camilleri, Andrea. *The Shape of Water.* Translated by Stephen Sartarelli. New York: Viking, 2002.

———. *The Snack Thief.* Translated by Stephen Sartarelli. New York: Viking, 2003.

(*) Capatti, Alberto, and Massimo Montanari. *Italian Cuisine: A Cultural History.* Translated by Aine O'Healy. New York: Columbia University Press, 2003.

Cappellani, Ottavio. *Sicilian Tragedee.* Translated by Frederika Randall. New York: Farrar, Straus and Giroux, 2008.

Casadio, Giovanni, and Patricia A. Johnston, eds. *Mystic Cults in Magna Graecia.* Austin: University of Texas Press, 2009.

Collodi, Carlo. *Il viaggio per l'Italia di Giannettino: L'Italia meridionale.* Bergamo: Leading Edizione, 2006 [facsimile edition of the original, Florence: Felice Paggi, 1880].

Contini, Mila. *Friuli e Trieste in Bocca.* Palermo: Il Vespro, 1978.

Dalí, Salvador. *The Secret Life of Salvador Dalí.* Translated by Haakon M. Chevalier. New York: Dover, 1993.

Daly, Dorothy. *Italian Cooking.* London: Spring Books, 1959.

(*) David, Elizabeth. *Italian Food.* London: Macdonald, 1954.

(*) Davidson, Alan., *Mediterranean Seafood: A Comprehensive Guide with Recipes.* 3rd ed. Berkeley, California: Ten Speed Press, 2002.

de Montaigne, Michel. *The Complete Works: Essays, Travel Journal, Letters.* Translated by Donald M. Frame. New York: Alfred A. Knopf / Everyman's Library, 2003.

De Mori, Lori, and Jason Lowe. *Beaneaters & Bread Soup: Portraits and Recipes from Tuscany.* London: Quadrille, 2007.

(*) De Vita, Oretta Zanini. *Encyclopedia of Pasta.* Translated by Maureen B. Fant. Berkeley and Los Angeles: University of California Press, 2009.

———. *The Food of Rome and Lazio: History, Folklore, and Recipes.* Translated by Maureen B. Fant. Rome: Alphabyte Books, 1994.

Dickens, Charles. *Pictures from Italy.* New York: Coward, McCann & Geoghegan, 1974.

Douglas, Norman. *Old Calabria.* Boston: Houghton Mifflin, 1915.

———. *Siren Land.* London: Penguin Books, 1948.

Durrell, Lawrence. *Sicilian Carousel.* New York: Viking, 1977.

Facciola, Stephen. *Cornucopia II: A Source Book of Edible Plants.* 2nd ed. Vista, CA: Kampong Publications, 1998.

Flaubert, Gustave. *The Letters of Gustave Flaubert, 1830–1857.* Selected, edited, and translated by Francis Steegmuller. Cambridge, MA: Belknap Press of Harvard University Press, 1980.

Gavotti, Erina, ed. *Millericette.* Revised and expanded edition. Milan: Garzanti Editore, 1992.

Gissing, George. *By the Ionian Sea: Notes on a Ramble in Southern Italy.* London: Chapman and Hall, 1901.

(*) *Grande enciclopedia illustrata della gastronomia*. Milan: Selezione dal Reader's Digest, 1990.

Gray, Patience. *Honey from a Weed: Fasting and Feasting in Tuscany, Catalonia, the Cyclades, and Apulia.* London: Prospect Books, 1986.

Grimaldi, Gianni. *Liguria in bocca*. Palermo: Il Vespro, 1987.

Hawthorne, Nathaniel. *The French and Italian Notebooks (The Complete Works of Nathaniel Hawthorne, Vol. X)*. Boston: Houghton Mifflin, 1899.

Hazan, Marcella. *Amarcord: Marcella Remembers*. New York: Gotham Books, 2008.

(*) ———. *The Classic Italian Cookbook*. New York: Alfred A. Knopf, 1976.

Hellrigl, Andreas. *La cucina dell'Alto Adige*. Milan: Franco Angeli, 1985.

Helstosky, Carol F. *Garlic and Oil: Politics and Food in Italy*. New York: Berg, 2004.

James, Henry. *Italian Hours*. Fairfield, Iowa: First World Library Literary Society, 2007.

Kasper, Lynne Rossetto. *The Splendid Table: Recipes from Emilia-Romagna, the Heartland of Northern Italian Food*. New York: William Morrow, 1992.

Kurt, Eva. *Bolzano in bocca*. Palermo: Il Vespro, 1978.

Lawrence, D. H. *Twilight in Italy*. New York: Clarkson N. Potter, 1990.

Levi, Carlo. *Words are Stones: Impressions of Sicily*. Translated by Angus Davidson. New York: Farrar, Straus and Cudahy, 1958.

Maggio, Theresa. *Mattanza: Love & Death in the Sea of Sicily*. Cambridge, MA: Perseus, 2002.

Malaparte, Curzio. *The Skin*. Translated by David Moore. Boston: Houghton Mifflin, 1952.

Mallo, Beppe. *Calabria e Lucania in Bocca*. Palermo: Il Vespro, 1978.

May, Tony. *Italian Cuisine: The New Essential Reference to the Riches of the Italian Table*. New York: St. Martin's, 2005.

McPhee, John. *Oranges*. New York: Farrar, Straus and Giroux, 1967.

Morton, H.V. *A Traveler in Italy*. New York: Dodd, Mead, 1964.

Newnham-Davis, Lieut.-Col., and Algernon Bastard. *The Gourmet's Guide to Europe*. London: Grant Richards, 1903.

O'Faolain, Sean. *An Autumn in Italy*. New York: Devin-Adair, 1953.

———. *A Summer in Italy*. New York: Devin-Adair, 1950.

Pianigiani, Ottorino. *Vocabolario etimologico della lingua italiana*. Rome and Milan: Società editrice Dante Alighieri di Albrighi, Segati, 1907.

Pomar, Anna. *La cucina tradizionale siciliana*. Barcelona: Anthropos, 1984.

Riley, Gillian. *The Oxford Companion to Italian Food*. Oxford: Oxford University Press, 2007.

Roggero, Savina, *Come scegliere e cucinare le carni*. Milan: Arnoldo Mondadori, 1973.

(*) Root, Waverley. *The Food of Italy*. New York: Atheneum, 1971.

Sardo, Piero, et al., eds. *Two Hundred Traditional Types: Italian Cheese: A Guide to Their Discovery and Appreciation*. Bra: Slow Food Arcigola, 2000.

Simeti, Mary Taylor. *Pomp and Sustenance: Twenty-Five Centuries of Sicilian Food*. New York: Alfred A. Knopf, 1989.

Smollett, Tobias. *Travels Through France and Italy*. Edited by Frank Felsenstein. Oxford: Oxford University Press, 1981.

Villari, Pasquale. *Le lettere meridionali ed altri scritti sulla questione sociale in Italia*. Florence: Le Monnier, 1991.

Waters, Mrs. W. G., *A Cook's Decameron, a Study in Taste: Containing over Two Hundred Recipes for Italian Dishes*. Whitefish, Montana: Kessinger, 2009.

Wright, Clifford A. *A Mediterranean Feast: The Story of the Birth of the Celebrated Cuisines of the Mediterranean, from the Merchants of Venice to the Barbary Corsairs*. New York: William Morrow, 1999.

Yeadon, David. *Seasons in Basilicata: A Year in a Southern Italian Hill Village*. New York: HarperCollins, 2004.

SOURCES

There are Italian and Italian-American groceries all over America, able to supply many of the specialty ingredients called for in the preceding recipes. (The largest and most comprehensive of these is Eataly in New York City.) Most of the more obscure or specialized foodstuffs are also available within the United States through online ordering. Here is a list of valuable resources:

www.amazon.com. Truffle shavers (the stainless-steel kind are sharper and lighter than the wooden models), chitarra pasta cutters, couscousières (couscous pots), wheatberries, and spelt are among the many products available through various mail-order merchants via Amazon.

www.brownetrading.com. Maine shrimp, fresh in season, frozen otherwise; also good American and imported fish and shellfish of many other kinds.

www.cortibros.biz. A wide range of top-quality Italian cheeses (among them montasio, caciocavallo, and sometimes bitto and crescenza), pastas, and other specialty items (including pane carasau, maltagliati, Italian lentils, chestnut honey, cuttlefish and squid ink, white truffles, domestic Italian-style cured pork products, and roasted peeled chestnuts). The Web site lists a limited selection of products; call (800) 509-3663 to inquire about items not included online.

www.crimson-sage.com. Mentuccia (lesser calamint) plants.

www.dartagnan.com. A dependable source for wild game birds, wild boar, venison, hare, rabbit, and guinea hen, plus white truffles in season. (Wild game is sold fresh in season, frozen the rest of the year, and availability varies.)

www.dipaloselects.com. One of the few sources for dried peperoni di Senise, both dried and fried; also a good place to find bitto, caciocavallo, and other Italian cheeses.

www.gourmetsardinia.com. Corbezzolo (arbutus) honey and dried malloreddus pasta.

www.igourmet.com. Several varieties of canned French snails; the wild Burgundy petits are best. (I have been unable to find a source for imported Italian snails.)

www.murrayscheese.com. A dependable supplier of Italian cheeses, as well as American-made Italian-style salumi—prosciutto, lardo, guanciale, pancetta, speck, nduja, assorted salamis, etc.—from the best and closest-to-the-real-thing domestic producers: Cremenelli, La Quercia, Boccalone, and Fra Mani. (See also the salumi producers' own Web sites: www.cremenelli.com, www.laquercia.us, www.boccalone.com, and www.framani.com.)

www.nutsonline.com. Pistachio, chickpea, and chestnut flour.

www.ohnuts.com. Good-quality roasted peeled chestnuts.

www.pikeplacefish.com. Alaskan spot prawns, fresh in season.

www.preferredmeats.com. Goat and kid meat are available at halal butcher shops around the country, but Preferred Meats also sells them by mail order, along with excellent lamb, pork, and beef.

www.zingermans.com. Good Italian cheeses; Italian-style cured meats; and Senise-style dried, fried peppers.

Other sites useful for various Italian products include:

agatavalentina.com

gustiamo.com

www.pastacheese.com

supermarketitaly.com

INDEX